MOUNTAIN DIALOGUES FROM ANTIQUITY TO MODERNITY

MOUNTAIN DIALOGUES FROM ANTIQUITY TO MODERNITY

Edited by Dawn Hollis and Jason König

BLOOMSBURY ACADEMIC
LONDON • NEW YORK • OXFORD • NEW DELHI • SYDNEY

BLOOMSBURY ACADEMIC
Bloomsbury Publishing Plc
50 Bedford Square, London, WC1B 3DP, UK
1385 Broadway, New York, NY 10018, USA
29 Earlsfort Terrace, Dublin 2, Ireland

BLOOMSBURY, BLOOMSBURY ACADEMIC and the Diana logo are trademarks of
Bloomsbury Publishing Plc

First published in Great Britain 2021
This paperback edition published 2023

Copyright © Dawn Hollis and Jason König 2021

Dawn Hollis, Jason König and several contributors have asserted their right under the Copyright, Designs and Patents Act, 1988, to be identified as Authors of this work.

For legal purposes the Acknowledgements on p. xi constitute an extension of this copyright page.

Cover design: Terry Woodley
Cover image © The Greek theatre with Mount Etna volcano in the background, Taormina, Sicily, Italy. Frans Sellies/Getty

All rights reserved. No part of this publication may be reproduced or transmitted in any form or by any means, electronic or mechanical, including photocopying, recording, or any information storage or retrieval system, without prior permission in writing from the publishers.

Bloomsbury Publishing Plc does not have any control over, or responsibility for, any third-party websites referred to in this book. All internet addresses given in this book were correct at the time of going to press. The author and publisher regret any inconvenience caused if addresses have changed or sites have ceased to exist, but can accept no responsibility for any such changes.

A catalogue record for this book is available from the British Library.

A catalog record for this book is available from the Library of Congress.

ISBN: HB: 978-1-3501-6282-2
PB: 978-1-3501-9410-6
ePDF: 978-1-3501-6283-9
eBook: 978-1-3501-6284-6

Series: Ancient Environments

Typeset by RefineCatch Limited, Bungay, Suffolk

To find out more about our authors and books visit www.bloomsbury.com and sign up for our newsletters.

CONTENTS

List of Illustrations	vi
Notes on Contributors	vii
Series Preface	ix
Acknowledgements	xi
Note on Translations and Order of Chapters	xii

	Introduction *Dawn Hollis and Jason König*	1
1	Gessner's Mountain Sublime *Dan Hooley*	21
2	'Famous from all Antiquity': Etna in Classical Myth and Romantic Poetry *Cian Duffy*	37
3	The 'Authority of the Ancients'? Seventeenth-century Natural Philosophy and Aesthetic Responses to Mountains *Dawn Hollis*	55
4	Toward a Continuity of Alpinism in Antiquity, Premodernity and Modernity: Josias Simler's *De Alpibus Commentarius* (1574) and W. A. B. Coolidge's French Translation from 1904 *Sean Ireton*	73
5	Mountains and the Holy in Late Antiquity *Douglas Whalin*	89
6	Erudite Retreat: Jerome and Francis in the Mountains *Janice Hewlett Koelb*	109
7	Sublime Visions of Virginia: Thomas Jefferson's Romantic Mountainscapes *Alley Marie Jordan*	131
8	Edward Dodwell in the Peloponnese: Mountains and the Classical Past in Nineteenth-century Mediterranean Travel Writing *Jason König*	147
9	The Top Story: Truth and Sublimity in Patrick Brydone's Account of His 1770 Ascent of Mount Etna *Gareth D. Williams*	165
10	Mountains of Memory: A Phenomenological Approach to Mountains in Fifth-century BCE Greek Tragedy *Chloe Bray*	185
11	Mountains, Identity and the Legend of King Brennus in the Early Modern English Imaginary *Harriet Archer*	197
12	Upland on Mont Ventoux *Peter H. Hansen*	215

Bibliography	229
Index	249

ILLUSTRATIONS

5.1 A medieval rock-cut church in Ayazini, Phrygia, Turkey. Photograph: Douglas Whalin, 2013   92
5.2 Narthex of the Church of Saint Simeon Stylites at Qalʿat Simʿān, Syria (B_237). Photograph: Gertrude Bell, 1905. Gertrude Bell Archive, Newcastle University   99
5.3 Saint Auxentios and his holy mountains, from the Menologion of Basil II, eleventh century. Wikimedia Commons   102
6.1 Giovanni Bellini (*c.* 1430–1516), Italian. *Saint Jerome in the Wilderness*, *c.* 1450. Tempera on panel. The Henry Barber Trust, The Barber Institute of Fine Arts, University of Birmingham / Bridgeman Images   120
6.2 Giovanni Bellini (*c.* 1430–1516), Italian. *Saint Francis in the Desert,* 1480. Tempera and oil on panel. 49 x 55 in. Copyright, The Frick Collection, New York   123
8.1 J. Walker, 'Map of Greece', from Edward Dodwell (1819), *A Classical and Topographical Tour through Greece during the Years 1801, 1805, and 1806*, London: Rodwell and Martin: Volume I, facing p. x. Reproduced by kind permission of the Syndics of Cambridge University Library   153
8.2 'Mount Olympus as seen between Larissa and Baba', from Edward Dodwell (1821), *Views in Greece*, London: Rodwell and Martin. Humbox   159
12.1 Paul Cézanne (1839–1906). *Mont Sainte-Victoire and the Viaduct of the Arc River Valley*, 1882– 1885. Oil on canvas. 25¾ x 32⅛ in. The Metropolitan Museum of Art, New York   220

CONTRIBUTORS

Harriet Archer is a lecturer in early modern English literature at the University of St Andrews. She received her DPhil from the University of Oxford, and has taught at the University of Colorado, Boulder, and Newcastle University, where she held a Leverhulme Early Career Fellowship. Her first book, *Unperfect Histories: The Mirror for Magistrates, 1559-1610*, was published in 2017, and she is currently working on the intersections of early modern admonitory cultures with nonhuman agents and environmental discourse.

Chloe Bray is a Leverhulme Postdoctoral Fellow at the University of Heidelberg. She received her PhD from the University of St Andrews, where she held the St Leonards and Millar-Lyell Scholarships. Her research interests span classical Greek literature, with a focus on landscape, time and emotion. She has published on the concept of edges in Homer, in a chapter titled 'Limits of Dread: ἔσχατα, πεῖραρ and Dangerous Edge-space in Homeric Formulae', in *Landscapes of Dread in Classical Antiquity*, edited by D. Felton (2018).

Cian Duffy is Professor and Chair of English literature at Lund University, Sweden. He has published monographs, editions and articles dealing with various aspects of the intellectual life and cultural history of Europe during the Romantic period. Recent work includes the collection *Romantic Norths: Anglo-Nordic Exchanges, 1770-1842* (2017) and the edition *Percy Bysshe Shelley: Selected Poems and Prose* (ed. with Jack Donovan, 2018).

Peter H. Hansen is Professor of History and Director of International and Global Studies at Worcester Polytechnic Institute. His research investigates the intertwined histories of mountaineering and modernity. *The Summits of Modern Man* (2013) examined the transformation of the summit position – which had been reserved for God or the King before the eighteenth century – into a symbol of individual sovereignty and enlightenment. He is currently writing a book on commercialization and Mount Everest.

Dawn Hollis is a postdoctoral researcher at the University of St Andrews, working with Jason König on a Leverhulme Trust research project entitled 'Mountains in ancient literature and culture and their postclassical reception'. Her work on the history of mountains has appeared in *Alpinist* and *Interdisciplinary Studies in Literature and the Environment*.

Dan Hooley is Emeritus Professor of Classics at the University of Missouri. He has written a number of articles and book chapters on Roman poetry, climbing and mountain literature, and classical reception. His primary subject is classical satire, on which he has written two books, *Roman Satire* (2007) and *The Knotted Thong: Structures of Mimesis in Persius* (1997).

Contributors

Sean Ireton is Associate Professor of German at the University of Missouri. He has published journal articles and book chapters on diverse topics and authors, mainly within the realm of German Studies. He is the author of *An Ontological Study of Death: From Hegel to Heidegger* (2007) and the co-editor of two essay volumes on the cultural history of mountains: *Heights of Reflection: Mountains in the German Imagination from the Middle Ages to the Twenty-First Century* (2012); and *Mountains and the German Mind: Translations from Gessner to Messner, 1541-2009* (2020).

Alley Marie Jordan is currently pursuing a PhD in Classics at the University of Edinburgh, entitled '"The Most Roman of the Romanists": Thomas Jefferson's Classical Aesthetic, 1768–1826'. She researches classical reception in eighteenth-century gardens and architecture more broadly, and has published on garden grottoes for the *Journal of Garden History* and on classical reception in J. R. R. Tolkien's *The Lord of the Rings*.

Janice Hewlett Koelb is Adjunct Assistant Professor of English and Comparative Literature at the University of North Carolina at Chapel Hill. Her research focuses on the symbolically productive interplay of mind, landscape and cultural memory. She is Advising Editor of *Marcabru*, in the Gale Cengage series *Classical and Medieval Literature Criticism* (Layman Poupard) and the author of articles in *Florilegium*, *Arethusa* and *Interdisciplinary Studies in Literature and the Environment*. Her book, *The Poetics of Description: Imagined Places in European Literature* (2006), traces the Romantic development of classical *ekphrasis* as emotionally persuasive place description.

Jason König is Professor of Greek at the University of St Andrews. His books include *Athletics and Literature in the Roman Empire* (2005) and *Saints and Symposiasts: The Literature of Food and the Symposium in Greco-Roman and Early Christian Culture* (2012). He is currently working on a book on mountains in the literature and culture of the ancient Mediterranean.

Douglas Whalin is a research fellow at the Institute of Christian Oriental Research (ICOR) at The Catholic University of America. A social historian, his research interests include group identities and the development of Greek, Syriac and Coptic Christian literature. His forthcoming monograph, *Roman Identity from the Arab Conquest to the Triumph of Orthodoxy*, explores how Romanness was articulated and understood in the eastern Roman Empire and its neighbours at the end of late antiquity and the start of the early Middle Ages.

Gareth D. Williams is Anthon Professor of Latin Language and Literature at Columbia University, New York City. He is the author of several books on Ovid and Seneca and, most recently, of *Pietro Bembo on Etna: The Ascent of a Venetian Humanist* (2017).

SERIES PREFACE

While our intention in writing this preface was to provide a neutral introduction that could stand for the whole series, recent events are too dramatic and relevant to ignore. As we launch the series, and write this text, we are (hopefully) emerging from the ravages of the 2020 Covid-19 pandemic. Along with the climate crisis, this experience has increased awareness of human reliance and impact on the environments we occupy, dramatically emphasized human inability to control nature, and reinforced perceptions that the environment is the most pressing political and social issue of our time. It confirms our belief that the time is right to situate our current (abnormal?) relationship with nature within an examination of human interactions with the environment over the *longue durée* – a belief that has given rise to this series.

Ancient Environments sets out to explore (from a variety of perspectives) different constructions of the 'environment' and understandings of humankind's place within it, across and around the Mediterranean from 3500 BCE–750 CE. By 'environment' we mean the worlds of living and non-living things in which human societies and cultures exist and with which they interact. The series focuses on the *co-construction* of humans and the natural world. It examines not only human-led interactions with the environment (e.g. the implications of trade or diet), but also those that foreground earth systems and specific environmental phenomena; it investigates both physical entities and events and ancient, imagined environments and alternate realities. The initial and primary focus of this series is the ancient world, but by explicitly exploring, evaluating and contextualizing past human societies and cultures in dialogue with their environments, it also aims to illuminate the development and reception of environmental ideas and concepts, and to provoke a deeper understanding of more long-term and widespread environmental dynamics.

The geographical remit of this series includes not only the cultures of the Mediterranean and Near East, but also those of southern Europe, North Africa including Egypt, northern Europe, the Balkans and the shores of the Black Sea. We believe that encompassing this broader geographical extent supports a more dynamic, cross-disciplinary and comparative approach – enabling the series to transcend traditional boundaries in scholarship. Its temporal range is also far-reaching: it begins with the Neolithic (a dynamic date range, depending on location in the Near East/Europe) because it marks a distinct change in the ways in which human beings interacted with their environment. We have chosen *c.* 750 CE as our end date because it captures the broadest understanding of the end of Late Antiquity in the Central Mediterranean area, marking the rise of the Carolingians in the West, and the fall of the Umayyad Caliphate in the East.

Our series coincides with, and is inspired by, a particular focus on 'the environmental turn' in studies of the ancient world, as well as across humanities more generally. This

Series Preface

focus is currently provoking a reassessment of approaches that have tended to focus solely on people and their actions, prompting scholars to reflect instead (or alongside) on the key role of the environments in which their historical subjects lived, and which shaped and were shaped by them. By extending beyond the chronological and geographical boundaries that often define — and limit — understanding of the meaning of 'antiquity', we intend that this series should encourage and enable broader participation from within and beyond relevant academic disciplines. This series will, we hope, not only advance the investigation of ancient ecological experiences, but also stimulate reflection on responses to contemporary ecological challenges.

The editors would like to express heartfelt thanks to Alice Wright at Bloomsbury Press who first conceived of the idea and suggested it to Esther, and who has done so much to develop it, and to Georgina Leighton, in particular for her work in launching the series. We are extremely grateful to the members of the Series Board, who have provided such wonderful encouragement and support, and to our authors (current and future) who have entrusted their work to this 'home'. We have chosen the 'Mistress of Animals' or *Potnia Theron*, a figure found in Near Eastern, Minoan, Mycenean, Greek and Etruscan art over thousands of years, as the motif for the series.

Anna Collar
Esther Eidinow
Katharina Lorenz

ACKNOWLEDGEMENTS

Very few mountain ascents are made unsupported, and the completion of this volume is no different. We are very grateful to the Leverhulme Trust for their generous support of the wider project, 'Mountains in ancient literature and culture and their postclassical reception', of which it is a part. All of the papers included in the volume were trialled at a volume workshop in December 2018. We are grateful to the St Andrews School of Classics for funding that workshop, and to John Clark, Katharine Earnshaw, Jon Hesk, Jamie Hinrichs and Rebecca Sweetman for their insightful contributions to the discussion. Thanks also to the roundtable participants at our panel on 'Ancient mountains and their modern significance' at the 'Thinking Mountains' conference at Banff in October 2018 (Stephen Slemon, Dan Hooley, Carolin Roeder and Sean Ireton), and to the audience at that event. Finally, very many thanks go to Alice Wright, Georgina Leighton and Lily Mac Mahon at Bloomsbury for guiding us along the route to publication, and to the series editors and anonymous readers for their very helpful comments.

NOTE ON TRANSLATIONS AND ORDER OF CHAPTERS

Where not otherwise specified, translations of Greek and Latin texts are from the latest version in the Loeb Classical Library series.

We have chosen not to divide the chapters formally into subsections, in the hope that readers will be encouraged to explore for themselves the many different points of connection between different chapters in the volume. We have, however, arranged the chapters in thematically related pairs in order to offer one possible pathway through the volume; a number of other possible guiding threads are explored below in the introduction (see further below, 8–15). We open with two chapters that examine the use of classical ideas about mountains, one early modern (Hooley), the other focusing on the eighteenth century (Duffy). The eighteenth century was often taken as a watershed period, which saw the development of uniquely modern responses to mountains, as we shall see further in the introduction, but these two opening chapters give us a first glimpse of some of the continuities across that boundary. The chapters that follow examine in turn (among other things) the processes of compiling knowledge about mountains (Hollis, Ireton), mountains as spaces of retreat and holiness on the edge of civilization (Whalin, Koelb), mountains as objects of aesthetic judgement (Jordan, König), the process of representing human experience in mountain landscapes (Williams, Bray), and the links between mountains and identity (Archer, Hansen). We hope that those pairings will provide a strong outline structure for those who choose to read the volume from end to end.

INTRODUCTION
Dawn Hollis and Jason König

In his 1711 *Essay on Criticism*, Alexander Pope famously contrasts the initial, short-sighted enthusiasm for poetic achievement ('Short views we take, nor see the lengths behind') with the longer view that comes from experience ('Hills peep o'er hills and Alps on Alps arise').[1] These lines capture something of the experience of a mountain ascent, in which hours of staring at the ground in front of one's feet can give way to a very different view as the clouds lift or a ridge is crossed. They encapsulate, too, something of the exhilaration that comes from taking a long view of mountain history. You may be familiar with the mountain literature of one period, but suddenly new landscapes from other periods and places are opened up to view, connected in many ways with the slopes that are familiar to you, but also quite distinct in their character. Our aim in this volume is to give the reader access to precisely that kind of view, by setting each of the texts and periods considered in what follows not just within their own distinctive contexts but also in a relationship of interconnection and intervisibility with multiple other chapters in the history of mountains, from classical antiquity to the modern world.

The current contours of mountain studies

The study of mountains in modern scholarship has in many ways never been more vital, in the sense of being both active and necessary. Mountain studies, broadly defined, have attracted increasing attention over the past decade or so, especially in the sciences and social sciences, driven by pressing contemporary concerns. The world's mountains offer many powerful examples both of the physical impacts of climate change and of its socio-economic consequences for people dwelling in what are usually seen as 'marginal' environments.[2]

Mountains also inspire cultural fascination. In a scholarly context, this has been reflected in increasingly vigorous discussion in the humanities and from historical perspectives in particular. Important work has been done over the past decade, adding nuance and richness to our understanding of mountains in many different historical contexts: in ancient Mediterranean and Byzantine culture, in Renaissance and Enlightenment responses and in the eras of Romanticism and modern mountaineering.[3] Valuable efforts have been made to bring these perspectives into dialogue with scientific and social-scientific approaches.[4] However, researchers working in different historical periods have not always been in dialogue with each other. This volume responds to that situation by opening a conversation between different timeframes and disciplines within the humanities and by bringing the classical tradition of mountain engagement more into dialogue with its postclassical equivalents. As we shall see there are some precedents for this project, but they are relatively few and far between, and tend to take the form of single-authored works.[5] In *Mountain Dialogues* we have instead taken a collaborative approach, with the goal of generating new insights into the richness and interconnectedness of the different texts and cultures that we study.

Any longue-durée consideration of mountains in Western culture faces the challenge of a very long-standing but misleading perception which still casts its shadow over academic and especially popular writing on mountain history. This is the idea that the history of mountain experience in Europe is characterized by an eighteenth-century watershed, on either side of which can be found the 'mountain gloom' of premodern engagements, and the 'mountain glory' of modern ones. These terms are drawn from the seminal work on the topic by Marjorie Hope Nicolson, who published her *Mountain Gloom and Mountain Glory: The Development of the Aesthetics of the Infinite* in 1959.[6] In many ways Nicolson's work was new and revolutionary: she read works of early modern natural philosophy, or 'science', as literary texts and as harbingers of cultural and aesthetic change. At the same time, it was based on a conception that was already deep-rooted: by her own admission she set out to solve 'a basic problem in the history of taste' which predated her work by decades, namely the apparent dearth of positive responses to mountains in English literature from before around the end of the seventeenth century.[7] And it is in its titular, long-established claim, rather than in its methodology or nuanced textual analysis, that Nicolson's work has gone on to have the greatest influence. A large proportion of late twentieth- and early twenty-first-century accounts of mountain history, especially non-specialist accounts that deal with the subject in passing, cite Nicolson, often to support the simple 'fact' that Europeans in general did not appreciate mountains until the eighteenth century.[8] The idea has long since circulated in the popular historical consciousness: most prominently in recent years, Robert Macfarlane's bestselling *Mountains of the Mind* reiterated to tens of thousands of readers that three centuries ago, 'The notion barely existed . . . that wild landscape might hold any sort of appeal'.[9]

There have been attempts to move beyond this overly simplistic model, although more so in some areas of study than others. Scholars on the later side of the supposed eighteenth-century watershed, including several of the contributors to this volume, have developed far more complex understandings of modern responses to mountains. Peter Hansen, for example, has introduced the concept of 'the summit position', proposing that the idea of the individual, alone and first upon a mountaintop, was crucial to the development of both modernity and mountaineering (which were themselves, he suggests, mutually constitutive phenomena) in the late eighteenth and early nineteenth centuries.[10] Hansen's analysis of mountaineering as a practice intertwined with and productive of new ideas regarding the fashioning of the self, the imperatives of empire, and political and individual autonomy, has offered an important corrective to the tendency to write modern mountaineering history in wholly uncritical and celebratory terms as a narrative of progress. As Hansen's insights make clear, the successive conquests of the world's peaks in the nineteenth and twentieth centuries were much more than just natural and inevitable responses to new perceptions of 'mountain glory'. In their study of the contemporary socio-political status of mountains, Bernard Debarbieux and Gilles Rudaz have drawn attention to the lack of consensus regarding any bureaucratic or governmental definition of the term 'mountain', arguing that the idea of the 'mountain' is itself a culturally variable construct, and that the forms that construct takes impact on the ways in which governments engage with mountains and how people living in the mountains experience them.[11] With that complex and multifaceted picture in mind the idea of 'mountain glory' as the unvarying, default modern response seems simplistic and misleading. Meanwhile, Cian Duffy has re-minted the famous term 'classic ground' (originally used by Joseph Addison with reference to the culturally and historically rich landscape of Italy), to emphasize the ways in which eighteenth- and nineteenth-century travellers experienced the Romantic sublime not as a disinterested aesthetic response but as a sensation embedded in an awareness and indeed active construction of the historical associations of specific landscapes. Duffy's work challenges the idea that romantic engagements with landscape were free from any connection with the past: on the contrary a sense of history was an essential feature.[12]

Others have begun to challenge the idea of premodern 'mountain gloom'. In some cases that has involved shifting the concept rather than overturning it entirely: for example, Martin Korenjak and William Barton have suggested that the moment of transition from 'gloom to glory' should be located several centuries earlier than Nicolson had assumed.[13] Others have gone further, most prominently Janice Hewlett Koelb, who has challenged Nicolson's stereotypes of 'Christian distrust' and 'Roman distaste' for mountains by pointing to the writings of individuals such as Dante, Quintilian and Cicero, to demonstrate that the concept of 'mountain glory' was rooted in premodern and indeed classical precedents.[14] Koelb rightly emphasizes Nicolson's 'enduring service' to literary scholars in highlighting for the first time 'the turbulent crosscurrents among theology, humane letters, and scientific speculation about the natural world' during the seventeenth century. She concludes, however, that the narrative of gloom and glory has served 'as a simple framework on which to pin a complex set of facts. But the facts ultimately will not allow so simple a framework to stand'.[15]

Despite all of these developments, however, there is still a tendency among academic and especially popular historians working on modern responses to mountains to use this oversimplified image of 'mountain gloom' in their attempts to sum up the 'prehistory' of the phenomena in which they are interested. That standard move leaves the impression of preceding swathes of human history in which relatively little happened: in which people neither liked nor spent much time around mountains. Many dismissals of premodern mountain experience see little need to provide a citation, Nicolsonian or otherwise: it is an idea which has entered the sphere of generally accepted historical knowledge.[16] Of course, no-one could deny that some things did change in the eighteenth and nineteenth centuries. The period saw the development of a new vocabulary of emotional and aesthetic response to mountains, along with the development of mountain-climbing as a leisure pursuit. But our hypothesis in this volume is that the gloom-glory model leads to a vastly oversimplified image of premodern mountain engagement, and to a systematic failure to understand what we can gain by exposing texts from different centuries to the same questions within a comparative framework.

It is inevitably difficult to generalize about 'premodern' responses. There are different factors lying behind the continued devaluing of premodern mountain engagements for different disciplines and different periods. For the centuries immediately preceding the supposed eighteenth-century watershed it seems likely that academic attention has been limited in part because of these long-lasting assumptions about premodern dislike of mountains. Why develop a research proposal on something that is widely believed, in both popular and scholarly discourse, to have been non-existent?[17] Recent scholarly discussions of early modern mountains can be counted on one hand.[18] The medieval period has seen a similar neglect of historical mountain studies, which is only now beginning to be remedied.[19]

For the classical world the picture is rather different. It is hard to imagine many classicists taking seriously the claim that the ancient Greeks and Romans were entirely uninterested in mountains. For some the gloom-glory dichotomy might in fact look like a straw man that is so easy to dismiss that it is not worth considering. Even for Greek and Roman antiquity, however, there do seem to be factors that encourage the impression of a disjuncture between ancient and modern responses. There has been important work on the history and archaeology of ancient mountains, for example in relation to their role as places of sacrifice and worship of the gods, or on their contribution to the economy and identity of particular regions.[20] There has also been some work on literary responses to mountains, especially in the pioneering publications of Richard Buxton.[21] Nevertheless there is still a tendency in Classics as a discipline to underestimate the complexity and sophistication of ancient landscape description, perhaps not directly because of the Nicolsonian model, but rather for the related reason that ancient landscape engagement tends not to follow the Romantic pattern of aesthetically inflected set-piece description: it takes a considerable effort to see beyond that absence and to appreciate on their own terms the much more disjointed, understated ways of engaging with landscape that we find in ancient narrative.[22] There has also been very little interest among classicists in the challenge of engaging with modern mountain writing as a way of opening up fresh questions and perspectives on the ancient material, presumably from an assumption that ancient and modern mountain responses do indeed belong to entirely different worlds.

The continuing tendency to think in terms of a sharp dichotomy between premodern and modern responses – the latter characterized by the desire to conquer mountain summits, and to produce writings which dwell at length on the sublime beauties of the landscape – has several consequences. On the one hand, it can lead us to underestimate the similarities between modern and premodern engagements. At the same time, and paradoxically, it can lead us to underestimate the differences. Ancient, medieval, and early modern responses to mountains tend to be judged according to how far they measure up to their more 'highly developed' modern equivalents, rather than being analysed on their own terms. Two prominent examples include Petrarch's ascent of Mont Ventoux in 1336, and Conrad Gessner's sixteenth-century writings in praise of mountains.

Both of these figures have been hailed as 'modern', as rare exceptions to a rule of mountain distaste, although Petrarch has also been criticized for falling short of a true appreciation of the summit when he turned from the view towards a consideration of his own spiritual failings.[23] In reality, of course, neither Petrarch nor Gessner were remotely 'modern', and nor were they the only authors of their eras to acknowledge mountains; they are simply the ones most frequently noted by virtue of their surface similarities with modern modes of mountain writing.

The aim of this volume, by contrast, is to consciously step out of the shadow of mountain gloom and glory: to encompass a wider range of past mountain writing, and to highlight congruences between mountain engagements of different periods where they exist, but also to utilize a comparative approach precisely in order to emphasize what is distinctive about responses to mountains in different cultures and periods. In terms of the former goal, this volume promotes a greater appreciation of connections across time, with chapters tracing the influence of particular classical texts and ideas on later responses to the landscape, and highlighting the way in which what we might at first glance take as modern ideas are in some cases actually rooted in ancient precedents. At the same time, we aim to avoid a simplistic sense of the 'classical tradition' at work, or any suggestion that ancient, medieval, early modern and modern mountain engagements were straightforwardly the same. Instead, our argument is that responses across time need to be read as part of the same history and exposed to the same variety of questions and approaches in order to produce distinctive but mutually intelligible answers. Rather than just tracing genealogical connections between different moments of mountain engagement, we propose a dialogue: between responses to mountains from different periods, and between the methodologies of different disciplines.

In doing so, we are building on the nuanced paradigms and ways of thinking developed in discrete corners of mountain scholarship of the past decade, but crucially bringing them together in order to develop new ways of understanding mountains in a historical perspective. We believe that this kind of collaborative, cross-disciplinary approach is vital in enabling the humanities in general and historical subjects specifically to play a significant role within the wider field of mountain studies. As noted in the opening to this introduction, mountain research in the sciences and social sciences has been driven by undeniably urgent questions regarding the preservation of the environment and the experiences of societies whose cultures and economies are intertwined with mountain landscapes. It is therefore perhaps no surprise that the field is dominated by environmental, geographical and socio-economic approaches. The current state of play, however, underestimates the extent to which historical, humanities perspectives have the potential to speak to contemporary concerns.

Explicit engagement with current issues through the mountain histories of the past is not our main goal in this volume, but we do see it as a high priority for the future. It might help us, for example, to understand more clearly the cultural variability of human responses to mountains, and to raise the possibility of alternative models for mountain life which are quite different from those we are familiar with. It might also at the same time shed light on continuities between past and present which can help to combat simplistic notions of modern exceptionalism, whereby anthropocentric modes of engagement with mountains are celebrated or denigrated as uniquely contemporary phenomena. This volume does, however, aim to break some new ground in building consensus regarding shared concerns, questions and themes within historical mountain studies. Our hope is that an intensification of cross-disciplinary dialogue in this field will lead to a stronger sense of shared identity, and so in turn to an increased prominence within mountain studies more broadly, which will ultimately strengthen our ability as scholars of the past to speak to the present and future.

Mountain pathways

Of course, in crossing any mountain one must start from somewhere. In this volume, we take as our starting-point the literature and culture of the ancient Mediterranean world. Our initial invitation to our contributors was to consider, among other things, how far postclassical ways of thinking about mountains had been shaped by classical understandings, and how a comparative approach, in bringing ancient and modern material together, can help to generate both new methodological developments and also fresh perspectives on long-standing scholarly views. In that sense this volume aims to make a distinctive contribution to the series in which it is published, in proposing an interpretation of 'ancient environments' that extends into modernity. The history of ancient Mediterranean environments and landscapes does not stop at the end of late antiquity. If we want to understand that history in its full richness we need to take the opportunity to expose it to questions and challenges from other periods and disciplines, and we need to understand its afterlife. What does it look like not only to read ancient mountains through the lens of modern experiences but also, more radically, to read 'post'-classical experiences through the lens of ancient mountain engagements?

Historically, mountains stand as places of connection. Traditionally there has been a tendency to assume, particularly for premodern culture, that mountains were wilderness spaces that obstructed travel and exchange and kept their populations cut off from the outside world. Recent work, at least on classical culture, has argued precisely the opposite: that mountains were often zones of interconnection and communication that brought the communities on either side of them together.[24] The diverse contributors to this volume came together to present their papers in Scotland in December 2018, and over and over again we recognized connecting concerns between papers on different periods which would otherwise have never been brought into conversation with one another. Our experience of that workshop and of the resulting volume has been that the topic of mountains offers an exciting and valuable meeting-place for a variety of disciplines, genres and scholarly literatures.

The chapters that follow deal with a series of themes and questions which we see as central to the study of mountains in past contexts, and crucial to any attempt to understand the relationship between ancient Mediterranean engagements with mountains and their later equivalents. This volume makes no claims to be exhaustive. It is designedly far from comprehensive in its chronological and geographical coverage. Each of the chapters focuses on specific issues or moments: these are case studies within a broad history, portions of an as yet incomplete outline map of a vast territory. In the history of mapping, mountains have traditionally posed great challenges: mountain regions have often been left empty because of their inaccessibility and because of the challenges of high-altitude cartography. Many of the individual case studies in the volume deal with areas that are still more or less blank in the history of scholarship; some by contrast offer a fresh view of often-studied ground. Nevertheless, we do aim to cover a set of recurring issues that have emerged repeatedly in our discussions as core issues from many different periods and genres.

We have chosen not to divide the chapters formally into subsections precisely because we want to maximize the opportunity for readers to draw out for themselves the variety of possible connections between different chapters in the volume. We have also chosen to avoid a chronological organization for the chapters, so as not to detract from our aim of promoting interconnection and communication between the study of mountains in different periods: often, the most significant overlaps between chapters have little to do with chronological proximity. We have, however, arranged the chapters in thematically related pairs in order to offer one possible pathway through the volume.

Our two opening chapters consider the classicizing mountain responses of figures on either side of the supposed eighteenth-century watershed in mountain perceptions, offering us a first glimpse of some of the continuities across that boundary. Dan Hooley elucidates the 'mountain sublime' of the sixteenth-century botanist Conrad Gessner, and Cian Duffy explores the tensions between 'scientific' and 'literary' responses to volcanoes in the writings of the traveller Patrick Brydone and the poet Anna Seward.

Chapters three and four delve further into the relationship between past and present in a pair of texts dedicated to compilation of knowledge about mountains. Dawn Hollis charts the uneasy authority of classical texts in seventeenth-century attempts to understand the natural landscape, in the work of Thomas Burnet and his interlocutors, whilst Sean Ireton's chapter on W. A. B. Coolidge and Josias Simler unpacks the erudite complexity of a twentieth-century climber's translation of a sixteenth-century guide to the Alps which was in turn indebted to ancient impressions of the mountains.

Douglas Whalin and Janice Hewlett Koelb, in chapters five and six, turn our attention from mountains as spaces of knowledge-making towards traditions of thinking about mountains as spaces of retreat and holiness that are reused repeatedly over many centuries from the ancient world onward: Whalin offers an overview of late antique Christian construction of mountains, and Koelb focuses specifically upon mountains as motifs in the lives and later representations of the saints Jerome and Francis.

Alley Marie Jordan reminds us in chapter seven that those classical ways of thinking about mountain retreats could be found even as far afield as Thomas Jefferson's eighteenth-century Virginia estates. Both Jordan's chapter, and Jason König's contribution in chapter eight on the travel writing of Edward Dodwell, address the intertwining of classical ways of thinking about mountains with aesthetic concepts such as the picturesque and the sublime which became so prominent in eighteenth- and nineteenth-century landscape writing.

From there we return to the work of Patrick Brydone, another famous example of the Mediterranean travel-writing genre, in the chapter by Gareth Williams. Both he, and Chloe Bray in chapter ten, explore in different ways the relationship between representation and experience in mountain narratives. Williams looks at the constant tension between real, embodied experience and imagined, even fabricated representations of ascent in eighteenth- and nineteenth-century antiquarian mountaineering, and also in Petrarch's famous account of an ascent of Mont Ventoux in 1336 and Pietro Bembo's account of his ascent of Etna in 1493. Bray unpacks the phenomenologically resonant character of portrayals of landscape in classical Greek tragedy, for example Euripides' *Bacchae*, which not only represents mountains as places of mythological fantasy, but also prompts its audience members to recall their own bodily experiences of mountain landscapes.

Finally, chapters eleven and twelve consider mountains and the construction of national or regional identity. Harriet Archer focusses on a series of rich sixteenth- and seventeenth-century texts, including John Higgins' *Mirror for Magistrates*, in order to unfold the relationship between poetic allegory, mountains, and a Tudor sense of British identity. In turn, Peter Hansen takes a long view of the history of Mont Ventoux as the nexus for developing ideas of modernity and nationhood, from the much-interpreted ascent by Petrarch to the ambivalent visions of the summit position in the writings of Provençal poet and Resistance leader René Char. Hansen's chapter offers an apt conclusion to the volume by then gesturing 'upland' to the future of mountain environments and our relationship to them.

The above represents just one attempt at route-finding through the chapters of this volume. In the Greek poetry of Hellenistic Alexandria, from the fourth and third centuries BCE, and later in Roman elegy, the idea of the poet travelling an untrodden path, sometimes explicitly a mountain path, was routinely used as a metaphor for literary originality.[25] We hope that readers will look beyond the possible pairings we have outlined above in order to trace their own original connections between the chapters, texts, eras and contexts represented here. As a starting-point for that process, in the remainder of this introduction, we offer a number of alternative routes by drawing out some of the thematic clusters that we have been most struck by in our reading and in our conversations. These fall under four main and overlapping categories – temporality, knowledge, identity and experience – although we recognize that these themes are inevitably intertwined with each other.[26] Some of what follows expands upon the connections sketched already in the previous paragraphs; other sections draw attention to further areas of common ground.

Temporality

Mountains across human culture are often associated with the past, sometimes a very ancient past, in distinctive ways. These often involve imagining mountains as places of origin, as Hansen shows in his account of Cézanne's fascination with Mont Sainte-

Victoire as a place linked with the dawn of human existence. Richard Buxton has pointed out that mountains are 'before' in ancient Greek thought too, envisaged as places linked with the earliest human populations and with the pre-human.[27] The deep time of modern geological understanding of mountains, recently charted at length by Veronica della Dora, is another way of thinking about the antiquity of mountains,[28] but the uniqueness of that modern view has often been overstated. In her chapter in this volume Hollis demonstrates that early modern notions of geological temporality were themselves formed with reference to classical (and also biblical) ideas about the antiquity of mountains,[29] particularly their ideas of an original 'Chaos' in the early stages of creation. These ideas were used not as inert embellishments, but as crucial evidence, albeit less highly valued than the authority of Scripture or rational observation and inductive reasoning. Duffy similarly emphasizes that eighteenth-century understandings of the timescales of Etna's volcanic landscape are indebted to classical predecessors. Many different cultures, then, have shared a sense of mountains as places with a deep antiquity which stands as a puzzle to understanding and analysis.

The antiquity of mountains also has a historical and mythological dimension. Mountains are wilderness spaces, but they are also places of human culture and human history, and the tension between those two elements is one source of their fascination. During the last two centuries the human past of mountains has been envisaged most often in relation to the history of mountaineering: famous peaks gain much of their fascination from the stories of those who have climbed on them and died on them in the past. But that phenomenon is only one subset of a much older process of understanding mountain landscapes according to the stories that are associated with their slopes and summits. The connection between landscape and memory that Simon Schama traced influentially more than two decades ago has a long heritage stretching back into the classical past.[30]

Much of our discussion of that issue in what follows focuses on the distinctive relationship with the past that we see in the mountains of the Mediterranean. For centuries and even millennia the communities of mainland Greece and Asia Minor processed to mountaintops to sacrifice, as a way of acting out their connections with the divine and with the customs of their ancestors.[31] The status of mountains as places of mythological memory continued even into the Roman empire and beyond, for example in the work of Pausanias, who travelled in Greece in the second century CE, and whose work is full of descriptions of mountain shrines and mythological stories associated with them.[32] For the ancient world it was hard to separate mythological and scientific explanation, as Duffy illustrates in the case of Mount Etna: he sees them as 'blurring ... rather than reinforcing any sense of these as distinct ways of knowing and describing the world'.[33] One version of the history of these sites might emphasize the way in which those mythological associations died away in the postclassical world, or at any rate became more and more confined to literary game playing, but Duffy also demonstrates that the mythological strand in those discussions continued to have an influence over the modern accounts – we see traces of it absorbed and reconfigured within the empirical language of writing about Etna in the eighteenth century, or in Anna Seward's writings on the volcanic quality of eighteenth-century industry and technology. In later centuries too that very ancient classical past continued to have a powerful resonance, as highlighted by König in his study of nineteenth-century travel writers, who were similarly aware of the way in which ascending the mountains of Greece connected them with an ancient history and mythology that might be less conspicuously visible at ground level. Veronica della Dora has drawn similar conclusions, for example in writing about mountains as memory theatres for Mediterranean travellers in the eighteenth and nineteenth centuries.[34]

Side by side with these traditions of mythological and historical memory we also see an alternative strand in the association between mountains and the past in early Christian culture where the characterization of mountains as sacred spaces is repurposed to convey the holiness of the saints who now inhabit them, as Whalin details in his contribution.[35] The mountain now becomes a space of retreat: in that sense it is about as far removed from human culture as possible, and the association of the saints with these spaces is itself partly dependent on the kind of ancient connections that Buxton has traced, where mountains stand outside civilization, as the home of divine figures, marginal, prodigious creatures and strange happenings. At the same time, however, the image of the mountain retreat quickly becomes a deeply conventional, cultural one, whose resonances still have a hold not only in the Renaissance, as Koelb demonstrates, but even in Thomas Jefferson's eighteenth-century America, as we see in Jordan's chapter.

It is also evident, however, that the normal rules of time can be suspended or disturbed in mountain contexts. For example, as König further makes clear, mountains can possess a temporality which is startlingly different from that of the spaces around them: the association with classical antiquity that Edward Dodwell and his contemporaries sense as soon as they begin to ascend the mountains of mainland Greece is at odds with the present-day realities of Ottoman Greece.[36] Alternatively, and appropriately for this volume, different layers of time can co-exist with each other on mountains. Conrad Gessner's sixteenth-century mountain writings, explored in Hooley's chapter, resist any easy narrative of periodization, standing in a kind of 'diachronic continuum': 'Gessner presents the opportunity to identify strains of thought and sensibility that leak through literary-historical framings, permeate through periods',[37] attitudes and motifs that are associated with both modern and ancient. His immersion in ancient ways of thinking about the sublime, which at the same time feels closely familiar from postclassical aesthetic discourse, is a good example. The most unexpected version of that phenomenon, as Hansen shows for Mont Ventoux and for Mont Sainte-Victoire, is the way in which mountain pasts can resurface in the present or be reactivated for the future, disrupting the linear flow of history. That image of mountains as spaces that have the potential to disrupt a straightforward sense of temporality seems particularly appropriate to the way in which this volume aims to challenge our sense of a linear narrative of mountain history.

Knowledge

Another overarching theme that unites all of the chapters that follow is the relationship between mountains and human knowledge. How can we know a mountain? What range of techniques have humans as individuals and communities used in their attempts to make sense of mountains? What continuities and differences do we see in those techniques of knowledge and control over time? Some of the chapters following address that question of knowledge in very explicit ways, in engaging with ancient and modern scientific discourse:[38] examples include Hollis's account of the development of the geological thinking of Thomas Burnet, and Duffy's mapping of the influence of ancient scientific thinking over modern responses to Mount Etna. Ireton analyses a nineteenth-century mountaineer's heavily annotated translation of a sixteenth-century classic in mountain literature, revealing a text that takes an eclectic, encyclopaedic approach (again partly in an ancient tradition of scientific writing) to produce a vast and multifaceted account of all that can be known about the Alps. In all of these cases we can see that mountains have been objects of fascination over many millennia as challenges to human attempts at decipherment and comprehension.

These attempts at knowing mountains crucially draw on a range of traditions and inheritances crossing multiple genres and eras. Mountains are spaces which particularly lend themselves to a kind of multifacetedness, where many different texts and ideas can be placed side by side with each other. Here once again the chapters by Duffy and Ireton are particularly relevant, with their attention to the accumulation of knowledge and precedent, with classical accounts and responses integrated with post-Enlightenment ways of knowing. Mountains have also historically been understood through a merging of classical and biblical heritages, as revealed in Whalin's account of mountains in late antiquity, and in Koelb's close reading of the writings of Saint Jerome.

Moreover, mountains are never known in a vacuum. The ways of knowing mountains that we chart here are rooted not just in ancient precedents but also in contemporary debates and priorities. Hollis, for example, emphasizes the dual influence of classical and biblical traditions in early modern mountain knowledge, but also shows that representations of mountains in that period often made controversial theological and scientific interventions: discussions of the origins of mountains in the late seventeenth century intersected with urgent debates about the geological history of the Earth and the accuracy of Scripture.

Identity

Representations of mountains also contribute to formations of identity. In many cases their antiquity plays a key role in that identity-forming function: for example the multifaceted past (or pasts) of Mont Ventoux is precisely what has made it so powerful as a symbol of Provençal identity, as explored in Hansen's chapter. In Jordan's chapter, we see classical influences shaping a new national landscape, with Thomas Jefferson conceiving (and physically constructing) his self-consciously 'American' mountain-spaces with ancient villas and the ideals of retirement uppermost in his mind.

Mountain ranges often act as borders for particular regions, or alternatively as heartlands. Either way they often have a prominent and very public role in representations of national identity; Bernard Debarbieux and Gilles Rudaz have mapped out the varieties of that relationship exhaustively for the nineteenth and twentieth centuries.[39] Mountains are also spaces in which personal or local identities are articulated, sometimes in tension; the term 'mountaineer' is most commonly used today to express an individual's engagement with the sporting pursuit of climbing to the summit, but the older usage, meaning someone who lives in the mountains, is still embraced by some communities, such as in the Appalachian mountains of North America.[40] Archer's chapter on a series of English Renaissance texts explores a number of different ways in which mountains were used as vehicles for articulating national identity, including images of mountain peoples whose identity is shaped by the harshness of the land they inhabit. The principles of environmental determinism on which those images are based have a vast classical heritage that work on modern mountains and identity often fails to acknowledge.

In other cases the link with identity is tied up with the lived experience of local populations. Recent work on the anthropology of mountain communities has emphasized among other things the richness and creativity of their adaptive strategies, and the way in which that often leads in turn to a strong sense of autonomy and regional consciousness.[41] Whalin makes the same point for the mountainous regions of the ancient Mediterranean in the opening pages of his chapter, emphasizing the way in which they stood apart from the urbanized norms of the coastal plains that accommodated the majority of the inhabitants of the Roman empire. The recovery of these kinds of engagements – the everyday, the non-elite – is arguably a significant potential contribution that historical mountain studies can make to contemporary discussions, in providing historical contexts to the rights of mountain-dwellers to have a say over the future of the landscapes they inhabit.

Experience

Humans also know mountains by imagining them, and imagined landscapes can in turn shape real experience. This is a central factor in the link between mountains and identity, but it also lies at the heart of aesthetic responses to mountains. Often the two are connected with each other, as in Thomas Jefferson's powerful vision of the aesthetic qualities of the American landscape. This is shaped by an engagement with classical categories as well as with the distinctively eighteenth-century language of the sublime, in much the same way as Edward Dodwell's portrayals of the mountains of Greece (see Jordan's and König's chapters, respectively). Likewise, Jefferson's explicitly American vision of mountainous landscape simultaneously draws on and stands in rivalry with its European and especially English equivalents. Here aesthetics, imagination and political sense-making go hand in hand.

Indeed, one of the recurring themes of this volume is the tension between expectation and reality, between imagination and experience. The idealization of landscape is sometimes so powerful that it can overwhelm and condition our real experience – although idealized landscapes may also be contested sites, especially when they are linked with particular national or local identities. In this volume, Williams traces a tradition of ascent narratives in which literary expectations are the dominant shaping force: whether or not Pietro Bembo or Patrick Brydone really climbed Mount Etna, the most striking fact in their accounts, he suggests, is their literariness, their imagined quality – and of course there are long-standing similar debates about Petrarch's ascent of Mont Ventoux. The narratives they create are powerful and memorable, but a knowing reader will have some awareness of this veneer of fictionality, in fact will appreciate it as part of the conventional procedures of landscape representation. Historically, and perhaps even today, this process of stretching for an image of the mountain that is just out of reach but almost attainable, through the power of literary imagination, is a central part of the thrill in elite engagements with mountains.

It is tempting, of course, to contrast that kind of artificial literary experience with another strand in ancient and modern engagement with mountains that is bodily, tactile, sensory. Bray's chapter draws on phenomenological approaches to landscape from recent scholarship to highlight the importance of that theme even for ancient Greek literature, especially tragedy. We tend to imagine – because first-person accounts of the experience of ascent are rare in ancient texts – that the physical experience of climbing and walking in mountains was alien at least to the literary elite, but in fact we find traces of that kind of bodily response scattered right through the surviving evidence for the ancient world, often combined with an interest in the way in which mountains can be places of heightened sensory engagement. That said, we should not assume a tight distinction between the imaginary and the real. Portrayal of the real and the bodily can be just as conventional, constructed, fictional as more detached, aesthetic portrayals of landscape. In some cases, perhaps in all cases, what we are dealing with is as much as anything a 'reality-effect', rather than an unmediated portrayal of bodily experience. Bembo and Brydone are once again good examples, as Williams shows: their accounts are packed with very tactile details of ascent and descent that at first sight might seem to be a guarantee of authenticity, but that on reflection turn out to be paralleled within their source texts. It is also striking that this kind of phenomenological engagement is not separate from a historical sensitivity to the links between landscape and memory; rather those two perspectives have the potential to be intricately intertwined with each other. As illustrated in Bray's chapter, memory is aided and stimulated by the kinds of exertion and immersion that mountain travel involves, and potentially reactivated at a later stage by textual or auditory triggers.

Mountains are also, for many different authors and ages, places of pleasure. In many cases, of course, that pleasure is tied up with aesthetic appreciation. But it is clear that there is a whole spectrum of other possible foundations for positive response to the idea and the experience of mountains. As Hollis establishes, Thomas Burnet's seventeenth-century critics were clear that this had been the view of the ancients, and cited a range of classical texts on the links between mountains and paradise to demonstrate that; their response focuses on the conviction that mountains were places associated with God's goodness, and in many cases places of 'beautiful usefulness'. Elsewhere, as in Conrad Gessner's work, the pleasure of the mountains is much more personal, shaped by a wide-ranging sensory satisfaction which is connected with but not narrowly confined to the sublime. The language of the *locus amoenus*, the poetic stereotype of the 'beautiful place', is repeatedly applied to mountains – paradoxically so given the contrasting pull towards representation of mountains as wilderness – both in the ancient literature, for example in the late antique Christian texts that Whalin describes, and in many centuries of later writing. The eighteenth- and nineteenth-century versions of the sublime and the picturesque clearly do represent new departures in some respects (although even that assumption turns out be far less secure than has usually been assumed),[42] but in other ways they are just one small subcategory of a much larger and more ancient set of associations between mountainous landscape and pleasure.

In the end, however, we must remember that mountains were and are real places – places of work, economic productiveness, religious observance,[43] habitation – not just playgrounds for the imagination. The standard mythological image of mountain as wilderness space which we find in many of our ancient sources is contradicted by the material evidence: mountains were often inextricably intertwined with the culture of the cities and communities around them,[44] and that basic tension – of mountains both within and beyond human control – is crucial to our experience of these places even now.

Mountains could also be places of exploitation and human hierarchy. The ways in which mountains are experienced and imagined are of course deeply implicated in social, cultural and gender hierarchies, and vary according to perspective and privilege. We know that now for the mountaineering culture of the nineteenth and twentieth centuries, which in some of its manifestations had an elitist, even imperialist character. It has long been clear, from the work of Denis Cosgrove and others, that the concept of landscape whereby the earth's surface is subjected to aesthetic assessment from a position of detachment and elevation, developing from the Renaissance onwards, was closely linked with the priorities of elite self-definition.[45] Other discussions in this volume open up new chapters in that history. Particularly striking is Jordan's account of the contrast between Jefferson's idealized representation of his hilltop retreat at Monticello, which relied heavily on an all-mastering view from above, and the underlying experience of slavery which enabled it. König too shows how Edward Dodwell's assessment of the mountains of Greece, which claims mastery both over the classical past and over judgements of sublime and picturesque landscape, stands in contrast (as for many of his contemporaries) with a more negative attitude to the modern inhabitants of Ottoman Greece and of their ability to appreciate the territory that surrounded them.

The gendering of mountain experience, by contrast, is still little understood for many of the centuries we focus on in this volume. Recent work has shown that modern mountaineering has largely been constructed as a masculine endeavour, but has also highlighted the increasingly creative ways in which many generations of women climbers and inhabitants of the mountains have manipulated and challenged that heritage.[46] The premodern equivalent of that story still remains to be told. Many of the phenomena we examine in what follows, for example the link between mountaintops and saintly retreat, represent mountains as spaces occupied by men. However, even that tradition is open to challenge in late antiquity, for example through Egeria's late fourth-century CE account of her ascent of Mount Sinai as an act of Christian religious devotion, which is one of the first surviving first-person mountain accounts of any length.[47] Side by side with the link between mountains and marginal populations – divinities, holy men, mythical creatures – was an image of mountain wilderness as a feminine space, outside the masculine realm of urban civilization, most famously in the evidence for Bacchic ritual on Mount Parnassos and other Greek mountains where women celebrated the god Dionysus in a state of trance. Those assumptions about the wild, untamed places of nature as feminine spaces have a long afterlife, in opposition to the masculine-controlled spaces of urban civilization: they find distant echoes in Thomas Jefferson's gendering of nature as feminine as he looks down from Monticello 'into the workhouse of nature, to see her clouds, hail, snow, rain, thunder, all fabricated at our feet'.[48] The challenge for the future is to expand on that outline map of gender associations for other periods and other genres.

Finally, but perhaps most urgently of all given our current ecological concerns, one of the other very powerful ways in which we experience and imagine mountains is as spaces that can unsettle anthropocentric certainties about the human capacity to dominate the natural world. This makes them useful vehicles for thinking through questions that have been central to the ecocritical and environmental humanities; they provide us with powerful models against which to measure our own imaginings of what it means to be human in confrontation with the more-than-human world.[49] At the same time we also experience mountains in some contexts as environments which undergo physical change as a result of the human relationship with them. The stories told by environmental historians about the roots of our current environmental thinking have often been vastly oversimplified. One standard account suggests that we need to look to early Christian culture for the origins of modern anthropocentric treatment of the environment, which stands in contrast with Graeco-Roman closeness to nature.[50] Others see Greek and Roman culture, and especially the globalized world of the Roman empire with its alleged deforestation of the mountain slopes of the Mediterranean, as a precursor of modern environmental damage.[51] In practice the truth is a much more complex one.[52] In fact what we see across the many centuries examined in this volume is a tension between alternative views, a mosaic of different possibilities for interaction with the environment,[53] due in part to the extreme variability between different micro-regions, and in part to the sheer difficulty of summing up what mountains mean for human culture. On the one hand their bulk can seem intimidating, invulnerable, permanent, utterly insulated from the pinpricks of human intervention; on the other hand they can seem surprisingly fragile spaces in need of protection, as we see in Hansen's discussion of the way in which Mont Ventoux served as a beacon for environmental thinking in the nineteenth and twentieth centuries. Accepting the complexity of that history of mountains and the environment may make us less inclined to tell over-simplifying stories about the situation we face today.

The increasing prospect

The aim of this volume, to return to the passage from Pope with which we opened, has been to 'see the lengths behind' human responses to mountains in the past and the present. Pope's ode promises that the reader who takes the long view will be rewarded with 'New, distant scenes of endless science', and an 'increasing prospect' for their 'wand'ring eyes'.[54] Each case study in this volume accordingly offers a new addition to our understanding of the complexity of the mountain past, and of the way in which mountain encounters are so often marked by a palimpsest of earlier texts and ideas.

To be more specific, we hope that this volume will serve two key purposes in further expanding the prospects that are visible from and through the history of mountains. The first is to challenge the continuing influence of the traditional narrative of mountain gloom and mountain glory and the way in which it reinforces a sense of stark division between modernity and premodernity. Classicists, medievalists and early modernists alike have struggled independently with the epistemic limitations that dichotomy has placed on their research; this volume has brought together work from across these periods and disciplines with the goal of beginning to frame a new narrative or narratives.

The second, related purpose that we hope this volume will serve is as an exemplar for the ongoing study of mountains in past contexts. Our goal has been to model the value and importance of intervisibility and interconnection between scholarship on different periods and from different disciplines. We believe that research on human engagements with mountains in the past can help to raise new questions about contemporary concerns as we look towards the future for the world's mountain environments. We also believe that collaborative scholarship, with its capacity to highlight both shared ideas and diversity of perspectives between different cultures and different responses over time, is especially suited to enable this. In this volume, we have sketched out one possible set of views of 'the length behind'. We expect that there are many more 'distant scenes of endless science' to explore.

Notes

1. Alexander Pope, *Essay on Criticism* (1711), Part 2, lines 22 and 32.
2. See Price 2015. The journal *Mountain Research and Development*, founded in 1981, has been an important forum for the second of those issues especially. See also the work of the Mountain Legacy Project, 'capturing change in Canada's mountains' through the use of repeat photography to highlight the retreat of glaciers, loss of precipitation, and other forms of landscape change: http://mountainlegacy.ca/ (accessed 30 August 2020).
3. See further bibliography below on all of those periods, particularly notes 5, 10–14, 18 and 19. On modern mountaineering, the literature, both popular and academic, is vast; recent studies on the cultural and aesthetic contexts of mountaineering in the nineteenth and twentieth centuries have included Colley 2010, Davis 2011, McNee 2016, Anderson 2020, S. Bainbridge 2020, W. Bainbridge 2020, Pitches 2020 and Schaumann 2020; the last five were published after the final draft of this volume was completed and it has therefore not been possible to include a detailed account of them here.
4. The promotion of such conversations has been the aim of the triennial 'Thinking Mountains Interdisciplinary Summit' (2012, 2015 and 2018) hosted by the University of Alberta. The University of Alberta also plays host to 'Mountains 101', a Massive Open Online Course (MOOC) which is freely available to all and covers topics including the geological origins of mountains, their cultural significance through time, their climatological significance, and practical safety in a high alpine environment: http://thinkingmountains.ca/about.html

5. Notable precedents can be found in della Dora 2011, 2016a, 2016b: 147–75; see also Schama 1995: 383–513, who brings together texts from many different periods, classical texts included. Perhaps the most obvious precedent for the collaborative project we are engaged in here is Ireton and Schaumann 2012, which like our volume weaves together chapters by many different authors working on either side of the traditional eighteenth-century watershed that we discuss further below; and similarly Mathieu and Boscani Leoni 2005; Kofler, Korenjak and Schaffenrath 2010; Kakalis and Goetsch 2018.
6. Nicolson 1959. Nicolson herself borrowed the dichotomy from John Ruskin's essays on 'The Mountain Gloom' and 'The Mountain Glory', published in the fourth volume of his *Modern Painters* (Ruskin 1856).
7. One of the earliest expressions of this can be found in a letter written by William Wordsworth to *The Morning Post* in 1844, later republished in Grosart 1876: 325–33. The full and complex genealogy of the concept of mountain gloom and glory is further explored in Hollis 2019.
8. Studies that mention Nicolson's work explicitly include (among many others) Tuan 1971: 70–4; Thomas 1983: 258–60; Porter 2000: 34–6; Rigby 2004: 131–40; Isserman and Weaver 2008: 27, terming Nicolson's work 'the classic and still indispensable study of the origins of the mountain aesthetic'.
9. See Macfarlane 2003: 14 for this passage; also 22–31, which closely follows the work of Nicolson in focussing on the figure of the seventeenth-century natural philosopher Thomas Burnet, discussed also in Dawn Hollis's chapter in this volume, and 137–67. Works intended for general audiences produced long before *Mountains of the Mind*, and indeed before *Mountain Gloom and Mountain* Glory, expressed the same general view: see for example Brown 1934: 17, which opened with the assertion that 'it is common knowledge that mountains were once regarded as things of terror and horror'. For a good recent example aimed at a non-specialist audience, see Sanzaro 2018, who claims that 'the origins of mountain climbing lay in the middle of the nineteenth century. Before that, they were seen as landscapes of evil otherness, where the tempestuous gods exercised their wrath. The curious ventured not.'
10. Hansen 2013: 2–3, 16–17, and throughout.
11. Debarbieux and Rudaz 2015.
12. Duffy 2013: 7–10; see also Duffy and Howell 2011: 4.
13. See for example Korenjak 2017 and Barton 2017. Korenjak argues that sixteenth-century rather than eighteenth-century sources represent the beginnings of mountain appreciation in Europe, whilst Barton suggests that the more positive attitudes identified by Nicolson in English-language texts of the eighteenth and nineteenth centuries are present somewhat earlier in Neo-Latin writings.
14. Koelb 2009; and see also now Hollis 2019. That is not to say that ancient people did not experience dread in certain landscapes and in certain contexts: see Felton 2018.
15. Quotations from Koelb 2009: 464.
16. See for example: Black 2003: 3 and Smethurst 2012: 130, who gesture towards the changing responses of European travellers and British natural aesthetics respectively without reference to Nicolson; also Thacker 1983: e.g. 3–4; Ring 2000: 7–25; Bates 2000: esp. xvii–xviii and 1–11; Fleming 2000; Hiltner 2015: xv; Dhar 2019: 345, in the opening section of an otherwise excellent account of mountain travel writing.

17. For example, di Palma 2014: 10–11 expresses just such an assumption about the absence of sources regarding 'marginal or repellent landscapes' (among which she included mountains, for the premodern period), arguing that 'lingering in order to pen an extended description or to delineate a view was simply out of the question when the goal was to put as much space between one's self and the offending environment as quickly as possible'.

18. In addition to Korenjak, Barton, and Koelb, noted above, see also Hollis 2017a with key points (and an account of the resistance among the mountaineering community to any revision of the 'mountain gloom' narrative) summarized in Hollis 2017b. For the Renaissance, see Williams 2017 on Pietro Bembo's ascent of Etna.

19. For the medieval west see Thomasset and James-Raoul 2000, Société des historiens médiévistes 2004; Carrier and Mouthon 2011. For medieval Byzantine culture and its origins in late antique responses, see esp. della Dora 2016b. Anthony Bale has noted in as yet unpublished work the emotional experiences facilitated by mountains during late medieval pilgrimages through the Holy Land, in which summit viewpoints were mentally constructed (and frequently named) as mountains of 'joy', a complex and theologically-implicated sensation associated with setting eyes upon the pilgrim's ultimate destination: Anthony Bale, 'What did it mean, and how did it feel, to look out from a mountain in the Middle Ages?', University of Edinburgh, Centre for Medieval and Renaissance Studies, 9 February 2016; and http://blogs.bbk.ac.uk/research/tag/holy-land/ (accessed 30 August 2020).

20. On mountain societies and economies see among others Garnsey 1988, McInerney 1999, Horden and Purcell 2000, esp. 80–97, Roy 2009; on mountain religion, see Langdon 1976, Romano and Voyatzis 2010.

21. See Buxton 2013, and earlier versions in Buxton 1992 and 1994: 81–96; also König 2013 and 2016; de Jong 2018.

22. Cf. della Dora 2016b: esp. 2–10 on the importance of the concept of 'place' (*topos*) for understanding Byzantine engagement with space, and on the way in which that has been 'overshadowed' (3) by the concept of 'landscape'.

23. For Petrarch, see Williams 167–8 and Hansen 215–16, below. For Gessner, see Hooley 22–3, also below. On the adoption (or rejection) of Renaissance figures as precursors to modern mountaineering see also Hollis 2019: 1050–3.

24. E.g. see Thonemann 2011: esp. 239–40 on the way in which the cities clustered around the slopes of Mount Kadmos in the Maeander Valley shared the territory of the mountain as a common source of pasturage and timber. The degree of interaction between members of the elites on either side of the mountain is much more visible in the surviving evidence than their relationship with the more accessible cities of the plains below. Their shared use of the mountain, where their shepherds and timber-gatherers would have crossed paths with each other repeatedly, is surely one of the reasons for that. On mountains as places of travel and communication, see Horden and Purcell 2000: 130–2.

25. E.g., see Propertius, *Elegies* 3.1.17–18: 'My page has carried down this work by an undefiled track from the mountain of the sisters [i.e. the Muses], so that you can read it in peace'; one of the key influences over that passage is Callimachus, *Aitia* prologue 25–8 (although the untrodden poetic path in that case is not explicitly a mountainous one). See also Worman 2015 for repeated discussion of these and other related metaphors as vehicles for ancient literary self-definition.

26. The concept of cultural memory is relevant to this intertwining of temporality, knowledge and experience. E.g., see Meckien 2013 (summarizing unpublished works by Jan and Aleida Assmann): 'Cultural memory is formed by symbolic heritage embodied in texts, rites, monuments, celebrations, objects, sacred scriptures and other media that serve as mnemonic

triggers to initiate meanings associated with what has happened. Also, it brings back the time of the mythical origins, crystallizes collective experiences of the past and can last for millennia. Therefore it presupposes a knowledge restricted to initiates'; see also Assmann 2013. We are grateful to Janice Hewlett Koelb for drawing our attention to this passage; see also her chapter in this volume for further use of this concept of 'cultural memory'.

27. Buxton 2013: 20–1.
28. See della Dora 2016a: 141–55.
29. Cf. Schama 1995: 249: 'The possibility that mountain peaks and valleys might not be the accursed places of the world coincided with the recovery of classical texts of natural history, especially the many congested volumes of Pliny the Elder. To the first generation of Renaissance fossil-hunters and mineralogists, mountains began to seem as if they had their own histories to tell'; one might quarrel with Schama's conventional (and by his standards untypical) dismissal of premodern mountain engagement, but this acknowledgement of the importance of classical precedents is nevertheless suggestive for our goals in this volume.
30. Schama 1995: 383–513 on mountains.
31. See Langdon 1976; and cf. Bernbaum 1997 for a sweeping survey of the role of sacred mountains in many different cultures.
32. E.g. see Jost 2007.
33. Cf. Buxton 2016.
34. della Dora 2008a; cf. della Dora 2016a: 155–9.
35. Cf. della Dora 2016b: 147–75.
36. Cf. della Dora 2008a.
37. Hooley, this volume: 23.
38. Cf. Debarbieux and Rudaz 2015: 13–41 on 'The mountain as object of knowledge'; della Dora 2016a: 165–89.
39. Debarbieux and Rudaz 2015: esp. 45–71.
40. Cf. Debarbieux and Rudaz 2015 for the figure of the 'mountaineer' (i.e. mountain inhabitant) in national self-definition from the eighteenth century onwards.
41. E.g. see Brush 1984 for a concise and still thought-provoking statement of that claim.
42. E.g. see Porter 2016, with discussion in Hooley this volume; also König in this volume on the way in which the concept of the picturesque was often articulated through classicizing images of landscape.
43. Cf. above on Pausanias, with Jost 2007; also Bradley 2000 on evidence from prehistoric cultures for the use of natural features as sacred places, esp. 20–8 on the way in which Pausanias's account parallels the evidence for other cultures.
44. See Jameson 1989, König 2019.
45. See esp. Cosgrove 1984.
46. E.g. see Debarbieux and Rudaz 2011 and 2015: 229–34 on the potential role of women (not yet fully activated in their view) in sustainable mountain development; Louargant 2013 for a collection of articles covering among other things women's involvement in the masculine-dominated fields of twentieth-century mountaineering and mountain-guiding and the role of women in mountain economies.
47. See della Dora 2016a: 109–11.
48. Discussed below by Jordan, 133.

49. The bibliography within mainstream ecocriticism is now vast, but see especially Buell 2005 and more recently Clark 2019 for two accounts that are particularly valuable for mapping out new models of environmental criticism. For recent ecocritical engagement with classical literature and culture, see among others Schliephake 2017; Hunt and Marlow 2019.
50. See esp. White 1967.
51. For the argument that depletion of the environment led to the collapse of Roman civilization, see Hughes 1996; and McNeil 1992: esp. 72–4, summarizing the standard arguments for a very high degree of deforestation in classical antiquity; however, see also Horden and Purcell 2000: 328–41 on the importance of avoiding a simplistic view of catastrophic deforestation.
52. Cf. Armbruster and Wallace 2001: esp. 8–11, which similarly challenges the tendency of modern environmental history 'to characterize Western thought through the Enlightenment as profoundly environmental and deeply invested in the notion of human beings as separate from and superior to non-human nature' (9), arguing instead for a much less 'monolithic' account; Fitter 1995: 84–155.
53. Cf. Coates 1998: 12 (but not for mountains specifically): 'We are hard pressed to find a single doctrine of man-nature relations in any era... A number of attitudes, notions and orientations invariably coexist in often messy contradiction'.
54. Alexander Pope, *Essay on Criticism* (1711), Part 2, lines 24 and 31.

CHAPTER 1
GESSNER'S MOUNTAIN SUBLIME
Dan Hooley

An old story tells of the world's antediluvian perfection, a divinely-engineered, featureless sphere subsequently rent and fractured by a god's retributive flood into a chaotic mess of raised and jagged scars on the land: misshapen, sin-haunted mountains.[1] That mountains should be employed thus as an aetiological topography representing the condition of post-lapsarian humanity is unsurprising. Mountains, hills, outcroppings invariably signify, reflect human states of mind – guilt and fear in this case. But they can reflect otherwise too, as can be seen in yet earlier mountain figurations as dwellings of the gods and remote Edens, sites of pilgrimage or settings of, precisely, otherworldly beauty and psychic catharsis. Just as mountains separate and define landscapes, they orient perspective. Looking upward, one takes bearings on their peaks along any number of lines: geopolitical, mythopoetical, metaphysical, epistemological. Conversely, anyone climbing to or near their summits inverts perspective to the piedmont below, to ordinary life, to the place one has come from, and thus inward, where the conjunction of self and place can be configured.[2]

Which complicates the grand European narrative of mountain aesthetics, the idea that mountains, from an early certainty that they were grotesque malformations or impediments, found their terrible beauties only after Shaftesbury, Burke, Kant and others had provided us with the right ('Sublime') vocabulary to describe them.[3] It complicates too the perspectives of mountaineering historians like John Grand-Carteret and W. A. B. Coolidge who largely carry forward the traditional narrative that climbing for pleasure is a post-Romantic phenomenon, views that can be called out, as Martin Korenjak has done, for their failure 'to incorporate these texts into a meaningful account of the development of mountain perception, let alone to integrate them into a more comprehensive history of mentalities.'[4] It will not be the object of this chapter to attempt such a comprehensive history, but rather to attempt to shake off thinking about mountains in terms of historical periodicity and focus instead on nuanced continuity, wherein 'new' ideas find anticipations and echoes throughout the longue durée of mountain history. Mountains can be seen as impenetrable barriers or, alternatively, as markers of passage *through*, or, as the editors of this volume put it, 'zones of interconnection';[5] bearings can be taken from them as they are seen through time and space. My example will be the fascinating case of Conrad Gessner whose floruit comes some two centuries ahead of the Romantic turn and who represents an illuminating counter-example to traditional thinking about mountains on almost all points.

Gessner's mountains

Gessner (1516–65), a Zurich humanist and physician, was the leading Swiss scholar of his day. A genuine polymath, he published some seventy-two books in his relatively short lifetime,[6] across an extraordinary range of subjects: a *Universal Bibliography* of all known texts in the classical languages and Hebrew; monumental histories of animals and plants; essays on potions and remedies for plague; a history of languages; Greek and Latin lexica; scholarly editions of Marcus Aurelius, Aristotle and others; and oddities like his short treatise on milk products. He was in addition a talented illustrator as seen in his zoological and botanical catalogues. Having overcome humble beginnings by dint of talent, timely scholarships, and the help of teachers, he travelled for study and early employment to a number of European cities, finally settling back in Zurich where he remained as Professor of Philosophy for the rest of his life, foreshortened as it was by chronic ill-health and constant, poorly-remunerated work as teacher, physician and scholar.[7] Yet throughout his adult years, Gessner took delight in regular mountain walks, as he writes at the opening of his letter to Jacob Vogel (*De Montium Admiratione / On the Admiration of Mountains*): 'I have resolved, my friend Vogel, for as long as God grants me life, to climb some few mountains, or at least one, every year when plants are in fresh growth, for the sake of their study as well as for the health-giving exercise and spiritual enjoyments mountains afford'. He was not alone. A circle of friends around Gessner taken up with the enthusiasm for mountain forays included Vogel, Joachim Vadianus, Jean Du Choul, Josias Simler, Simon Grynaeus, Johannes Rhellicanus, Johannes Chrysostomus Huber, Benedict Marti and others.[8] Most were fellow physicians and natural scientists, as the latter discipline broke new ground in the mid-sixteenth century in Switzerland and beyond. Humanist philological zeal for recovering the scientific and other knowledge of Greece and Rome was in the late Renaissance giving way to the correction and augmentation (through observation of the natural world in particular) of the errors and limitations of even such prepossessing authorities as Aristotle, Theophrastus and Pliny the Elder. In the botanical realm especially, specimen gathering and gardens, herbaria, observation, description, and the constant communication of enthusiastic naturalists would lead, in a remarkable historical efflorescence, to the vast catalogues of plants and animals produced by Gessner and others, themselves setting the stage for revolutions in taxonomy that would occur in the next century.[9] Gessner's mountain rambles were undertaken largely in these interests, hence his stated preference for rambles with like-minded, well-educated companions. But he is unusual in foregrounding the aesthetic elements and palpable joys of mountain travel itself. In his mountain epistles, alpine landscapes, not botanical specimens, occupy his attention and are rendered in language readers have found so singular. Gessner's science was, indeed, complemented by a humanist-informed, Zwinglian theology, which identified, as did that of Calvin, a deep connection between creator and natural creation, instilling in those landscapes a sense of wonder calling for deeper inquiry.[10] His science and religion were of a piece.[11] Evidence of that connection is virtually everywhere latent in his alpine descriptions even when it is not as explicit as in the familiar opening to *On the Admiration of Mountains*, where the ascent brings one ever closer to the 'contemplation of the supreme architect'.[12]

But to claim that Gessner and this group could constitute an early phase in the history of proper alpinism is in almost all discussions doubted: Gessner like his contemporaries (it is said) climbed only in order to observe plants or for other scientific reasons; he did not climb for sport or leisure; he was surely not a competent mountaineer in the sense that the term would have in the age of Whymper, Mummery and Stephen; he did not climb to the summits of mountains but only as far as his interests led him; the sixteenth-century upsurge of mountain interest in Switzerland particularly represented a false start to something more mature and different in kind after the mid-eighteenth century, or more exactly after the ascent of Mont Blanc by Paccard and Balmat in 1786, and the turn of the nineteenth century, when alpine ascents substantially increased in number; he was not yet part of a movement that changed the way people saw mountains.

The truth value of nearly all of these claims can be qualified. Most of them derive from established assumptions, fixed bearings in the history of mountain sensibility. Gessner 'must' be an outlier, clearly post-'gloom' but earlier than the full throated, aesthetically informed perspectives of later. So a quirky 'between'. But slot in another lens, that of climbing *per se*, and he lies somewhere in the late-middle of the recorded history of mountain ascents, that is, well after Livy's description of Philip's ascent of Haemus and numerous other classical accounts.[13] Pull the frame in closer, that of his local Swiss community of lettered and scientific men, and we see that Gessner's climbs were not uncommon; indeed the definitively comprehensive work on early alpinism was written after Gessner's death by his protégé and friend, Josias Simler.[14] Again, shift the focus to recorded descriptions that register pleasure and beauty in mountains, and Gessner seems to be back at the beginning of an understanding that would become ours.[15] Gareth Williams identifies Gessner's 'rapturous sense of engagement with mountain nature that appears proto-Romantic in its release of feeling',[16] a quality that he discusses in Pietro Bembo's account of his 1493 ascent of Aetna. In fact, there is in Gessner much that seems proto-Romantic, including, as Williams says, the exaltation of individualism.[17] But historical periodicity does create problems of fit, so that with such figures as Gessner we end up using verbal shims, qualifiers like 'proto-', 'pre-', 'early', 'incipient', or 'post-' when we tweak them into the narratives of intellectual history. Such narratives are tagged to both chronological and ideological lines, and thus dictate the terms of critical regard, assuring that any particular body of work will be understood in relation to recognized sequential signposts – themselves constructions of long-entrenched views. I want to argue here that Gessner presents the opportunity to identify strains of thought and sensibility that leak through literary-historical framings, permeate through periods (without approaching the dubious status of eternal truths, permanent or fixed values), connecting our stories about aesthetics and mountains.

Gessner's two alpine letters are relatively brief. The first, *de Montium Admiratione* (*DMA*) was published in 1543 as an epistolary introduction to an exposition on *Milk and Milk Products* (*Libellus de lacte et operibus lactariis*) – a subject surprisingly dear to his heart as we learn in his second text, the *Descriptio Montis Fracti* (*DMF*). *DMA* initially gives the appearance of a record of desultory mountain impressions: a discussion of why their great mass does not sink into the earth, their endless supplies of water, wood and minerals, the delicate yet enduring snows of their peaks, the imaginary creatures of myth that reside there, the nature of their trees, the delights to be had high in the mountains. The *DMF* of twelve years later is a rather more occasional document, recording a recent climb with three friends[18] of the Gnepfstein or Mittaggüpfi, on the western ridge of the Pilatus massif looming over Lucerne. Its opening refers to his regular annual habit of climbing mountains, as at the opening of his earlier piece, later maintaining that he has summited other, higher mountains than this one. The Pilatus climb was, after all, undertaken only as a holiday excursion to view the lake on the massif where the ghost of Pontius Pilate resided, as legend had it, menacing the locals who feared destructive storms should the small tarn be disturbed.[19] By Gessner's time only a remnant of superstition remained, and, when led by a certified guide who could guarantee no mischief, the ascent became very popular. Gessner's description records impressions on the way: plants, fruit and berries encountered, descriptions of the landscape, the pleasures of eating and drinking in the mountains, all leading to an extensive digression on the gratifications of all five senses to be had there.[20] A generalizing excursus on the particular joys of mountain travel with the right friends follows, continuing on with a discussion of its value to health and well-being, and of its rough comforts. At last comes a description of the tarn of Pilate itself, a reasoned disquisition on the implausibility of superstitions lurking about the place, and a brief account of the descent.

Adumbrating the sublime

Thus summarized, the two texts do not appear to offer much to mountain aesthetics. Yet the frequently quoted opening of *DMA* addressed to Jacob Vogel, is remarkable:

> I have resolved, my friend Vogel, for as long as God grants me life, to climb some few mountains, or at least one, every year when plants are in fresh growth, for the sake of their study as well as for the health-giving exercise and spiritual enjoyments mountains afford. For what immense pleasure and delight of spirit do you reckon there are in gazing in wonder at a great mass of mountains, and in raising one's head high, as it were, among the clouds! In some fashion or other, the mind is overwhelmed by their astonishing heights, and is swept up into contemplation of the supreme architect.[21]

Frequently observed is the surprising enthusiasm for mountainscapes. Surely that, but his rhetoric specifies. 'I have resolved henceforth … for as long as God grants me life, to climb'. Gessner's resolution is not to 'study' but, first, every year *to climb*; the focus is clearer in his Latin where the crucial verb is delayed to a position of emphasis at the end of a longish preamble: *Constitui posthac, Aviene doctissime, quamdiu mihi vita divinitus concessa fuerit, quotannis montes aliquos, aut saltem unum conscendere.* The objects of study and healthy exercise of mind and body come afterward, in a circumstantial clause. Then a dramatic shift as the tenor becomes declamatory: 'For what great pleasure, what delights ...!' as Gessner's language plays out, enacting ascent: the spirit is 'moved at the sight of a great mass of mountains' and is suddenly *there* 'holding one's head high, almost among the clouds' (*apud tamquam inter nubes attollere*). And at this point agency inverts, for like the eye the mind is *overwhelmed* and *drawn upward* to the contemplation of God by the mountains themselves. The experience is as close as a rationalizing scholar and scientist of the mid-sixteenth century could come to rapture (*rapitur ad contemplationem*).

Gessner's formulation sounds prescient of much later Romantic inflections of natural landscapes, though there are parallels among contemporaries.[22] Gessner is distinct, however, in drawing his language predominantly from classical sources. Historically and by education positioned in an intellectual framework that viewed classical writers as both anciently authoritative and, paradoxically, new sources of knowledge, Gessner looked to Graeco-Roman texts for orientation. Examples of Greek and Roman *physiologia* (writings on the nature of the physical world), geography, topography and natural history informed his work; as did the ancient tradition of *paradoxa*, descriptions of the uncanny and surprising (Gessner's *Historia Animalium* included specimens of unicorns and dragons). Which is not to say that Gessner sought out the extraordinary, but that his scientific inquiries were characteristically sourced in the discussions of particularly Aristotle, Theophrastus, the medical writers, and others where surprise and novelty could be found. Gessner alludes both substantially and incidentally to classical sources throughout both his mountain essays, and at times does more than allude, as in his explanation of the rise and longevity of mountains:

> For why do mountains in the long march of time not subside? Why are they not destroyed by the storms to which they are perpetually exposed, or by torrents of rain? Certainly because of fire, it being the cause of both the generation and perdurance of mountains, as demonstrated in the testimony of the philosopher Philo.[23] In fact when fiery matter buried in the earth erupts by its natural force, it tends toward its appropriate place, and whenever it finds an opening, small as it may be, it lifts upward with it a good deal of earthly matter – as appears in the craters of Aetna – as much as possible. As soon as this very earth breaks out, it is borne up in a compact path. And again, this earthly matter is driven along following the fire, and rising to a great height is drawn into a narrow shape, and finally stops as though at the point of a sword, imitating the shape of the fire. Then, in as much as the lightest and heaviest elements, naturally opposites, necessarily contend with one another, each is pulled by its own gravitation to its proper place, and yet they are drawn apart by the force of the other. Consequently, the fiery substance taking the earth skyward with it is pulled back by the weight of the heavier earth; but this mineral substance, weighted down by its own mass, is on the other hand raised upward by the fire's natural power and, finally and with difficulty overcome by the fire's prevailing and elevating force, is deposited on high in fire's realm and remains there. For this reason, fire is the *habitus*, or condition, as the Stoics say, of the

mountains, the constraint by which mountains are bound, which starting at their center extends in every direction, reaching to their furthermost extremes.[24]

'As demonstrated in the testimony of the philosopher Philo...' – the movement from the Stoicizing Middle Platonist Philo of Alexandria (20 BCE–50 CE) to Gessner's scientific appreciation of the mountain world is seamless, Gessner's rather tortuous and protracted orogenic account being an extended translation of Philo's Greek.[25] And again in the following section, translating Philo:

> Further, (to return from my digression) some say that the cause of mountains arising and experiencing no diminution with declining age is their similarity to trees, but these people are clearly uninformed. For, they will declare, just as trees lose and regrow their leaves with the changes of the seasons, so too certain parts of mountains break away and are replenished in turn, even though this growth becomes apparent only after a long period of time. For trees are endowed with a more rapid nature and grow more quickly, but mountains slowly. So, we are told, the newer parts of mountains are scarcely observed by our senses except after a lengthy period of time. I leave these people to their own speculations.[26]

Gessner's wholesale appropriation of Philo raises questions. He might, of course, simply have been convinced by the Stoic-inflected explanation, or, composing his letter hurriedly, neglected to integrate the idea more satisfactorily. But in following Philo's brusque rejection of what would seem to some a more natural explanation – certainly nearer to a modern understanding of non-volcanic orogeny – in favour of a rather arcane if spectacular process couched in language that cloaks it in portentous mystery, Gessner does seems to be foregrounding, even highlighting, an aetiology that strikes him as more impressive and awe-inspiring than the more prosaic processes of erosion and uplift. Philo's own language of dismissal ('these people seem to have no knowledge of the way in which mountains come to be, otherwise they would probably have held their tongues in shame', Philo, *On the Incorruptibility of the World*, 134) suits as well, for that such miracles as mountain heights could be born of such mundanity is beneath contempt. They are born instead, Philo and Gessner maintain, by spectacular forces, fierce struggles between primal elements of earth and fire, fraught with ebbs and flows until resolved in triumphant stasis, the Stoic *Logos*, Fire itself (ibid. 136).[27]

The poets too (Homer, Virgil, Ovid) come into play, and draw the discourse in similar directions. Homer for instance at *DMF* 204-6: 'For which of the senses does not enjoy its own particular pleasure? In respect to the sense of touch, the whole body afflicted by heat is exceptionally restored by a breeze of cold mountain air, which blows from every side over the whole surface of the body and is drawn fully into the lungs; as Homer says, "the chill blast of Boreas revived him"'. The modestly misquoted reference is to *Iliad* 5.697-8, describing an exhausted and wounded Sarpedon, favourite son of Zeus, being revived by a gust of cool wind. The image conjured by the quotation, however, is a little at odds with the robust healthiness of brisk mountain breezes Gessner is praising here. Sarpedon's death at the hands of Patroclus in Book 16 of the *Iliad* is given full, tragic scope in the poem, as the distraught king of the gods anguishes over whether he can save his son from the overweening *aristeia* of the Greek hero. Did Gessner simply like the conceit of life-giving breath and seize on a likely, modified quotation from Book 5 to underscore it, or does the citation's clear foreshadowing of tragic fate in Book 16 lend a shadow of darkness and mortality to surface salubrity? In support of the latter notion, one could observe that Gessner has, a few lines earlier, glossed Epicurus' theory of pleasure this way:

> But since the impulse of the body's pleasure through which the senses are soothed responds to a tension or remission of the opposite condition, as in a balance where one part rises higher by as much as the other is weighed down, where no contrary and unpleasant feeling of the senses precedes, no pleasure can follow ... And so when at once we rest from the hardest labor, cool ourselves from great heat, drink after great thirst, eat after exceptional hunger, especially with a mind both calm and carefree to the greatest extent possible, delighting in the pleasant society of friends, companionship, and conversations – who would not judge this the greatest of pleasures?[28]

The greatest of pleasures are dependent, à la Heraclitus, on the greatest of miseries: relieving cold and heat, life and death. So with a simple breath of fresh air, an allusive turn (to Sarpedon's revival) that wittingly or not brings the mind back to an altogether darker moment, and substantial ballast to what could otherwise be an idealizing bit of bucolic atmospherics.[29]

But the bucolic in *DMA* does in fact become interesting:

> And so since this force of all the elements and of all of nature manifests itself most intensely there, it is no wonder that people of old marveled at a certain divinity in the mountains and imagined many mountain-inhabiting gods, like Fauns, Satyrs, and Pan, to whom they attributed goat-like feet, calling them half-goats ('goat-footed' and 'goat-legged' in Greek), on account of the rough severity of the mountain terrain and because these animals delight in mountain pastures. They also imagined these same creatures to be terrifying, because in thinking of these forested and elevated places a sense of astonishment arises in the mind somehow greater than that originating in human affairs.[30]

There follows another half paragraph on Pan and 'his son' Bucolion and the sundry nymphs said to frequent mountain spaces.[31] One fascinating aspect of the passage is its placement, sandwiched as it is between the two parts of Gessner's orogeny borrowed from Philo: that is, after Philo's words have described the rise of mountains in terms of primal elemental conflict, terrifying and sublime in its power. Here, mountain landscapes are inhabited by incarnations of that same power: 'since this force of all the elements of nature manifests itself most intensely there, it is no wonder'. Some of these creatures are the stuff of quaint myth, and Gessner treats them so, as in his catalogue of all possible mountain nymphs. But of Pan particularly, the rhetoric becomes more serious: 'Pan especially, dweller of mountain places, represents the world whose primary forces, as I've said, reside in mountains and there exercise their power most abundantly'.[32] Pan, force of nature, mountain landscapes, virility and panic—as an early edition of Liddell and Scott's Greek Dictionary informs us: 'τὸ πανικόν with or without δεῖμα, panic, fear ... any sudden terror, without visible cause, was ascribed to Pan, who ... assisted the Athenians at Marathon by striking such causeless fear into the enemy'.[33] So, as in the passage just above, '[t]hey also imagined these same creatures to be terrifying, because in thinking of these forested and elevated places a sense of astonishment arises in the mind somehow greater than that originating in human affairs'.[34] Gessner's Latin is more forceful, culminating as it does with his strong, three-word evocation of the shaken or staggered human mind: *stupor animis oboriatur*. But at the end of this section, almost as if he has gone too far, Gessner is quick to return to a more decorative bucolic mode: the muses and Diana dwell there too.[35] After all, 'these are matters of fable, of course'. Yet what lies beneath the surface seems to be what really matters to Gessner as he closes the passage: 'within the husks of myth lie seeds of truth'.[36]

This is then not a decorative classicism but rather a concerted use of specifically classical material to layer in a subtext of a certain kind of grandeur, awe, splendour, *gravitas*, and even terror. Gessner counts it wisdom 'to contemplate earthly paradise with the eyes of body and mind, among which wonders not the least are the raised and jagged peaks of mountains, their inaccessible precipices, vast ridges rising to the sky, steep rocks, and dark forests'.[37] Such heights and grandeur, psychic transport, physical and conceptual vastness, the very idea of the inaccessible, particularly as prompted by features of nature, are all elements of the sensibility commonly designated sublime – a vast subject itself, particularly after the later formulations of Burke, Kant and many others. But, as James Porter has recently argued, energetically tackling the notion that the language and aesthetics of the sublime is a modern invention, one can discern a long premodern tradition preoccupied with the idea: 'Far from being a principle of rhetorical criticism that emerged late in the day, the sublime proves to have been widely available as a category of aesthetic and non-aesthetic judgment, experience and value, one that helped shape Greek and Roman thought from its earliest beginnings to its final appearances, and from there passed on to modernity'.[38] He floats a modern working conception: 'simultaneously fascinating and fearful, [the sublime] object resists integration into one's frameworks of understanding ... [it] produces profound mental or spiritual disruption, be this momentary or lasting – it is like a shock of the Real'.[39] Classical sources for or instances of the sublime Porter treats, among others in his extensive survey, include the pre-Longinian critical and rhetorical traditions, the Presocratic natural philosophers, Dionysius of Halicarnassus, the Euphonists Pausimachus of Miletus and Andromides, Demetrius, Aristotle, the fourth-century rhetoricians, ancient comedy and tragedy, Homer, Lucretius, Plato and of course the familiar *locus classicus* for the idea, Longinus (called so, but of unknown identity, first to third century CE). Gessner was familiar with most of these texts himself, as well as with their language and themes – featuring mighty natural forces, heights and depths, fear, awe, cosmic scope and so on. How he employed some of these sources can be seen in the passages selected above, where Philo's explanation of the birth of a mountain, in its dramatic inconcinnity with the conversational tenor of Gessner's essay in its other parts, introduces a startling strangeness, a literally alien discursive element that takes the mind aback, a 'mental disruption'. It can be seen too in the Homeric adaptation, intended to lend weight, scope, intimations of mortality, and in the case of the creatures of Arcadian myth, the outright confrontation with the powers resident in mountainscapes and the impact on the human mind they can induce.

Longinus' *On the Sublime* itself, the key text for transmission of the notion of the sublime into modernity via Boileau's French translation, was in Gessner's day emerging into European consciousness after a long hiatus: Francisco Robertello's edition of Longinus was published in Basel in 1554, a year before Gessner's *DMF*.[40] Longinus' text deals for the most part with sublimity in the context of rhetoric and poetry, that is, as a modality of expression, heightened sensibility and poetic register. But its Chapter 35 treats sublimity in nature, which becomes a key element in the thought of later theorists. It is not known whether Gessner read some version of Robertello's edition, but we do know that Gessner was aware of Longinus' treatise: his *Bibliotheca Universalis* notes 'a Greek opusculum of Dionysius Longinus preserved in Rome', and an incomplete version in private hands.[41] Longinus' relevance to the tenor of Gessner's mountain writing is readily apparent, and if the emphasized words below are not evidence for explicit borrowing, they are a strong indicator of shared ideas associated with the sublime (italics are mine):

> If anyone wants to know *what we were born for*, let him look round at life and contemplate the *splendor, grandeur, and beauty* in which it everywhere abounds. It is a *natural inclination* that leads us to *admire* not the little streams, however pellucid and however useful, but the Nile, the Danube, the Rhine, and above all the ocean. Nor do we feel so much *awe* before the little flame we kindle, because it keeps its light clear and pure, as before the fires of heaven ... We do not think our flame more worthy of *admiration* than the *craters of Etna*, whose eruptions bring up rocks and whole hills out of the depths, and sometimes pour forth *rivers of the earth-born, spontaneous fire*.
>
> Longinus, On the Sublime, 35.3-5; tr. Russell

Compare Gessner's *DMA*:

> ... the human race has been placed in the world to see in [the earth's] *wonders some greater, indeed the greatest, power*. ... Students of wisdom will set out to look upon the *wonders* of this earthly paradise with the eyes of mind and body: among which not the least are the raised and jagged peaks of mountains, inaccessible precipices, vast ridges rising to the sky, steep cliffs, and dark forests ... Thus of all nature's elements and varieties, the greatest *astonishment* is to be found in the mountains. There it is possible to see the 'vast weight upon the land', as if earth were vaunting its power and making trial of its strength in so lifting such a mass ... There are also

fires within, through which metals are forged as though by smiths ... And too, there are places where *flames break out, as on Aetna, Vesuvius*, and the mountain near Grenoble.[42]

In both cases, there is reference to an innate disposition to prefer the great and massive to the small and domestic, shared instances of volcanic mountains, and just as crucially the psychological impact – 'wonders' and 'astonishment' – of the disparities of power and scale.[43] Longinus' treatise throughout, and not only in this chapter on the material sublime, is an extended analysis of a state of mind, and that is in fact what Gessner reveals as well.[44]

But the direct influence of Longinus is unnecessary to the case that Gessner was influenced by the ancient tradition of the sublime. As already mentioned, a significant number of Greek and Roman writers not only employed the language of the sublime, but featured it, as Porter has shown, as a conceptual category in common classical currency. To take another relevant example, the Gessner passage just above is intriguingly nested around a lengthy quotation from his friend Simon Grynaeus (1493–1541) on the nature of mountains from the latter's *Notiunculae in librum Aristotelis de Mundo* (*Notes on* de Mundo, or *On the Universe*), then thought to be Aristotle's and transmitted along with his authentic corpus.[45] *De Mundo* is itself an exercise in sublime rhetoric, as its opening preface declares:

> Many a time ... has philosophy seemed to me a thing truly divine and supernatural, especially when it has *exalted itself to the contemplation of the universe* and sought to discover the truth that is in it; the other sciences shunned this field of inquiry because of its *sublimity and grandeur* [*hypsos kai megethos*];[46] philosophy has not feared the task or thought itself unworthy of the noblest things but has judged that the study of this is by nature most closely related to it and most fitting.

The treatise that follows celebrates philosophical judgements of the nature of the cosmos, and of natural forces and features, finally attributing the loftiest status to the God/Nature/Necessity transcending it all and holding it in sublime balance.[47] Gessner's opening of *DMA* echoes that move, leaping as fully as did the author of *de Mundo* into the rhetoric of the sublime. If anything Gessner delineates the process more clearly: 'in some way, the mind is overwhelmed by the astonishing heights, and is caught up (*rapitur*) in contemplation of the supreme architect'.[48] Gian Biagio Conte (1994) produces an intriguing corollary to both the author of *de Mundo* and Gessner in his discussion of the sublime in Lucretius:

> In the sublime the didactic impulse (as urgent as a holy mission) and the reader's structure have a model to which the poet adapts his discourse and the reader his behavior. Once its hidden laws have been shown, the grandiose and sublime nature functions like a mirror, reflecting the beholder's mind: it becomes a structure acting in the spectator's consciousness ...

his ibi me rebus quaedam divina voluptas
percipit atque horror, quod sic natura tua vi
tam manifesta patens ex omni parte retecta est.
At these things, as it were, some godlike pleasure and a thrill of awe seizes on me, so that thus by thy power nature is made so clear and manifest, laid bare to sight on every side.

Lucretius, De Rerum Natura 3.28-30[49]

Read thus, even the didactic elements, scientific curiosity, and underpinning of religious conviction, always prominent in Gessner's two essays, function vitally not only in representing a sublime sensibility in describing or 'admiring' mountains, but as well in transmitting a heightened awareness in his readers.

It is tempting, finally, since Gessner has invoked Epicurus conspicuously in his digression on the pleasures of the senses, to see a link with Lucretius' simple pleasures of the senses in a natural setting at 5.1379-87, where he describes the origins of music in an Epicurean *locus amoenus*:

> People learned to imitate with their lips the liquid notes of birds before they could, in chorus, delight their ears with music ... [and reeds taught them the] tuneful plaints the flautist's fingers play on the pipe, discovered amid pathless woods and forests and glades, amid the solitary haunts of shepherds and the peace of the open air.

Which music the sublimities of Gessner's rhetoric take to the heights:

> The sweet songs of birds in the woods delight as well, as does, finally, the silence of solitude. Nothing can grate on the ears here; there is nothing to annoy; there are no disturbances or city fracases, no disputes of men. In this deep and almost religious quiet, from the exalted ridges of mountains you might almost hear, if such exists, the harmony of the spheres.[50]

Gessner's words can thus soar as they do moving from aural pleasures to those of sight in a passage describing the visual delights of mountainscapes in his *DMF*.

> Sight is delighted by the marvelous and unaccustomed aspect of mountains, ridges, rocks, forests, valleys, rivers, springs, and meadows. As to color, everything is for the most part green and in flower. And with respect to the features observed, the sights of crags, boulders, twisting byways, and other particulars are marvelous and rare, wonderful both for their shape and for their height and magnitude. If one wishes to extend the gaze of the eyes, broaden the vision, look far and wide, and take in everything, there are overlooks and rocky promontories on which you might already seem to be situated with your head among the clouds.[51]

But in those 'valleys, rivers, springs and meadows ... green and in flower' we are reminded that Gessner was nothing if not a synthetic thinker, drawing upon Epicurean, Stoic and Aristotelian ideas, the rhetorical registers of the sublime, and in this case and as earlier, the imaginative landscapes of the bucolic. Gessner's bucolic, as in *DMA*, can be haunted by Pan's infectious terrors, and so touched by the sublime, but may also find itself, with a kind of easy shift that evidences no hard lines between registers, in the gentler, imaginative hills and mountains of Arcadia and Sicily: 'you will see fields and green forests into which you could walk; or look even closer and discern dark valleys, shady rocks, hidden caves'.[52] Lucretius, no programmatically bucolic poet himself but here looking back to a golden age, again may inform (*De Rerum Natura* 5.1392-96 (~2.29-33)):

> Often, therefore, stretched in groups on the soft grass hard by a stream of water under the branches of a tall tree, they would delight their limbs at little expense, especially when the weather smiled and the season of the year painted the green herbage with flowers.

Along with the conspicuous raptures Lucretius records, pastoral's *locus amoenus* has its place too. Gessner also visited his mountains when they were green and in flower, to botanize and savour their sights. In his *DMF* he speaks glowingly of the strenuous physical efforts mountain ascents require, the pleasures of exertion and relaxation. He relishes witty conversation with friends on the climb, relishes equally the cheese and milk provided by his mountain hosts and a sound night's sleep in their fragrant and, as he says, health-giving lofts: 'At night, your breathing will be much more easy and salubrious. Hay will be your pillow, your mattress piled all beneath you, and as a blanket spread over you'.[53] The rains come to his sunlit mountainscapes only late, at the close of the Pilatus climb, delaying his descent and keeping him, one might guess contentedly, on the mountain a bit longer:

> We, however, leaving Pilate's lake and in order to return quickly since the day was already waning and there were signs of evening rains, climbed a rise to the left and walked back over a road easy enough for cattle to use ... And so just before nightfall we returned to the city, delayed a while on the mountain by the rains.[54]

Virgil's image at the close of his first *Eclogue* (79-83), with its poignant comforts (for the refugee Meliboeus) – as well as its ominously sublime shadows – might be a suitable emblem for Gessner's end of day: 'Here you can rest the night with me, on a bed of green boughs; I have sweet fruit, soft chestnuts, and an abundance of good cheese. And, already, the chimneys of distant cottages send up their smoke and greater shadows fall from high mountains'.

Back in Zurich, and displaced from them in his quotidian life and labours, Gessner would frequently have gazed at the icy-white peaks of his beloved Alps twenty or so miles south of the hills of the city with a longing to return, as he himself testifies. A world apart, up and over there, and better. This real and figurative distance – the gap wherein the mind constructs the image of a mountain that lives in experience, desire and memory – is the space where notions of alpine sublimity can take root and grow, extending forward and back. Gessner's sublime mountains may be seen to exist in a kind of open diachronic and even organic continuum, rather than as specimens in the superseding and displacing march of intellectual history.[55] Standing against the sky and anchored as they are in classical thought, Gessner's mountains are perforce as conceptual as they are real, founded on idea and irrupted rock. Both enabling perspective.

Notes

1. Thomas Burnet in his *Sacred Theory of the Earth* (the first part of which was first published in Latin in 1681) looks back to sources of the notion in biblical and other early creation myths, amply contextualized and supplemented by Nicolson 1959: 72–112, and discussed further at length by Dawn Hollis in this volume.
2. Petrarch's account of his ostensible 1336 climb of Mont Ventoux, to take an early example, flips the expected outward summit perspective inward, a turning point of reflection and self-assessment largely in spiritual terms. See among others Ascoli 1991 *passim*, Williams 2017: 96–7 and 100 and Hooley 2012: 21–3.
3. The modern *locus classicus* for the traditional narrative is Nicolson 1959. As the editors note in their introduction it is altogether too easy to read Nicolson simplistically and find easy fault with a dated paradigm. In other cases, critical response can be informed, as in the case of Porter 2016, and brusque: 'In a word, the recent picture of the emergence of the sublime in the early modern era gets things wrong at both ends: it is the product of bad classical philology (narrow *Wortphilologie*) and of triumphalist history that has nothing in fact to celebrate. The discovery of the natural or aesthetic sublime in the eighteenth century was not "a result of one of the most profound revolutions in thought that has ever occurred," any more than it can be said that the ancient Greeks and Romans lacked an aesthetic or some other appreciation of the power of hills' (49–50), in the context of a broader discussion of European 'misinheritances' of the classical sublime at 36–51. In respect to mountaineering history, Hollis 2017a and 2017b, Korenjak 2017 and others have chipped steadily away at the central conclusions of Nicolson and others by pointing out omissions in their consideration of classical, medieval, and early modern texts.
4. Korenjak 2017: 181. Sean Ireton in his chapter considers the complicated case of the learned Coolidge more substantially, but as a practising Victorian mountaineer invested in the sensibility and language of first ascents, class exceptionalism, and national pride, Coolidge appears to have looked on pre-golden age climbing with a dismissive eye.
5. This volume, 6.
6. Some eighteen works remained unpublished at the time of his death, most subsequently published.
7. Josias Simler wrote the first biography of Gessner: *Vita clarissimi philosophi et medici excellentissimi Conradi Gesneri Tigurini*, published in 1566. Henry Morley's biographical essay (1871) is based on it. Among others, Serrai 1990 offers much detail; also useful is Fischer 1966. Wellisch 1975, is good on Gessner's financial struggles and life in general; he gives a full list of biographical treatments of Gessner at 231–6.
8. Ogilvie 2006 presents a good overview of Gessner and others in the context of the rising discipline of natural science in the European sixteenth century. See also Durling 1965 on

Gessner's *Liber Amicorum*, a guest log of friends and scientific and scholarly visitors, some 227, covering only the last ten years of his life.

9. Ogilvie 2006.
10. See Hansen 2013: 40.
11. Staedtke 1965: 239. See Serrai 1990: 52–68 for more on Gessner's Zwinglianism. So close was the Zwinglian connection between nature and creator as to 'superficially imply pantheism' as Stephens 1986: 86 says, qualifying that by noting the 'utter dependence of creation on the creator'. See too Nicolson's 1959 discussion of Luther and Calvin, at 96–104.
12. See further below, 24–5.
13. Coolidge's edition of Simler itemizes several, but see Korenjak 2017: 184 for others and an up-to-date bibliography.
14. *De Alpibus Commentarius*.
15. Barton 2017: esp. 68–71 discusses Gessner's contributions to chorographic description and their relation to developments in landscape painting.
16. Williams 2017: 108.
17. See Hansen 2013: 1–3, and fascinatingly throughout. Also, Ireton's discussion of Hansen in his chapter on Coolidge in this volume.
18. Peter Hafner, Peter Boudin, and Johann Thomas, surgeon, pharmacist, and painter respectively: see Serrai 1990: 49.
19. One of three Pilate-haunted peaks; the others were 'Mt. Sibillini (2,476 m) in central Italy and Mount Pilat (1432 m) in the Cevennes': Korenjak 2017: 188.
20. See Barton's chapter '*Geographia, prospectus, pictura*', 2017: 67–113.
21. *DMA* iii–iv. The parenthetical page numbers are keyed to the Latin text to be found in Coolidge 1904. The translations are my own, drawn from a complete translation of the two texts forthcoming in Ireton and Schaumann 2020. I am grateful to the editors for permission to utilize material from that translation for this essay.
22. Williams 2017: 109, n. 177, citing Freshfield 1904: 449, points out similar language in Benedict Marti, Professor of Greek and Hebrew at Bern and friend of Gessner, writing in 1558-9: 'These are the mountains which form our pleasure and delight when we gaze at them from the higher parts of our city and admire their mighty peaks and broken crags that threaten to fall at any moment ... Who, then, would not admire, love, willingly visit, explore, and climb places of this sort? I assuredly should call those who are not attracted by them dolts, stupid dull fishes, and slow tortoises ... In truth, I cannot describe the degree of affection and natural love with which I am drawn to mountains, so that I am never happier than on the mountain crests.' Also, Ogilvie's 2006 description of the renaissance naturalist Carolus Clusius (1526–1609): 'Clusius' publications ... sparkled with their author's joy in tramping through the woods and fields, watching plants, plucking some to take home and transplant and leaving others to observe the following season' (48).
23. Philo Judaeus, also called Philo of Alexandria, *On the Incorruptibility of the World* 25.
24. *DMA* viii–x.
25. Whether or not the text is the work of Philo or not has long been in question, support leaning lately toward authenticity.
26. Ibid. x–xii = Philo, *On the Incorruptibility of the World* 132–4.
27. Clearly both Philo and Gessner see orogeny only as volcanic, and this accords with widespread classical thought. See Seneca's *Natural Questions*, 6.9-31 which deals with various

28. *DMF*, 204.
29. Provisionally in support, depending whether it can be assumed Gessner had read Lucretius (see below, note 41), is *De Rerum Natura* 3.117–29, esp. 128–9: *est igitur calor ac ventus vitalis in ipso / corpore qui nobis moribundos deserit artus* ('there is therefore a vital heat and wind in the body itself which leaves our limbs at the point of death').
30. *DMA* 10: x.
31. Bucolion is generally held to be the illegitimate son of Laomedon and Calybe; cf. Homer, *Iliad* 6.21 and Apollodorus 3.12.3. Gessner's source for the Pan-parentage is unclear, though scattered references can be found in fragments. Cf. Wathelet 1988: 366.
32. *DMA*, x.
33. Fourth edition, 1855, 1033. The current *LSJ* in its otherwise admirable efficiency drops this phrasing.
34. Ibid.
35. Cf. Lucretius, *De Rerum Natura*, 4.572-94.
36. *DMA*, x.
37. Ibid. iv.
38. Porter 2016: xix.
39. Ibid. 5.
40. But after the 1543 publication of *DMA*. Since Robertello prepared his edition in Italy, its Basel publication does not make it likelier that Gessner had read any part of that particular text. But there were manuscripts circulating earlier throughout Europe. Gessner does make note of Robertello's edition of the military writer Aelianus Tacticus in his *Bibliotheca*.
41. See Steppich 2006: 63. Cf. Josias Simler, ed., *Bibliotheca Universalis*, Zurich, 1574, p. 171. As Porter explains (1–2) the primary, tenth-century manuscript 'attributes the work to Dionysius Longinus on the title page where the essay begins ... while the table of contents that appears at the front of the codex assigns the title to "Dionysius *or* Longinus"'. The private library where the partial Longinus manuscript resided was gathered by Diego Hurtado de Mendoza, Charles V's ambassador to Venice. Gessner met the curator of the library, Arnout van Eynhouts, in 1543 and became familiar with the collection, as Wellisch tells us (1975: 159).
42. *DMA* iv. The last instance refers to a burning methane flare near Grenoble.
43. The comments of James Beattie (eighteenth century) on sublimity offer a later point of comparison: 'The most perfect models of sublimity are seen in the works of nature. Pyramids, palaces, fireworks, temples ... are mighty efforts no doubt, and awaken in every beholder a pleasing admiration; but appear as nothing when we compare them, in respect of magnificence, with mountains, volcanoes, rivers, cataracts, oceans, the expanse of heaven, clouds, and storms': *Dissertations Moral and Critical*, 186; quoted in Brady 2012: 179.
44. As Conte 1994: 19 puts it: 'the *hypsos* is not just a *genus scribendi* but a *genus vivendi*, not just a formal procedure but a psychological state and mode of behavior, that of *megalophrosyne*, of mental grandeur.'
45. Published in Basel in 1533. The passage Gessner quotes is found on pp. 166–7.
46. Possibly the earliest instance of *hypsos* in the sense of 'sublime'; see Porter 2016: 475.

47. The sublime for the author of *de Mundo* is this universal divine coherence; it would find substantial echo in the Zwinglian Protestant Gessner. Porter discusses *de Mundo* at ibid. 473–83.
48. *DMA* ii–iv. Here too Gessner seems very close to Lucretius. He was aware of the text well enough to include references in his *Bibliotheca* and a Lucretian distich at the head of his edition of Stobaeus in 1543. Lucretius' famously soaring preamble praises the philosopher Epicurus whose thought transcends the constraints of conventional ideas and ascends to the very boundaries of the universe. Lucretius' atomist physics and rejection of divine influence would not have comported well with Gessner's religious dispositions but, if indeed he had read the text in full, they would have offered glimpses of the terrifying sublimities of oblivion and the micro- and macroscopic vastnesses of the deep universe. On Lucretius and the sublime, see Conte 1994: 1–34 and Porter 2016: 445–54.
49. Conte 1994: 22.
50. *DMF* 206–8.
51. Ibid. 206.
52. Ibid. 206.
53. Ibid. 214.
54. Ibid. 220.
55. The close of Peter Hansen's chapter in this volume (225) is relevant: (speaking of Mont Ventoux) 'moments of its past are not as distinct as geological strata or archaeological layers'.

CHAPTER 2
'FAMOUS FROM ALL ANTIQUITY': ETNA IN CLASSICAL MYTH AND ROMANTIC POETRY
Cian Duffy

Mountain ranges feature prominently in the cultural landscape of late eighteenth- and early nineteenth-century Britain. The Alps, the Pyrenees, the Scottish Highlands, Snowdonia, the English Lake District: these are the high places of British Romanticism. These ranges were explored, mapped, climbed; they became the focal points of debates about the age of the earth and the forces which shape it; they were painted and modelled; and they were made the subjects of, and the settings for, countless works of prose, verse and drama, some long forgotten, and some ranked now amongst the greatest works of English literature. It is from the engagement with these places during the Romantic period that we have inherited some of our most powerful and most enduring attitudes to mountains.[1]

Alongside these celebrated ranges, two isolated peaks also lift their heads above the landscape of British Romanticism: the Italian volcanoes, Vesuvius and Etna, the latter 'famous from all antiquity', as John Dryden the younger, the son of the poet, reminds us in his posthumously published *Voyage to Sicily and Malta*.[2] The description and study of these volcanoes by travellers and natural philosophers in the second half of the eighteenth century played a key role in the development of the modern scientific discipline of geology and was at the heart of one of the major scientific controversies of the day: whether water or volcanic activity was the primary agent of geomorphic change.[3] Interest in Vesuvius, in particular, was further augmented by the rediscovery in the middle of the eighteenth century of the cities of Pompeii and Herculaneum, casualties of the pyroclastic eruption of 79 CE described in two letters to Tacitus by Pliny the Younger, whose uncle was killed during that eruption.

At the same time, volcanoes and volcanic eruptions became a recurrent trope of late eighteenth- and early nineteenth-century British writing across a range of different genres and areas of enquiry. So popular, indeed, did the figure become that by the second decade of the nineteenth century, Lord Byron could dismiss it as a 'tired metaphor': 'So let the often used volcano go. / Poor thing! How frequently, by me and others, / It hath been stirred up till its smoke quite smothers' (*Don Juan*, 13.285–8). The multivalence of the volcano trope in the writing of the period is well exemplified by a letter which Byron wrote to his future wife, Annabella Milbanke, on 29 November 1813, in which he describes 'poetry' as 'the lava of the imagination whose eruption prevents an earthquake'.[4] Volcanoes and volcanic eruptions served as metaphors (and sometimes as similes) for everything from artistic inspiration to political revolution. And this is to say nothing at all of their frequent depiction in visual media (paintings, panoramas), travel accounts, expedition narratives and popular entertainments.[5]

None of this, of course, will be especially new to scholars of British Romanticism. The role of volcanoes in the development of 'natural philosophy' and the place of volcanic symbolism in the works of individual Romantic-period authors and artists has been well documented.[6] One part of the story of the Romantic volcano remains, however, to be told: the legacy of classical engagements with Etna to the representation, conceptualization and figurative appropriation of the volcano in late eighteenth- and early nineteenth-century British writing. That legacy is my subject here. More specifically, this essay will examine the interaction between classical accounts of Etna and other developing genres of describing and representing that mountain in some influential eighteenth-century accounts, including those given by John Dryden the younger and by the Scottish traveller and natural philosopher Patrick Brydone.[7] In paving the way for the modern science of volcanology, such writers, I argue, both retain and depart from the tropes of classical writing about Etna, and, in so doing, enable new figurative appropriations of the volcano and volcanic processes in late eighteenth- and early nineteenth-century English poetry. As an example of such classically-derived appropriations, the essay will conclude with an examination of the use of volcanism as a figure for industry in the poems written about the ironworks at Coalbrookdale by the poet Anna Seward, well-known in her day as the 'Swan of Lichfield', and by Seward's friend and contemporary, the poet and polymath Erasmus Darwin, one of the founders of the Lunar Society of Birmingham, in his *Botanic Garden*.

'Pour forth a blazing stream': classical accounts of Etna

On a voyage to Sicily and Malta at the start of the eighteenth century, the young John Dryden and his companion – a Mr Cecil: probably John Cecil, 6th Earl of Exeter – were making a comparatively ambitious extension to the European Grand Tour. The Tour was normally (though by no means exclusively) the preserve of young aristocratic men and those tutors, artists, family members or guardians who might journey with them.[8] Amongst its ostensible pedagogic purposes was the study of the remains of the classical and Renaissance cultures whose textual and visual artefacts continued to form the basis of the education of aristocratic youth across Europe well into the nineteenth century. Hence Italy remained the primary destination of the Tour: Italy, which Joseph Addison, in his *Letter from Italy*, describes as 'classic ground' – a landscape familiar to the imagination of educated European travellers before they arrived there because of its many literary associations, a landscape where 'the Muse so oft her harp has strung / That not a mountain rears its head unsung'.[9]

Vesuvius, just outside Naples, normally the southern terminus of the Grand Tour, was frequently visited. But Sicily and Etna were well off the beaten track for British travellers in 1700 – and indeed remained so almost eighty years later: when Patrick Brydone published his influential *Tour Through Sicily and Malta* in 1773, he noted in his 'Advertisement' that 'had there been any book in our language on the subject of the following Letters, they should never have seen the light'.[10] Despite the relative lack of first-hand, contemporary information, however, Dryden's and Cecil's evident familiarity with classical literature meant that when they arrived in Sicily on Sunday 7 November 1700, they arrived at a place both foreign and familiar.[11] And this paradox is best exemplified in one of the high points (in various senses) of their visit: Etna, 'or as they now call it Mongibello', which, as we have seen, Dryden reminds the reader, was 'famous from all antiquity for it's [sic] vomiting up fire'.[12] But of what, precisely, did this 'fame' consist for Dryden and his classically-educated contemporaries at the beginning of the eighteenth century? As Hyde points out in 'The Volcanic History of Etna', classical authors believed Etna to be the highest peak on earth. In *Pythian* 1, for example, Pindar, writing in 470 BCE, describes it as 'a skyward column' (κίων δ᾽ οὐρανία).[13] But where was Etna on the cultural map of Europe in 1700?

The entry for '*Ætna*' in the influential *Classical Dictionary* published by the English lexicographer John Lemprière in 1788 opens, interestingly enough, not with information about classical sources, but rather with physical details of elevation, circumference and supposed age ('about 3000 years'), and estimates some '100 eruptions' between the birth of Pythagoras and the Battle of Pharsalus, which brought to an end the Roman Civil War fought between Gaius Julius Caesar and Gnaeus Pompeius Magnus.[14] On this estimate of eruptive activity, Lemprière further speculates that 'the silence of Homer on the subject' might be 'considered as proof that the fires of the mountain were unknown in his age'.[15] Following these nods towards contemporary natural philosophy, Lemprière then summarizes the two primary explanations of Etna's eruptions in classical mythology: 'the poets supposed that Jupiter had confined the giants under this mountain, and it was represented as the forge of Vulcan, where his servants the Cyclops fabricated thunderbolts'.

The former explanation – that Zeus, having defeated the rebellion against his rule by the offspring of Gaia and Uranus, imprisoned them under Etna, where their throes produced earthquakes and eruptions – finds its most canonical expressions in the *Theogony* of Hesiod and in the *Aeneid* of Virgil. In the *Theogony*, it is not one of the giants but rather the Titan, Typhon, who is buried beneath Etna:

> And when [Zeus] had overpowered him, scourging him with blows, [Typhon] fell down lamed, and the huge earth groaned; a flame shot forth from that thunderbolted lord in the mountain's dark, rugged dales, as he was struck, and the huge earth was much burned by the prodigious blast, and it melted like tin when it is heated with skill by young men in well-perforated melting-pots, or as iron, although it is the strongest thing, melts in the divine earth by the skilled hands of Hephaestus when it is overpowered in a mountain's dales by burning fire. In the same way, the earth melted in a blaze of burning fire.
>
> Hesiod, *Theogony* 857-67[16]

The iron-working imagery used by Hesiod here, and the explicit reference to Hephaestus, the god of fire and metalwork, remind the reader of the other mythological association of Etna as the smithy where the thunderbolts of Zeus, and the other weapons of the gods, are forged.[17] The *Prometheus Bound* combines these two myths into a single scene.

Following his defeat by 'the unsleeping weapon of Zeus, the downrushing thunderbolt breathing out flame', Typhon had 'his strength thundered out of him and reduced to ashes':

> And now he lies, a sprawled, inert body, near the narrows of the sea, crushed under the roots of Mount Etna; on its topmost peaks Hephaestus sits forging red-hot iron, and from hence one day will burst forth rivers of fire, devouring with their savage jaws the smooth fields of Sicily with their fine crops. Such is the rage in which Typhos will boil over.
>
> [Aeschylus],[18] *Prometheus Bound* 358–71

The future volcanic 'rage' imagined here is usually read as a rhetorical anticipation of the devastating eruption of Etna in 479 BCE, also described by Pindar, in *Pythian* 1, when from the 'depths' of the mountain 'belch forth holiest springs of unapproachable fire', 'rivers of lava pour forth a blazing stream', and 'a rolling red flame carries rocks into the deep expanse of the sea with a crash' (Pindar, *Pythian* 1.21-4). But the combined emphasis on spectacular destruction and concomitant creation in these early accounts of Etna would leave a considerable legacy to eighteenth-century debates about the agencies of geomorphic change.

In the *Aeneid*, Virgil identifies the giant Enceladus rather than the Titan Typhon as the prisoner of Etna, in a celebrated passage that is both powerful as spectacle and effective as detailed observation on the components of an explosive eruption:

> There lies a harbour, safe from the winds' approach and spacious in itself, but near at hand Aetna thunders with terrifying crashes, and now hurls forth to the sky a black cloud, smoking with pitch-black eddy and glowing ashes, and uplifts balls of flame and licks the stars – now violently vomits forth rocks, the mountain's uptorn entrails, and whirls molten stone skyward with a roar, and boils up from its lowest depths. The story runs that Enceladus' form, scathed by a thunderbolt, is weighed down by that mass, and mighty Aetna, piled above, from its burst furnaces breathes forth flame; and ever as he turns his weary side all Trinacria moans and trembles, veiling the sky in smoke.
>
> Virgil, *Aeneid* 3.570-82[19]

As noted, the emphasis here is on the sublime destructive power of Etna in eruption. But the extent to which Virgil's speaker discriminates between the different components of the event – the column of 'black cloud' and the occlusion of daylight, the projection ('vomiting up') of material from inside the crater, and the production of liquid lava ('boils over') – also points to the parallel tendency in classical writing to offer what we would now consider empirical as well as mythological explanations for Etna's eruptions.

This parallel, empirical discourse about Etna finds its most canonical expression in the work of Virgil's contemporary Titus Lucretius Carus who, in his *De rerum natura*, seeks to explain 'in what ways the flame is excited which suddenly roars out of the vast furnaces of Etna' (Lucretius, *De Rerum Natura* 6.680-2).[20] Lucretius's motivation for this project is important and reflects the wider aims of *De rerum natura*. He offers his explanation of Etna's eruptive violence specifically in response to the 'panic fear' provoked by 'the fiery tempest which arose and held supreme dominance over the fields of Sicily' during the eruption of 121 BCE, in which the city of Catania was totally destroyed (6.641-3). Such fear can be allayed, Lucretius suggests, not by appeals to myth, but by resituating such local disasters within a wider, systematic understanding of natural processes:

> in considering these matters you must cast your view wide and deep, and survey all quarters far and abroad, that you may remember how profound is the sum of all things … If you keep this steadily before your mind, comprehend it clearly, see it clearly, you would cease to wonder at many things.
>
> 6.647-54

This is exactly the language that eighteenth-century natural philosophers would often use to explain how the rational mind must seek to overcome the overwhelming affective power of sublime sights like Etna in order to formulate systematic, empirical explanations of such spectacular natural phenomena. Nor should this be thought mere coincidence: the methodological and epistemological paradigms of Lucretian thought exerted, as a number of scholars have shown, significant influence on the development of natural philosophy in the early modern period and in the eighteenth century.[21] And indeed, the explanation given by Lucretius for the eruptions of Etna – that they are produced by the interaction of superheated wind and water in caverns beneath the mountains – left its own specific legacy to debates about volcanism in the late eighteenth century.[22]

Johnston reads Virgil's account of the eruption of Etna in *Aeneid* 3 as evidence that:

> phenomena such as this were too dramatic to be restrained to non-mythological interpretation [and that] Virgil, to the extent that Lucretius persuaded Romans to cast aside these mythological associations, can be said to have 'remythologised' Lucretius' volcanoes for posterity.[23]

As noted, however, one of the most striking things about Virgil's lines is not the extent to which they demarcate between mythological and scientific explanation but rather the extent to which they combine empirical description with myth – blurring, I would suggest, rather than reinforcing any sense of these as distinct ways of knowing and describing the world. In this respect, then, my reading of classical writing about Etna here follows Richard Buxton in his excellent essay on 'Mount Etna in the Graeco-Roman *imaginaire*'. As Buxton makes clear, 'imaginative and speculative interest' in Etna in classical antiquity encompasses 'a wide range of different types of discourse: mythological/religious, historical, geographical, geological, botanical, political, philosophical'.[24] Ultimately, Buxton argues, such writing illustrates the relative 'absence of boundaries' between these different discourses and particularly between what Buxton characterizes as 'mythical and scientific explanations of "natural" phenomena'.[25] In his survey of

'Earthquakes and volcanoes in Latin literature', Smolenaars similarly finds a 'wedding of science and poetry' in a number of classical responses to the phenomena, where 'any distinction between mythological and scientific beliefs seems deliberately blurred'.[26]

This 'interplay and co-identification of science and poetry'[27] in classical writing about Etna specifically is perhaps best exemplified in the Latin poem the *Aetna*, once attributed to Virgil, but most likely dating from the first century CE, and which has, as Johnston notes, 'strong Lucretian echoes'.[28] Hyde suggests that the now relatively little-known *Aetna* is valuable as 'the most detailed and scientific description of any phase of nature which has come down to us from antiquity'.[29] Johnston, similarly, reads the *Aetna* as an unsuccessful attempt to 'demythologize the phenomenon'.[30] However, as other scholars have argued, the relationship between empirical description and myth in the poem is more complex than these estimations allow. Buxton, for example, notes that 'the scientific/non-scientific boundary' is 'remarkably porous' in the poem,[31] whilst for Welsh, the *Aetna* altogether 'collapses the distinction between scientific enquiry and poetry about such enquiry'.[32] Nor is such a 'collapse' by any means unique to the *Aetna*. We have seen it in Virgil's account of an eruption in the *Aeneid*, and Buxton points to further instances in the 'anthropomorphic-anatomical metaphoricity'[33] used by Lucretius in his attempt at a rational explanation of eruptions, and in the various mythological, historical and observational perspectives invoked by Strabo in his accounts of volcanism in his *Geography*. 'Virtually every passage', Buxton says of his survey of classical writing about Etna, 'can be said to involve more than one type of discourse'.[34]

In sum, then, educated eighteenth-century visitors to Sicily inherited from classical writing about Etna not just a set of recurrent tropes linking the volcano with destruction and creation, but also an entire episteme. Our modern, 'two cultures' conception of the arts and the sciences as discrete and distinct means of knowing and describing the world, which emerges from the eighteenth-century practice of natural philosophy, is markedly absent from the classical writing about Etna which would have been the primary source of information about the volcano for Dryden and Brydone when they made their respective voyages to Sicily.[35] Such writing is, rather, pre-disciplinary. It is a mode in which figurative and observational descriptions are overlapping rather than opposed forms of representation. And it is this mode, as well as specific, local patterns of image and association, which eighteenth-century writing about Etna takes up and transforms. Classical texts, in short, provide not only the imagery but also the idiom out of which the modern, scientific study of Etna emerges in eighteenth-century natural philosophy.

'This amazing mountain': eighteenth-century visitors to Etna

The influence of classical writing about Etna on Dryden's five-page account of the volcano in his *Voyage to Sicily and Malta* is immediately apparent. Not only, as we have seen, does he note that the mountain is 'famous from all antiquity', but his explanation of the grounds for this fame – 'for it's [*sic*] vomiting up fire' – uses the exact figure preferred by classical authors to image eruption: vomiting. Pindar's seminal account in *Pythian* 1 describes

Etna as a mountain 'from whose depths belch forth holiest springs of unapproachable fire' (τᾶς ἐρεύγονται μὲν ἀπλάτου πυρὸς ἁγνόταται ἐκ μυχῶν παγαί) (Pindar, *Pythian* 1.21-2); Virgil, as we have seen, says that Etna 'violently vomits forth rocks, the mountain's uptorn entrails' (*scopulos avulsaque viscera montis / erigit eructans*) (*Aeneid* 3.575-6); and Lucretius explains how 'hot fire with quick flames … throws itself upwards straight through the mountain's throat' (*excussit calidum flammis velocibus ignem, / tollit se ac rectis ita faucibus eicit alte*) (Lucretius, *De Rerum Natura* 688-9). These are exactly the images used by Dryden to describe Etna's eruptive activity: the mountain is 'famous' for 'vomiting up fire'; it has a 'mouth of fire' through which it can be seen 'voiding' an 'immense quantity of liquid fiery rock'; sometimes 'many fiery mouths' can be seen beneath the main crater; and an inactive crater filled with ash is a 'mouth all choked up'.[36]

In classical texts, such anthropomorphic imagery has, of course, its origins in the myth of Typhon or Enceladus imprisoned under Etna and literally 'vomiting up fire'. But in Dryden's *Voyage*, this context is absent – he makes no mention of the myth. In other words, the figurative language of classical writing about Etna is transformed, in Dryden's *Voyage*, into the literal language of empirical, natural philosophy – and a boundary between genre (figurative/literal) and discipline (poetry/science) begins to become visible where it was not, previously, to be found.

In addition to this structural, epistemic debt to classical writing about Etna, Dryden's account also has two very specific, local borrowings. He describes, following Pindar and many others, the 'wonder' of seeing at the summit 'so much snow remain unmelted near so much flame and smoak'.[37] And he notes, with for example Strabo, that the vast quantities of volcanic ash deposited on the lands adjacent to the volcano, whilst initially destructive, in the long term 'fatten and cherish the soil' and make the country 'extream fertile' and the vines especially 'fruitful'.[38] Both of these tropes would become recurrent in eighteenth-century writing about Etna, and especially the latter, as natural philosophers increasingly attempted to relocate the spectacle of volcanic eruption within a longer term, systematic history of geological processes operating over 'deep time' – a project which, as we have seen, also informed the account of Etna given by Lucretius in *De rerum natura*.[39]

A similar indebtedness to classical writing about Etna can be seen in what was arguably the most influential and certainly the most widely read first-hand, contemporary account of 'this amazing mountain' written during the eighteenth century: the extended description given by the Scottish traveller Patrick Brydone in Letters VI–XI of his *Tour Through Sicily and Malta*.[40] Dawn Hollis has shown how each of the elements of Brydone's response to the volcanic sublime, 'the aesthetic, the empirical and the cultural', as well as the interaction between those elements in his account, are 'evident in earlier', and especially in classical, responses to the mountain.[41] I have elsewhere demonstrated the key role played by Brydone's account of Etna in the formulation and dissemination in the late eighteenth century of the concept of geological 'deep time'.[42] What I want to focus on here is the extent to which classical sources specifically influence Brydone's central perception of the age of the volcanic landscape and of the uniformity over time of volcanic processes. Empirical observation of the depth of the lava flows from historical and recent eruptions of Etna is, as I show in *The Landscapes of the Sublime*, an essential foundation for Brydone's understanding of 'deep time' – but so too, I want to argue here, is the historical data which he sees embodied in classical responses to the volcano.

Brydone describes 'the examination of Aetna' as 'one of the greatest objects of our expedition'.[43] But, like Dryden before him, Brydone was visiting a mountain already familiar to him through its classical associations, 'celebrated in all ages' as he puts it.[44] Brydone concludes his final letter about Etna with a review of 'the various fables and allegories to which it has given rise', noting that 'it is so often mentioned by the ancient writers, that it has been said of Aetna, as well as of Greece: *nullum est sine nomine saxum*' ['no stone without a name'].[45] In this review, Brydone mentions and sometimes quotes key classical descriptions of the volcano, including those by Pindar, 'the philosophical poet' Lucretius and Virgil, discussed above, as well as others by Diodorus Siculus and Thucydides.[46] The account given by Pindar, Brydone thinks 'the most satisfactory of all', because it 'conveys a clearer idea both of the mountain itself and an eruption of the mountain', despite Pindar having 'still kept in view that absurd and ridiculous idea of the ancients, that Jupiter had buried the giants below mount Aetna'.[47] Brydone also notes various classical speculations about the mountain, such as those concerning its age and elevation, as well as various semi-historical legends surrounding it, such as the stories that 'the emperor Adrian and the philosopher Plato' had undergone the 'labour' of an ascent of the volcano in order 'to see the rising sun from the top'.[48] He pays particular attention to the Greek-Sicilian philosopher Empedocles, 'a native of Agrigentum', whom various classical authors, including Strabo, say lived near the summit of Etna and died after falling or throwing himself into the crater.[49]

In Strabo's *Geography*, Empedocles leaps to his death and his fate is revealed only when one of his brass sandals is found 'a short distance outside the rim of the crater, as though it had been thrown up by the force of the fire' (εὑρεθῆναι γὰρ ἔξω μικρὸν ἄπωθεν τοῦ χείλους τοῦ κρατῆρος, ὡς ἀνερριμμένην ὑπὸ τῆς βίας τοῦ πυρός) (Strabo, *Geography* 6.2.8). In Brydone's day, and for long after, 'the ruins of an antient structure, called *Il Torre del Philosopho*', circa 450 m from the summit, was 'supposed to have been built' by Empedocles 'who took up his habitation here, the better to study the nature of mount Aetna'.[50] Brydone, combining an appreciation for the beauties of the night sky at such an elevation with his own sense of himself as a natural philosopher, remarks: 'had Empedocles had the eyes of a Galileo what discoveries must he not have made'.[51]

Brydone's familiarity with classical descriptions of Etna is also visible through the tropes and images which he uses throughout his account. He makes frequent reference to 'the great mouth of the volcano' and its 'vomiting out torrents of smoke' and 'dreadful' 'torrents of fire'.[52] He notes the 'astonishment' produced by seeing at the summit 'in perpetual union, the two elements that are at perpetual war': 'an immense gulph of fire, for ever existing in the midst of snows that it has not the power to melt; and immense fields of snow and ice for ever surrounding this gulph of fire, which they have not power to extinguish'.[53] And he comments upon how some of 'the old lavas' have been transformed into 'fertile fields and rich vineyards', an effect which he attributes to 'the vast quantity of nitre contained in the ashes of Aetna': a landscape reduced to 'black and barren matter' in the wake of an eruption is transformed 'in process of time' to one of the 'most fertile soil upon earth'.[54] These reflections partake of the central argument in natural philosophy that Brydone makes in his account of Etna: that the apparent catastrophe of volcanic eruption has creative and regenerative potential if viewed as part of a long-term, systematic history of natural processes. And the key component here is, again, time: 'what time must it require to bring it to its utmost perfection', Brydone asks of the fertile landscape around Etna, 'when after 2000 years it is still in most places but a barren rock?'[55]

Brydone's formulation of the concept of 'deep time' in his account of Etna depends, as I have said, primarily upon empirical observation of the landscape. But such observations are significantly buttressed in Brydone's *Tour* by the use of classical descriptions of Etna as evidence for the uniformity of volcanic processes over time. Empirical observations constitute a record of the 'depth' of time involved in shaping the visible landscape whilst classical sources verify the notion of the same processes operating over that time.

Hence, in his account of Etna, Brydone frequently remarks how classical accounts of Etna and its eruptions are entirely consistent with what he sees before him today, and upon the implications of that consistency for the timescales involved in the volcanic landscape. Some of these are mere passing observations, such as Brydone's remark that Etna 'is as much celebrated by the ancients as the moderns, for the variety of its odoriferous productions [i.e. gases]'.[56] But others are much more substantive and significant in terms of their implications for natural philosophy. Foremost amongst these we might cite Brydone's discussion of Pindar's 'most satisfactory' account in *Pythian* 1, composed some 2,200 years earlier.[57] This celebrated passage, Brydone says, not only 'shews to a demonstration, what has been much disputed, that Aetna was in these early ages, of as great an elevation as at present' but also that the lava flows from Etna – the bedrock of Brydone's argument for 'deep time' – behaved the same way in the past as they do in the present.[58] 'But what pleases me most in this [Pindar's] description', Brydone writes:

> is, that it proves beyond the possibility of a doubt, that in these very remote [i.e. ancient] eruptions, it was common for the lavas of Aetna to run a great way out to the sea. – The conclusion, I think, is fully as just, and perhaps not less sublime, than the 'avolsaque viscera montis erigit eructans' of Virgil.[59]

Just such an extensive flow, Brydone knew, had occurred in recent history, during 'the great eruption of 1669', when the lava from Etna 'scaled the walls' of Catania, destroying the city, 'and poured its flaming torrent into the ocean'.[60] Once again, then, the comparison of classical with modern accounts of Etna provided for Brydone indisputable ('beyond the possibility of a doubt') and 'sublime' evidence of the uniform and systematic operation of volcanic processes over substantial periods of time.

'All the pomp that mighty ETNA boasts': from classical to Romantic

The increasing divergence in the latter part of the eighteenth century of what we would now consider 'scientific' writing from literary and other responses to landscape has been well documented by scholars such as Heringman, O'Connor, Rudwick and others, often as part of a wider history of the emergence of scientific disciplinarity and the modern episteme from the eighteenth-century practice of 'natural philosophy'. In the specific context of responses to Etna, the emergence of a more 'scientific' way of writing about the volcano is well exemplified by the description of it given by the English diplomat and antiquarian William Hamilton in Letter IV of his *Observations on Mount Vesuvius, Mount Etna, and Other Volcanos* – which is conspicuous, from our point of view here, for making no other substantive reference to classical accounts of Etna than to note the stories concerning Empedocles and Hadrian.[61] Whilst they may have been increasingly relegated to the footnotes of this new, empirical genre, however, both the imagery and the modes of classical responses to Etna continued to influence the figurative appropriations of volcanism in late eighteenth-century and Romantic-period British poetry. On some occasions, this classical influence was direct, but on others, it was mediated through texts like Brydone's *Tour*. To illustrate this continued classical legacy, I want to turn, in closing, to the engagements with volcanism by Anna Seward in her poems 'Mount Etna', 'To Colebrooke Dale', and 'Colebrook Dale', and by Erasmus Darwin in 'The Economy of Vegetation'.

In 'Mount Etna', Seward makes explicit her familiarity with Brydone's account of the Sicilian volcano. Although first published in the *Poetical Register* for January 1807, Seward's subtitle informs the reader that the poem was 'Written many Years back, after having read Mr. Brydone's *Tour thro' Sicily*'.[62] Teresa Barnard has recently argued that because of the 'limited educational prospects and restricted travel opportunities' available to women like Seward, works such as Brydone's *Tour* offered a 'reassuring substitute for a lack of the university education and classical languages received by her male peers'.[63] Reading such works, and responding to them in poetry, became, in Barnard's analysis, a key means for such women writers to engage with stereotypically 'masculine intellectual subjects'.[64]

Seward's poem 'Mount Etna' certainly follows Brydone's account closely, acknowledging direct borrowings in footnotes. She praises the Scotsman's 'faithful pages' which 'paint' for the 'kindling eyes' of the reader's imagination the 'sublime' scene of 'all the pomp that mighty ETNA boasts' (lines 1–3, 6). Having tracked this 'pomp' across twenty-two quatrains, however, Seward strikes a different chord in the final three stanzas of her poem. Returned from her imaginative expedition, facilitated by Brydone's 'faithful pages', to the slopes of Etna, Seward's speaker concludes by giving thanks for the contrast between those distant Sicilian scenes and her own island home:

> Here, while we rove beneath thy wayward skies,
> Lov'd Albion, zon'd by Ocean's azure wave,
>   To NATURE let our hearts thanksgivings rise,
>   For all she banish'd as for all she gave!
>
> That not on *our* cold mountain heights reside,
> On Snowdon, or Helvellyn's peak sublime,

Th' ETNEAN GRACES; – in their ardent pride,
And baleful charms, *exil'd* this happier clime

lines 89–96; Seward's emphasis

In the contrast which Seward's speaker draws here between the quasi-Satanic 'GRACES' of Etna – those 'BRIGHT DESTROYERS' (line 100), with their 'ardent pride' – and the 'cold' 'sublime' of the graces who inhabit British mountains, we can see, obviously, a contrast between different kinds of physical geography. But we can also detect some other, stereotypical dichotomies, familiar from eighteenth-century cultural and imaginative geography: notably, the opposition between paganism and Christianity, and between the supposedly fiery, Catholic culture of Italy (soon to become the staple of Gothic romances) and the restrained, Protestant ethos of Britain. 'NATURE', Seward's speaker implies, is to be thanked for *these* differences too.

Broadly contemporary with Seward's 'Mount Etna' are two other poems, however, which register her sense that 'Lov'd Albion' is coming increasingly under threat – and which register that threat using volcanic imagery which derives ultimately, via both Brydone and Erasmus Darwin, from classical writing about Etna. These are the two poems that Seward wrote about the development of industrial ironworks at the nearby town of Coalbrookdale in Shropshire, which she visited in 1787: the sonnet 'To Colebrooke Dale', which was first published in *Original Sonnets on Various Subjects* in 1799, although Seward probably wrote it in 1790, when she composed her considerably longer poem 'Colebrook Dale'.[65]

Coffey (2002) and Setzer (2007) have both recently read these poems from the perspective of environmentalist and eco-feminist criticism, seeing them as part of a debate between Seward and her friend and would-be mentor, the natural philosopher and poet Erasmus Darwin, over the virtues and costs of technological progress.[66] For Coffey, Seward's Coalbrookdale poems respond quite deliberately to Darwin's discussion of the area in 'The Economy of Vegetation', where he 'celebrates' in both the main text and the notes 'the potential of science and technology to capitalize on the natural resources found in the vale'; Seward, by contrast, focuses on the extent to which the 'industrial processes' lauded by Darwin have 'spoiled' the 'natural beauty' of the area.[67] Setzer, in a parallel reading, sees Seward's Coalbrookdale poems responding to a (masculine) tradition of topographical poetry, which includes Pope's *Windsor Forest* and Darwin's *Botanic Garden*, and using 'images of sexual violation' to argue against the 'industrial degradation' of the landscape.[68]

Building on this scholarship here, I want to focus on the ways in which Seward's poems use volcanic imagery derived ultimately from classical sources to figure the industrial processes that she sees as destroying the bucolic landscape of Coalbrookdale. Such imagery, I will argue, is not only central to Seward's concerns about industrialization but also forms an important component of her writing back against Darwin's *Botanic Garden*, where classical tropes are used to celebrate volcanic activity as a metaphor for industry.

As both Coffey and Setzer note, Seward's first response to Coalbrookdale is given in a letter of 6 October 1787 to her friend William Hayley, the biographer of William Cowper, written shortly after her visit:

> A friend in Shropshire has lately shewn me the wonders of Colebrook Dale. We passed a fine autumn day in exploring the features of that scene, where we find, in such uncommon union, the dusky, noisy, assiduous, and indeed stupendous efforts of art, and romantic nature; – where the Cyclops usurp the dwellings of the Naiads and Dryads, and drown, with their dissonance, the woodland song; light their blazing fires on each of the many hills, and, with their thick black smoke, shroud, as with a sable crape, the lavish woods and fantastic rocks; sully the pure waters of the Severn, and dim the splendour of summer's sun.[69]

Although it has not previously been noted by scholars, the imagery which Seward uses here to describe the 'uncommon union' of 'art' and 'romantic nature' is both implicitly and explicitly volcanic. Implicitly in the 'blazing fires' and 'thick black smoke' which 'shroud' the landscape, 'sully the pure waters', and 'dim the splendour of the summer's sun' – we recall Virgil's account in *Aeneid* 3 of an eruption of Etna 'veiling the sky in smoke' and Brydone's revision of that passage in his account of an eruption, when 'clouds' from Etna 'darken the face of the sun, covering up this scene, under a veil of horror and of night; and laying waste every field and vineyard'.[70] And explicitly in that the 'woodland' domain of 'the Naiads and the Dryads' is being 'usurped' by the industrial activities of 'the Cyclops'. Etna, we recall from Lemprière's *Classical Dictionary*, was often 'represented as the forge of Vulcan, where his servants the Cyclops fabricated thunderbolts'.[71] In the opening of 'The Economy of Vegetation', Erasmus Darwin recalls this same tradition 'when of old, as mystic bards presume':

> Huge Cyclops dwelt in Etna's rocky womb,
> On thundering anvils rung their loud alarms,
> And leagued with VULCAN forged immortal arms'
>
> lines 157–60[72]

In her description of Coalbrookdale, in other words, Seward implies that those 'BRIGHT DESTROYERS' who were safely distant in her poem 'Mount Etna' now threaten the landscapes of 'Lov'd Albion'. The threat to the landscape from industrial activity is figured in terms of the destructive power of volcanic activity – but without any sense of the regenerative potential noted in both classical sources and in eighteenth-century works like Brydone's *Tour*, Hamilton's *Observations* and Darwin's *Botanic Garden*. And this is exactly the same anxiety which marks, in exactly the same terms, Seward's two poems about Coalbrookdale.

In her Petrarchan sonnet 'To Colebrooke Dale' Seward evidently versifies the volcanic imagery of her letter to Hayley. Seward's speaker laments that the 'GENIUS of Colebrooke' has proved 'faithless' to his 'charge' to protect the 'woods and vales' and 'rocks and streams' formerly sacred to 'poetic dreams' and 'Naiads and Nymphs' (lines 1–4). These are (as in Seward's letter) now being occupied by 'the swart Cyclops': 'dark-red gleams / From umber'd fires' are visible 'on all thy hills', whilst 'the beams / Solar and pure' are being shrouded 'by columns large / Of black sulphureous smoke, that spread their veils / Like funeral crape' and 'pollute thy gales, / And stain thy glassy floods' (lines 5–12).

It is certainly possible to read, following Coffey and Setzer, an element of sexual violence in the overthrow of the (female) Naiads and Dryads by the (male) Cyclopes – albeit remembering that the 'GENIUS' of Coalbrookdale is explicitly identified in the first line as male. But the primary figurative context here is certainly volcanic, an association made all the more visible by Seward's adding a detail not present in her letter, namely that the 'columns' of 'smoke' are 'sulphureous'. Classical accounts of Etna in eruption, and perhaps especially Virgil's descriptions of Etna in the *Aeneid* and of the Cyclopes in the *Georgics*, seem the obvious precursor texts here, along with Darwin's use of classical ideas about Etna in the opening of 'The Economy of Vegetation'.

This same volcanic imagery remains at the core of Seward's much-extended second poem on the subject: 'Colebrook Dale'. Here the 'grace' and 'bloom' of 'violated COLEBROOK' are the result of 'the Genius' having been 'brib'd' by 'Plutus', the Greek god of wealth (lines 1–4). And the consequences for 'the pearly-wristed Naiads' and 'the watry sisters' are again expressed in terms of the devastation of eruption in the linking of Cyclopes, the denizens of the forges of Etna, with industrial development:

> Now we view,
> Their fresh, their fragrant, and their silent reign
> Usurpt by Cyclops; – hear, in mingled tones,
> Shout their throng'd barge, their pond'rous engines clang
> Through coy dales; while red the countless fires,
> With umber'd flames, bicker on all thy hills.
> Darkn'ing the Summer's sun with columns large
> Of thick, sulphureous smoke, which spread, like palls,
> That screen the dead upon the sylvan robe
> Of thy aspiring rocks; pollute thy gales,
> And stain thy glassy waters
>
> lines 20–30

The destruction wrought by industry on the once bucolic landscape of Coalbrookdale is, in short, imaged as the devastating effects of volcanic eruption, but without the sense visible in some classical texts and in most eighteenth-century works of natural philosophy of the regenerative potential of volcanism. No fertility seems likely to follow in Seward's poem. Industry merely 'transforms' these once 'Tempean vales' into a 'gloomy Erebus', into the underworld of Greek myth – and of course, as Brydone reminds us in his *Tour*, classical sources often also associated Etna with the underworld: 'it is still very generally believed here [i.e. in Sicily]', he remarks, 'that Aetna is the mouth of hell'.[73]

As noted, Coffey and Setzer have argued persuasively that Seward's two poems about Coalbrookdale can be read as early examples of what we might now consider environmentalist or eco-feminist responses to industrialization. Both, in particular, read Seward's poems as a writing back against Darwin's unquestioning defence of technological progress in *The Botanic Garden*, a writing back given all the more force by the fact that Darwin had incorporated into *The Botanic Garden*, without acknowledgement or permission, Seward's own 'Verses Written in Dr. Darwin's Botanic Garden'. In Seward's Coalbrookdale poems, then, we can read in the struggle between Naiads and Cyclopes a mythologization not just of different visions of the British landscape but also a mythologization of ideological and personal tensions between Seward and Darwin. However, and more specifically for our purposes here, we can furthermore read Seward's overwhelmingly negative use of volcanic activity as a figure for industry in her Coalbrookdale poems as a significant counterpart to Darwin's much more positive figurative deployment of volcanic processes in 'The Economy of Vegetation'.

I have already noted Darwin's invocation of classical stories that placed the Cyclopes in the workshop of Hephaestus on Etna. That invocation forms part of the larger apostrophe to the 'Nymphs' with which 'The Economy of Vegetation' begins after the initial exordium taken from Seward. In Section III, Darwin follows the 'Nymphs' beneath 'Earth's vaulted roofs of adamantine rock' to see 'the billowy Lavas, as they boil' at the centre of the earth (lines 138, 140). These subterranean 'fires' provide 'genial warmth' for 'the incumbent land' in a process that Darwin figures as maternal:

> So when the Mother-bird selects their food
> With curious bill, and feeds her callow brood;
> Warmth from her tender heart eternal springs,
> And pleased she clasps them with extended wings
>
> lines 144–8

Darwin then describes an eruption: 'from deep cauldrons and unmeasured caves / Blow flaming airs, or pour vitrescent waves' (lines 149–50). This is an impressive aesthetic spectacle, at least if the viewer is safely distant: 'sea-wildr'd crews', Darwin writes, in a passage recalling *Aeneid* 3, 'the mountain-stars admire, / And Beauty beams amid tremendous fire' (lines 155–6). At this point, Darwin introduces the stories told by 'mystic bards' about the Cyclopes and their 'thundering anvils' located 'in Etna's rocky womb', a maternal image which echoes his earlier account of the volcanic 'Mother-bird', and which introduces now the arrival of 'Venus' (classical goddess of love, and wife of Hephaestus) in the 'dark abode', where 'with radiant eye She view'd the boiling ore ... And beauty blazed amid eternal night' (lines 161, 166 and 172).

In this extended invocation of classical myths about Etna, then, Darwin forges (if the pun may be forgiven) a complex connection between volcanism and (maternal) creativity which is entirely consistent not only with classical but also with more recent, eighteenth-century writing about the long-term, regenerative effects of volcanic processes, and with his own understanding of industry and technology as fundamentally progressive forces, which have a 'beauty' of their own. And it is precisely this kind of connection which Seward seems to counterpoint in her use of volcanic imagery in the Coalbrookdale poems, where the Cyclopes of industry destroy the beautiful rural landscapes formerly sacred to naiads and dryads.

The rhetorical tussle which I have been charting between Seward's Coalbrookdale poems and Darwin's *Botanic Garden* is indicative of the extent to which figurative appropriations of volcanoes and volcanic processes continued in parallel to the more strictly scientific approaches to the phenomenon taken by Hamilton and others. Arguably, Seward and Hamilton represent opposite poles of the disciplinary divide between artistic and scientific modes of describing the world which emerged from the practice of natural philosophy, with writers like Brydone and Darwin still inhabiting that earlier, pre-disciplinary mode so often also visible, as we have seen, in classical accounts of Etna. What the engagements with volcanism by Seward and Darwin do make abundantly clear, however, is the continued and rich legacy to late eighteenth-century and Romantic-period British poetry of classical writing about volcanoes and about Etna in particular: 'that venerable and respectable father of mountains', as Brydone calls it in his *Tour*.[74]

Notes

1. For the emergence of 'romantic' attitudes to mountain landscape and the continued legacy of those attitudes see, for example: Nicolson 1959, Ring 2000, Macfarlane 2003, and Duffy 2013.
2. Dryden 1776: 25.
3. For a detailed history of the debate between the so-called 'Neptunist' and 'Plutonist' schools of thought in eighteenth-century speculation about earth history, see Rudwick 2005 and Heringman 2004: 105–6 and 200–6.
4. Byron 1982 3: 179. For 'the recurrence of volcanic tropes in Byron's poetry' and its role in contemporary critical responses to his work, see Coghen 2015: 79.
5. For 'the eruption of a volcano' as an 'old faithful subject of London pictorial exhibitions' in the late eighteenth and early nineteenth centuries, see Altick 1978: 171.
6. As in Matthews 1957, Ashburn Miller 2009, Duffy 2013: 68–100 and Coghen 2015.
7. In her chapter in this volume, Dawn Hollis examines the 'ongoing influence of classical ideas and writings' (56) about mountains on the earlier history of natural philosophy in the seventeenth century. Hollis (2020) considers Brydone's account of Etna in relation to a number of early, classical, medieval and early modern accounts, all of which, she argues, 'are rooted in a clear sense of the landscape as imbued with cultural, largely classical, memory' (page numbers for this piece not available at time of writing). I return to her argument later.
8. Influential studies of the Grand Tour include: Black 1992, Buzard 1993, and Chard 1999.
9. Addison 1701: lines 12–14. For detailed consideration of the kind of imaginative geography involved in Addison's concept of 'classic ground' and its significance for writing about landscape in the eighteenth century and Romantic period, see Duffy 2013: 8–17.
10. Brydone 1773: I, 'Advertisement'. The editor of Dryden 1776, which was published posthumously, three years after Brydone 1773, quotes this same passage from Brydone, emphasizes Dryden's 'originality', and presents his *Tour* as a 'proper companion to Mr. Brydone's', printing it 'in the same size and manner, that both may be uniformly classed together when bound' (v–vii). These claims to originality refer, of course, to the entirety of Dryden's and Brydone's journeys to Sicily and Malta, and not only or specifically to their respective accounts of Etna.
11. This is not, of course, to imply that no other travellers had visited Etna or written about it. As Williams 2017 shows, the Italian scholar and churchman Pietro Bembo describes in his *De Aetna* an ascent which he made in 1493, during a two-year stay in Sicily. Like Dryden and

Brydone centuries later, Bembo's account is heavily influenced by what Williams 2017: 7–8 calls 'the Etna idea': the collection of tropes surrounding the volcano inherited from classical literature. But in the seventeenth and eighteenth centuries, contemporary, published descriptions of Etna in English or other modern European languages were scarce. Hollis (2020) considers as important hypotexts for Brydone's description of Etna not only Bembo's account, but also the discussion of volcanism in Thomas Burnet's *Sacred Theory of the Earth* (1684, 1690) and in Athanasius Kircher's *Mundus Subterraneus* (1665).

12. Dryden 1773: 25.
13. Hyde 1916: 401, quoting Pindar, *Pythian* 1.19.
14. Lemprière 1788: s.v. '*Ætna*'; no page numbers.
15. Hyde 1916: 401 speculates that Homer's account, in *Odyssey* 9.481-7, of the Cyclops throwing rocks at the departing Odysseus might be an oblique reference to a powerful eruption.
16. Classical and postclassical accounts sometimes conflate or confuse the two wars fought by the gods of Mount Olympus, led by Zeus: the Titanomachy and the Gigantomachy. The first was fought between the Olympian gods, who were victorious, and an older race of Gods, the Titans, who inhabited Mount Othrys; the second was the subsequent war between the race of Giants, who were descended from the Titans, and the Olympian gods, who again emerged victorious.
17. As in, for example, Euripides, *Cyclops* 599, and *Trojan Women* 200–3. For examples of a later Roman tradition which locates the smithy of Vulcan (the Roman equivalent of Hephaestus) on the island of Vulcano, just off the Sicilian coast, cf. Virgil, *Aeneid* 8.416-22 and Pliny the Elder, *Natural History* 3.8.93-5.
18. The text is traditionally attributed to Aeschylus, but both date and authorship are disputed.
19. For a detailed study of this passage in relation to the wider engagement with volcanoes in Virgil's work, see Johnston 1996, who observes in these lines from *Aeneid* 3 'the combined physiology of a quasi-human Mt. Aetna and of the Titan Enceladus' (56).
20. Another example of this discourse can be found, for example, in Strabo, *Geography* 6.2.8.
21. On this aspect of the influence of Lucretius, see for example Johnson and Wilson 2007 and Johnson 2015.
22. See Lucretius 6.680-702; and cf. Plato *Phaedo* 111 c-e; and Strabo, *Geography* 6.2.10. In a footnote to his account of a volcanic eruption in 'The Economy of Vegetation' (discussed below), for example, Erasmus Darwin explains that 'the immediate cause of volcanic eruptions is believed to be owing to the water of the sea, or from lakes, or inundations, finding itself a passage into the subterraneous fires' (Darwin 1791: 14). For discussion of the classical theory, see Brydone 1773 1: 75-6. Percy Bysshe Shelley also draws on the theory in *Prometheus Unbound* 2.4.
23. Johnston 1996: 58, quoting Hardie 1986: 178.
24. Buxton 2016: 26.
25. Ibid.
26. Smolenaars 2005: 313.
27. Welsh 2014: 99.
28. Johnston 1996: 58. Williams 2017: 8 notes a similar 'doubleness' of mythic and empirical discourses in classical responses to Etna and in Bembo's *De Aetna*.
29. Hyde 1916: 410. Hyde expresses reservations about what he feels to be 'grave faults of style' in the poem, but recent assessments have been more favourable: see, for example, Kruschwitz 2015.

30. Johnston 1996: 58.
31. Buxton 2016: 34.
32. Welsh 2014: 99.
33. Buxton 2016: 33.
34. Ibid. 38.
35. The expression 'the two cultures' was coined by Snow 1959. On the inter- or pre-disciplinary nature of eighteenth- and early nineteenth-century writing about earth history, see Rudwick 2005: 48–58 and *passim*.; Heringman 2004: 192–210 and 276–7; and Duffy 2013: 69–71 and 100–1.
36. Dryden 1776: 25–8
37. Ibid. 25. Cf. again Pindar *Pythian* 1.20-22 on 'snowy Aitna, nurse of biting snow all year round, / from whose depths belch forth holiest springs / of unapproachable fire'.
38. Dryden 1776: 29. Cf. Strabo, *Geography* 5.4.8: 'at Catana [now Catania], it is said, that part of the country which had been covered with ash-dust from the hot ashes carried up into the air by the fire of Aetna made the land suited to the vine'.
39. Rudwick 2005 remains the seminal cultural history of the formulation, during the eighteenth and early nineteenth centuries, of the concept of geological 'deep time', i.e. that the earth was immeasurably older than the 6,000 years allocated by established chronologies deriving ultimately from the work of James Ussher, who proposed 22 October 4004 BCE as the date of creation.
40. Brydone 1773: I, 140. For the wide readership and commercial success of Brydone's *Tour*, see Sher 2006: 92, 346 and 454.
41. Hollis 2020.
42. Duffy 2013: 72–86.
43. Brydone 1773: I, 151
44. Ibid. I, 196
45. Ibid. I, 246. Brydone quotes Lucan on the ruins of Troy in *Pharsalia* 9.973.
46. Brydone 1773: I, 249.
47. Ibid. I, 250.
48. Ibid. I, 183. *Historia Augusta* 1.13.3 records that the emperor Hadrian ascended Etna in 125 CE. In Brydone's day, Aelius Spartianus was believed to be the author of this life of Hadrian, but scholars today dispute both the date of composition and the author(s) of the *Historia*. Diogenes Laërtius, *Lives and Opinions of Eminent Philosophers* 3.18 says that Plato 'made three voyages to Sicily, the first time to see the island and the craters of Etna' – although this does not, of course, count as evidence of an actual ascent.
49. Brydone 1773: I, 199.
50. Ibid. I, 183. Various later 'structures' were subsequently built on the site, with the most recent being destroyed in an eruption in 2002.
51. Ibid. I, 185
52. Ibid. I, 196, 181, 197, 173.
53. Ibid. I, 173–4.
54. Ibid. I, 113, 115.
55. Ibid. I, 115–16.

56. Ibid. I, 234.
57. Ibid. I, 249.
58. Ibid. I, 250–1.
59. Ibid. I, 251.
60. Ibid. I, 163.
61. See Hamilton 1774: 78, 82. In this respect, Hamilton's approach to the classical heritage of Etna is markedly different from the treatment of mountains in Burnet's *Sacred Theory of the Earth* and other, contemporary seventeenth-century engagements with mountains, which, as Hollis shows in this volume, often retain, even as they ostensibly eschew, classical tropes and modes.
62. Seward 2016: 43. Barnard 2015: 43 provides a useful contextualized and descriptive account of Seward's poem, which she reads as a 'tribute to Brydone's Etna'. Seward's sonnet translated from the Italian of Vicenzo da Filicaja 'On Catania and Syracuse Swallowed Up by Earthquake' (which Barnard 2015 does not mention) may also owe something to her reading of Brydone.
63. Barnard 2015: 44, 51.
64. Ibid. 51.
65. As Seward's titles make clear, various spellings of Coalbrookdale were current in the late eighteenth century.
66. Barnard 2015 does not consider Seward's Coalbrookdale poems whilst discussing Seward's 'Mount Etna'.
67. Coffey 2002: 142.
68. Setzer 2007: 70.
69. Seward 1811: 1.338–9.
70. Brydone 1773: 1.127.
71. Lemprière 1788: '*Ætna*'; no page numbers.
72. For the placing of the Cyclops at Etna in classical literature see, for example, Virgil, *Aeneid* 8.416-53, and *Georgics* 4.170-75. See also Brydone 1773: I, 84 and 90.
73. Ibid. 1.165.
74. Ibid. I, 109.

CHAPTER 3
THE 'AUTHORITY OF THE ANCIENTS'? SEVENTEENTH-CENTURY NATURAL PHILOSOPHY AND AESTHETIC RESPONSES TO MOUNTAINS[1]

Dawn Hollis

'Tis true, the Poets who were the most ancient Writers amongst the Greeks, and serv'd them both for Historians, Divines, and Philosophers, have deliver'd some things concerning the first Ages of the World, that have a fair resemblance of truth ... but ... we will never depend wholly upon their credit, nor assert any thing upon the authority of the Ancients which is not first prov'd by natural Reason, or warranted by Scripture.[2]

Thomas Burnet, *The Theory of the Earth* (1684)

In 1684 the natural philosopher Thomas Burnet threw an intellectual grenade with his *Sacred Theory of the Earth*, a translation and expansion of his 1681 *Telluris Theoria Sacra*. Burnet sought to provide a mechanical explanation for key moments of Scriptural history and eschatology – the Creation, the Flood and the Apocalypse – and in so doing to produce a rational explanation for the current form of the Earth. Burnet posited that the Earth had originally formed out of the 'Chaos' into a paradisiacal 'Mundane Egg', with a smooth surface uninterrupted by mountains or seas.[3] Over time, the rays of the sun heated the waters upon which the surface of the Earth rested and, at 'the appointed time ... that All-wise Providence had design'd for the punishment of a sinful World', caused the waters to burst open the shell of the egg.[4] This cataclysm was none other than the universal flood, or 'Deluge', and as the waters receded they revealed 'the true aspect of a world lying in its own rubbish': continents separated by seas and bisected by mountain ranges.[5] Ultimately, this broken form would meet its end at the Conflagration, which would begin with the eruption of 'the *Burning Mountains* or Volcano's of the Earth', and which would set light to the storehouses of coal and other fuels secreted in the bowels of the Earth.[6] At the last, 'every mountain and hill' would be brought low, a 'huge mass of Stone ... soften'd and dissolv'd'.[7] Out of the roiling matter of the previous Earth – a second Chaos, so to speak – would form the New Earth: paradise, without oceans or hills.

Burnet's *Theory* rippled through the intellectual world of late seventeenth-century Britain and Europe and, ultimately, through the modern historiography of mountain experience and landscape aesthetics. In his own time, Burnet inspired a horde of critics. The *Theory*, however, could not be silenced, seeing six further editions between 1697 and 1759. Authors now credited with articulating early eighteenth-century definitions of natural sublimity went to the mountains with Burnet in mind; Joseph Addison even wrote a Latin ode to the *Theory*.[8] This chapter will focus on the *Theory* and the flurry of responses produced in its aftermath from 1685 to 1700, with a focus on two key issues: the aesthetic reception of mountains, and the ongoing influence of classical ideas and writings on the natural philosophic thought of the late seventeenth century.

In his treatment of mountains, Burnet presents a contradiction: he wrote that his desire to investigate their origins had been prompted by his awed impression of them as objects with 'the shadow and appearance of [the] INFINITE', but his *Theory* ultimately posited that they were nothing but the shattered ruins of God's original Creation, visible monuments of humankind's sinfulness. In modern scholarship, Burnet's positive response to mountains has been interpreted as him giving *new* voice to a hitherto-unknown appreciation for them. Meanwhile, his more negative depictions of mountains as disordered ruins have been seen to represent long-standing early modern attitudes of distaste towards them.[9] This chapter will reorient this assessment, by emphasizing the extent to which Burnet's respondents challenged his denigration of mountains with reference to a wide variety of positive arguments for them as original creations of God. Contrary to previous assessments, I argue that Burnet was representative of early modern attitudes not in his dismissal of mountains, but in his approval of them, and that it was in his attempt to remove mountains from the narrative of creation that he was heterodox.

In terms of the influence of classical ideas, the Burnet debate occurred during the midst of the 'Quarrel of the Ancients and Moderns', in which writers and thinkers wrangled over the value which should be placed on ancient texts.[10] Simultaneously, a crux of the debate itself was the level of dependence that should be placed upon different sources of natural knowledge: Scriptural, empirical and, indeed, classical. Burnet was criticized for over-dependence on ancient insights by respondents who would themselves, in the next textual breath, quote passages out of Ovid. This chapter will explore the instances in which discussions specifically regarding mountains either drew upon or rejected classical knowledge. These were concerned with the origin (or not) of mountains out of the original chaos, and their aesthetic identity as objects worthy of paradise. As such, the defence of the value of mountains launched in response to Burnet's *Theory* both relied upon ancient knowledge and evoked a sense of the antiquity of the human enjoyment of mountains.

The Burnet debate, mountains, and the 'ancients' and the 'moderns'

Before considering the moments of intersection between mountains and classical knowledge in the Burnet debate it is necessary to trace the broad contours of the controversy and the general attitudes which its participants expressed regarding the use and value of 'ancient' insights. The debate spanned more than a dozen volumes, published over the course of almost twenty years. Clergymen and mathematicians alike wrote long treatises and parodic dialogues in response to Burnet, and almost every aspect of his original work and thinking was considered and critiqued.

It is important to emphasize that the debate was not strictly *about* mountains. They were certainly a chief feature, and I would argue that the passions of Burnet's respondents were particularly excited by his suggestion that mountains, far from being the admirable creation of God, were ruinous remnants of God's punishment of sinful mankind. However, there were yet more crucial matters at stake. Burnet's *Theory* marked an attempt to provide a rational explanation for events recorded in Scripture, which sometimes required him (at least according to his accusatory respondents) to place his own intelligence above the evidence of the Bible. The *Theory* was written during a period in which, as Paolo Rossi has put it, seventeenth-century natural philosophers were beginning to stare into 'the dark abyss' of deep time[11] – and to wrestle with the corresponding idea that the Earth might be far older than Scriptural evidence allowed.[12]

The problem of deep time was accompanied by similarly huge questions: how had the Earth come into being, mechanically speaking, and how had it changed since creation? These questions could be answered with reference to the 'Book of Nature' – the physical Earth, perceived to be a second form of divine revelation – but what to do when human interpretations differed from God's literal revelation as found in the Bible? This is why Burnet's theory provoked so much vociferous reaction: because his answers had the potential to 'strike at . . . the very *Foundation*' of religion itself.[13]

Rather ironically, given the response he received, Burnet's professed intention in his work was to 'silence the Cavils of Atheists'.[14] He was a Cartesian, meaning he held to a mechanistic view of the Universe: one which God could create and then set on autopilot. Above all he resisted theories which relied on regular miraculous intervention, or which expected God to 'do and undo' as He went along.[15] A truly divine Creation, in Burnet's view, was one which was so well-designed that it required no subsequent intervention. This view made both the Scriptural account of the Flood, and extant explanations of it, difficult for Burnet to stomach.[16] A point which made Burnet particularly anxious was the account in Genesis of the Earth being 'covered' by the waters of the Deluge (Genesis 7.20). However, there was clearly not enough water in the Earth to achieve this: if one took it out of the sea, the laws of hydrodynamics (which Burnet understood even if he would not have used the term) meant it would slip right back in again.

However, it was not just the volume of water which concerned Burnet: he was also deeply troubled by the mountains themselves. In the panegyric praise of mountains for which he would later become most famous, Burnet wrote that

> The greatest objects of Nature are, methinks, the most pleasing to behold . . . there is nothing that I look upon with more pleasure than the wide Sea and the Mountains of the Earth. There is something august and stately in the Air of these things that inspires the mind with great thoughts and passions. We do naturally upon such occasions think of God and his greatness.[17]

However, Burnet quickly suggested that this divine sense of appreciation was mistaken; 'these Mountains we are speaking of, to confess the truth, are nothing but great ruines', admirable only insofar as the 'old Temples and broken Amphitheaters of the *Romans*' are worthy of attention as memorials of 'the greatness of that people'. Burnet presents his sense of wonder at mountains – which in his use of the plural pronoun he acknowledges is a common response – as a mirage which most people do not move beyond: 'the generality of people have not sence and curiosity enough to raise a question concerning these things'.[18] Of course, Burnet himself is different: it was his first impression of the Alps and Apennines as 'wild, vast, and indigested heaps of Stones and Earth' which drove him to seek 'some tolerable account how that confusion came in[to] Nature'.[19] If people would only look and think, as he did, they would realize 'what a rude Lump our World is which we are so apt to dote upon'.[20]

Burnet's *Theory* thus killed two birds with one stone, for it suggested that the mountains, far from being *covered* by the waters of the Deluge, were the result of it. As such, it solved the problems posed by a Flood which would otherwise require God to miraculously make and unmake a sufficient volume of water to drown the mountains, and which ran contrary to the Cartesian view of a God great enough to design a world in which He did not need to intervene. It also satisfied Burnet's sense that God was too good to have included such disordered objects as mountains in His original act of creation.

Burnet's earliest and most vociferous respondents were Herbert Croft, the eighty-five year-old Bishop of Hereford, and Erasmus Warren, a rector in his mid-thirties serving a parish in Suffolk. Croft deemed Burnet's *Theory* to be the expression of 'a grave and sober madness', and feared that it made Scripture 'a Nose of Wax, to be shaped and fitted ... to this Mans ridiculous inventions'.[21] Croft saw Burnet's theory of the Deluge as nothing but a '*Præludium* to usher in his rare Conceit of a new World' – or, rather, an old world, Burnet's vision of a paradisiacal flatland. Croft's response to the topography of this imagined world was scathing and sarcastic: as he noted, 'It wants onely one thing; There is a not a Mountain in all his World ... from whence you might have a large prospect of this delicious Land'.[22] He also grasped at the inherent contradiction in Burnet's simultaneous denigration and praise of mountains, quoting the passage given above before elaborating that

> surely all men who behold these things have the same delightful contemplation, as he acknowledges to have felt, when he beheld them; and yet we never looked upon them as broken ruined fractions of a former Structure, which we poor Souls never dream'd of, till his Theory gave us notice of them.[23]

Warren highlighted the same inconsistency in Burnet's judgement of mountains, and came to the same conclusion – that it was in his approval of mountains that he expressed received opinion, and in his denigration of them that he diverged from it.[24] Warren was the only critic to whom Burnet would publicly respond: over the course of the two years following Warren's *Geologia* (1690), Burnet would publish two replies and Warren a further two counter-responses.[25] Warren defended mountains as both beautiful and useful objects clearly designed by God. Not only were they the 'Tornings, and Carvings, and ornamental Sculptures' of nature, which represented 'the marvellous and adoreable

Skill of her *Maker*', but they were also immensely valuable to humankind, 'in Bounding Nations; in Dividing Kingdoms; in Deriving Rivers; in Yielding Minerals; and in breeding and harbouring innumerable wild Creatures'.[26]

Some dozen authors – too many to treat individually here – responded to Burnet over the course of the final decade of the seventeenth century, and Warren's dual recognition of the beauty *and* use of mountains figured prominently for many of them. The philologist Richard Bentley insisted that the 'irregularities' of mountains were vital for 'all the conveniences and comforts of life', in part due to their role in storing metals; without which, he argued, humankind would be 'bereave[d] ... of all arts and sciences, of history and letters' and even of religion itself.[27] This mountainous utility was not secondary to their beauty but inherent to them, for, according to Bentley, 'all bodies are truly and physically beautiful ... that are good in their kind, that are fit for their proper uses and ends of their nature'.[28] John Beaumont, a medical practitioner who became fascinated with the internal workings of the earth after befriending miners in the Mendip Hills, expressed a similar impression in a more allusive way:

> We find the Ancients call'd the Earth δημήτηρ our Mother Earth; for as *Plato* says, the Earth does not imitate a Woman, but a Woman the Earth: and they compar'd the Mountains on the Earth, to the breasts of a Woman: and indeed ... we shall find that the Mountains are no less ornamental, and of necessary use to the Earth for affording continual streams of fresh Waters to suckle all her Productions; than the protuberant Breasts of a Woman are, both for beautifying her Person, and yielding sweet streams of Milk for the nourishment of her Children.[29]

This same sense was expressed consistently throughout the debate: Burnet's awestruck experience of mountains was perfectly common, because mountains – in their beautiful usefulness – were quite clearly designed and created by God, and thus worthy objects of awe.

As Beaumont's reference to 'the Ancients' would suggest, classical knowledge or ideas figured frequently over the course of the Burnet debate. Indeed, the appropriate application of classical knowledge formed a particular point of contention, secondary only to fervent opinions held and expressed regarding the appropriate interpretation of Scriptural evidence. As shown in the quote opening this chapter, Burnet outlined three resources to which a natural philosopher could turn in constructing their theories: Scripture, reason and classical knowledge. For Burnet, these sources of knowledge and insight existed in a clear hierarchy: 'Reason is to be our first Guide', supported by 'further light and confirmation from the Sacred writings'. He justified giving primacy to reason by virtue of the fact that it, like Scripture, had been gifted to humankind as a form of revelation – although many of his respondents would deem this to be virtually atheistical arrogance. The 'Testimonies of the Ancients', on the other hand, were a clear last: Burnet suggested that what 'truths' ancient culture did have access to were merely received from even earlier antiquity, and that the 'grounds and reasons of them' were not understood by those who recorded them. As such, Burnet promised his reader that he would 'only make general reflections upon' classical sources, 'for illustration rather than proof of what we propose; not thinking it proper for an English Treatise to multiply citations out of Greek or Latin Authors'.[30]

Just as Burnet's critics identified the inconsistency in his responses to mountains, so too did they highlight that he failed to practise what he preached in his use of ancient sources. Herbert Croft commented that 'Sometimes he favours much of the Heathen Humour', whilst Erasmus Warren mused that it would have better had Burnet 'kept to his word' regarding his lack of reliance on the 'authority of the Ancients', rather than diverting from 'sober truth' and pursuing 'superstitious knowledge' and the 'Dreams' of 'Poets'.[31] One respondent, Samuel Parker, alluded to Burnet's reliance on ancient texts in a quip steeped in irony. His 1700 essay regarding the *Theory* took the form of a dialogue between one 'Philalethes' (lover of truth) and 'Burnetianus' (a 'Burnet fan'). The latter asks 'What becomes then of the Authority of the Ancients?', followed by the ironic aside 'not to cite'em particularly'; Parker's point being that Burnet cited them to excess.[32]

Some authors critiqued not only Burnet's use of the Ancients but the writings of the Ancients themselves. John Keill, a mathematician, was scornful of philosophers both ancient and modern who 'have maintained opinions more absurd than can be found in any of the most Fabulous Poets, or Romantick Writers'. Keill took particular pot-shots at Anaxagoras, Heraclitus, Xenophanes and Epicurus as representatives of 'the Ancients', and reserved particularly fierce criticism for Descartes as the leader of 'the Moderns'.[33] A year later, Keill would criticize natural philosophers who relied on ancient writers simply because they lived closer in time to the Deluge, pointing out that for all this they still 'did not live within some thousands of Years of the time, when this change was suppos'd to be made'. More than that, these same authors 'have said a thousand other things, that neither the *Theorist* nor any body else can believe'.[34] Ironically, Burnet also made his own critique of ancient philosophy, dedicating some time to dismantling the Aristotelian concept of the eternity of the Earth. One of his arguments against this idea was that had the Earth existed from eternity, it was impossible that the ancients should have been 'so ignorant', having had endless generations to develop their understanding: 'How imperfect', Burnet asked, 'was the Geography of the Ancients … their knowledge of the Earth … their navigation?'[35] Both Burnet and many of his respondents, therefore, articulated perceptions of ancient knowledge as, at best, secondary to the more reliable resources of reason and Scripture, and at worst as superstitious, flawed or even ridiculous.

These articulations, however, did not tell the whole story. Some participants in the debate had only positive things to say about classical knowledge. Beaumont, in keeping with his easy reference to 'the Ancients', given above, offered a general defence of pre-Scriptural natural knowledge. He termed ancient philosophers 'Men of Sense', who possessed 'an enquiring and restless Genius'. He even argued that, since *Moses* (supposed to have authored Genesis) 'had his learning from the *Egyptians*', one 'cannot think the Antients so ignorant in that kind, as some may otherwise imagin them to have been'.[36] The parson-naturalist dedicated an entire chapter of his *Miscellaneous Discourses* (1692) to 'The Opinions of the Ancient Heathen Philosophers, and other Writers concerning the Dissolution'.[37] Moreover, even the most staunch critics of Burnet's use of classical knowledge could not help but refer to it themselves. As will be seen in the remainder of this chapter, Croft, Warren and Keill all drew upon 'the authority of the Ancients' in seeking to construct their arguments against Burnet. With regard to mountains, ancient knowledge proved particularly pertinent in discussions of their origination out of a Chaos, and their aesthetic value as objects worthy (or not, as Burnet claimed) of a place in paradise.

The formulation of the Chaos

The key to Burnet's thesis that the antediluvian Earth was formed without mountains was his understanding of the Chaos. The concept of the Chaos (χάος) was central to ancient Greek cosmogony. Burnet's essential argument was that the Chaos separated matter according to its density, which then formed into the Earth according to the principles of gravity, with the heaviest matter at the core and lighter matter, such as water, forming an outer layer.[38] This water was then covered by small earthy particles so light that they had been thrown up by the motion of the Chaos, and which ultimately formed the thin shell of what Burnet termed the 'Mundane Egg', another concept with deep classical antecedents.

Burnet was more than conscious of the fact that he was drawing on classical tradition in his construction of the Chaos: indeed, he turned to classical mythology to justify his vision of a peculiarly ordered 'chaos'. He noted that

> the Ancients in treating of the Chaos, and in raising the World out of it, rang'd it into several Regions or Masses, as we have done; and in that order successively, rising from one another ... and therefore they call it the Genealogy of the Gods.[39]

Burnet went on to comment that 'those parts and Regions of Nature, into which the Chaos was by degrees divided, they signifi'd ... by dark and obscure names, as the *Night*, *Tartarus*, *Oceanus*, and such like', and that the 'Ancients ... made *Contention* the principle that reign'd in the Chaos at first, and then *Love*', representing the same division of elements, followed by union, as presented in his *Theory*. Here, Burnet echoes both the writings of Aristophanes (*Birds* 693-9), and the *Theogony* of Hesiod (115-125), both of which depict the mythological figure of Chaos as the first of the primigenial gods to appear, with Eros following and, in the case of Aristophanes, mating with Chaos to produce humanity. Burnet was careful to emphasize that these ideas supported his own argument, not because they offered reliable natural-philosophical evidence in and of themselves, but rather because his theories explained 'notions which we find in the writings of the Ancients figuratively and darkly deliver'd'.[40] Just as his work set out to offer a rational interpretation of Scripture, so too – he claimed – did his explication of the Chaos enlighten some of the stranger passages of classical literature.

The concept of the Mundane Egg receives similar treatment:

> this notion of the *Mundane Egg*, or that the World was *Oviform*, hath been the sence and Language of all Antiquity, Latins, Greeks, Persians, Egyptians, and others ... I

thought it worthy our notice ... seeing it receives such a clear and easie explication from that Origin and Fabrick we have given to the first Earth, and also reflects light upon the Theory it self, and confirms it to be no fiction.[41]

Here, ancient knowledge – though 'explicated' by Burnet's *Theory* – is also given credit for confirming his own arguments. In his conclusion regarding the form of the antediluvian Earth, Burnet reiterates his triumvirate of sources of knowledge, and their appropriate application, commenting that, as it is 'proved by Reason, the laws of Nature, and the motions of the Chaos; then attested by Antiquity ... and confirmed by Sacred Writers', he and his readers can comfortably 'proceed upon this supposition, *That the Ante-diluvian Earth was smooth and uniform, without Mountains or Sea*'.[42] What is particularly intriguing about this passage – alongside the fact that it reiterates the connection between the form of the Chaos and the mountain-less Earth – is that here, Burnet places Scripture in the role of confirming that which was attested by antiquity: a far cry from his initial promise to utilize 'the authority of the Ancients' for mere illustrative and confirmatory purposes.

Burnet's critics rightly identified his theory of the Chaos as a crux in his argument for the form of the antediluvian Earth, and unsurprisingly disagreed with his vision of its formulation. Herbert Croft, despite referring in derisory fashion to Burnet's interest in 'the several vain opinions of Heathen Poets or Philosophers' (which he characterizes as '*Ignes fatui*', a will-o'-the-wisp), roots part of his criticism in what he sees as Burnet's generalization of ancient opinion. 'I desire him to tell us', the elderly bishop stated, 'whether all the ancient Heathens were of this opinion', concluding that they in fact offered multiple models not just for the Chaos but for the general mechanics by which the world originated. Croft's rare reliance on ancient ideas is followed by a sting in the tale: 'this Chaos', he concludes, is clearly 'an Idea framed out of his [Burnet's] own brain', and therefore worthy of being rejected 'as we do *Epicurus's* Atoms'.[43] This passage sees the ancient and the contemporary reflecting poorly on one another: ancient knowledge is akin to invention, but Burnet is also implicitly equated with an ancient philosopher who in the seventeenth century was frequently associated with atheism and immorality.[44] For Croft, Burnet's *Theory* is nothing more than a conjured will-o'-the-wisp, made all the more suspect by his reliance on ancient writings.

Other critics, in contrast, drew directly on ancient literature to contradict Burnet's interpretation of the Chaos. Erasmus Warren argued that Burnet's idea of the orderly accretion of the Chaos could not have occurred because it would have taken far too long; longer, certainly, than the 'Divine Account' of the seven days and nights of Creation.[45] The fine particles which made up the crust of the Earth would also have had to accrete to an incredible thickness, formed by 'inconceivable Quantities of little Particles' to create a crust that would one day form 'the highest Mountains' of the Earth. More than this, the crust would have had to have been '*somewhat* bigger' than indicated by the current height of mountains, for 'the Mountains are now worn ... *lower* than they were', an idea which Warren states as fact, with reference to Aelian's *Varia Historia* (8.11).[46]

Later respondents to Burnet would turn to an author more in the modern mainstream of classical literature. John Beaumont argued that Burnet's concept of the Chaos was far too orderly, and gave no credit to the contrary, fermenting nature of the substance 'as all Antiquity has represented it'. For evidence of this, one need 'go no further than *Ovid*, who has represented the Nature of a *Chaos*, as well as any of the Antients':

>   ---*Congestáque eodem*
> *Non bene junctarum Discordia semina rerum.*
>   --- And mingled there
> The jarring Seeds of ill-joyn'd beings were . . .

>   ---*quia corpore in uno*
> *Frigida pugnabant caldis, humentia siccis*
> *Mollia cum duris, sine pondere habentia pondus.*
>   ---'cause in one Masse
> The cold things fought with hot, the moist with dry,
> The soft with hard, the light with contrary.[47]

Of all Burnet's critics, Beaumont quoted the *Metamorphoses* at greatest length, but several others alluded to the text as well. Archibald Lovell mused that Burnet had failed to represent 'a True and Original *Chaos*, which was no more but what the Poet says, *rudis indigestaq;* [sic] *moles*, bare and indigested matter, void of all Form, but susceptible of any that it should please an Almighty Creator to stamp upon it'.[48] Samuel Parker, his tongue firmly in cheek but clearly alluding to the same passage out of Ovid, characterized the ancient vision of the Chaos as 'a mere Hotch-potch of matter, a rude, undigested Mixture . . .'[49] Even John Keill, despite his declared distaste for classical sources, wrote as follows: 'certain it is that in such a great heap of matter, and so different mixtures of all sorts, *Mollia cum duris, sine pondere habentia pondus...*' (*Metamorphoses*, 1.20: 'The Soft and Hard, the Heavy and the Light').[50] Drawing on this description, Keill suggested it was far more likely that the Chaos was a liquid full of solid lumps which, following the principles of Archimedes, would float like icebergs – forming mountains present from the very beginning of the world.[51]

Crucial to Burnet's argument for a mountain-less antediluvian Earth was a Chaos which divided matter by mass, and allowed the construction of his smooth, uniform 'Mundane Egg'. He leaned heavily on the declared authority of the ancients in doing so, but his critics did not have to look far when deconstructing his arguments to find classical antecedents to support a Chaos far more suited to the original formation of mountains.

Paradise and the ancient aesthetics of mountains

In the sixth book of the *Aeneid*, Aeneas travels to the Elysian Fields to speak to his father, Anchises. He is guided by the Cumaean Sibyl, who inquires of a group of souls – headed by Musaeus of Athens – where they might find the father of the Trojan hero. Musaeus responds in a passage rich with landscape description:

> In no fix'd place the happy souls reside.
> In groves we live, and lie on mossy beds,
> By crystal streams, that murmur thro' the meads:
> But pass yon' easy hill, and thence descend;
> The path conducts you to your journey's end.
> This said, he led them up the mountain's brow,
> And shews them all the shining fields below;
> They wind the Hill, and thro' the blissful Meadows go.[52]

The topography of paradise formed one of the cruxes of Burnet's argument. In both Burnet's *Theory*, and the responses to it, ancient conceptions of precisely what paradise looked like provided important supporting evidence.

Burnet's case was that there was nowhere in the current form of the Earth that satisfied the definition of paradise and thus, by extension, the Earth must have changed drastically since Creation. Burnet located paradise in the smooth, flat, antediluvian Earth which rose out of the Chaos as he had interpreted it. He turned to both biblical and classical sources to elaborate upon the supposed characteristics of paradise – all of which, he argued, were far more likely to occur with the notable absence of mountains. Burnet identified corollaries to the Christian paradise in a variety of classical topoi; the Golden Age, which he deemed to be 'contemporary with our *Paradise*', but also specific locations such as the Elysian Fields, the Fortunate Isles, the Gardens of the Hesperides and Alcinous, Ogygia (the home of the goddess Calypso), and Taprobana (a real place, modern-day Sri Lanka).[53]

Through these, Burnet highlighted characteristics which classical authors ascribed to paradise and which, he argued, would also have been extant on the surface of his sea-less, peak-less 'Mundane Egg'. The first of these characteristics, present in accounts of the classical Golden Age, was 'a perpetual Spring, and constant serenity of the Air'.[54] This was a feature also of Burnet's theorized original, or 'Primigenial' Earth, thanks in part to its upright axis (Burnet suggested that the disruption of the Deluge had caused the present-day tilt), but also because winds 'could not be either impetuous or irregular in that Earth; seeing there were neither Mountains nor any other inequalities ... to stop them or compress them'.[55] Supporting evidence for this could be found in both Virgil and Ovid:

> Such days the new-born Earth enjoy'd of old,
> And the calm Heavens in this same tenour rowl'd:
> All the great World had then one constant Spring,
> No cold East-winds, such as our Winters bring.
>
> Virgil, Georgics 2.336-9[56]

> The Spring was constant, and soft Winds that blew
> Rais'd, without Seed, Flow'rs always sweet and new.
>
> Ovid, Metamorphoses 2.107-8[57]

Ovid also gave the account, which Burnet pointed to, of Saturn, 'an Ante-diluvian God, as I may so call him', being ousted by Jupiter, who introduced the four seasons.[58] Burnet goes no further along this particular line, although the implication is clear; the disruption of the Deluge which he recounts in his *Theory* is clearly hinted at in the changing of the guard from Saturn to Jove recounted in the *Metamorphoses*. Burnet also emphasized that 'they' – i.e. the Ancients – also 'supposed this perpetual Spring … in their particular *Elysiums*', a thing he could easily demonstrate 'from their Authors' if it were not for the fact that it would 'multiply Citations too much in this place'.[59]

The second common feature of both the ancient Golden Age and the antediluvian Earth was that of human longevity. This feature, 'however strange soever, is well attested, and beyond all exception, having the joynt consent of Sacred and Profane History'.[60] Burnet likewise avoided choosing to 'multiply Citations' here, merely insisting in broad-brush terms that

> all Antiquity gives the same account of those first Ages of the World, and of the first men, that they were extreamly long-liv'd. We meet with it generally in the description of the Golden Age; and not only so, but in their Topical *Paradises* also they always suppos'd a great vivacity or longævity in those that enjoy'd them.[61]

Such an opinion, Burnet noted, was not merely his own impression: '*Josephus* speaking upon this subject, *saith* the Authors of all the learned Nations, *Greeks* or *Barbarians*, bear witness to *Moses*'s doctrine in this particular'.[62] In this case, Burnet drew upon ancient writings to intervene in a debate surrounding Scripture. Turning to classical accounts of Paradise offered confirmation that longevity truly was a feature of the antediluvian Earth.

The third characteristic was the fertility of the soil and production of animals from said soil: 'All Antiquity speaks of the plenty of the Golden Age, and of their *Paradise*, whether Christian or Heathen'.[63] Once again, Burnet gestured towards ancient perceptions in general but avoided highlighting specific texts, noting that

> The Ancient Poets have often pleas'd themselves in making descriptions of this happy state, and in admiring the riches and liberality of Nature at that time, but we need not transcribe their Poetry here, seeing this point is not, I think, contested.[64]

Just as grapes and honey flowed more freely in the antediluvian Earth, but now 'must be squeezed out, and are more bitter', so too was the world as a whole more productive, even to the point of spontaneously generating animals – another claim made by Burnet to support a mechanistic understanding of Creation. He suggested that this was evidenced in Scripture, arguing that Moses 'seems to suppose that the Earth brought … [animals] forth as it did Herbs and Plants', but went into far greater depth in arraying relevant ancient sources.[65] Asserting that there was really no difference between the 'Seeds out of which Plants rise, and the Eggs out of which all Animals rise', he suggested that 'the warmth and influence … imputed by the Ancients to the *Æther* was surely sufficient to bring such earth-born eggs into fruition'.[66] He acknowledged that 'this opinion of the spontaneous Origin of the Animals ... hath lain under some *Odium*, because it was commonly reckon'd to be *Epicurus*'s opinion particularly' – Epicurus an ancient, as noted above, who was viewed with ambivalence – but insisted that the concept 'was not at all peculiar to *Epicurus*', and could be found in the writings of the Pythagoreans and the Egyptians too.[67]

Burnet concluded that the 'three general Characters' of his theorized antediluvian Earth could also be identified as 'the chief ingredients of the Golden Age, so much celebrated by the Ancients'.[68] He deployed both specific ancient material and general assertions of the opinions of 'the ancients' in support of his model of an antediluvian Earth, with the first characteristic – that of a serene atmosphere – in particular linked to the absence of mountains. His use of classical material here focused on the environmental realities of his proposed antediluvian world.

Burnet's interlocutors also drew upon ancient discussions of paradise, although they did not focus, as he did, upon the physical or meteorological details provided by these accounts. Rather, they emphasized the frequent inclusion of mountains within ancient depictions of paradise, in order to demonstrate that the appreciation of mountains as having aesthetic value was not just their own 'modern' opinion, but the indubitable taste of 'the ancients' as well.

Erasmus Warren, for example, attacked Burnet's use of ancient material in his discussion of paradise, witheringly observing that 'poets ... are by no means to be regarded in this matter. They are Men of wit and licentious fiction ...', and questioning whether ancient recollections of a 'Golden Age' might in fact refer to the era immediately following, rather than preceding, the Deluge.[69] Nevertheless, Warren was not above asserting, in his general defence of mountains as the original creation of God, that 'It is well known also, that many of the Learned Ancients have taught, that Paradise was situate upon high Mountains'.[70] John Beaumont offered a similarly unreferenced and generic pair of assertions regarding both sea and mountains. Of the sea, which he treated first, he observed that 'we find the Ancients so fond of a Sea, that scarce any of them describe a terrestrial Paradise, but mention a Sea with it'. Moving later to the question of mountains, he elaborated that 'indeed as the Ancients (according to what I have intimated before) scarce ever describ'd a Paradise without mentioning a Sea, so they seldom did it without naming Mountains'.[71] In each of these examples, 'the Ancients' are treated in general terms.

It was not until the intervention of Richard Bentley that a respondent to Burnet cited specific ancient sources in order to support the argument that mountains had a place in paradise and were thus aesthetically valuable. Among Bentley's plentiful criticisms of Burnet was the case, extensively made, that a mountainous Earth was superior to a mountain-less one:

> Are there then such ravishing Charms in a dull unvaried Flat, to make a sufficient compensation *for the chief things of the ancient Mountains, and for the precious things of the lasting Hills?*
>
> Deuteronomy 33.15[72]

In support of this, Bentley swiftly moved from biblical citation to a discussion of ancient responses. Citing Aelian's *Varia Historia* 3.1, he asked the reader to consider 'What were the *Tempe* of *Thessaly*, so celebrated in ancient story for their unparalleled pleasantness, but a Vale divided with a River & terminated with Hills?' He turned next to 'all the descriptions of Poets ... when they would represent any places of superlative delight', emphasizing first that 'They will never admit that a wide *Flat* can be pleasant, no not in the very *Elysian Fields*; but those too must be diversified with depressed Valleys and swelling Ascents'. This comment is paired with a series of marginal quotations from Virgil's *Aeneid*, including phrases alluding specifically to the passage given at the opening of this section. Bentley places a modern poet alongside this ancient one, commenting that 'They [poets] cannot imagin even Paradise to be a place of Pleasure nor heaven it self to be Heaven without them [mountains]', with marginal notes gesturing towards John Milton's 1667 *Paradise Lost*.[73] As poets, Milton, Virgil, and other ancient writers represent a jury delivering 'the sentence of Mankind' regarding the beauty, value and long existence of mountains.

This aesthetic point is also a religious one, or, as Bentley puts it, 'another Argument of the Divine Wisdom & Goodness'. It is a sign of the goodness of God that the world should be 'distinguished with Mountains and Valleys, ... and that because of the τὸ βέλτιον, it is better that it should be so'.[74] Far from supporting Burnet's argument for a flat antediluvian Earth, the consensus of his respondents – vague though many of their allusions may have been – was that 'the authority of the Ancients' supported the idea of mountains as being beautiful, and thus worthy elements of God's original creation.

Conclusion

This chapter has demonstrated two key points. First, that the overwhelming consensus of the Burnet debate, despite the opinions of Burnet himself, was that mountains were objects of value which had clearly been designed by a beneficent God for the benefit of mankind; and second, that despite a surface-level rhetoric throughout the debate which largely denigrated classical knowledge, the 'authority of the ancients' in fact loomed large as multiple authors sought to understand the origin and nature of the natural world with reference to past ideas. Of course, none of this is to say that ancient knowledge or ideas went uncontested, but it is evident that foundational ideas regarding the formation of the Earth (and thus its geology) were widely accepted, with little more required for supporting reference than a brief tag out of Ovid. Even more compellingly, 'the Ancients' were drawn upon as arbiters of natural aesthetics: if *they* could not imagine paradise without mountains, how could Burnet be right in saying that they were the unsightly ruins of the Flood?

One potential critique of the material explored in this chapter is that the 'classical reception' evident in the Burnet debate was not always particularly good Classics; both Burnet and his respondents frequently referred with frustrating vagary to 'the Ancients' as a whole, and where specific texts were invoked the corpus which they apparently drew upon, once reconstructed, looks notably small (Ovid and Virgil seem to have formed a good majority of it). However, I would argue that in some respects that is precisely the point. Previous works attempting to reconstruct the 'literary heritage' of early modern discussions of mountains have carried out their own surveys of the classical (and biblical) material relating to mountains.[75] Such surveys may be valuable as points of comparison, but they are problematic in two ways. Firstly, they risk being selective in a fashion which reproduces the modern presumption that positive responses to mountains belong largely to the postclassical, post-Romantic era. Secondly, in terms of unpicking the classically-influenced mountain ideas of the late seventeenth-century it does not particularly matter what citations a modern survey of ancient literature can find if they were not the citations which were prominent in the minds of the authors of the time: the 'literary heritage' thus traced ignores the more important contours of what was actually *inherited* from the classical corpus. It also does not particularly matter whether Burnet's critics were correct in attesting that 'the Ancients ... scarce ever describ'd a Paradise ... without naming Mountains'. What matters is that his critics believed that to be the case.

Burnet's *Theory* – and the furore surrounding it – represents the wider late-seventeenth-century natural-philosophical project of seeking to understand the origins of the world, in the midst of a moment of strife in the intellectual history of early modern Europe. New ideas of deep time and geological change were challenging what had hitherto been theological certainties regarding the age and creation of the world, and confidence in the authority of ancient sources of knowledge were on the wane, alongside a growing sense that, perhaps, the 'moderns' might rightfully step out of the shadows of their classical forbears. At the same time, this period by no means saw the outright rejection of Scriptural knowledge, and, to a lesser extent, the 'authority of the ancients' continued to hold some sway. In the Burnet debate, mountains stood at the nexus of new, ancient and biblical ideas about the world. The traditional narrative of 'mountain gloom and glory' sees mountains as subject to the same flux, with old, negative ideas giving way to new, positive attitudes. The above reading of the Burnet debate would suggest the contrary; that, with the exception of Burnet, natural philosophers of the late seventeenth century could trace deep antecedents for the aesthetic appreciation of mountains.

Notes

1. The initial research underpinning this chapter was undertaken for my MPhil thesis, and I am grateful both to the AHRC for supporting that research and to Alexandra Walsham for her expert and generous supervision of it. More recent thanks are due to Jason König for his ever-insightful comments.
2. Burnet 1684–91: I, 4.
3. Ibid. I, 52–65.
4. Ibid. I, 72.
5. Ibid. I, 110.
6. Ibid. II, 55.

7. Ibid. II, 111, with reference to Isaiah 40.4.
8. Addison 1699.
9. Burnet 1684–91: I, 139–40. The most enduring interpretation of Burnet as the vocalizer of a new attitude towards nature can be found in Nicolson's seminal *Mountain Gloom and Mountain Glory* (1959), and is reiterated in Macfarlane 2003; see also Wragge-Morley 2009.
10. See Levine 1999.
11. On deep time, see also Duffy in this volume, 43–5.
12. Rossi 1984: ix. As Rossi emphasizes, the idea of the relatively recent origin of the Earth (*c*. 4000 BCE) was also challenged in the same period by attempts to synchronize different cultural chronologies (for example ancient Egyptian and Chinese) with biblical chronology.
13. Warren 1690: sig. A3v.
14. Burnet 1684–91: I, 17.
15. Ibid. I, 20.
16. The *Theory* was also not wholly about the Deluge. However, Burnet's explanation of it underpins all of his subsequent discussions regarding Paradise, the original Earth, the Conflagration and the Earth still to come.
17. Burnet 1684–91: I, 140.
18. Ibid.
19. Ibid. This passage is potentially an allusion (conscious or not) to Ovid's *rudis indigestaque moles* – see below for more explicit references to the same.
20. Burnet 1684–91: I, 151.
21. Croft 1685: sig. A6r and br. Croft associates the expression 'grave and sober madness' with Seneca, giving the Latin as '*Sobrie insanire, & per gravitatem furere*'.
22. Ibid. 136.
23. Ibid. 142.
24. Warren 1690: 146.
25. See Warren 1690; Burnet 1690; Warren 1691; Burnet 1691; Warren 1692.
26. Warren 1690: 147.
27. Bentley 1693: 38.
28. Ibid. 37.
29. Beaumont 1693: 56.
30. Burnet 1684–91: I, 3–4 and 6.
31. Croft 1685: a5r-a5v; Warren 1692: 264–5.
32. Parker 1700: 5.
33. Keill 1698: 2–5 and 11–12.
34. Keill 1699: 41–2.
35. Burnet 1684–91: I, 34 and 39–40.
36. Beaumont 1693: 10. In making this argument he was articulating a wider early modern belief: see Assmann 1998.
37. Ray 1692: 28–38.
38. Burnet 1684–91: I, 51–60.

39. Ibid. I, 63.
40. Ibid. I, 64.
41. Ibid. I, 65. The oviform shape allowed, Burnet argued, for the motion of rivers around an otherwise smooth globe: I, 227–8.
42. Ibid. I, 65.
43. Croft 1685: 144–5. Despite Croft's general scorn for 'the ancients', he does – without any sense of irony – draw on them for the occasional witty tag, for example commenting (with an obvious stab at Burnet, sig. A7r) 'the more we study, the more we come to know our own ignorance, as that Wise man said, *Hoc unum scio, me nihil scire*' (a phrase widely attributed to Socrates).
44. For the ambivalent early modern reception of Epicurus, see Wilson 2009: 267.
45. Warren 1690: 48.
46. Ibid. 49. An entirely separate chapter could be written on the connection between early modern ideas regarding the heights of mountains and classical knowledge and methods for measuring altitude; for a dated but valuable introduction to this area, see Cajori 1929.
47. Beaumont 1693: 26–7. The lines quoted are from Ovid, *Metamorphoses*, 1.8-9 and 1.18-20.
48. Lovell 1696: 14, quoting Ovid, *Met,* 1.7.
49. Parker 1700: 5.
50. Keill 1698: 50. Translation (not in Keill) given from George Sandys' 1632 Ovid.
51. Ibid. 50–1.
52. Dryden 1697: 389, 6.914-21 (6.673-8 in the Loeb Latin text). Dryden's *Virgil*, composed between 1694 and 1697, marks a translation more or less contemporaneous with the Burnet debate, and also one which has gone on to become an – or even the – iconic early modern English translation of a classical text.
53. Burnet 1684–91: I, 176–7 and 252–3.
54. Ibid. I, 177.
55. Ibid. I, 196 and 224–5.
56. Ibid. I, 177. The translation is as given in Burnet (who also included the Latin).
57. Ibid.
58. Ibid. I, 177–8.
59. Ibid. I, 178.
60. Ibid. I, 180.
61. Ibid. I, 181.
62. Ibid., referring to Josephus' *Jewish Antiquities*, 1.4.105-8. Burnet's use of Josephus here and elsewhere suggests that he viewed him, a Jewish if not a Christian author, as distinct from (and more reliable than) his 'pagan' forbears.
63. Ibid. I, 181.
64. Ibid. I, 182.
65. Ibid. Burnet cites Genesis 1 verses 11 and 24 – the first dealing with herbs and grass, the second with animals, but both featuring the phrase 'Let the earth bring forth' (King James Version).
66. Ibid. Burnet again quoted Virgil's *Georgics* (2.325-6), suggesting an analogy between the effect of the aether on the Earth and the 'irradiation of the Male' upon the female: 'In fruitful show'rs of Æther *Jove* did glide / Into the bosom of his joyful Bride'.

67. Ibid. I, 182–3; cf. 62, above on the rejection of Epicurus' theory of atomism.
68. Ibid. I, 183–4.
69. Warren 1690: 263.
70. Ibid. 208.
71. Beaumont 1693: 55–6.
72. Bentley 1693: 39–40.
73. Ibid. 40.
74. Ibid. 40–41.
75. Nicolson 1959 dedicates her first chapter to 'The Literary Heritage' of seventeenth-century English attitudes to mountains, suggesting that 'the early Greeks had shown some of the awe and aversion of many primitive peoples in the face of a Nature they did not understand', whilst 'the Latin attitude towards mountains … remained almost consistently adverse' (38–9); see the introduction, above for further discussion, and for recent critiques of Nicolson, esp. Koelb 2009. More recently, Barton 2017: 15–58, offers an overview of Latin and biblical responses to mountains, concluding that 'the lack of aesthetic judgements of the mountain or mountain environments in the biblical tradition – just as in the Classical – is clear' (58).

CHAPTER 4
TOWARD A CONTINUITY OF ALPINISM IN ANTIQUITY, PREMODERNITY AND MODERNITY: JOSIAS SIMLER'S *DE ALPIBUS COMMENTARIUS* (1574) AND W. A. B. COOLIDGE'S FRENCH TRANSLATION FROM 1904

Sean Ireton

In his *De Alpibus Commentarius* from 1574, the Swiss theologian and classicist Josias Simler consulted all the extant texts that ancient Greek and Roman authors had written about the Alps, supplementing them with updated information from his contemporaries. Simler's *Commentarius* is the first work devoted exclusively to the Alps and sums up the knowledge pertaining to the region from antiquity through the early modern era. The French translation from 1904 has become a classic of Alpinist history in its own right: *Josias Simler et les origines de l'alpinisme jusqu'en 1600* (*Josias Simler and the Origins of Alpinism up to 1600*). As the title indicates, this work is more a contextual transformation than a mere textual translation. The instigator of this scholarly enterprise, the American-born historian and mountaineer William Coolidge, further included notes, appendices and a wealth of surplus material such that Simler's roughly 150-page treatise is transmuted into an approximately 900-page tome; indeed, into a kind of proto-databank of the Alps, one that not only quantitatively augments but radically reinvents the original sixteenth-century 'encyclopédie alpine' for a twentieth-century audience.[1] The encyclopedic nature of Simler's *Commentarius* lies in its wide-ranging coverage of Alpine geography, hydrography, climatology, mineralogy, botany and zoology as well as more specific mountain phenomena such as storms, avalanches and glaciers. The *meta*-encyclopedic aspect of the fin-de-siècle French 'translation' lies in its collage-like organization and its self-aware stance as a work published in the wake of the glory days of Alpinism. If Simler's Latin tract, composed at the height of the early modern era, can be said to link the (Mediterranean) classical tradition with the incipient (Central European) modern age, then Coolidge's *Simler* opus further reinforces these links from the vantage-point of modernity, specifically post-golden- and silver-age Alpinism and its ensuing decades of mobilized mountain conquest.[2] Nevertheless, as further indicated in the title, the cutoff year of Coolidge's historical investigation is 1600, which for him heralds a kind of blackout in the development of Alpinism, one that lasted from the Thirty Years' War to the era of vigorous Swiss Alpine exploration during the second half of the eighteenth century embodied by the likes of Horace-Bénédict de Saussure, Marc-Théodore Bourrit and the lesser-known Benedictine Père Placidus à Spescha.[3]

It is crucial, however, to note that this historical hiatus posited by Coolidge does *not*, in substance, correspond to the pivotal shift between the seventeenth and eighteenth centuries signalling the cultural dichotomy of premodern gloom versus modern glory, as famously adumbrated by Marjorie Hope Nicolson and later propagated in much of the academic discourse on mountain aesthetics.[4] Granted, the time intervals seem to neatly overlap, but Coolidge is merely postulating a brief epistemological gap in an otherwise longstanding tradition of encyclopedism or knowledge-ordering vis-à-vis the history of human engagement with mountainous environments, a gap resulting from the chaos and ruin of decades-long pan-European warfare.[5] And a roughly 150-year lull in activity, whether physical or scholarly, is by no means equivalent to a drastic historical break or wholesale epistemic rupture. As both Simler and Coolidge – the latter even more so thanks to his broader encyclopedic knowledge (which of course stems from his 'modern' access to a greater wealth of documentary materials) – make abundantly clear, the history of human-mountain interaction firmly extends back to antiquity. In other words, Simler's and Coolidge's respective texts give deep and detailed testimony of a non-dichotomous continuity of Alpinism from antiquity to premodernity – and, by extension, to the era of high modernity during which Coolidge carried out his meta-translational enterprise (initiated in 1895 but mainly conducted between 1899–1903). In the following, I will outline these two Alpine classics and highlight some of the key arguments contained therein concerning the history of mountaineering in Europe. Given the length and breadth of these encyclopedic compilations, the one a vast accumulation of textually ingested authorial knowledge, the other a dazzling display of scholarly erudition combined with a seemingly infinite collation of *inter*texts functioning within a larger *intra*textual corpus, my approach will necessarily be more selective than exhaustive. In the end, my chapter intends to offer an overarching framework, one that remains perhaps more thematic-heuristic than chronological-historical, but that nevertheless aims to contextualize the rest of the contributions in this volume. At the same time, my focus on select accounts, events and trends in the history of Alpinism, as transmitted by Simler and Coolidge, may yield pointers that help illumine or reinforce continuities in human intercourse with mountains from the classical to early modern age – and perhaps beyond. But first, some brief historical-biographical remarks on both authors are in order.

Coolidge and Simler: biographical backgrounds

William Augustus Brevoort Coolidge was 'an American by birth, a Briton by education, a Frenchman (and particularly a Dauphinois) by adoption'.[6] In more precise bookend biographical terms, he was born in New York City in 1850 and died in Grindelwald, Switzerland, in 1926. Between these two stations of his life, the scion of a wealthy cosmopolitan family in America and a retired mountaineer residing in the heart of the Bernese Alps, he was educated in Paris and England, specifically Oxford, where he won a French scholarship in 1871 and taught history until 1896. All the while, he climbed extensively in the Alps. By his own reckoning, between the years 1865–1900 he had undertaken 1,750 mountain forays of which 900 resulted in summit ascents. He first visited the Alps under the mentorship of his aunt, Meta Brevoort, a pioneering climber in her own right.[7] Known as 'the young American who climbs with his aunt and his dog', Coolidge was accompanied on most of his excursions by Brevoort (until her death in 1876) and by Tschingel (until her death in 1879), a beagle mix named after a glacier pass in the Bernese Oberland. Tschingel, or at least her detail-obsessed human master and chronicler, could in fact boast of having crossed thirty-six high passes and climbed thirty peaks, eleven of them ranking as first canine ascents.[8] While Coolidge cannot be considered an expert mountaineer in terms of pure technical climbing ability let alone agility, he possessed great endurance and boundless perseverance. Indeed, such was his amateurishness on rock and ice that he always relied on a professional guide, usually the Grindelwald native Christian Almer and, later, Almer's sons Ulrich and Christian Jr. (It was from Almer that the teenage Coolidge received Tschingel, as a kind of a consolation prize following a failed attempt of the Eiger in 1868.) Nevertheless, despite his lack of technical Alpine knowhow, Coolidge has earned himself a place in the sporting history of Alpinism for three main reasons: (1) he was one of the first to engage in winter mountaineering, thereby accomplishing many off-season first ascents; (2) he preferred to use high bivouacs rather than rely on established lower-lying huts, a practice that shortened summit bids and ultimately helped increase his number of ascents; (3) much of his climbing activity was focused on the French Dauphiné, a wild and underexplored region at the time and still somewhat off the beaten track of most mountaineering itineraries. In fact, two topographical features of this subrange bear his name today: a mountain called Pic Coolidge (3,774 m/12,382 ft) and the Couloir Coolidge on the far more prominent Mont Pelvoux (3,946 m/12,946 ft).

An active high-mountain trekker and productive peak-bagger, Coolidge was an even more prolific writer, eventually becoming 'the Boswell of the Alps' and, in more superlative terms, 'the greatest Alpine historian that the world has ever known'.[9] On a side note, Coolidge was anything but a proper Victorian in terms of his social etiquette and personal demeanour. As a professional historian, he was fault-finding and petty; he for instance once condemned an entire book because the author had used the wrong accent (presumably in a French word). As a human being, he could carry grudges to the extreme, if not to the grave – for example against Edward Whymper.[10] In more objective scholarly terms, he contributed more than 230 articles to the *Alpine Journal*, which he also edited from 1880 to 1889; published in nearly thirty other periodicals dedicated to Alpinism; composed scores of encyclopedia entries; and wrote, co-wrote or collaborated on a total of sixty-one books. As his biographer Ronald W. Clark notes: 'never before was such an excessive accumulation of Alpine knowledge made available'.[11] His two crowning achievements are *The Alps in Nature and History* (1908) and the text under consideration here: *Josias Simler et les origines de l'alpinisme jusqu'en 1600* (1904). What Clark says about Coolidge's numerous guidebooks – that they 'categorized, rationalized, and codified the Alps'[12] – certainly applies to this latter work, which constitutes a peculiar palimpsest of intra-intertextuality carried to the extreme. Some basic facts about his *Simler* book and, as one prominent reviewer remarks, the 'somewhat intricate system of pagination'[13] of this highly heterogeneous work can be summed up as follows. It consists of:

- over 200 pages of prefatory, introductory and bibliographic matter, written in French (except for the original Latin of a seminal text by Conrad Gessner that will soon be discussed in more detail);
- 307 pages of main text, which includes the original Latin of *De Alpibus Commentarius* and the French translation on facing pages;
- 130 pages of notes on the *Commentarius*, in French;
- 197 pages of appended texts ('pièces annexes'), eighteen in all, mainly in Latin and in French translation, consisting of key documents that attest to the history of mountain climbing, from the ascent of Mount Haemus in 181 BCE by Phillip of Macedon to a previously obscure account of Alpine travels throughout the Duchy d'Aosta between 1691 and 1694;
- 63 pages of notes *on* these appendices, in French;
- 29 pages of index.

Again, all totalled, *Josias Simler et les origines de l'alpinisme jusqu'en 1600* amounts to over 900 pages. As the opening lines of Douglas Freshfield's review in the *Alpine Journal* express in half-exasperated, half-humorous fashion:

> 'Prodigious!' is the adjective which will best express the feelings of the man of average strength and prehensile grasp who is fortunate enough to receive the edition *de luxe* of this portly and strangely proportioned volume. Most possessors even of the ordinary edition will, we fancy, after gazing for a few days at Mr. Coolidge's monumental work, follow the present writer's example and send it off to their binder to be bisected, an operation which the arrangement of the text happily renders not impossible.[14]

As for Simler, here are some basic facts, as represented in typically meticulous fashion by Coolidge himself in a fifteen-page biographical 'sketch' toward the beginning of his book. Josias Simler was born in 1530 and died, just two years after the publication of *De Alpibus Commentarius*, in 1576. He spent nearly his entire life in the canton of Zurich, interrupted only by his studies in Basel and Strasbourg. His surname, alternatively spelled with one *m* or two, proves interesting from a philological standpoint. Technically speaking, it should be spelled Sim*m*ler, since his forebears were bakers that provided the local Benedictine monastery in Rheinau with daily bread or rolls (southern German/ Austrian/Swiss = *Semmel*). But, as Coolidge points out, although 'Simmler' is the more accurate spelling based on family history and trade, 'Simler' was the version that Josias tended to use in his professional capacity as an author (rather than baker). Most of Simler's writings focus on his native Switzerland, especially its geography and history, for instance *Vallesiae et Alpium Descriptio* (1574) and *De Helvetiorum Republica* (1576).[15]

He also wrote a biography of his mentor and friend Conrad Gessner (alternatively spelled 'Gesner', though for other reasons than in Simler's case),[16] himself a quintessential Swiss citizen-spokesman and central figure in the history of Alpinist discourse. Indeed, Gessner's treatise *De Montium Admiratione* (*On the Admiration of Mountains*) from 1541, also discussed in Dan Hooley's chapter above, is included as the opening text in Coolidge's book, both in the original Latin and in French translation (more on this connection later). As for Simler, *his* signature mountain treatise, *De Alpibus Commentarius*, went through three editions – 1574, 1633 and 1735 – before Coolidge reissued and recast it in 1904.

Josias Simler et les origines de l'alpinisme jusqu'en 1600

As Coolidge points out in his biographical sketch, Simler was not an 'Alpinist' in a modern sense, nor can his treatise be considered a product of 'Alpinist' history as we understand it today.[17] For Coolidge, there existed a fundamental difference between modern versus early modern concepts of 'Alpinism' or, more generally, mountain exploration and endeavour. In Simler's time (before 1600), the focus lay on lower slopes, where botanical studies were able to be carried out. Many of the early writers on the Alps, from Gessner during the mid-1500s all the way to Albrecht von Haller in the mid-1700s, were, after all, botanists rather than geologists and glaciologists like their scientific counterparts in the nineteenth century. Before the modern era, at least according to Coolidge in his biographical chapter on Simler, mountains were simply not climbed and high passes were crossed only by soldiers, shepherds, pilgrims, merchants and government officials on state business – but never for the sake of pure sport. Indeed, except for Aegidius Tschudi, who trekked to the top of St Théodule Pass (3,295 m/10,810 ft) between Zermatt and the valley of Aosta in 1528, no authors who wrote about the Alps before 1600 ever attained snowy heights. This includes Gessner, whose famous ascent of one of Mount Pilatus's subpeaks did not carry him beyond the modest elevation of 1,919 m/6,296 ft.[18] Simler himself contracted gout at an early age (twenty-nine) and thus would not have been able to engage in much Alpine ambulation in the first place. Nevertheless, as Coolidge proceeds to argue, if one defines 'Alpinism' in a broader sense, namely as 'la science des Alpes',[19] then Simler and his contemporaries rightfully rank high (figuratively) in the history of this tradition and its discourse. Though they may not have been physically familiar with the mountains that towered around them and everything they wrote about was, in effect, 'second-hand' knowledge,[20] they are still 'Alpinists' in a premodern sense of the word. In fact, by these early metrics, Simler can be considered 'the first "Alpinist"' as his book '*sums up* clearly, methodically and in a precise fashion the data that one possessed about the Alps, from all possible points of view, back then in the sixteenth century'.[21] Coolidge goes on to speculate that Simler would have been able to accomplish far greater things, both in terms of scholarship and the mountaineering ventures predicated thereupon, had he lived in a later era. The implication here, of course, is that Coolidge sees himself as fulfilling this function, creating an even more cumulative and definitive encyclopedia of the Alps, indeed 'a complete monograph of Alpinism up to 1600'[22] whose ultimate ambition, if not conceit, is to surpass its early modern predecessor and ostensible translational sourcebook. Simler's own sources range from numerous classical Greek and Latin authors (e.g. Polybius, Ptolemy and Strabo; Silius Italicus, Livy, Tacitus and Pliny the Elder) to a handful of medieval historians (all of them obscure by today's standards) to his own Swiss contemporaries (most notably Gessner, Tschudi and Johann Stumpf). Coolidge in fact provides a 'List of Authors Cited by Simler,'[23] one that amounts to ten pages, almost half of which is taken up with a list of ancient authors.

Simler's *De Alpibus Commentarius* comprises approximately a third of the total text of *Josias Simler et les origines de l'alpinisme jusqu'en 1600*, although this fraction includes the pages of the facing French translation. The actual Latin text therefore makes up only about one-sixth of Coolidge's book and does not even begin until after 192 pages of preliminary material, including a short preface and long introduction, neither of which can truly be called 'ancillary' in terms of importance. Already in the preface, which contains the usual obligatory acknowledgements and previews of content, Coolidge seems compelled to address a seemingly minor matter, one that however separates him from his predecessor in terms of a provincial, and arguably petty, aspect of Alpinism. Coolidge, that is, feels the need to justify why his translation of a prominent Swiss author was published in France, more precisely in Grenoble, rather than in Switzerland. (The fact that it was translated by an American expatriate and longtime resident of Britain, whose native tongue was not French, is never once broached.) Given the dominance of Swiss mountains, authors and cartographers in Alpinist discourse from the early modern to modern eras – e.g. Josias Simler, Conrad Gessner, Thomas Schöpf, Johann Jakob Scheuchzer, Albrecht von Haller, Élie Bertrand, Gottlieb Sigmund Gruner, Horace-Bénédict de Saussure, Marc-Théodore Bourrit, Jean-Jacques Rousseau, et al. – his point may be well taken, but the argumentative lengths to which he goes in order to defend his book seem rather bizarre. Ultimately, he is endorsing the subrange and greater Alpine region that he became most closely attached to as a mountaineer: the Dauphiné Alps of southeastern France. In the process, he outlines four reasons for the publication of his book in a city that lies removed from the main stage of Alpinism in central Switzerland: (1) In his *Commentarius* Simler himself reports on various places in Dauphiné, in one instance even singling out Grenoble; (2) The second and 'best' French translation of Simler's other major work, *De Helvetiorum Republica*, was carried out by a Dauphiné native, namely the Protestant theologian Innocent Gentillet; (3) The first technical ascent or true rock-climb (*grimpade*) carried out in the Alps, that of Mont Aiguille in 1492, took place in Dauphiné not far from Grenoble; (4) In *On the Admiration of Mountains*, Conrad Gessner alludes to a geographical-geological phenomenon situated in the proximity of Grenoble: la Fontaine Ardente or 'Burning Fountain', a methane gas source that produces an aboveground flame. In sum, two of the 'Seven Wonders of the Dauphiné' (natural and manmade sites located throughout this former French province) figure 'intimately'[24] in Simler's treatise: Mont Aiguille and la Fontaine Ardente. One senses here, in Coolidge's prefatory argument, a kind of inferiority complex toward the storied history if not sublime majesty of the Swiss Alps, especially as some – indeed, perhaps all – of the above reasons seem rather tenuous if not downright arbitrary. Nevertheless, two of them prove to be critical in the history of Alpinist discourse and are worth dwelling on, especially as Coolidge himself dwells on them in his introductory chapters.

Since Gessner's *Epistola ad Jacobum Avienum de Montium Admiratione* or *Letter to Jacob Vogel on the Admiration of Mountains* ranks as one of the foundational documents in the history of Alpinism and, more specifically, Alpine aesthetics, it is only fitting that Coolidge incorporated and translated it as a kind of overture to his book, situating it between the preface and lengthy, detail-laden introduction. As he states in the former, this text 'constitutes one of the charters of Alpinism'.[25] Gessner, like Simler, was a key conduit between antiquity and premodernity with respect to scientific knowledge about the natural world. In his letter, Gessner can even be said to adopt a 'modern' attitude toward mountains, whose summits he seeks out at least once a year 'for the sake of … health-giving exercise and spiritual enjoyments'.[26] Given the greater scope of mountain-climbing discourse, it is striking that Coolidge opens his book with Gessner's mountain manifesto, whereas he relegates Petrarch's more canonical Mont Ventoux epistle to the chronologically arranged 'Pièces annexes'. Indeed, here it occupies the chronological spot of 'No. 9', sandwiched between the ascents of Canigou (2,784 m/9,134 ft) in the Pyrenees by Pierre III of Aragon sometime during the late thirteenth century (probably 1285) and of Rochemelon or Rocciamelone (3,538 m/11,608 ft) in the Graian Alps by Bonifacio Rotario in 1358. The subsequent historical ascent included in the appendix, consisting of five archival records appearing in print for the first time, is that of Mont Aiguille (2,085 m/6,841 ft) by Antoine de Ville and his team of seven or more companions[27] on 26 June 1492. Earlier, in his introduction, Coolidge stresses the historic magnitude of this event, especially with respect to the question of 'modernity'. It is therefore worth retracing this summit siege and exploring some of its historical records, all within the greater context of both athletic and academic mountain exploration from the classical to the modern age.

For Coolidge, Antoine de Ville's letter to the President of the Parliament of Grenoble documenting his ascent of Mont Aiguille[28] is more than just a 'charter' of mountaineering (recall his characterization of Gessner's *De Montium Admiratione*). It is the veritable '"Magna Carta" of Alpinism'[29] and the historical 'starting point of modern Alpinism'.[30] Obviously, the year in which this ascent occurred is felicitously significant, and Coolidge even intimates that 1492 is 'the beginning of modern history in general'.[31] As mentioned earlier, de Ville's enterprise is also 'modern'[32] insofar as it was the first technical ascent conducted within the greater Alps; it relied on such innovative mountaineering – yet established military – devices as ladders, ropes and grappling hooks. There are three further reasons for its importance according to Coolidge: (1) Félix Perrin, Coolidge's principal collaborator on the *Simler* book, had long studied this peak and climbed it several times; (2) Coolidge himself believes he was the first foreigner to have scaled it; and (3) de Ville's letter written from the summit is a seminal testimony in the history of Alpinism. On a more personal-sentimental note, Coolidge has a special interest in this ascent 'because it was accomplished in 1492, the year when my homeland, North America, was discovered, and because the peak in question rises in Dauphiné, the land that could almost be called my adopted home.'[33] As Coolidge sums up his views concerning the critical stations of this late medieval to early modern historical arc: Petrarch was 'the first Alpinist inspired by the love of mountains'; Bonifacio Rotario was 'the first person to climb a high snowy summit'; and Antoine de Ville was 'the first rock climber' (*grimpeur*) within the greater expanse of the Alps.

Peter Hansen has written insightfully on this monarch-mandated mountaineering enterprise, which the French King Charles VIII foisted upon his artillery officer Antoine de Ville.[34] In fact, the only reason why de Ville's groundbreaking climb was recorded in the first place was so that 'the royal exchequer would reimburse his expenses'.[35] As Hansen notes more broadly, here with respect to Coolidge's book: 'apart from one ascent by a "primitive guide", almost all the ascents Coolidge could document were expressions of monarchical authority – the sovereign on the summit'.[36] In other words, Aldo Leopold's environmental-ethical injunction of 'thinking like a mountain' is here transformed into 'thinking like a state', which is itself an historical modification of Petrarch's 'thinking like a self'. For Hansen, these three basic attitudes toward mountain climbing – the fashioning of the self, the imperative of empire and the interactive rapport between humans and the natural world – represent fundamental tensions not of modernity, but of 'modern*ities*'. As Hansen argues: 'mountain climbing did not emerge as the expression of a preexisting condition known as "modernity", but rather was one of the practices that constructed and redefined multiple modernities during debates over who was first [to set foot on the summit]'.[37] Mountaineering is thus contemporaneous with enlightenment, not a result or consequence thereof. To complement Hansen's argument, one might say that, just as enlightenment in the Kantian view is not necessarily a fixed historical period in the development of humanity but rather a continual process in the self-emancipation of the human being, mountain climbing is an analogous ongoing enactment of the modern condition. Even Leslie Stephen, who adopts an otherwise rigid dichotomous view that the Alps did not become a 'public playground' until around 1760 (after the Seven Years' War),[38] sees a more general, processual connection between Alpinism and enlightenment: 'The history of mountaineering is, to a great extent, the history of the process by which men have gradually conquered the phantoms of their own imagination'.[39] In alternative terms, here with echoes of Johann Jakob Scheuchzer and, more recently, Fergus Fleming: the thresholds of mountain modernities are all about killing, or at least exorcizing, Alpine dragons.[40]

Hansen, in sum, problematizes the basic notions or constructs of 'late medieval', 'early modern' and 'modern'. Such a conceptual corrective is not without import for this volume, both for the historical-theoretical parameters behind it and the scholarly contributions contained within it. In more concrete terms, the historiographical cliché of Petrarch as the 'first modern individual' (cf. Ernest Renan, Georg Voigt, Jacob Burckhardt and Ernst Cassirer) is itself an ideological construct that arose during the nineteenth century. If nothing else, Petrarch is a figure who blurs the otherwise neatly drawn lines between historical eras, one whose *existential* moment of mountain glory proved transitory compared to his ensuing and far more abiding experience of mountain gloom, when his summit perusal of St Augustine's *Confessions* put both him and his premature sense of 'modern' individuality back in their humble 'premodern' place.

Coolidge's *The Alps in Nature and History* as parallel text

As the previously cited review of *Josias Simler et les origines de l'alpinisme jusqu'en 1600* laments: 'Yet it is difficult not to wish that Mr. Coolidge would digest his vast store of knowledge into some independent form that would be likely to attract a greater number of intelligent readers'.[41] Four years after the publication of his gargantuan *Simler* book, and a mere two years after this *Alpine Journal* review, Coolidge would do just that: issue something more authorially independent and more digestible to the reader: *The Alps in Nature and History* (1908). Yet a closer look at this 440-page text reveals that it may not be such an autonomous achievement after all, for it evinces numerous similarities, in terms of both structure *and* content, to Simler's original *Commentarius*. These correlations not only speak for the fundamentality of Simler's sixteenth-century compendium for subsequent mountain discourse; they also offer initial attestation of – or least toward – a typology of Alpinist literature. In more philological terms, Coolidge used if not appropriated a great deal from Simler's 'systematic account',[42] updating of course certain information in the wake of the 334 years that separate these two works of scrupulous scholarship. Indeed, some of these updates can already be found in Coolidge's own – even more systematic – account from 1904, which, as previously discussed, is a kind of magnification and modernization of Simler's 1574 treatise. The basic upshot of this complementarity, if in part supplementarity, is that *Josias Simler et les origines de l'alpinisme jusqu'en 1600* and *The Alps in Nature and History* can be read, and more generally regarded, as 'co-texts', both predicated on the same premodern urtext. But again, in the so-called 'history of Alpinism', periodization tends to be more fluid than fixed. More specifically, Simler's 'early modern' *Commentarius* proves to be presciently 'modern', as a structural and thematic comparison with Coolidge's second major opus will reveal.

Obviously, the greatest degree of divergence between the two texts concerns post-1600 facts and figures. This includes much of the information found in the long chapter entitled 'The Political History of the Alps',[43] the shorter one on 'Modern Mountaineering in the High Alps',[44] and the various sections outlining ascents up until 1865, the year of the Matterhorn conquest-catastrophe that signalled the end of the 'golden age' of Alpinism.[45] In other words: phenomena pertaining to a chronologically 'modern' era, one that postdates Simler's historical age. These segments of *The Alps in Nature and History* are the only ones that offer genuinely fresh material not already found, or at least not in some measure addressed, in the *Commentarius*. Conversely, the former text lacks the latter's chapters on hydrography and mineralogy,[46] though one could consider Coolidge's early chapter on glaciology[47] as a latter-day scientific equivalent of Simler's sixteenth-century hydrographical observations. Otherwise, both books overlap to an astounding degree, though not necessarily in the same sequential order. In the following, I will give a rough sketch of their many parallelisms, whereby I intend to bring out, in somewhat structuralist fashion, the typological correspondences between these two historically distanced Alpinist texts. At the same time, beyond such formalistic features of typology, several thematic or more substance-based commonalities will inevitably emerge, attesting to a rich continuity in Alpinist discourse between the late sixteenth and early twentieth centuries.

Both *De Alpibus Commentarius* and *The Alps in Nature and History* open with two chapters that seek to define the Alps, both in terms of etymology and topography. Coolidge, for his part, places especial emphasis on the native notion of an *alp* or *alpe* as a *sub*-Alpine pasturage, which of course seems paradoxical given its modern mountaineering meaning. Both texts further contain chapters on flora and fauna. Whereas Simler's features separate ones on (a) trees and (b) shrubs and plants, Coolidge's is restricted to Alpine flowers. Simler's consideration of endemic animals is relatively brief, covering quadrupeds such as the Alpine ibex (*bouquetin* or *Steinbock*), the chamois (*chamois* or *Gems*) and the marmot; and various ornithological species belonging to the grouse subfamily and Lagopus genus (basically diverse types of ptarmigans). The parallel chapter in Coolidge's work showcases the same examples but adds others such as the brown bear, the white hare, the stone-marten, the common fox, the bearded vulture (*Lämmergeier*) and the golden eagle. It should be noted that Coolidge outsourced these flora and fauna chapters (to George Yeld and Howard V. Knox, respectively) and that they thus remain the only ones that do not directly issue from his own pen. As for the chapters on 'The Tribes of the Alps' ('De Gentibus Alpinis'/'Les peuplades des Alpes') and 'The Alpine Folk', they are also thematically analogous. While Simler surveys, in somewhat static schematic fashion, a host of ethnic groups indigenous to the Alps, which from an historiographical standpoint means those 'peoples vanquished'[48] by the Romans, Coolidge is more diversified in his approach, dealing with the political allegiances, native languages and religious denominations of the broader Alpine populace. In the process, he arrives at some interesting conclusions or at least propositions. For instance, he points to 'the connection between the free air of the Alps and that of a republican form of government'[49] and puts forth the more radical ethno-political thesis that 'The Alps, in short, far from having hemmed the "Wandering of Nations" at any date from the fifth century onwards, have rather served as a great highway, with many branching byways, which have led the wanderers up and down, right and left, in zigzags and by straight lines, till the labyrinth seems to lack any clue whatsoever'.[50]

This latter statement anticipates his subsequent remarks on intercultural exchange in chapter VII, 'The Great Historical Passes of the Alps'. Here Coolidge argues that the geologically 'mighty barrier'[51] of the Alps is riddled with numerous passages that helped foster contact and even forge close bonds between inhabitants of separate, indeed geophysically separated, valleys. In more provocative terms, he points out 'the paradox that mountain ranges unite rather than divide, while a physical obstacle in a valley will prove far more potent by cutting off the lower from the higher portion.'[52] His detailed depictions and deeper deliberations on Alpine passes (complete with accompanying maps) correlate with three successive chapters in the *Commentarius*,[53] which boast a wealth of historical facts: 'Quinam primum Alpes transierint'/'Premiers passages à travers les Alpes' ('First Passages across the Alps'); 'De itinere Annibalis per Alpes'/ 'Passage des Alpes par Hannibal' ('Hannibal's Journey through the Alps'); and 'Alpium celebriora itinera'/'Les Routes les plus célèbres à travers les Alpes' ('The Most Famous Routes of the Alps'). Even greater depth and breadth can be found in the respective sections dealing with the various Alpine subranges. Simler discusses seven of these, all of which Coolidge also covers (though the precise appellations have in part changed over the centuries). These include the Maritime Alps, the Cottian Alps, the Graian Alps, the Pennine Alps, the Vallis Alps, the Lepontine Alps the Rheatian Alps and the Julian/Carnic Alps. Coolidge, for his part, divides the Alps into twenty groups.[54] His additions are notable for two main reasons. For one, he includes territory in eastern Switzerland, Austria, Bavaria and northern Italy or southern Tyrol (e.g. the Dolomites) that were simply beyond the epistemological purview of someone even as erudite as Simler, who, living in Zurich during the sixteenth century, was far removed from these eastern Alpine chains and the limited localized knowledge about them. Secondly, Coolidge inserts a section on the Dauphiné Alps, which, as mentioned above, is a region explored relatively late in mountaineering history and moreover largely pioneered by him and his aunt.

Finally, some mutual details concerning technical mountaineering matters prove even more illuminating in view of the greater question of historical continuity. Coolidge's chapter on 'Alpine Guides' has informational precedents in Simler's chapter on 'De itinerum Alpinorum difficultatibus, et periculis, et quomodo hæc superari possint'/'Difficultés et dangers des passages à travers les Alpes et moyens d'en triompher' ('On the Difficulties and Dangers of Alpine Journeys, and the Manner in Which They Are Overcome'). This section offers fascinating observations about everything from mountain weather and snow conditions to requisite Alpine equipment and survival techniques. Simler's descriptions here seem strikingly modern, as they reflect practices described in contemporary mountaineering manuals.[55] Indeed, according to scholar-climber and recent translator of this chapter into English, Alan S. Weber, it 'represents the first Alpine climbing guide'.[56] It contains, for instance, detailed information on avalanche formation and survival; roped glacier travel and knowledgeable guides; the prevention of hypothermia, frostbite and snow-blindness (although these modern specialized terms are not used per se); and the use of rudimentary forms of alpenstocks, crampons, climbing ropes, glacier goggles and snowshoes. And all the while, as added historical attestation of these diverse Alpine phenomena and Alpinist paraphernalia, Simler invokes ancient authors such as Claudian, Silius Italicus, Strabo and Xenophon. The arc from antiquity to premodernity, perhaps even all the way to modernity, thus manifests itself here *in nuce*. To give readers a better sense of these forward-thinking explanations and procedures, I cite the following passage on glacier travel, specifically on the avoidance of falling séracs and looming crevasses, here taken from Alan S. Weber's English translation contained in his anthology on mountaineering from 200 BCE to 2003. It is of course typical for Simler, and naturally part of my ongoing argument, that he cannot but ground his premodern Alpine commentary in a more originary, classical source of knowledge. As Simler writes and Weber translates:

> The ice in the Alps not only makes the paths dangerous because it is slippery, but it creates even greater difficulties ... Strabo mentions these dangers in the following words: 'blocks of ice, perilously situated on the heights, fall down, entirely covering the pathways and rushing down to the vallies [*sic*] below. Often in fact, the new ice covers the old, especially when snow falls before the sun has entirely melted the icy crust which covers the soil'. In addition, this old ice, upon which one is often forced

to walk, is pitted with deep crevasses 3 or 4 feet wide, and often even larger, into which every fall would undoubtedly be fatal. It often happens that these crevasses are hidden under freshly fallen or blown snow. Therefore travelers who cross the Alps hire locals who know the region to guide them; these guides gird themselves with a rope to which they also attach several of those who are following them. Those who proceed first sound the way with a long baton and search the crevasses in the snow attentively, and if from carelessness a guide falls in one, the others tied to the rope catch him and draw him out.[57]

Summit summation

As William Barton has recently stated in his assessment of early modern mountain aesthetics: 'While Simmler's work is based firmly on the ancient tradition, it is not restricted by these roots to a one-dimensional view of the mountain landscape. Simmler's mountain attitude is complex and multifaceted'.[58] Coolidge's *Josias Simler et les origines de l'alpinisme jusqu'en 1600* is an even more multifaceted, indeed seemingly inexhaustible, text that opens multiple avenues of discussion with respect to human interactions with mountain environments.[59] Although its historical framework and geographical perspective are restricted, namely antiquity through the early modern era ('jusqu'en 1600') and the greater compass of the European Alps ('alpinisme' in a more literal-localized sense), it raises numerous questions that bear on the periodization of mountaineering history as well as the delineation of Alpinism in general, far beyond the frontiers of the actual range that lent its name to the now global practice of mountain climbing.[60] In the twenty-first century, Peter Hansen has of course problematized the former issue. Yet Coolidge and Simler, the latter with far less historical hindsight, also narrate Alpine-related events, encounters and phenomena that transcend static historiographical categorizations of Alpinism, writ both large and small. The fact that Coolidge further includes copious intertexts that reflect on the human experience of climbing mountains throughout the European continent, from the eastern Mediterranean to the Pyrenees, underscores their fundamental orographical rather than mere geographical importance. Indeed, Coolidge foregrounds his mammoth opus with Gessner's letter on the admiration of mountains; that is, with a more existential than historical meditation on the alpine (here deliberately writ small) experience, regardless of precise locality or temporality. And to close here with Gessner, who, like Petrarch, transcends such historical taxonomies as antiquity, premodernity and modernity: 'Thus, the greatest wonder of nature's elements and diversity is to be found in the mountains'.[61]

Notes

1. Coolidge 1904: clxii. As a general practice, I will translate Coolidge's French into English, except for short citations that contain obvious cognates and possess a certain rhetorical flair, like the one here.

2. The golden age of Alpinism designates a period of intense summit pursuits, mainly by British climbers, that began with Alfred Willis's ascent of the Wetterhorn in 1854 and ended in 1865 with Edward Whymper's (catastrophic) conquest of the Matterhorn, the last unclimbed giant of the Alps. The subsequent silver age focused on less dominant yet still challenging peaks and lasted until 1882, with the ascent of the Dent du Géant by W. W. Graham and his party.
3. Coolidge 1904: viii and xiii.
4. Nicolson 1959. For two recent and nuanced critiques of this aesthetic paradigm, an (adversely) influential one for mountain studies, see Koelb 2009 and Hollis 2019. Despite these, and other, principally periodization-based critiques, Nicolson's major blind spot lies in her exclusive focus on British mountain discourse and her utter neglect of the far more nuanced Continental – especially Swiss – tradition.
5. Since Coolidge, other scholars have postulated a similar decline in mountain interest during the seventeenth century after a flourishing period of inquiry throughout the sixteenth. See for example Korenjak 2017. In his extensive bibliography, Korenjak points to several sources that make this claim, though he himself goes to great lengths in his own lengthy article to refute it.
6. C. E. F. 1905: 568.
7. Williams 1973: 49–51.
8. This includes Mont Blanc, whose summit had previously been attained by a dog, but one that had been carried by a human; Tschingel was the first to reach the top by the power of her own four legs. For intriguing (as well as entertaining) details regarding Tschingel, ranging from her pioneering Alpine-canine climbs to her penchant for red wine and weak tea, see Clark 1953: 155–63.
9. Clark 1953: 147; 145.
10. Coolidge's 'issues' with Whymper concerned the latter's (supposed) shoddy scholarship rather than his seminal mountaineering feats. In the 1880 edition of his classic book *Scrambles amongst the Alps*, Whymper, for instance, referred to Frederick Gardiner (a friend of Coolidge's who made the third ascent of the Matterhorn as 'J. Gardiner.' And even though this error was corrected in the main text of subsequent editions (namely those from 1893 and 1900), the oversight remained in their respective indices. As if this 'heinous crime' (Clark 1959: 132) were not enough, Coolidge was never able to forgive Whymper for reporting that he (Coolidge) had climbed only one of the subsidiary peaks rather than the main peak of the Ailefroide in the Dauphiné Alps.
11. Clark 1959: 130.
12. Ibid. 138.
13. Freshfield 1906: 76.
14. Ibid. 76.
15. The former work was originally published along with the *Commentarius* in the same volume (entitled *Vallesiae Descriptio, libri duo: De Alpibus Commentarius*) as the first of the two tracts, running from pages 1 to 65, followed by the *Commentarius*, which runs from pages 66 to 124.
16. Generally speaking, 'Gesner' is the Latin version and 'Gessner' the autochthonous German-Swiss spelling. Gessner always signed his surname according to the latter orthography but, interestingly, spelled his first name with a Latinate C rather than a Germanic K.
17. See Coolidge 1904: clviii–clxiii.
18. Coolidge's elevation figures differ slightly from these updated data. As a general practice, I will give currently agreed-upon measurements of summit elevations rather than those provided by Coolidge in his *Simler* book.

19. Coolidge 1904: clx.
20. Ibid. clx, clxiii
21. Ibid. clxiii
22. Ibid. xi.
23. Ibid. clxxix–clxxxix.
24. Ibid. ix.
25. Ibid.
26. Gessner 2020: 30. This new scholarly translation of Gessner's classic text, undertaken by Dan Hooley (also a contributor to this volume), will surely supersede the previous one by H. B. D. Soulé (see Gessner 1937: 5–15), which has long been out of print. For another, more readily available translation, see Gessner 2003.
27. These figures vary depending on the historiographical source. Cf. Coolidge 1908: 207; and Hansen 2013: 22. The original French document specifies, however, that de Ville had 'plus de diz avecques moy, tants gens d'église que autres gens de bien' / 'more than ten with me, clergymen as well as other respectable people' (Coolidge 1904: 'Pieces annèxes', 171).
28. The rocky peak does not really resemble an aiguille/needle/pinnacle, at least from most perspectives, but rather a massive anvil or stump. However, the locals referred to it as 'The Needle' or *l'Agulle* in the regional-historical dialect. Furthermore, given the fundamental differentiation in orological nomenclature between rounded and sharply formed summits (cf. French: *dôme* vs. *aiguille*; German: *Dom* vs. *Spitze*), this moniker is understandable. Nevertheless, one cannot fail to note an obvious geomorphological difference between, say, Mont Aiguille and the Aiguille du Midi of the Mont Blanc massif. The former's designation as 'Mont Inaccessible' in an illustration from *Les Sept Miracles de Dauphiné* (1701) is, at any rate, a more accurate appellation, though the book's insistence that the mountain resembles an 'inverted pyramid' (see Hansen 2013: 24, Figure 4) seems not only inaccurate but far-fetched. On the other hand, Coolidge's later characterization of Mont Aiguille as a 'wonderful freak of nature' (1908: 207) strikes me as perfectly apt.
29. Coolidge 1904: xxxiv.
30. Ibid xxxiii.
31. Ibid. xxxv. Coolidge also mentions, parenthetically and somewhat enigmatically, the year 1494. He does so perhaps in allusion to the Treaty of Tordesillas, an edict that created an imaginary geopolitical line in the middle of the Atlantic Ocean, dividing the entire known – and unknown – world between Spain and Portugal.
32. Coolidge will later temper this view, stating that 'this amazing expedition of 1492 . . . has a distinct flavor of the Middle Ages' (1908: 207), perhaps because it is reminiscent of a siege upon the fortified walls and battlements of a medieval castle.
33. Coolidge 1904: xxxiii.
34. Hansen 2013: 22–7.
35. Ibid. 25.
36. Ibid. 25.
37. Ibid. 3.
38. Coolidge pinpoints the same pivotal year as 'the origin of serious mountain climbing' (1908: 210).
39. Quoted in Hansen 2013: 4.

40. Compare the notorious superstitious 'dragon discourse' of the otherwise enlightened and scientific-minded Scheuchzer; and also, more generally, Fleming 2000.
41. Freshfield 1906: 77.
42. Coolidge 1908: 410.
43. Ibid. 75–149.
44. Ibid. 239–57.
45. Ibid. 199–238. This was also a critical year for Coolidge in terms of his nascent Alpine career, for that summer, at the age of fifteen, he visited the Alps for the first time, even stopping over in Zermatt a month after the Whymper party accident on the Matterhorn. From here, in fact, he sent a letter to his mother, written on hotel note-paper featuring an image of the Matterhorn to which he added two dots indicating 'where they [the victims] fell from, and where they fell. A horrible distance'. See Clark 1953: 146; and, for a facsimile of the letter, 150.
46. Coolidge 1904: xvi and xvii.
47. Coolidge 1908: chapter III, 'The Snowy Region of the Alps'.
48. Coolidge 1904: 239.
49. Coolidge 1908: 59.
50. Ibid. 58.
51. Ibid. 150.
52. Ibid. 151.
53. Coolidge 1904: iv, v, vi.
54. Coolidge 1908: chapter XIII, 279–372; and, more conveniently, appendix I, 373–96.
55. The longstanding American classic *Mountaineering: The Freedom of the Hills*, first published in 1960 and now in its ninth edition, particularly comes to mind in this regard. Indeed, with respect to its miscellaneous mountain-related topics, Simler's account reads like a precursor to this current comprehensive guide on the sport of mountaineering. See especially Linxweiler and Maude 2017: chapter 2: 'Clothing and Equipment'; chapter 16: 'Snow Travel and Climbing'; chapter 17: 'Avalanche Safety'; chapter 18: 'Glacier Travel and Crevasse Rescue'; chapter 25: 'Alpine Rescue'; chapter 27: 'The Cycle of Snow'; and chapter 28: 'Mountain Weather'.
56. Weber 2003: 22. To be realistic, a sustained in-depth comparison between Simler's sixteenth-century reflections on Alpine travel and any recent handbook on the sport of alpinism is simply not tenable, indeed may well be unreasonable, given the countless advances in outdoor equipment, climbing techniques and general knowhow over the last several decades. Nonetheless, *typological* correspondence is no less important than content-based conformity, at least here with respect to an historical phenomenon like mountaineering, which has undergone an extreme degree of technologization, sub-specialization and even professionalization within a relatively short period of time. For a sense of this rapid advancement if not epistemic evolution of the sport, one need only compare the first edition of the abovementioned *Mountaineering: The Freedom of the Hills* from 1960 with the ninth edition from 2017. Whereas the former consisted of 430 pages, the latter contains 624. The qualitative or content-based difference between the two editions is even more profound, particularly in terms of new climbing practices and ethics. Despite these disclaimers, Simler's chapter on Alpine 'Difficulties and Dangers' seems *far* ahead of its time.
57. Simler 2003: 24.
58. Barton 2017: 19.

59. A similarly rich study, though without quite the historiographical diversity of original records and documents, let alone intertexts, is John Grand-Carteret's *La montagne à travers les âges: Rôle joué par elle, Façon dont elle a été vue*, which was published in two (voluminous!) volumes in 1903 and 1904, precisely when Coolidge's *Simler* opus was released. The first volume covers 'Des temps antiques à la fin du dix-huitième siècle' ('From Ancient Times to the End of the Eighteenth Century') and consists of 560 pages, including 307 illustrations; the second examines 'La montagne d'aujourd'hui' ('The Mountain of Today') and comprises 494 pages, including 350 illustrations. This prodigious (not to mention portly and strangely proportioned) study warrants however its own separate discussion.

60. On this problem of periodization, especially as pertains to the so-called early modern versus modern eras, see Mathieu 2005 and Korenjak 2017.

61. Gessner 2020: 31.

CHAPTER 5
MOUNTAINS AND THE HOLY IN LATE ANTIQUITY
Douglas Whalin

When the virgin Thekla came to this country, passed its borders, and arrived at the mountain peak, she in turn brought Apollo low and silenced him. And even up to our time she has made that most vocal of oracles to sit in utter silence, opposing it with the voice of the Lord and King, saying, 'Silence! Be quiet!' Accordingly, the oracle is silent and still and cowers in fear. [Apollo] departed, so I believe, from his own tomb and his locale, abandoning this site – whether one wishes to call it a tomb or a sanctuary – to poor and simple men, who devote themselves to prayers and supplications to be hereafter a dwelling place for God. This is the preamble of the miracles of the martyr.

Miracles of Saint Thekla, 1.2[1]

The *Miracles of Saint Thekla* tell of the saint's posthumous activities beginning, as quoted in this passage, with the martyr's spiritual battle against the god Apollo, expelling him and claiming his mountain sanctuary in Cilicia as the home for her own cult centre. The *Miracles* were written in the fifth century CE about a first-century saint (she was reportedly a companion of Saint Paul according to the apocryphal *Acts of Paul and Thekla*). Thekla's story builds upon and engages with pre-Christian traditions and locations while seeking to establish a new framework for their interpretation and transmission. This vignette encapsulates the way in which the centuries-long process of Christianization played out through the social landscape as well as the literal landscape of the late antique Roman world.

At its maximum, late antiquity encompasses the half-millennium from the third through eighth centuries CE. Across political history, the arts, philosophy, religion and society at large, this period is characterized by the repurposing of classical Graeco-Roman models into new forms.[2] In all aspects of life, including the engagement with landscape, this meant an ongoing dialogue with and transformation of ideas and attitudes inherited from the classical past, and the reconciliation of them with a changing world. Although Christianity became the dominant religion in the Roman and post-Roman world, nowhere was society uniformly Christianized. The integration of this new religion into existing literature and other art forms was an evolving process, often contentious and ongoing throughout late antiquity.[3] In this period, generations of thinkers struggled to articulate and define the relationship between the cultural inheritance from their polytheistic 'pagan' ancestors and their new monotheistic Christian faith.[4]

Mountain Dialogues from Antiquity to Modernity

By focusing on this period of change and transition, this chapter offers a bridge between ancient and early modern understandings of mountains explored elsewhere in this volume. It seeks to convince readers that this bridge was significant and is worth considering. It does so through asking several key questions. Did 'classical' concepts of mountains and landscape disappear at the end of antiquity, and if so, how? In what ways did literature regarding mountains interact with wider debates about the proper relationship between Christian and non-Christian cultural heritages?

To explore these questions, this chapter examines social engagement with mountains through three major paradigms. First, it will look at mountains as spaces of everyday existence, drawing principally on archaeological sources. This will seek to ground the subsequent discussion of literary and social landscapes in daily physical realities. Second, it will survey literature for descriptions of, and thus attitudes about, mountains. Authors in late antiquity struggled to reconcile classical and Christian cultural influences and to decide what had to be preserved, replaced, or rejected, and mountains provide a prism for understanding this wider process. Finally, this chapter will look at the Christianization of mountain landscapes through the establishment of saints' cults and monasteries. This intersection of literature and landscape will tie the chapter together, as we take an overview of the physical appropriation of the classical world into a Christianized one. The mountain landscape of Greece and the eastern Mediterranean was at once unchanged and profoundly altered.

Mountains and everyday life

The transition from the classical to the late antique period passed with little note or disruption to mute landscapes of the Mediterranean and to the great majority of people who inhabited them. Constantine moved the Roman capital in 324 CE to the re-founded city of Byzantium (officially renamed New Rome, but colloquially referred to as Constantinople), but the Roman world enjoyed a continuity of laws, traditions and government stretching back to the early Republic.[5] The peaks which dominated the imaginations of audiences attending performances of Euripides, Sophocles and Aeschylus in the fifth century BCE, as described in Chloe Bray's chapter in this volume, still stood over the cities and farms inhabited by their descendants. Above those fields and cities herdsmen led their flocks on the seasonal trek from mountain to valley and back, hunters found game, the same passes constrained and directed the flow of travellers overland, and sites which provided natural defences were utilized as they had been in millennia past and would be in centuries to come. The people who inhabited the lands continued to speak Greek, read and transmitted the works of classical authors, whose style they admired and emulated, and in turn produced original literature of their own time.[6] The world of late antiquity was closely interconnected with the classical past through shared language, history, literature, and, not the least of all, its mountainous landscape.

Civilization around the Aegean was, and still is, largely restricted to coastal plains, hemmed in by sea and mountains. On the Asian side as one proceeds eastward and inland, hills and mountains give way to the central Anatolian highlands, a semi-arid landscape which differs markedly from the coastal plains which access it from north, west and south. Late antiquity represented a period of continuity for many urban spaces as well – often the final phase of such before layers of disruption coinciding with invasions and large-scale social disruption in later centuries – with most of the great cities of the classical period continuing as centres of urban life.[7] Across the landscape in cities and in the countryside, 'pagan' shrines were transformed in a variety of ways – some abandoned, some de-sanctified, some rebuilt and Christianized.[8] Even as some sites were destroyed or abandoned in the seventh century, many other classical cities continued to be inhabited throughout the middle ages.

The empire's civil administration depended upon cities – organized physically and socially along Graeco-Roman lines – as administrative centres. In turn this shaped the world of the Roman *literati*, the elite-educated men who overwhelmingly dominate written sources. The system worked well with the inherent logic of human habitation patterns on the Mediterranean's fertile and well-defined coastal planes, from which it had emerged.[9] However, as one moved further inland and higher in elevation, the abundance of villages and relative lack of cities naturally created challenges for Roman bureaucratic systems.[10] The Hellenization of inland and eastern Anatolia had begun with Alexander's conquests nearly a millennium earlier, but was not complete by the end of antiquity. Among the more radical departures from the conventions of classical city building were the troglodytic, rock-cut cities of the region's upland interior. Although the origins of many of these rock-cut sites dated far back into the second millennium BCE or earlier, the classical and late antique periods saw changes to the fabric of these settlements which aligned them more closely with the norms of the wider Graeco-Roman world. This included adapting the built-architectural monumental language of the Christian church to the medium of excavated rock, an architectural form at once heavily influenced by classical inheritance whilst being comprehensively un-classical (Fig. 5.1). While notable examples may be found concentrated in Phrygia and Cappadocia, perhaps the most famous example is Amaseia in the Pontus, the birthplace of one of antiquity's greatest geographers, Strabo.[11]

Traditional building programmes in the style of coastal cities can also be found in highland cities. The remains of villages and cities clinging to the sides of mountains attest to the penetration of the urban life characteristic of Roman civilization even in the regions' highlands.[12] Two particularly well-preserved and well-excavated examples are the cities of Arykanda in Lycia and Sagalassos in Pisidia. The former is in the mountains of southeast Anatolia above the classical sites of Xanthos and the pre-Christian cult site of Letoon, while the latter lies inland from the port of Perge. Both were flourishing regional centres in antiquity situated along roads near passes which constrained and directed traffic between the coast and the highland plateaus of Anatolia's interior.

Arykanda perches above the valley of the river Arycandus which cuts a deep, narrow gash through the limestone on its way out of the mountains. The valley and hillsides were covered in forests of the native Lebanese Cedar in antiquity, and thus formed an important source of shipbuilding materials.[13] The site is dominated by the peak now

Figure 5.1 A medieval rock-cut church in Ayazini, Phrygia, Turkey. Photograph: Douglas Whalin, 2013.

known in Turkish as Bey Dağ, which at 3,086 m elevation is one of the highest in Lycia. The name 'Arykanda' is of Hittite origin, but few remains from the second millennium BCE have been found on the site. Clear evidence has been found for continual inhabitation from the fourth century BCE to at least the sixth/seventh centuries CE. The main city itself had all of the trappings of a classical city, with multiple agorae, churches, a necropolis, odeon, stadion, regularly-organized street plan, theatre and walls protecting its most exposed approaches. The city's largest bath house was accompanied by a gymnasium and fed by aqueduct from regional springs, and excess was stored in a large cistern cut directly into bedrock. However, following these few centuries as a bustling local centre, the main urban site was abandoned in favour of smaller, more protected settlements nearby and the human habitation patterns of the region returned to the state of small villages and herders which had dominated before the city's existence.[14]

The city of Sagalassos in Pisidia had a similar story. It is located about 1,500 m above sea level on the southern slope of Mount Ağlasun, whose highest peak reaches 2,045 m. Although today a visitor is greeted by a sparse subalpine landscape of grasses and small bushes with rocky limestone outcroppings, in antiquity the mountain was covered in oak and pine forests.[15] The city's classical phase began in the Hellenistic period and continued into the seventh century CE. By the Roman period, Sagalassos sat at a crossroads where the main road crossing from Pamphylia to the Anatolian plateau intersected regional routes connecting the city to its hinterland. The city is structured around a series of terraced agorae and public spaces which open out to commanding views of the valley and mountains beyond.[16] The city's use as an urban centre ended abruptly in the later sixth or early seventh century at approximately the same time as at Arykanda, in this case possibly due to an earthquake devastating the city's water supply systems. But as at Arykanda, the local population dispersed to villages. One fortress-settlement on a neighbouring hilltop (called a *kastron* in medieval Greek), only a few hundred metres from the city's edge, remained strategically important until the Seljuk conquest of the region in the twelfth century CE.[17]

Graeco-Roman urbanism originated in the geographical context of the Mediterranean coastal planes, but by late antiquity penetrated the mountains which overlooked the Aegean basin. However, as seen above, it found mixed success establishing itself there – indigenous living patterns like rock-cut troglodytic settlements endured, and the cities were more vulnerable to collapse than their coastal counterparts due to extremes of environment, climate and susceptibility to political instability. Where similar patterns in the archaeological record appear (such as adding monumental Christian buildings to urban patterns which were otherwise little changed from classical precedent), they were carried out in ways which adapted broader Mediterranean patterns to specific local needs.[18] Mountain life resisted conforming to the norms of coastal Mediterranean civilization even as it was systematically influenced and shaped by it.

Reconciling literary tradition with a new faith

For late antique authors, there was often a tension between their classical education and their faith as they struggled with questions about whether and how to integrate the 'pagan' Greek forms which they read, admired and often emulated into the intellectual structures of Christianity.[19] Writing about the landscape and their physical world provided these authors with a way to explore their own society and their relationship to it.

The struggle to reconcile Christian and pre-Christian traditions and knowledge occurred across the breadth of literary genres.[20] Mountains often appear in literature alongside desert and wilderness – sometimes interchangeably so. Even though we know from archaeological evidence that such a dichotomy was not absolute in practice, mountains as wilderness oppose civilization – not human habitation in the broadest sense, but more narrowly urban Roman Mediterranean civilization.[21] There were people who lived in the mountains, and life there resembled that elsewhere in the Roman world in many ways, but mountains and their residents existed outside mainstream society conceptually, and to a certain degree physically as well. Basil of Caesarea (d. 379), Gregory of Nazianzus (d. 390) and Gregory of Nyssa (d. *c.* 395) epitomized many of these contradictions in their lives and their writings. They are collectively known as the Cappadocian fathers, for all three were originally from the mountainous highlands of central Anatolia, a landscape which is at the heart of some of their surviving writings. In Basil of Caesarea's *Epistle* 14, written to Gregory of Nazianzus, we can see the dual strands of Basil's education in the Greek *paideia* and in the Christian faith as he describes a mountain wilderness in tropes both classicizing and Christianizing:

> There is a high mountain, covered by forest and a clear, cold stream flowing from the north. A broad plain spreads out at its base, continuously nourished by the moisture from the mountain. Growing around the place is a forest with trees of every colour and shape, almost like a fence, so that it surpasses even Calypso's island, which Homer showed to be greater than every other marvel.[22] And it is not much inferior to an island, because it is encircled by defences on every side. Deep ravines break around it on two sides, while on the other, under an overhanging bank, a swift river flows, continuous and inaccessible. The mountain extends from here to the other side, to a crescent-shaped bend where the ravines intersect, which walls off the passage from the base. There is only one entrance across it, and I am its master. From my home there is another pass, rising up to the crest of the ridge above. There the plain spreads out before this vision, and the river which descends from the heights to flow around it is, it seems to me at least, no less a delight than the vision offered by the Strymon from Amphipolis... To me and to anyone else, the river appears very sweet to behold, yielding sufficient support for those who dwell around it from the uncountable multitude of fish nourished in its pools. What is necessary to say about the breath of the earth or the breeze from the river? Another might marvel at the many flowers or the melodious birds, but I have no leisure to hold such things in my mind. But the greatest thing we are able to say about this land is that, being well suited to bear produce of every kind, it nurtures the fruit which is most pleasant to me of all, that is quietness; it is not just that it is removed from the urban bustle, but it is even unfrequented by travellers apart from those who come among us for hunting. It is nurturing to beasts and other things, but there are no bears or wolves such as you have, but it supports herds of deer and wild goats and hares and others of that same sort.
>
> Basil of Caesarea, Epistle 14

In Basil's letter, reality and imagination blend together interchangeably. Basil's mountain refuge is described as an enclosed space, an obstacle challenging to access and traverse, both anchoring him in creation and separating him from a variety of dangers. The location is Edenic, free from predators and filled with trees, streams, and otherwise bountiful in its resources which are useful to people. Although a Church father writing to another Church father, his one major literary reference is Homer's *Odyssey*, showing the enduring power of pre-Christian literature as a common cultural reference point. Although obviously 'pagan' literature, Homer's texts remained the cornerstone for Greek *paideia* long after Christianization of the culture.[23]

However, although both Basil and Gregory were educated using these common 'pagan' cultural forms, for Basil his mountain Eden represents an opportunity to categorically reject mainstream society, an urban world which he finds in conflict with his faith and his personal predispositions. His mountain is not devoid of human life – he evokes encounters with peasants, travellers and hunters – but it is free from Graeco-Roman civilization. For Basil, his mountain was a contemplative retreat away from the temptations which filled late antique city life.[24] At the same time, he approached the mountain as a landscape which was his to master and tame. One can find echoes of Basil's mountain retreat in the writing of Saint Jerome, as explored in Koelb's chapter in this volume, as well as much later in Jordan's chapter on Thomas Jefferson's romantic hermitage of Monticello.

Hagiography represented the literary record of the life and miracles of a holy person. Whether martyrs or confessors, saints were recognized for their Christian virtues, made evident through their miracles, which made them closer to God than their fellow men. As a result, saints bypassed the institutional structures of church and state, creating the potential for unmediated access between believer and God. Their ability to attract followers and mediate problems balanced out their potential uncontrollability; for all of the dangers that they presented to the late antique church, they were indispensable motivators of the masses and evidence for God's continued involvement in the world. Hagiographies were written with the specific agenda of establishing and memorializing the sanctity of their protagonists. Their purpose was not just to reassure believers but to convince sceptics.[25] As such, while they often contain invaluable historical data, their overall setting was realistic – an allegorical account of the world which was plausible in the eyes of writers and readers with respect to both its mundane and spiritual truths – rather than factual in the strictest understanding of the word.

These holy men and women were not just independent of worldly institutions, they were often celebrated for the rejection of inherited social roles and for their retreat to the solitude of the wilderness – a wilderness which was often, specifically, a mountain. In the *Life of Saint Macrina*, a fourth-century saint, the author Gregory of Nyssa gives the following summary of the pious life and early death of one of her brothers, Naukratios:

> Approaching his twenty-second year, Naukratios gave demonstration of his educational achievements before a public hearing, so that everyone in the theatre who heard was overwhelmed. But by some divine foresight he disdained everything in his hands, and so he departed for a solitary and impoverished life, according to some great impulse of intention. He brought nothing with him except himself, and one of his slaves named Chrysaphios, on account of his friendship with him[26] and his own resolve to enter into this life. And so Naukratios lived by himself, in a place on the banks of the Iris. The river Iris flows through the middle of the Pontus, although it begins in Armenia before coming to our region, and eventually its stream disgorges into the Euxine (Black) Sea. Along this the young man found a place in the deep forest, a luscious hollow concealed by the rocky slope which stretched out above. There he lived, being far removed from the urban hubbub and the business of soldiers and those who speak in courts of law.
>
> Gregory of Nyssa, *Life of Saint Macrina* 8.4-22

In this Edenic setting he lived a simple life of poverty for five years until his sudden and unexpected death. The initial measures of the young man's success are in terms of upper-class, urban, public, Roman life, which he rejects by departing for a solitary life in the countryside. His wilderness is not harsh but filled with 'luscious' growing things, echoing the Edenic language found in Basil of Caesarea's epistle above. It is crucial to note that his 'solitude' in practice is only a matter of degree – he is accompanied by a servant, and maintains social connections to his family, especially his mother.[27] For him, this little patch of wilderness provided a physical manifestation for his spiritual rejection of the 'classical' urban life.

Although Macrina's brother had the misfortune of dying young, and his pious vocation is preserved only as a short vignette within the broader account of her life, the trope of the young, classically educated Christian retreating to the mountains in search of a more complete spiritual education is found scattered throughout hagiographical literature. In his *Life of John Chrysostom*, John's contemporary and hagiographer Bishop Palladius of Aspuna writing in the first half of the fifth century reports that in his youth John's education was patronized by his local bishop. However, this was not sufficient for the young man:

> When his conscience pricked him, he was not satisfied with the work of the city. Even though he was in the vigour of his youth and his thoughts were sound, he went up to a nearby mountain. He was moulded by an elder named Syros, attending with self-control and faithfully imitating his hardy training. There [John] stayed four years, fighting against the rocky cliffs of luxury. Once he gained easy supremacy over these things, not so much by work as by reason, he withdrew to a grotto, alone, as he strove toward the unknown. He spent twenty-four months there, enduring much sleeplessness, thoroughly learning Christ's covenants in order to banish ignorance. For two years he did not recline either at night nor during the day, deadening his gastric system until the power of his kidneys was overcome by the cold. Being no longer strong enough to be useful to himself, he came back again to the harbour of the Church.
>
> Palladius of Aspuna, *Life of John Chrysostom* 28.14–29.4

John Chrysostom's mountainous retreat is initially clearly framed in juxtaposition with Antioch, the thoroughly Graeco-Roman urban environment in which he had lived and where, of course, local ecclesiastic institutions were situated. This account also employs the mountains as a metaphorical juxtaposition with the urban world – the city, home to the 'rocky cliffs of luxury', contrasts with the spiritual wholesomeness of the inhospitable wilderness. Syrus was clearly a pious and virtuous mentor for the younger man, and his isolation from both Church and society served to lend authenticity to his personal authority. John's time in the mountains was both one of spiritual growth and physical deprivation – and the physical toll ultimately necessitated his return to civilization. Despite the dangers, in Palladius' account mountains function as an authentic and legitimating space, filled with spiritual parallels to their earthly realities. In Christian

Mountains and the Holy in Late Antiquity

literature, mountains are the background for spiritual travellers, inhabited by lonely ascetics and other holy men and women whose physical and spiritual life sets them apart from the conventions and institutions of urban civilization and the church.

Focusing on mountains delineates a few key contour lines of the late antique debate between and reconciliation of 'pagan' and Christian heritages. These tensions are part of an ongoing process whereby individuals actively rethought their relationship to multiple traditions simultaneously, providing various answers to these same fundamental questions. Especially in Basil's epistle, we can see an attempt to present a Christianized concept of an Edenic mountain retreat in the language, style, and trappings of the classical 'pagan' ekphrastic tradition. While his was not the only solution articulated for this problem, it would be one of the most influential for how Christians in subsequent centuries conceived of their relationship to the ancient world. How these classically-educated Christian authors discussed the natural world – and particularly how they treated mountains – sheds light on the nature of the classical/postclassical divide, and how very difficult it is to find and define.

Holy men, holy mountains

Religious mountains infiltrated the late antique imaginations through two major models or precedents: biblical mountains and holy mountains associated with specific saints' cults. Mounts Sinai, Horeb, Carmel, Calvary and Tabor were not just literary places but physical locations in the Roman provinces of Syria, Palestine and Egypt.[28] They inspired pilgrims to visit and patrons to found churches and monasteries either atop or alongside them. Numerous mountains were mentioned in the Bible, but only some became sites which were culturally significant and symbolically resonant for Christian patronage in late antiquity. These physical locations provide pilgrims then and now with a way to map the spiritual world onto the physical one, often in locations which they singled out in literary praise for their exceptional nature.

Although the caves of individual hermits and ascetics dot the slopes of Mount Sinai and its neighbours, the principal monastic foundation there is Saint Catherine's monastery which sits in a valley at the mountain's base. In continuous use since its foundation in the mid-sixth century, this institution's ancient library has preserved a wealth of manuscripts and art.[29] It survived conquests and the conversion of the local Bedouin peoples to Islam because it continuously attracted pilgrims and financial support from Christians native to the Levant and Egypt, from Romans and the Constantinopolitan church, and from Latins especially from the period of the Crusades onward.[30] The mountain today is a living link with the late antique world, testament to the power which the choices made in this time have had as precedent for later generations.

Mount Tabor also formed an important geographical link with the biblical past, albeit one without the same unbroken continuity. The transfiguration represents a significant moment in accounts of Jesus' life. As described in the synoptic gospels, Jesus, accompanied by three disciples, ascended the mountain to pray. At the summit, visions of the prophets

Moses and Elijah appeared and conversed with Jesus, the vision concluding with a voice from the heavens calling Jesus 'son'.[31] Located about 18 km west of Lake Galilee, Tabor stands above the plain of northern Palestine as a regional landmark reaching a height of 575 m. It was an important stop for pilgrims visiting the holy lands, and even served as the seat for the local bishop during the early Abbasid period in the eighth and ninth centuries. Although the current Church of the Transfiguration was only built in the early twentieth century, it sits atop the archaeological remains of several previous churches, various incarnations of which date to the late antique and Crusader periods.[32] Holy mountains, like the monastic communities who lived upon them, existed in a state of tension between inaccessibility and prominence, themes which become more conspicuous in the context of post-biblical holy sites.

Sacred topography was not a static resource. Although the number of biblical mountains was finite, Christianity was a living tradition with the potential to create new holy spaces. Sacred objects and meanings could be transported, and new sites of exceptional sanctity could be created to join biblical antecedents. An important early precedent for this was Saint Anthony the Great (c. 251–356), an Egyptian desert hermit whose life was immortalized in a hagiography written by Athanasius of Alexandria (c. 298–373). This account of Anthony's life played a key role in standardizing and popularizing hagiography as literature, while the physical location of Anthony's desert hermitage attracted followers who established an eponymous monastery in the Red Sea Mountains southeast of modern Cairo – one of the oldest continuously operated monasteries in the world.[33]

The number of holy mountains grew as biblical antecedents were joined by promontories made holy by saints and their followers. In the early fifth century, Simeon Stylites the Elder (c. 390–459) gained fame and a widespread cult following as one of the first and most prominent 'pillar saints'.[34] The pillar atop which he spent the final three decades (according to hagiographical tradition) of his life became the focal point for an important regional pilgrimage site. A large church and monastic complex was built up around the pillar in late antiquity which attracted pilgrims well into the middle ages. Known as *Qalʿat Simʿān*, its ruins are, at least for now, part of the 'Ancient Villages of Northern Syria' UNESCO World Heritage site.[35] Although not a very high mountain in absolute sense, the site commands the local landscape, and as such has been a regional strategic asset in numerous wars, unfortunately including the current civil war in the country.[36] The interaction between Simeon, the mountainous landscape of northern Syria, literary accounts of his life, and the efforts of his followers after his death to create lasting monuments to his memory, form an important precedent for how we can think about the intersection of Christianity and mountains in late antiquity more broadly.

The life of Simeon the Elder, who was born in a small village in the Roman province of Cilicia, has been preserved in several hagiographical accounts. In Greek, his biographies are short or generally late in date, but a surviving Syriac *vita* likely dates to shortly after Simeon's death.[37] According to this Syriac life, Simeon felt an ascetic calling at a young age. He became disenchanted with communal monasticism, and sought ways to remove himself from society to dedicate himself to pious activity – a common hagiographical

Mountains and the Holy in Late Antiquity

trope. He tried living in a hole dug in the monastery's garden, as well as a cave not far from the monastery.[38] But over time, tensions grew between Simeon and the other monks (he could hardly have contributed equally to fulfilling the community's earthly needs being so ostentatiously removed from the world), and so Simeon chose to depart and seek his own spiritual path in the wilderness.

His wanderings took him 'to a certain mountain which was in the town of Telneshē',[39] where he performed a number of miracles and began to develop a reputation as a holy man and to attract followers. 'The Saint's fame began to be talked about in the world, and men began to flock to him from everywhere',[40] but reports of his being a miracle worker brought widespread attention, and this fame in turn doomed the saint's attempts to escape this world. Once the saint decided that neither constant movement across the landscape nor retreating into a cave were sufficient for his needs, he took to living atop a series of ever-taller pillars, the last and tallest of which he reportedly remained atop for over thirty years. In elevating himself up on a pillar, Simeon at once removed himself from the world and stood on display as an exemplar above it for all to see. In effect, Simeon made for himself a private mountain in miniature, set atop the mountain in Telneshē. The church at *Qalʿat Simʿān* was built around his final tallest pillar, which itself became a major pilgrimage site even in the saint's own lifetime (Fig. 5.2). The monastery memorialized the saint's physical abode even as it transformed the landscape immediately around it.

Figure 5.2 Narthex of the Church of Saint Simeon Stylites at Qalʿat Simʿān, Syria (B_237). Photograph: Gertrude Bell, 1905. Gertrude Bell Archive, Newcastle University.

Besides the mountainous physical geography of the village of Telneshē where Simeon established himself, mountains factor prominently into a few other places in the narrative. When Simeon cured a young woman from a nearby village of her lifelong paralysis, she and her grateful father 'ascended the entire length of the mountain,' where he built for her a cell in which she resided for 'all the days of her life',[41] abandoning the traditional social role of wife and mother which she would otherwise have been expected to fulfil. The short miracle story of this anonymous woman ascetic confirms that the pull of sacred geography was independent of gendered social constructs. As this chapter's opening quote from the *Life* of St Thekla already suggested, for late antique Christians mountains were not an essentially male space.[42] A mountain hermitage allowed a saint to transcend and escape society, a place where they could positively define their own otherness.

The concerns of mountain life appear in other miracles performed by Saint Simeon. Two vignettes tell of difficulties created by wild beasts for rural inhabitants – travel was interrupted, children and the weak would disappear, and hunters were mobilized to attempt to deal with the threats.[43] Of course in the story these very mundane troubles were only solved through the saint's miraculous intervention, but the realism of the setting and the problems which people faced align with what one would expect to find based on other sources. Most peculiar, however, is the story of the supernaturally moving mountain:

> A certain mountain was near the village, about two miles off, and it kept creeping nearer little by little until it touched the border of the village. And from under it was heard the sound of waters, mighty as the abyss, and from their fear all the inhabitants of the village had forsaken it and fled. It was fearful, because they saw the mountain creeping and coming to bury them. And when they saw that calamity was fated for them, and there was no help anywhere, the presbyter arose and brought his whole village, from the greatest even to the smallest, and came to the blessed Mar Simeon. When they entered, they all cast themselves down before him and told him the whole matter. He said to them, 'In the name of our Lord Jesus Christ, take three stones, and make three crosses upon them, and go fix them before it, and there keep vigil three days and celebrate the mass. And I have confidence in the Lord that it will not come any nearer'. And our Lord did there a great sign. For they went and did as he had commanded them, and on the third day of a sudden was heard from beneath the mountain the sound of a mighty crash like thunder, and the mountain sank away. And there went up from beneath it many waters and covered all that land. Then our Lord dried them up, and after three days the water was all swallowed up, and no damage was done. The mountain had become level with the earth and was like a plain. They sowed it with legumes and got from it two hundred *cors* [~2400 bushels].
>
> *Life of St Simeon Stylites*, 562–3[44]

There may be a natural explanation for such an event – Syria, like the rest of the eastern Mediterranean, was and is tectonically active. Thinking of the passage in terms of a spiritually-informed realist perspective though, a mountain suddenly appearing, transforming, and vanishing was for fifth-century author and audience alike in keeping with their understanding of the world on the one hand and of the miraculous power wielded by a saint on the other. From a narrative perspective, however, this wandering mountain seems to function metaphorically for concerns over the power and mystery of the wilderness, its ability to encroach on human life, and the desire to overcome and tame such a threat to peoples' benefit. In Simeon's hagiography, mountains are not some passive setting for his story to play out, but integral to his life's work and purpose. This miracle presents a different variation on the trope of the wild mountain being tamed by humans and ultimately brought under cultivation for their benefit.

Saint Auxentios (*c.* 420–14 February 473) was a contemporary of Saint Simeon the Elder. Also born in Syria, he moved to Constantinople at a young age intending to pursue a career in the imperial service, but quit in *c.* 442 to follow a solitary spiritual vocation. He first resided on Mount Oxeia (on the Asian side of the Bosporus, possibly located near Istanbul's modern suburbs of Kartal and Pendik), where he lived for a decade. However, he was compelled to attend the Council of Chalcedon in 452 where he had to defend himself against rumours of heresy – evidence for one of the ways which the institutional church could curb and control saints in their own lifetime. Afterward Auxentios again retired to a solitary life, atop a new mountain 'for this other one, which the locals called Skopos, rose above the clouds, being very steep and most rugged'.[45] Located about 5 km west of Mount Oxeia, Skopos would be known to later generations as Mount Auxentios (Fig. 5.3). Like Anthony and Simeon, considered above, Auxentios attracted followers and other ascetics eager to live up to his example. The saint did not organize them into a community, but after his death his successors established a monastery around the stories of his miracles and the artefacts of his life.[46]

Called 'that great mountain' by patriarch Nikephoros in his *Brief History*,[47] in its time Mount Auxentios was every bit as culturally resonant as the earlier monastic centre at *Qal'at Sim'ān* or the later monastic complexes at Meteora and Athos, although unlike the other examples very little physically remains of its complexes. Rising a modest 428 m in elevation and situated 12 km southeast of Chalcedon (Constantinople's principal Asian suburb), the mountain today known as Kayışdağ was situated very close to the heart of imperial and ecclesiastic power, while being firmly outside it. Archaeological remains were recognizable near the summit until 1960, when they disappeared as a result of work on a military installation.[48] The mountain was both a religious locus and proximate to the imperial capital of Constantinople, attracting pilgrims and monks for the next thousand years.

Besides the grotto of Saint Auxentios near the summit, over time the mountain became home to six monasteries, founded between the sixth and thirteenth century; the three earliest, that of Saint Auxentios, the Monastery of Trichinarea and that of Saint Stephen the Younger, are of particular interest here. The origins of the former began in *c.* 460, when a single pious woman named Stephanis came to the mountain wishing to live an ascetic life under Auxentios' direction. The saint accepted, and she settled a short distance from his grotto. There her solitary life quickly formed the nucleus for a community

Figure 5.3 Saint Auxentios and his holy mountains, from the Menologion of Basil II, eleventh century. Wikimedia Commons.

of women ascetics. Within Auxentios' own lifetime, Stephanis had gained seventy companions, a community which became the Trichinarea monastery. This institution survived until the fourteenth century when the region was occupied by the Turks.[49]

Saint Stephen the Younger (715–67) lived on the mountain as a hermit and monk, founding an eponymous monastery there in *c.* 760. The *Life of Stephen the Younger* was written in or around 807, within living memory of the saint's life and death. As a document, his hagiography was a microcosm of the mountain community at the turn of the ninth century. It was commissioned by *abba* Epiphanios, an ascetic monk living on the mountain who had been Stephen the Younger's student, on behalf of the nuns at the Trichinarea monastery.[50] In this text, the mountain serves as a powerfully unifying landscape between the text's subject (Stephen the Younger), patron (*abba* Epiphanios), and intended audience (nuns at the Trichinarea). The terms used to describe the landscape are bold and draw deeply on biblical and historical precedent:

> As one approaches across the Gulf of Nicomedia, there is a mountain opposite the city on the side of the district of Bithynia, and to those wishing to be saved it is wholly delightful. Far loftier than all the other peaks which lie around it, cold and dry, I shall concisely say it touches heaven. For if someone called it a mountain of God, and Mount Horeb, Mount Carmel or Mount Sinai or Tabor or Lebanon or even the holy city, as if it lay in the country of Jerusalem, they would not err against propriety. Here is a place of salvation. The place draws into itself those who will be saved. Truly, Jerusalem is there. So on this holy mountain, to which familiarity has

fixed with the name of Saint Auxentios both today and for ages past, succeeding generations of fathers have reigned. They confined themselves within the holy grotto, until they found paradise in the abode of death.

Stephen the Deacon, *Life of Stephen the Younger* 11.21-34[51]

Again, note the appearance of Edenic imagery in connection with solitary ascetic life on the mountain. The author, Stephen the Deacon, situates the mountain experientially first – as a notable landmark for travellers crossing the sea of Marmara toward Constantinople – but then elevates it into the realm of sacred biblical geography. In it, all of the major biblical sites are brought from Syria and the Egyptian desert to the Bosporus. Mount Auxentios stood as equal to, and replacement for, the biblical mountains which, after the seventh century, were no longer easily accessible to Christian Romans. The mountains around the Aegean were well on their way to becoming a new holy land for the empire's Christians.

Looking further into the medieval period, the process of Christianizing the peaks of classical Greece continued as an ongoing process for millennia. Today, two of the best-known Aegean monastic complexes are Mount Athos and Meteora. Although they are later in origin than the other mountain monasteries covered in this chapter, they are extremely well-documented, giving a very clear picture about how these sacred medieval mountains appeared in practice. Mount Athos, rising from sea level to 2,033 m in height on the easternmost branch of the Chalcidice peninsula, emerged as a holy mountain in the ninth century.[52] The monasteries there were physically removed from Thessaloniki and Constantinople but perched atop one of the most prominent landmarks of the northern Aegean.[53] The monasteries at Meteora in central Greece were not organized into monastic communities until the fourteenth century, but their dramatic inaccessibility overlooking the plains of Thessaly again situates these as spiritual sanctuaries removed from the world while at the same time being there for all to see.[54] The same patterns of inaccessible prominence which characterized late antique Christian mountains survive to today.

Mountains and the classical inheritance

Across late antique literature and society, there are a few commonalities to the way in which mountains were treated. Whether conceived of metaphorically or described in rather literal terms, mountains are situated in opposition to the civilized society of Graeco-Roman urbanism. However, it is key to note that this is not invariably a bad thing. Many of these Christian authors were, to one degree or another, sceptical of and ambivalent towards their own society. Going to a mountain or living on it was a difficult reality for many, but a fantasy indulged in by some others – themes which resonate with later periods explored in this volume.[55] In the imagination, mountain life provided a way to remove oneself physically and mentally from the pressures of the urban world – whether they be the influences of education and fields of knowledge (such as medicine and astronomy) perceived to be insufficiently Christianized, or institutions which were too worldly. Mountains provided a way to articulate this apprehension, to imagine alternatives, and to reflect the concerns of a society for itself as its members struggled to integrate competing cultural traditions.

The concept of late antiquity seeks to reclaim serious study of a time which, not all that long ago, was dismissed as the Dark Ages. It is a relatively new scholarly field, pioneered above all by Peter Brown in the last quarter of the twentieth century, and as such it entirely postdates Nicolson's *Mountain Gloom and Mountain Glory*. It rejects the idea of a sharp historical or cultural break, and instead frames this as a transitional period between classical antiquity and the middle ages. The way in which people who lived in the Greek heartland in this period interacted with and wrote about mountains has proven to be a microcosm for their efforts to reconcile classical and biblical traditions more broadly. This chapter points to still more questions about the nature of this transition: did these same patterns hold true for people and authors in Latin-dominated western Europe? How was the reception of classical and biblical antiquity in Latin challenged by widespread first-hand experience with the Aegean and the Levant during the period of the Crusades? To build a metaphor around the volume's theme, the 'classical tradition' was not a bridge spanning a chasm anchored on either end by the Second Sophistic and the Renaissance, but a path across the slope, explored and maintained by thinkers of every generation who perpetually had to consider anew their relationship with the past – be it enshrined in literature or in the landscape itself.

Let us conclude by continuing from where the opening quotation left off. After silencing Apollo's oracle and cleansing his mountain sanctuary for Christian worship, Thekla continued her campaign against pagan mountain shrines:

> Thekla made war against the nearby peak, which was formerly called Mount Kokysion, but to which the passage of time, remoulding it in accordance with an old myth, has given the appellation as a holy place of Athena *kanétis* – as if the mountain were Athena's temple! This mountain was taken away from the demon and was placed under the rulership of Christ, exactly as it was from the beginning. And now the place is occupied by martyrs, just as a most lofty citadel is occupied by generals and military commanders, and it is inhabited by holy men, since the shield-bearing and city-defending Pallas Athena was unable to fend off the assault of an unmarried, foreign, and naked girl.
>
> *Miracles of Saint Thekla* 2.1[56]

The *Miracles of Saint Thekla* were written in fifth-century Cilicia, about the posthumous deeds of a saint who lived in first-century Rome. As with the passage which opened the chapter, this vignette tells us how the late antique mountain landscape was imagined as a battleground where pagan shrines were redefined, sometimes quickly and messily, in a process of Christianizing the classical landscape. Its story started when a female Christian saint attacked and seized the holy site of Apollo, a male 'pagan' deity, making it hers. As elsewhere, what appears at first glance as a story of conflict and incompatibility instead shows signs of sustained engagement and considered re-use of pre-Christian forms and attitudes. Indeed, the *Miracles of Saint Thekla* stands out from many hagiographical texts for its prodigious quantity of classical references and the high-literary register of its language.[57] Far from tainting the landscape, the one-time status of the mountaintop as home to a pagan sanctuary added prestige and lustre to the saint's triumphant conquest of the peak. For late antique authors and inhabitants alike mountains, as with all things from the classical pagan past, could be reconciled with their new Christian faith.

Notes

1. Translations in this chapter are my own unless otherwise specified. This translation from Talbot and Johnson 2012: 13.
2. Late antiquity is traditionally marked off from classical antiquity by the 'Crisis of the Third Century' (235–284 CE), a fifty-year period when the Roman Empire was wracked by political, social and economic turmoil. Its end is usually dated to *c.* 750 CE, which marked the final disappearance of the 'Justinianic plague', as well as the Abbasid Revolution which brought the end of rapid Islamic expansion and the stabilization of a new and radically different political order across western Eurasia. See, for example, Brown 1989; Bowersock, Brown and Grabar 1999; Clark 2011.
3. Considerable recent attention has been given to revising the triumphalist narrative of Christianity in late antiquity: see especially Cameron 2011; Salzman, Sághy and Lizzi Testa, 2016.
4. For recent overviews of the field, see Cameron 1999; Gemeinhardt 2012; Stenger 2016.
5. And would endure in unbroken continuity until the fall of Constantinople to the Ottomans in 1453: Kaldellis 2015.
6. On the transmission of ancient learning, see Reynolds and Wilson1991; Johnson 2006 .
7. Jacobs 2012; Busine 2015.
8. Hahn 2008; Frankfurter 2018.
9. The 'classical city' is characterized by specific features which by late antiquity across the Mediterranean could include but were not limited to: walls, public baths, gymnasium, temples and/or Christian basilicae, theatre, hippodrome/circus, odeon, bouleuterion/senate house and other civic buildings, agora/forum, extramural necropolis, public water storage and collection systems, and organized street plans: Lavan and Bowden 2001; Rizos 2017.
10. Cooper and Decker 2012: 15.
11. Ibid. 19–20; König, 2016: 65–6.
12. Sanders 2004; Athanassopoulos 2010.
13. Robinson and Wilson 2011.
14. Harrison 2001: 38–47; Bayburtluoğlu 2005.
15. Waelkens 1993: 37–8.
16. Harrison 2001: 62-3.
17. Waelkens 1993: 48–9.
18. For more on the broader regional patterns, see especially Drake and Brown 2006; Sweetman 2015.

19. Kakavoulis 1986.
20. This included many 'scientific' fields, which then were conceived of as natural philosophy: Bernard 2018.
21. Buxton 1992; Langdon 2000.
22. Homer, *Odyssey* 5.63–74.
23. Allen 1987; Kahlos 2012; Elsner 2013. The comparison with the river Strymon at Amphipolis, which seems to be mentioned primarily for the purpose of demonstrating the authors' wide travels and familiarity with classical Greek locations, may be a part of this same learned play with the cultural inheritance from the pagan past.
24. della Dora 2016b: 171–2. This may also be read as a reversal of Christ's time in the desert, where he was tempted by the devil, at Matthew 4:1-11; Luke 4:1-13.
25. Sarris, Dal Santo and Booth 2011.
26. This could alternatively be translated as 'on account of his (Chrysaphios') usefulness to him (Naukratios)'.
27. This seems to invite comparison to the 'solitude' which Henry David Thoreau enjoyed at Walden Pond, where he nonetheless relied on his mother to wash his clothes and provide him with food, and where he regularly entertained friends.
28. della Dora 2016b: 148–55.
29. Evans 2004; Shams 2011.
30. della Dora 2016b: 155–6.
31. Matthew 17:1-8; Mark 9:2-8; Luke 9:28-36.
32. della Dora 2016b: 156–7.
33. Gabra and Vivian 2002; Louth 1988; Dunn 2000.
34. Stylies were ascetics (there are surviving accounts of both men and women) who lived on a platform atop a pillar (*stylos* in Greek), sometimes with a small shelter against the elements, often without. Platforms were reached by ladder, which both physically removed the saints from pilgrims who might visit and placed their lives on full display, and ascetics reportedly remained atop their platforms for years at a time. Delehaye 1962. On the question of whether or not there were pre-Christian precedents, see Frankfurter 1990: esp. 188–91.
35. 'Ancient Villages of Northern Syria, UNESCO World Heritage Centre': http://whc.unesco.org/en/list/1348/ (accessed 25 August 2020).
36. R. Spencer (2016), *The Telegraph*, 13 May 2016: https://www.telegraph.co.uk/news/2016/05/13/syrian-monastery-where-st-simeon-sat-on-a-pillar-for-four-decade/ (accessed 25 August 2020).
37. Syriac is a dialect of Aramaic which was widely spoken across the Middle East and Levant in the first millennium CE. The language is closely associated with the spread of Christianity across Asia and remains a liturgical language for churches across western Asia and India – the Syriac translation of the Bible, called the *Peshitta*, predates Jerome's Latin *Vulgate* by over a century. Its large literary corpus was heavily influenced by Greek, and Syriac played a key role mediating the translation of classical Greek knowledge into Arabic in the early Islamic period: Brock 2006.
38. Lent 1915: 121.
39. Ibid. 121, 123. In another place, locals from the region are referred to collectively as 'the inhabitants of the mountain': 140. A subsequent passage describes when people were summoned to the saint's pillar, 'many people gathered there, a countless multitude. The

mountains were covered, and the *mandra* [the 'enclosure' containing Simeon's column] was filled inside and out with men and women': 178.

40. Ibid. 132–3.
41. Ibid. 126.
42. The *vita* of the eighth-century saint Anthousa of Mantineou claims that, as a youth, she 'lived in mountains and caves' and studied under a monk named Sisinios who lived outside of normal society. See Talbot 1996: 1 who observes that tropes connecting the saint to mountains and wilderness are clearly not limited by gender, despite the fact that women's hagiographies are relatively scarcer than men's.
43. Lent 1915: 147–8, 163–5.
44. Ibid. 146–7.
45. ἄλλο δὲ λίαν ἄναντες καὶ ὑπερνεφὲς καὶ τραχύτατον (Σκοπὸν τοῦτο καλοῦσιν ἐγχώριοι) κατειλήφει (Clugnet 1903: 10).
46. Janin 1975: 44.
47. Mango 1990: 154–5.
48. Janin 1975: 43–4.
49. Ibid. 45–6.
50. Auzépy 1997: 87 (French translation 179); Kazhdan and Talbot 1998: 94–5.
51. Auzépy 1997: 102 (French translation 195).
52. See della Dora 2011. Mount Athos, of course, cast a very long shadow over the course of classical Greek history. According to Herodotus, it was the site where Darius' fleet was wrecked in 492 BCE, and where Xerxes dug a great canal in order to bypass its stormy tip for his invasion of 480 BCE: Herodotus, *Histories* 6.44, 7.22-5.
53. Iozzo, Borghesi and Magnelli 2001; Speake 2002 and 2018.
54. della Dora 2012 and 2016b: 158–9; Poulios 2014.
55. See Koelb and Jordan in this volume.
56. Tr. Talbot and Johnson 2012: 15.
57. Ibid. x–xii.

CHAPTER 6
ERUDITE RETREAT: JEROME AND FRANCIS IN THE MOUNTAINS
Janice Hewlett Koelb

The Greek word *oros*, inadequately translated as 'mountain', enfolds an old conception obscured by the preoccupations of modern tourism, mountaineering, geology and – crucially – by the absence of a single word to convey *oros* into modern English. *Oros* has nevertheless persisted as a stable concept whose defining properties are not dictated by the anachronistic convention of measuring height above a standardized geodetic reference point, but rather by local cultural geography, as Buxton explains:

> An *oros* is not the plain (where you grow corn and fight in phalanx), nor is it the city or the village (where you live) ... [N]either is it an acropolis, that fortified height, often also religious centre and symbol of political power, *within* the city. An *oros* is a height outside inhabited and cultivated space ... [I]n a specifically Egyptian context, *oros* may signify the desert (near or far) in contrast with the fertile and cultivable Nile Valley.[1]

The striking Egyptian example shows that what we call 'desert' the Greeks called *oros*, because the sands (only modestly elevated compared with European mountains) were markedly outside the zone of settlement and cultivation. Thus while any 'mountain' in English would be a variety of *oros* for the Greeks, not every Greek *oros* is a mountain to our minds. The nuanced cultural geography implied by *oros* matters if we wish to discern 'mountains' over centuries of Western thought and experience; re-conceptualizing the cultural memory of mountains in terms of *oros* can lay open to view an afterlife of classical landscape that has been hidden in plain sight.[2]

Oros enfolds a cultural understanding of mountains as liminal spaces that mediate between civilization and barbarism, culture and nature, the familiar and the alien, the human and the divine, the past and the present. This mediating quality of mountains plays an especially prominent role in the lives of Jerome (*c.* 347–420) and Francis (*c.* 1181–1226), two Christian saints whose reception is intimately bound up with mountain sojourns during which new and enduring connections were forged between such opposing forces. These saints, as fashioned by themselves or re-fashioned by others, are depicted as engaging in activities that align with the mediating character of the *oros*: remembering, reading or writing. This chapter will show how the autobiographical writings and later accounts and depictions of Jerome reveal the intertextual fusion of the Virgilian past not only with the wilderness of the Hebrew prophets but also with Renaissance reflections on the restorative value of erudite rural retirement. Two canonical mountain landscapes of Giovanni Bellini will illustrate how the symbolically productive characteristics of ancient mountains were creatively realized as naturalistic landscapes in fifteenth-century Venice.

Giovanni Bellini (c. 1435–1516) took an intertextual approach to legend and history in his early *Saint Jerome in the Wilderness* (Fig. 6.1). Bellini's approach came to fruition in his *Saint Francis in the Desert* or *in the Wilderness* or *in Ecstasy* (Fig. 6.2), as the same painting is variously known. The slippage is telling. The setting may be either Monte Subasio, on whose western shoulder lies Francis's home town Assisi, or La Verna, an isolated mountain to the north. The mountains are as literary, as real, and as creatively imagined as the wilderness in which Bellini situated his *Saint Jerome*. These Quattrocento mountains refract the same symbolic valences Buxton detected in the Greek *oros*: real and imagined Greek mountains are 'outside and wild', a place for outsiders and fugitives; 'mountains are before', the place where it all began; and mountains are a 'place for reversals' and epiphanies, the place where the divine and the human come together.[3]

When Bellini's *Saint Francis* visibly realized mountain landscape as an articulate vehicle for spiritual meaning, cultural memory and humanistic integration, he was making visible in the mountains near his home what had been implicit in Jerome's letters: mountains as *locus amoenus* (pleasant place), a topical term whose cultural geography (for reasons to be discussed) became bound up with the liminal cultural geography of the *oros*. But if the idea of a saint's mountain as *locus amoenus* seems implausible, even oxymoronic, the place to begin is by noting a certain misconception of the moral status of landscape before the seventeenth or eighteenth century.

The moral status of medieval landscape

Long before Marjorie Hope Nicolson advanced the notion that Christians distrusted mountains, the intellectual ground had been prepared for her theory to flourish as a special case of a widespread general idea about Christians in the natural world. This general idea is that before the Renaissance or thereabouts (however dated), Europeans had long been under the spell of a Dark Age rendering them incapable of enjoying nature or natural beauty. Kenneth Clark, for example, begins his magisterial *Landscape into Art* (1949) by disparaging the lack of naturalistic verisimilitude in medieval art; for him such styles evidence 'mistrust of nature'.[4] He cites the authority of St Anselm (c. 1033–1109), Archbishop of Canterbury, who 'maintained that things were harmful in proportion to the number of senses which they delighted, and therefore rated it dangerous to sit in a garden' with its many sensory delights. 'This, no doubt, expresses the strictest monastic view. The average layman would not have thought it wrong to enjoy nature; he would simply have said that nature was not enjoyable.'[5] But Anselm himself undermines Clark's assessment of what the average layman is capable of enjoying: Anselm assumes that gardens delight the senses and therefore *must be enjoyable*, presumably to Clark's average layman and everyone else, including Anselm. For Anselm, gardens are dangerous precisely because he *knows* they delight the senses of human beings, all of whose instincts generally trouble the archbishop. Anselm's ascetic brief is against the *pleasures* of the senses; there is no point in discouraging activities that tempt nobody. Secular medieval literature is replete with pleasurable love gardens, trysts and lavish feasts.

While asceticism is a genuine philosophical outlook, and certainly predates Christianity, not even early Christian saints are univocal on the moral status of the natural world. Countering Clark's gloss on Anselm, we have (to give only one example), a hymn by Saint Ephraem of Syria (306–73) evoking the beneficent pleasures of landscape:

> If you wish to climb to the top of a tree, its branches range themselves under your feet and invite you to rest in the midst of its bosom, in the green room of its branches, whose floor is strewn with flowers. Who has ever seen the joy at the heart of a tree, with fruits of every taste within reach of your hand? You can wash yourself with its dew and dry yourself with its leaves. A cloud of fruits is over your head and a carpet of flowers beneath your feet. You are anointed with the sap of the tree and inhale its perfume.
>
> *Hymn of Paradise* 9.5-6[6]

The point of Ephraem's hymn is that if the natural world can be as innocently joyful as nesting in the green room of a tree, then paradise, the unseen 'joy at the heart of the tree' must be even more so. Ephraem's figurative language is persuasively vivid because he knows that people enjoy trees and many other earthly delights.

The figurative language alludes more broadly to the notion that there are two revelations of God's mind, and both are sacred: the book of scripture, a verbal text, and the book of nature that communicates non-discursively and elicits a non-discursive response that the mind may be able to instantiate through art. Ephraem's art was writing, as was Jerome's, as was Francis's; Bellini's was painting. Both divine revelations, written scripture and the non-discursive natural creation, are vehicles of spiritual meaning in portraits of Jerome in the mountains with a book or books. The overarching theme of such pictures is that spiritual integrity can be recovered or deepened through simultaneous immersion in both revelations. The mountain, understood as *oros* outside the civilized centre, is a privileged site for such immersion.

Depictions of voluntary exile to the *oros* can be ambiguous though. Does the image celebrate the values of an Anselm or an Ephraem?

> One might expect the natural setting for a painting of St Jerome to be consistently austere as the accessory of his self-mortification. We know from Jerome's own account that his life while in the desert was one of vigorous penance . . . ; but the desert or wilderness in early Christian thought is a mesh of contradictions . . . the haunt of demons and the realm of bliss and harmony with the creaturely world.[7]

Can the same mountains be demonic and Edenic? The contradiction may not be sharply evident to the modern viewer, who may approach depictions of Jerome in the belief that nature must not have, or should not have afforded pleasure to an ascetic Christian saint. But the innocent joys of nature are presented in the letters of Jerome himself, usually through literary remembrances of Virgil.

A fugitive from Rome: Jerome retreats to the *oros*

Jerome was born into a wealthy cosmopolitan Christian family in Stridon (near Aquileia), educated in Rome under the distinguished pagan grammarian Aelius Donatus, and credited with founding ascetic monasticism.[8] As a young man in Aquileia, Jerome and his friends were 'united in the closest friendship' until what Jerome describes only as 'a monstrous splitting asunder' prompted him and a few friends to head East to cure their souls. Along the way their paths diverged; Jerome stopped a while at the country home of his equally scholarly Christian friend, Evagrius (345–99). While Evagrius's home and collegial friendship offered all the spiritual amenities of rural solitude, Jerome found himself compelled to leave after an overwhelming sense of guilt incubated a visionary dream. He recounted the episode several years later, in a letter to Eustochium, a sixteen-year-old girl whom he admonished to remain chaste and avoid temptation of every description, including – for he presented himself as an avuncular expert witness – the conversations of married women and the seductions of lecherous priests who may come to call. The long letter, perhaps his most famous, offers intimate glimpses into this urbane intellectual's troubled state of mind: 'I still could not bring myself to forego the library which I had formed for myself at Rome with great care and toil. And so, miserable man that I was, I would fast only that I might afterwards read Cicero'. To make matters worse, 'after floods of tears' he 'would once more take up Plautus'. Now settled in the view that a passion for Cicero and Plautus was imperilling his immortal soul, and near death from a fever, Jerome dreamed that at the direction of Christ he was scourged for his classical reading. To redouble the pain, he was 'tortured more severely still by the fire of conscience' and vowed never again to possess or read worldly books (Jerome, *Letter* 22.30).[9] The company of the liberal, syncretic Evagrius was apparently now intolerable, for neither Evagrius nor any other friends could be persuaded to join Jerome in the sort of penitence he had in mind.[10] Evagrius, at some point reportedly in love and tempted to have an affair, later retreated to a syncretic penitential community in the Egyptian *oros* and distinguished himself as one of the Desert Fathers. Jerome later denounced his friend and host as a heretic for (among other reasons) not rejecting classical philosophy.[11] Jerome may or may not have observed the letter of his vow to abjure worldly books, but his writings suggest that his mind had already been irremediably shaped by classical reading committed forever to memory.

The pattern of seeking solitude within a like-minded community, as Jerome had done when he joined Evagrius, would repeat itself and is crucial to understanding the nature of Jerome's ascetic solitude and the *social* appeal of the *oros*, Egyptian or otherwise; a place at once apart, approachable, sustainable and spiritually supportive of whatever penitence one felt compelled to embrace. Jerome's penitence entailed a five-year sojourn

(374–9), followed by a return to the city. As in Greek myth and drama, *oros* and *polis* interact in the story of Jerome, but more dynamically.[12] He took his urban anxieties to a mountain community, along with his cultural memory, his studies, and his desire for conversation; and then he returned with the fruits of his learning.

Jerome retired into the *heremus*, his late Latin term for the Chalkidean 'desert', or 'wilderness', or Italian *solitudine*, as *heremus* is variously translated. For English speakers, 'desert' and 'wilderness' evoke particular kinds of landscape, perhaps the Sahara as depicted in film or the mountain forests sought by North American tourists. *Heremus*, from the Greek *erēmos*, is usually translated as 'desert' or 'wilderness'. But the root of the Greek has to do with solitude, not topography or climate;[13] whence Latin *solitudo*, translated into English as either 'state of being alone', to denote a mental state, or as 'desert' or 'wilderness'; or even 'unfrequented part of a street' to denote an urban space, but never as 'mountain/s'. What warrant is there for stretching the definition of 'mountain'[14] to include Jerome's place of retirement, whatever he called it?

A precise geological term came into English late in the nineteenth century to describe where Jerome got away from it all: *massif*, a compact cluster of hills or mountains.[15] In geological terms, Jerome retired to the limestone massif bordering the ancient city of Chalkis ad Bellum, in modern Turkey close to the Syrian border. But to characterize the cultural geography, rather than the geology, the Greek term *oros* is the perfect fit. The Chalkidean massif rose up to modest elevations (by mountaineering standards) from what was then a fertile river valley. The massif was just outside the zone of town settlement or agriculture, and literally at the boundary of Roman civilization. Chalkis, now in ruins, formed part of the Roman *limes* marking the border of the empire, and was a caravan stop on the road to nearby Antioch.[16]

Although Jerome could not persuade his friends to come along, his solitude was not a lonely exile into uncharted territory. He joined an established community where, with permission, one might live modestly without foregoing the innocent amenities of civilization: sufficient food and water for an abstemious diet, books and writing materials, and reliable mail service on Roman roads. Indeed, Jerome submitted a formal letter of application to Theodosius, apparently the head of the institution,[17] petitioning to 'embrace your admirable community' and to secure the penitential benefits of retirement from Rome. Jerome likened his lost soul to the proverbial sheep astray from the flock, to the prodigal son astray from the father, and finally to Aeneas at sea after fleeing the dangerous affair with Dido. He confessed to Theodosius: 'I have begun not so much to abandon my vices as to desire to abandon them' (Jerome, *Letter* 2).[18] Such free interweavings of the Bible and Virgil, 'above all others the pagan who bridged the gap between paganism and Christianity',[19] characterize Jerome's letters and helped guarantee Virgil's unbroken canonical stature throughout Christendom.

Jerome ultimately abandoned the Chalkidean version of solitude, just as he had abandoned Evagrius's country home, because he was contemptuous of colleagues who challenged his doctrinal views.[20] He was grateful though to one person: a Jewish Christian anchorite from whom he learned, with much difficulty, both to speak Hebrew and to read the Hebrew Bible. Thus Jerome in the mountains, while imitating the wilderness excursions of the prophets, enjoyed the good fortune of a native-speaking guide who led him through a foreign textual wilderness mirroring the geographical Judean wilderness not so very far to the south. Text, *oros*, and religious vocation were now securely interfused. Like many a biblical or Greek protagonist, Jerome was tutored and initiated in the mountains, and returned to the city.[21]

Jerome resumed his scholarly religious vocation, first in Antioch (379–81) and then in Rome, the centre of Christianity and of the multicultural civilization that had educated him in his youth. It was as though he brought the mountains back into the city as protection against the manifold corruption he feared; for good or for ill, he resumed his ministry. It was in Rome in 384 (five years after quitting the mountains) that Jerome wrote the letter to young Eustochium describing his anti-classical dream. The same letter also vividly describes why he particularly sought the mountainous terrain surrounding his living quarters: 'How often, when I was living in the desert (*heremo*) in the vast solitude (*solitudine*) which gives to hermits a savage (*horridum*) dwelling-place, parched by a burning sun, how often did I fancy myself among the pleasures of Rome!' Burning in the sun was not a curricular requirement of the institution, but he imposed it upon himself as well as other privations: sackcloth, cold drinking water (i.e. no wine), raw food. 'I had consigned myself to this prison, where I had no companions but scorpions and wild beasts' on the outside; inwardly he was 'filled with bitterness', and haunted 'amid bevies of girls ... dancing girls'. Dreading the shelter of his little room because it held his transgressive secrets, he ventured out into the mountains that a thousand years later would provide the setting for depictions of Jerome in penitence in the wilderness: 'I used to make my way alone into the desert (*deserta*). Wherever I saw hollow valleys, craggy mountains, steep cliffs, there I made my oratory, there the house of correction for my unhappy flesh' (Jerome, *Letter* 22.7). For Jerome the mountain landscape was not the 'haunt of demons' stereotyped in modern scholarship. For the haunt of demons was experienced in his mind, and the demons were dancing girls. He sought refuge in the valleys, crags and mountains of the massif from their unrelenting pursuit; it may be the case that what prompted his penitence in the first place had more to do with sharing the agonies of lovesick Evagrius than with his inability to forego a passion for merely reading about such matters in Plautus.

The easy intertextuality of Jerome's application letter – from stray sheep to prodigal son to terrified Aeneas – foreshadowed him contending with the dancing girls. Although Jerome never did fully understand the relationship between his own fantasies and his troubling and dangerous obsession with preserving the sexual honour of girls, he did moderate his views on the value of self-mortification and, after a stint at Rome, eventually sought a version of erudite solitude more in keeping with old Roman ideals.

After Jerome's protector Pope Damasus died in 384, the new Pope Siricius made clear that he considered the learned but extreme and irascible Jerome a rival. Life became sufficiently unpleasant that Jerome was soon driven from Rome.[22] In 384 or 385, while mulling over where to escape Siricius and the mobs who accused him (not without cause) of leading young virgins to purify themselves by fasting to the point of ruining their health and ending their lives,[23] Jerome wrote a wistful letter evidencing his ambivalence about the sort of place that is amenable to the spiritual life. The addressee was an older female colleague Marcella (325–410). On this occasion, less than a year after the letter to young Eustochium, severe privation had no role in the ideal Christian retreat from the evils of Rome; instead Jerome praised country life in rhetorical terms that mark him as the person he was educated to be: an urban Roman intellectual with a culturally ingrained attraction to the virtues and pleasures of rural retirement. Jerome's letter gives the old topos a Christian inflection:

> As our barque has now been shaken by tempestuous winds, now holed upon rugged rocks, let us take this first chance and make for the haven of a rural retreat. Let us live there on milk, on the bread we bake for ourselves, and on the greenstuff that we water with our own hands, country delicacies, cheap and harmless. If thus we spend our days, sleep will not call us away from prayer, nor overfeeding from study. In summer the shade of a tree will give us privacy. In autumn the mild air and the leaves beneath our feet point out a place for rest. In spring the fields are gay with flowers and the birds' plaintive notes will make our psalms sound all the sweeter.

Jerome was clearly more in Ephraem's camp than Anselm's here: he imagines a *locus amoenus* where birdsong would sweeten the psalms. Concerning winter, his tone took a more practical (and notably non-ascetic) turn: in the unlikely event that firewood need be purchased, 'certainly as far as I know, I shall escape the cold at a cheaper rate'. As for Rome, she can 'keep her bustle for herself', namely the evils traditionally cited by the Roman moralists: 'the fury of the arena, the madness of the circus, the profligacy of the theatre' (Jerome, *Letter* 43.3) Moreover, Jerome contrasted the moral degeneracy of urban leisure with an erudite Roman's praise for the salutary intellectual activities afforded by rural *solitudo*: reading and study.

He reminded Marcella that Ambrose 'supplied Origen with parchment, money, and copyists' for his voluminous writing, and that Ambrose never dined with Origen 'without something being read' (Jerome, *Letter* 43.1). Jerome then issued the perennial lament of a scholar and teacher, the lax literacy of his contemporaries: 'If we spend more than an hour in reading, you will find us yawning and trying to restrain our boredom by rubbing our eyes; then, as though we had been hard at work, we plunge once more into worldly affairs' (Jerome, *Letter* 43.2). Jerome's plea for reading and study in rural solitude was well-crafted to persuade Marcella, for she was the educated daughter of a senator, a chaste widow and a scholar in her own right. Marcella often hosted Jerome in her Aventine palace where she encouraged and collaborated with him on his translations from the Hebrew and Greek, as Evagrius had done in his Greek-speaking country home. Jerome was, in a way, returning her hospitality. She declined the offer.[24] He made his way East, eventually settling in Bethlehem.

In 411, a quarter-century after Jerome wrote his valedictory letter to Marcella on the virtues of rural retirement, he reflected on the value of his long-ago sojourn in the *oros*, the site of the self-fashioned prison he had so vividly described to Eustochium decades earlier. The 411 letter offers advice this time to a married man, Rusticus, in search of where and how to live the devout Christian life. The circumstances were unusual. Rusticus and his wife had vowed never to consummate their marriage. After breaking their vow, his wife left him to do penance for her sin, but Rusticus wavered in whether or not to follow her example into a life of chaste solitude. Here as elsewhere Jerome's usage of the word *solitudo* enfolds both a psychosocial state and an imagined landscape: 'The sons of Jonadab', explained Jerome, 'lived in tents which they pitched whenever night came on', and when attacked by the Chaldeans were forced to take refuge in cities. Likewise for himself (and in contradistinction to the earlier wilderness-prison), 'a town is a prison, and the wilderness paradise' (*mihi oppidum carcer est et solitudo paradisus*) (Jerome, *Letter* 125.8). Where Wright translates *solitudo* as 'wilderness', Fremantle translates 'solitude'.[25] Since Jerome's biblical context is a disturbed nomadic community, translation is a difficult call. Both renderings of Latin *solitudo* together convey Jerome's meaning where no single English word would suffice.

The letter urged Rusticus not to follow in the self-abnegating footsteps of young Jerome in penitence, but rather to leave his mother and join a supportive monastic community that instantiated the same rural values and pleasures Jerome had praised in his invitation to Marcella. The solitude depicted for Marcella, so reminiscent of the solitude praised by Roman intellectuals who sought rural retreat in mountain villas, is in Jerome's settled opinion the solitude that cured his soul. As he remarkably confessed, it was not the lonely fasting that subdued his 'natural heat', those dancing girls who chased him out of his room into the mountains; it was the struggle to learn to speak and read Hebrew in the *oros* that had tempered his soul (Jerome, *Letter* 125.12).

Jerome's monastic ideal fuses two Roman themes: cultivating one's food in a beneficent setting, and cultivating one's soul by reading: 'Always have a book in your hand; learn the psalms word by word'; he urged, and enjoy the blessings of honest work and simple food:

> Make creels of reeds or weave baskets of pliant osiers. Hoe the ground and mark it out into equal plots, and when you have sown cabbage seed or set out plants in rows, bring water down in channels and stand by like the onlooker in [again Virgil's] lovely lines (*pulcherrimorum versuum*):

> > Lo, from the channeled slope he brings the stream,
> > Which falls hoarse murmuring o'er the polished stones
> > And with its bubbling flood allays the heat
> > Of sun-scorched fields.
>
> Jerome, *Letter* 125.11[26]

After Virgil's description of a channelled mountain torrent, a harmonious collaboration of nature and art, hill and plain, Jerome's own lovely words then cover the gamut from fruit-grafting to fishing to bee-keeping and the lessons to be learned from the tiny creatures (*in parvis corporibus*) (Jerome, *Letter* 125.11), just as Virgil had done in the *Georgics*. The ideal ascetic monk turns out to be a skilful Roman gardener with books, pausing in his labours to gaze upon water gushing from the mountaintop over polished stones into his *locus amoenus*.

The montane *locus amoenus*

Jerome's and Virgil's gardeners merge in a late antique *locus amoenus* in the mountains, a culturally unifying variant of *locus amoenus* that would flourish in medieval and Renaissance literature and art. As with other classical *topoi*, 'the artistic development of a *locus amoenus*' is not mere imitation of a formula but a spontaneous creation, 'and even in ... schematized form [is] activated' by the poet or artist's 'distinct aesthetic feeling'.[27] The distinct feeling we have seen unfolding in Jerome's quest for a spiritually harmonious place was shaped by the expressive resources of myth and cultural memory offered by classical tradition and the evolving Judeo-Christian idea of paradise. E. R. Curtius conveys the meaning of the classical *topos* through several examples, including the six 'charms of landscape' enumerated in Libanius (*c.* 314–93): 'causes of delight are springs and plantations, and gardens and soft breezes and flowers and bird voices'.[28] The 'plantations' in Libanius's list is a reminder that a *locus amoenus* could be imagined early on as a liminal and unifying place, a place outside the city where what occurs naturally collaborates with what humans introduce, as in Jerome's *Georgics* passage. The attractive mix of the wild and the cultivated is as old as Homer's description of the artisan Calypso's seductive abode at *Odyssey* 5.57-73.

The value of recognizing a text such as Calypso's abode or – much later on – Milton's Eden as a *locus amoenus* is not that we can classify it as an object with certain topical features (trees and so forth) and call it a day. The topical features of Milton's seventeenth-century *locus amoenus* are overt signs of something much deeper: the intertextuality of Milton, Dante, and their humanistic and biblical predecessors, including Jerome, who forged a bond between classical *locus amoenus* and biblical Eden. The earthly paradises of Dante and Milton are fresh likenesses of the lovely place upon the original mountain whence flows the branching river out of Eden: 'the garden at the beginning of the world'.[29] 'Mountains are before', as Buxton puts it. Moreover, paradise in its earliest development 'embraces both garden and pasture. The Hebrew Bible already contains pastoral images; later Christ is portrayed as both pastor and sheep; ... both the Good Shepherd and the Sacrificial Lamb'.[30] The confluence of all these features, classical and biblical, provides one of the '"pastoral occasions" [for] the construction of meaning in landscape' during the Renaissance: 'the saint in a landscape, ... an analogue to the shepherd in his pleasant place'.[31] Jerome's complex mountain experience became a perfect early occasion for constructing the meaning of landscape in the Renaissance.

The personal and cultural memory of mountain and text transformed Jerome's penitential *oros* from prison to paradise, from sun-parched hills to a montane *locus amoenus* with reviving waters: heaven on earth, a landscape of the highest moral status. Jerome's feat of memory, at first glance either false idealization or rhetorical ornamentation, may be more precisely described as recovering a suppressed dimension of what Jerome had actually experienced at Chalkis. 'Jerome's desert on the northern border of Syria was populated by many other monks and hermits as well as the local peasantry, and lay close to a fertile river basin'.[32] The habitat supported more than scorpions and wild beasts that, along with the demonic dancing girls, haunted Jerome's tormented inner world. While roaming the mountains and cliffs, Jerome had ample opportunity to pause by one of the streams watering the valley below to gaze like Virgil's gardener upon rural mountain life. The Mediterranean landscape, as much as its textual analogues, informed the monastic ideal Jerome inspired others to realize on the ground.

While the prison-to-paradise transformation vividly illustrates how the beginnings of ascetic monasticism intersect with 'classical and humanist explorations and celebrations of rural retirement',[33] the classical continuity is deeper still, extending its roots far into culturally widespread ancient taboos of mountains as restricted or even ritually quarantined sacred space. The ancient *oros* could be a dangerous place, a place of exile; or a place of initiation and divine illumination; or a place of reversals and unions of opposites. The categories overlap. The *oros* is 'outside and wild', beyond normal urban experience; but, crucially, the *oros* is one pole in symbiotic interaction with the deepest concerns of the *polis*. In Greek drama, '*oros* and *polis* often constitute two of the significant spaces' orienting the action. Exiles and initiates do return and bring a new order, as did the heroes who returned to transform the city after tutelage in the mountains.[34] For Jerome, the cultural hero of early Christianity, the distance between the Roman centre and the tutelary *limes* was on an imperial scale, and his return both shaped the Roman Church and provided later generations with a humanistic model for collapsing distinctions between the pagan and the Christian. In Italy a millennium later, mountains could be 'a landscape of sacred discourse',[35] a distinctively modern union of mountain landscape and sacralized text, both penitential *oros* and *locus amoenus*. Jerome in letters and legend inspired the unlikely interweaving of these contrary symbolic valences.

Giovanni Bellini's Jerome: the *oros* as prison and paradise

'Myths ... refract, transforming the world by a process of selective emphasis and clarification, and exaggeration'.[36] Just as in mythical and literary depictions of actual Greek mountains, the symbolically productive qualities of Jerome's *oros* are refracted, intensified and combined in visual depictions of Jerome in the wilderness. While Jerome's own story of how he experienced, remembered, and internalized the *oros* was inflected by his Roman education as much as by biblical accounts of the wilderness, the folklore that had sprung up around his journeys was as well-known as his writings. The legends of the saint as redacted into a single story in the thirteenth-century *Golden Legend*, completes the verbal frame we need for beginning to read pictures created centuries after his death.[37] These pictures feature a protagonist almost as important as Jerome, a denizen of the mountains not mentioned in Jerome's writings: the lion, a rehabilitation of the 'scorpions and wild beasts' that had figured forth his mental torment. The lion became a symbol of the Resurrection and a particular attribute of the saint.[38]

The Golden Legend has it that a lion with a crippling thorn in its paw approached Jerome while he was residing in a Bethlehem monastery. Only Jerome, convinced that God sent the lion for a reason, is calm and compassionate enough to remove the thorn and persuade the others to welcome the grateful lion into the community as a working brother tasked with guarding their donkey. The natural sleep habits of the lion prove ill-suited to twenty-four-hour guard duty; and soon enough the donkey is stolen by merchants while the donkey grazes and the lion dozes. Falsely accused of eating the donkey, the lion is reassigned to the donkey's burdensome chores. After a year of this unjust punishment, the lion spots the donkey leading a camel caravan and brings him back, along with all the thieving merchants and camels. The remorseful merchants pay restitution in Egyptian oil, and promise oil to light the monks' lamps for posterity.[39]

The Golden Legend also rehearses certain vivid details from the letters – scorpions, girls, penitential suffering and the like – in addition to the folkloric story summarized above. Although the historical Jerome neither attests to living in a monastery nor to befriending a lion, the culturally potent idea of a monastery, the legend's colourful objects and actors, and the symbolic resonance of both lion and donkey proved irresistible to artists: camels, thieves, doubting brothers, caravans and Egyptian oil all found their way into the iconography of Jerome. It is important to note that portraits of Jerome typically reference the other prominent fact of his actual life: the scholarship, always betokened in art by a scene of reading in the company of the legendary lion, whether the scene is indoors or in the wilderness. Thus the verbal frame for any picture of Jerome in a landscape can present ambiguities of story and setting that may or may not be resolvable to the satisfaction of viewers who may (albeit unconsciously) expect a picture to capture a single moment in time in a particular setting. A portrait (then and now) can, however, characterize its human subject by layering or otherwise arranging symbolic and anachronic elements within a single thematically unified composition. In such portraits, setting has as much a role in dramatizing human character as does the face and body, and as strong a narrative role as the verbal materials informing the portrait. When setting organizes our perception of the human subject and his story, the picture admits of readings that heavily depend on the viewer's understanding of how pictures do or do not tell stories and reveal character.

A case in point is Giovanni Bellini's earliest surviving independent work,[40] *Saint Jerome in the Wilderness* (Fig. 6.1). This *Jerome* is one of many pictures in which elements of the landscape serve to dramatize the spiritual crisis of Jerome, but Bellini's youthful effort is an original presentation of the ambivalent *oros* as both prison and paradise. Andrews resolves the tension by showing how the composition suggests an allegorical narrative:

> [it] is dominated by the steep diagonal of the foreground cliff, and then by the abrupt horizontal division between flat, tawny desert and rolling green background. A path perfunctorily rendered by one or two brushstrokes is the only link between these two landscapes. Jerome's position within this mixed landscape expresses his predicament. His chosen dwelling is the rocky den in the desert . . ., but the choice he has made to relinquish the more comfortable world is dramatized by allowing

that forsaken world to appear as the background. Jerome is in sight of it here, as a way of figuring his consciousness of the life deliberately left behind. There is a correspondence between the meagre-fleshed saint and the parched leafless tree that is the only vegetation in the desert.[41]

Upon closer inspection of the sunlit mid-ground (Andrews' tawny desert with only a leafless tree), we find that Jerome's donkey has wandered out of his legendary pasture,

Figure 6.1 Giovanni Bellini (c. 1430–1516), Italian. *Saint Jerome in the Wilderness*, c. 1450. Tempera on panel. The Henry Barber Trust, The Barber Institute of Fine Arts, University of Birmingham / Bridgeman Images.

where he was lost and found by the lion, into a topographically accurate equine *locus amoenus*: a fragrant hay-meadow newly mown and raked, with the haystack still standing nearby, and fresh gleanings to nibble from the ground. Renewable annual nourishment flourishes here besides the blasted tree, with all the classical and Christian resonance of death, resurrection and *reverdie*, on a permanent grassland formation among the steeper hills. Bellini's green hills bear no trace of Rome or urban development; the hills cannot signify the forsaken world. The only architectural structure is a building sketched into the hillside, its rectilinear corner one of several instances where the drawing shows Bellini, still working in his father's shop, cautiously experimenting with the new science of perspective drawing.[42] Moreover, the sketch of the plain building, suggesting the legendary monastery, motivates the path down from the hill to the meadow.

The tawny meadow modulates into the tawny foreground in the lion's shadow, where another denizen of both meadows and Christian iconography, the rabbit, peeps out from its burrow, straight out from the picture plane to the viewer, as if surprised and immobilized by the attention. Because a rabbit is capable of conceiving a second litter while already pregnant, she was thought to achieve this feat without male assistance and thus became a symbol of the Virgin Mary (and by a syncretic route the spiritual godmother of the Easter Bunny), and more generally a symbol of the rich rewards of chastity, innocence and spring.[43] Although rabbits often appear in pictures of saints (where their significance varies), here the conventionally symbolic animal is naturalistic as well. It helps characterize a coherent, familiar landscape whose convincing verisimilitude holds a familiar story together from beginning to end as we comprehend the narrative and iconographic elements of the picture.

The point of the story, the restoration of spiritual integrity, is figured visually by the integrity of the landscape and its reassuring vegetation cycle, and intertextually by the legends and letters that constitute the verbal frame not only of the whole picture but also specifically of the distinctive scene of reading, speaking and listening that dominates the foreground as the ostensible subject matter. The scene almost audibly proclaims the salvific power of Jerome's literariness; even the lion takes notice, leaving the donkey unmolested and enjoying himself on the meadow. The foreground scene plainly depicts Jerome among cliffs and mountains where he made his oratory. The lion has been domesticated by Jerome's compassionate attention to its wound. The crag, by offering a seat and lectern, has been domesticated as well. Jerome adapts his needs to the crag, and the crag reciprocates. The sinewy contours of the rock face follow the contour of Jerome's upraised arm, even bending a bit as if it had an elbow; the same contour follows the lion's back down into the foreground separating light from shade. The compositional alignment reinforces the unified strength and heavenward direction of man, beast and mountain. Graphical alignments and thematic features such as the 'found' bench and the tame lion blur distinctions between the natural, the domesticated and the artefactual. Here Jerome and the lion share a pleasant place for spiritual nourishment that mirrors and balances the nutritional amenities enjoyed by the donkey in the meadow.

The donkey, both in legend and in this picture, behaves like a normal donkey; but Jerome's companionable lion is purely legendary, a fasting and forebearing lion more interested in Jerome's words than in the tasty prey nearby. His upraised paw, mirroring Jerome's heavenward gesture, is bloodied with a stigma-like red spot where the thorn once was; the spot, highlighted by a single bright brush-stroke indicating where the thorn had been, marks the lion as a Christ-symbol and underscores the resurrection theme. Jerome's lion frequently accompanies him in art from at least the fifteenth century, whether the saint is pictured in the wilderness or in town in his study.

Both topics, Jerome in his study and Jerome in the wilderness, dominate visual representations of Jerome. The saint is typically either in a comfortable study or in a harsh wilderness vividly emphasizing the penitent body, rather than in the more amenable wilderness depicted by Bellini and by Jerome himself in his Virgilian description of the ideal monastery.[44] It is telling that Jerome set forth his monastic *locus amoenus* in a letter sent not from any monastic establishment but from his study in Bethlehem, the site of the fictive monastery in the legend of the lion, and also the city where he lived for the last fifteen years of his life. At his final residence, the historical Jerome wrote and translated with the assistance of scribes and thanked the 'Lord that from a bitter seed of learning I am now plucking sweet fruits' (Jerome, *Letter* 125.12). His initiation in the mountains was psychologically painful; but the mountain landscape, with its rough peaks and fertile valleys, was amenable enough to sustain him materially and intellectually for five years and to yield his true vocation in town. Of any personal adventures in basket-weaving or tree-grafting Jerome tells us nothing; his study was his pleasure garden. Thus the idea of a contemplative private residence became conflated with the idea of clerical monastic retreat.

We have seen from Jerome's letters how crucial reading and writing were to his mental states, both disturbed and revived, and to both the mountains and the urban centre in which he began and ended his circuitous journey into the transformative *oros*. Of the two topics, scholarship and wilderness, 'the mature scholar at ease in his study in town, is thematically *more* prominent in *early* art than Jerome, the penitent in the wilderness'.[45] This tradition encouraged Jerome's association with the mediating discourses of Italian humanism. By the Quattrocento, representations of Jerome in his study began to be 'almost indistinguishable from the representations of the father of humanism, Petrarch.' Jerome was understood as Petrarch's 'ancient forerunner, devoting himself to philological study, to translation from Greek into Latin and to the establishment of texts'.[46] What has concerned us here is Bellini's hybrid of humanistic scholarship and mountain landscape: Jerome in a somewhat domesticated *oros* with a foreground scene of reading.

The gentler fifteenth-century Jeromes in a wilderness, inspired by Bellini's vision of a place that is at the same time *oros* and *locus amoenus*, are classically Roman in their rhetorical character: usually 'small, produced for private contemplation, [offering] sophisticated urban collectors models of thoughtful life led apart from society in an orderly bounteous suburb'. The theme, bringing 'man, animals and nature so intimately together, was favored especially in Venice', a development for which Giovanni Bellini is chiefly responsible.[47] Bellini also led the way in integrating the old medieval subject of Jerome the scholar with the newer Jerome in the wilderness, by depicting Jerome in a carefully improvised oratory in the shade with the stone lectern and bench. Bellini's integrating vision sharpened for the viewer the initiatory event of reading and contemplation in the actual Chalkidean massif, but remembered and re-imagined as the paradise of Jerome's classically-inflected writings about the right kind of solitude and how best to institutionalize it for others. Bellini's fifteenth-century Jerome inhabits mountains of cultural memory: at once symbolic and legendary, akin to the literary landscapes of both the ancient Hebrews and Romans, and immediately available to sojourners in the montane back-gardens of Italian towns.

Bellini's Francis: a gardener-saint in the mountains

Young Bellini's experiment in superposing legend, actual local topography and Jerome's epistolary descriptions of contemplative rural retirement came to fruition in his *Saint Francis in the Desert* (Fig. 6.2). The two works share 'broad aspects of theme and design and landscape', 'a peaceful pastoral countryside', 'similar wild and domesticated animals', and many of the same symbolic motifs (minus the lion).[48] Like Jerome, Francis is

Figure 6.2 Giovanni Bellini (*c.* 1430–1516), Italian. *Saint Francis in the Desert*, 1480. Tempera and oil on panel. 49 × 55 in. Copyright, The Frick Collection, New York.

portrayed voluntarily exiled in the mountains to recover or deepen his spiritual integrity. Francis, a saint and poet who unlike Jerome did not leave a rich autobiographical record, could nevertheless be imagined in the fifteenth century as kind of latter-day Jerome in studious retirement, born and bred in thirteenth-century Italy, and recapitulating in expanded form the humanistic values associated with the Jerome of tradition. Like Bellini's *Jerome*, his *Francis* presents its theme by alluding to well-known events in the saint's hagiography without unambiguously presenting any single one of them.

The location is most likely La Verna on Mount Penna in the Apennines; a geologist has attested to how accurately the rock formation is depicted.[49] Bellini's La Verna affords a more sustainably inviting *locus amoenus*, a more perfect model than Jerome's *oros* had been, of thoughtful life in a humanistic mountain landscape. At the same time, the landscape unifies a constellation of symbols rooted in the Old Testament and in what was already a rich tradition of Franciscan sources.[50] Although La Verna is associated with Saint Francis, no single real or imagined event at La Verna is unambiguously depicted in the painting. Francis in legend is marked with five stigmata, documenting him as an emblem of Jesus the man who suffered in the world we know. In the picture, the wounds are inconspicuous; at least two are missing entirely. The saint's open arms might also suggest stigmatization; but the conventional posture is kneeling, and the saint 'does not raise his arms and hands in the familiar manner'. The rest of the usual stigmatization iconography is missing, muted or transformed. Most notably the 'seraph, the central symbol of the event, fails to appear in the heavens'. Another possible occasion is suggested by the slip of paper tucked under his rope belt, as if inspired in the midst of composing the *Canticle of Brother Sun*, with its famous apostrophe to Brother Sun and Sister Moon; a persuasive reading were it not for the fact that Francis did not compose the *Canticle* there.[51] And so it is with other attempts to identify the depicted occasion. The slip of paper and the careful avoidance of a clear iconographic programme are among the features that frustrate any attempt to read the picture as any one moment in the legend of the saint.

Instead of representing one narrative moment, Bellini's intertextual layering presents the *locus amoenus* as a sacred niche in mountains that are amenable both to human artisanal intervention and to communion with the natural world. The sheltered *studiolo* maintained by its gardening resident realizes in miniature Jerome's ideal monastery. A pair of sandals casually left to the side of a bench betokens comfort in the real world as much as it alludes to Moses removing his sandals on holy ground after seeing the burning bush on the mountain at Exodus 3.5. Here, though, holy ground is the topographically accurate Mount Averna. The vines, the hedge, and the raised bed of carefully laid up stone watered with a jug from the nearby streamlet and planted with juniper, mullein and oris root, all betoken some commitment to staying awhile and to returning.

> *Saint Francis in Ecstasy* offers the most satisfying image of the saint who, more than any other, identified with the natural world. In his own poetry Francis had sung the praises of God in all his creation, detailing in his *Canticle* . . . a litany of natural forces and forms – from 'brother sun' and 'sister moon' to 'mother earth who maintains and governs us and puts forth different fruits with colored flowers and grass'.[52]

The saint's open posture, standing outside his little study with the Bible on the lectern, proclaims full receptivity to nature not as a thing apart from the divine but nature as divine revelation on a par with scripture. The painting visually realizes the *Canticle*'s 'intense feeling of solidarity between humankind and the natural order in relationship to God ... an experience of the world as a single harmonious theophany'.[53] The surrounding landscape prepares the viewer as well as Francis for 'an experience of contemplative renewal' in the world we all share: 'the landscape with its broad horizon is so perfectly adapted to accommodate the constellation of symbols, while always maintaining ... verisimilitude'.[54]

The painter's mature approach to picturing a narrative of spiritual experience is similar to the one he practised in the *Jerome*, if it is now fair to say that the intensity of Francis' nature mysticism admits of narrative treatment at all. Bellini hated stories, according to Pietro Bembo: his invention was always imaginative, 'accommodata della sua fantasia'.[55] He painted what he wished to paint, and in his own manner. He painted religious subjects when moved to do so, even when requested to do otherwise by Isabella d'Este. She once commissioned an antique fable; he remitted a Virgin and Child.[56] He did not need a religious figure as a screen or pretext for painting landscape. He needed the right saint to express his *fantasia* concerning the beauty of the world, and he needed the luminous Italian landscape to express what he wished about the character of the saint.

Bellini achieved these reciprocal goals by claiming the graphical and iconographical freedom to make light itself an actor in landscape painting. 'More than any of his Italian contemporaries, Bellini strove to recreate our visual experience of the world – the physical act of seeing – as a metaphor for our experience of the sacred'.[57] Instead, for example, of personifying divine presence as a seraph in the sky, Bellini brightens the light in the upper left into an actor whose influence seems to bend the laurel tree in the direction of Francis. Francis's gaze at the same time greets the brightening sky as if it were the person 'Sir Brother Sun, / Who is our day, ... , shining with great splendor. / From you, most high, he takes his meaning';[58] Bellini shows us the landscape as seen by Francis, a mystic in ecstatic surrender to an unseen God who is the source of natural abundance. Visual and metaphorical light – light as divinity, learning, poetical inspiration, as well as the everyday blessing of ordinary ocular light – controls both the overall mood of the painting and the viewer's visual attention to carefully drawn details that manifest divinity as natural beauty: 'here Bellini established the basic configuration of the saint in nature: his isolation and envelopment, his communing with the light, his distance from the city, the rustic bower of his cave, the stillness'.[59]

One of the strangest things about this basic configuration, so appropriate to the author of the *Canticle*, is that it did *not* establish a new mode of painting Francis '*nel deserto*' (the earliest attested reference to this painting's subject matter). Bellini's utterly fresh way of representing Francis did not gain traction until late in the sixteenth century. Only then did the idea of Francis the rural saint begin to flourish in visual art.[60] Francis, the *Canticle* notwithstanding, had neither a traditional association with classical pastoral nor a visual tradition of being depicted out-of-doors. Instead, it was Jerome's life, wilderness legend, and Virgilian celebration of rural life that encouraged re-visioning *him* as the classical/Christian mediator with 'a natural home in the landscape'. Venetian artists, 'by locating [Jerome] in a more familiar and accessible setting ... not only domesticated that wilderness but thereby reaffirmed its pastoral situation'.[61]

The *Saint Francis*, 'the absolute masterpiece of devotional painting in the second half of the fifteenth century',[62] displays the fourteenth- and fifteenth-century Italian fusion of Christian and pagan discourse in its full rhetorical radiance. The saint's study, now fashioned as a *locus amoenus* far more comfortably domesticated than Jerome's improvisational oratory in the mountains, is the abode of Francis the monk and poet. The scene could well have illustrated Boccaccio's 1388 humanistic defence of the divine collaboration of poetry and mountains, *Genealogia Deorum Gentilium*: 'Poetry, ... while she dwells in heaven ... moves the minds of a few ... to a yearning for the eternal, lifting them by her loveliness'; she draws those few minds 'into pouring forth most exquisite discourse from her exalted mind'. When poetic Muses descend to perform their sacred ministry, a montane *locus amoenus* is their haunt: if Poetry 'leave her lofty throne, and descend to earth with her ... sacred Muses, she never seeks a habitation in the towering palaces of kings or the easy abodes of the luxurious; rather she visits caves on the steep mountainside, or shady groves, or argent springs, where are the retreats of the studious'. Poets are drawn to the mountains, continues Boccaccio in a Trecento ekphrasis of mountain glory: mountains are 'the region of stars, among the divinely adorned dwellings of the gods and their heavenly splendors' (Boccaccio, *Genealogia Deorum Gentilium* 14.4).[63] The heavenly splendour of mountain solitude attracts not only inspired poets but 'Paul the Hermit ... and many other reverend and holy men' who created the poetry of the Bible (14.11).[64] Jerome himself was the standard Renaissance authority for defending the Bible as poetry.[65]

Boccaccio's montane *locus amoenus*, where the gods dwell and the studious find refuge, is amenable to those with pure and simple material needs. It is the sort of Virgilian retreat that the rhetorically-trained Jerome imagined for himself and Marcella, and that he later modulated into the ideal monastery landscape. In Boccaccio's words: 'There the beeches stretch themselves, with other trees, toward heaven; there they spread a thick shade with their fresh green foliage ... there, too, are clear fountains and argent brooks ... and there the flocks and herds, the shepherd's cottage or the little hut untroubled with domestic cares; and all is filled with peace and quiet'; natural pleasures 'soothe the soul; then they collect the scattered energies of the mind' (14.11).[66] Boccaccio's divine mountains and Bellini's Franciscan *locus amoenus* embraced Jerome's biblical and classical *oros*, and integrated the symbolically productive qualities of both into the Italian mountains of their own experience.

Conclusion

The cultural memory of ancient mountains is available to us through the words and artefacts that depict them, but only inasmuch as we can decipher their manifold meanings. It is inadequate, as Buxton has shown, to look up Greek *oros* in a dictionary and translate it as the 'mountain' of current usage, if we wish to see the symbolically productive characteristics of the Greek *oros*. While English *mountain* does not function as *oros*, the *oros* as generally understood by the Greeks has flourished as a type of cultural landscape under many different names, as has been shown in this study of Jerome and Francis.

Oros enfolds an ancient understanding of mountains as liminal spaces that mediate between opposing forces: civilization and barbarism, culture and nature, the familiar and the alien, the human and the divine, the past and the present; and later, the Christian and the pagan. This mediating quality is prominent in the lives and legends of Saint Jerome and Saint Francis, whose mountain sojourns forged for Christianizing Europe new and enduring connections among such disparate and contending forces. The cultural integration that began to be achieved as early as Jerome's fourth-century scholarship was recognizably modern, humanistic, and grounded as much in Jerome's lived experience in actual mountains as in biblical landscape and the ineradicable memory of Virgil's mountains.

When Jerome, an erudite Roman, retreated for five years to the Chalkidean massif, he began to master Hebrew and, as attested by his letters, brought the imagined Virgilian past into geographical and cultural intersection with the biblical wilderness nearby and with Roman reflections on the restorative spiritual value of erudite rural retirement. A millennium later, Giovanni Bellini depicted both Jerome and Francis (as a latter-day Jerome) in contemporaneous Italian mountains, and in a way that aligned not only with art and documents available to Bellini but with the mediating character of the ancient *oros*. Thus Bellini visibly realized his own familiar mountain landscapes, not distant ones, as articulate vehicles for spiritual meaning, cultural memory, humanistic integration and the restoration of spiritual integrity.

Bellini's mountains, like the *oros* of ancient Greek cultural imagination, remained a liminal place for temporary fugitives from the city. Mountains are 'before', a place where, as in Eden, the original harmony among humans, divinity and the natural world could be found; or where, in the particular case of Jerome, the Hebraic foundation of Christianity could be fully encountered in its original articulation. Mountains are a place for reversals and epiphanies, as experienced in Jerome's perceptual transformation of prison into paradise; or a place where Christian and pagan divinity can become one, as they do in Francis's vision of Brother Sun illuminating a *locus amoenus*. The humanistic phenomena examined in this chapter served the imaginative needs of an increasingly complex civilization that, unlike that of the Greeks, attempted to embrace only one sacralized text as replete with knowledge of what has been and what is to come. For Europe was and remains inextricably bound to classical texts asserting their own powerful claims to canonical status, and to an ancient idea of mountains as liminal places where opposing forces are mediated and a new integration is forged.[67]

The story of erudite retreat, integration, and return to civilization traced in this chapter is but one example of how Buxton's method in glossing *oros* may be fruitfully generalized to other European mountains and still more generally to other symbolically productive landscapes that sometimes surprisingly turn out to be *oros* by another name.

Notes

1. Buxton 1992: 2.
2. For cultural memory, see the introduction to this volume, note 26.
3. Buxton 1992: 7–9.
4. Clark [1949] 1979: 5.
5. Ibid. 3.
6. Translation from Russell 1997: 13–14. For a verse translation from the Syriac, see Brock (1990).
7. Andrews 1999: 32.
8. Wright 1933: vii.
9. Translation from Fremantle 1980: 35.
10. Ibid. xvii.
11. Ibid. 274, n. 4; 448, n. 2.
12. For mountains in tragedy, and the relationship between city and wilderness, see Bray in this volume.
13. Beekes 2010: s.v. 'erēmos'.
14. *Oxford Latin Dictionary*: s.v. 'solitudo'.
15. *Oxford English Dictionary*: s.v. 'massif'.
16. Kelly 1975: 26–7.
17. The addressee may have been the Theodosius who resided in a different anchorite establishment, where Jerome may have stopped on his way to Evagrius: Kelly 1975: 41, n. 26.
18. Translation from Fremantle 1980: 4.
19. Highet 1985: 72.
20. Jerome, *Letter* 17, with translation in Fremantle 1980: 20–1.
21. For Greek examples, see Buxton 1992: 12.
22. Wright 1933: viii–xi; xviii.
23. Fremantle 1980: xviii.
24. In 410 Marcella's palace was sacked. She was eighty-five and did not survive the year: Wright 1933: x.
25. Wright 1933: 411; Fremantle 1980: 247.
26. Jerome quotes Virgil, *Georgics* 1.108-10.
27. Hardison and Behler 1993: 1294.
28. Curtius 1983: 195–200.
29. Russell 1997: 13.
30. Ibid. 14.
31. Rosand 1992: 161–3.
32. Lillie 2007: 32.
33. Andrews 1999: 33.
34. Buxton 1992: 7, 9.
35. Lillie 2007: 35.

36. Buxton 1992: 7.
37. On the 'verbal frame' as 'all the discourse surrounding a work of art', including the title, museum labels and writings about the subject matter and artist's motivation, see Sayre 2009: 64–9.
38. Hall 1974: 193. In art, an attribute is a 'symbolic or decorative object conventionally associated with a given individual or activity'. Animal attributes are common: Juno's peacock, Poseidon's bull, Athena's owl, the Nemean lion of Hercules. *Concise Oxford Dictionary of Art Terms* (Clarke 2010): s.v. 'attribute'.
39. de Voragine 2012 (tr. Ryan): 599–601.
40. Goffen 1989: 4.
41. Andrews 1999: 36.
42. Goffen 1989: 4.
43. Lagomorphs have two uteri. Pliny the Elder (*Natural History* 8.81.218–19) considered hares capable of hermaphroditism, whence chaste conception.
44. Meiss 1974: 134.
45. Ibid. 134.
46. Ibid. 134. On Petrarch as the supposed paternal figure not just of humanism but modernity, see Hansen's chapter in this volume, 215–16.
47. Ibid. 19–20.
48. Ibid. 20–2.
49. Ibid. 22.
50. Gentili 2004: 172.
51. Meiss 1964: 21.
52. Rosand 1988: 64.
53. Moloney 2013: 83.
54. Gentili 2004: 173. The complexity has inspired much commentary: for a bibliography see Rutherglen and Hale 2015.
55. Letter from Bembo to Isabella d'Este, 11 January 1506, quoted in Meiss 1964: 34. For English translation, see d'Este 2018: 151.
56. For Bellini's fraught relationship with Isabella, see Bätschmann 2008: 102–5.
57. Goffen 1989: 107.
58. Translation from Moloney 2013: xxiii.
59. Rosand 1988: 64.
60. Meiss 1964: 21.
61. Rosand 1988: 65–6.
62. Gentili 2004: 172.
63. Translation from Osgood 1930: 24–5.
64. Ibid. 56.
65. Ibid. 149, n. 10.
66. Ibid. 56–7.
67. For mountains as sites for intertwined cultural perceptions, see König in this volume. For integrating Christian and pagan traditions, see Whalin. For Monticello as a site for constructing American identity from ancient and contemporaneous materials, see Jordan.

CHAPTER 7
SUBLIME VISIONS OF VIRGINIA: THOMAS JEFFERSON'S ROMANTIC MOUNTAINSCAPES
Alley Marie Jordan

Introduction

Before and after the American Revolution of 1776, Thomas Jefferson, plantation owner, co-author of the Declaration of Independence and later third President of the United States, curated the mountainous Virginia landscape in his classical imagination. Jefferson's experiences with mountains extended primarily to the hills of his native Virginia, especially the plantation atop his 'little mountain', Monticello in Albemarle County, and the famous 'Natural Bridge' rock formation in Rockbridge County. Jefferson's treatment of those places reveals an American searching for an ancestral identity amongst fluctuating politics and ideologies. Jefferson's classical identity manifested itself not just in his attitude to mountains, however, but also in his philosophy. Jefferson drew on Epicurean ideas, through Horace, Lucretius and Virgil, as a language and philosophy through which to articulate his classical imagination of Monticello. Jefferson first documented his fascination with Epicureanism in 1799; it lasted until his death in 1826. Epicureanism was, above all, concerned with the pursuit of happiness, as was Jefferson atop his mountain. According to William Temple in his 1731 *Upon the Gardens of Epicurus*, a copy of which Jefferson owned, all ancient philosophers agreed 'that happiness was the chief good, and ought to be the ultimate end of man; that as this was the end of wisdom, so wisdom was the way to happiness'.[1] In line with that opinion, Jefferson was chiefly concerned with achieving happiness through learning, especially through classical learning. Thus, the idea of his mountain was as an Epicurean oasis – a place of learning, retirement and nature.

Despite Virginia's transition from a colony to a state, Jefferson's transition from a local lawyer to a Founder, and the United States' transition from a small republic to an expanding empire, Jefferson's classicizing vision of the Virginian landscape remained remarkably stable, as did his Epicureanism. He drew heavily on Roman poets such as Lucretius, Horace, Virgil and Statius. Jefferson's classical education, interests and substantial library of classical texts were far from unique among the Virginia gentry.[2] However, Jefferson's use of the classical heritage was in some respects very distinctive, not least in the way he used it to construct a particularly American image of Virginia's landscape.

The aim of this chapter is to draw attention to two specific aspects of that engagement. The first is the way in which Jefferson aligned his experience of Monticello with classical images of mountains and of the countryside more generally as places of retreat, and with the Epicurean goals of tranquillity alongside retirement. The second goal is to elucidate the ways in which Jefferson infused America's sublime natural monuments with imagery drawn from the English picturesque, which was itself indebted to classical traditions, such as the pastoralism of Virgil and Theocritus before him.[3]

Monticello as an Epicurean retreat

As a young man during 1771, Jefferson wrote to his future brother-in-law, Robert Skipwith, inviting him to his mountaintop under construction:[4]

> Come to the new Rowanty, from which you may reach your hand to a library formed on a more extensive plan ... A spring, centrally situated, might be the scene of every evening's joy. There we should talk over the lessons of the day, or lose them in Musick, Chess, or the merriments of our family companions. The heart thus lightened, our pillows would be soft, and health and long life would attend the happy scene.[5]

Jefferson wrote of Monticello as the 'new Rowanty', likely a reference to the ancient Assyrian area of Rowandiz. A century or so later, the Oxford Assyriologist, Archibald Henry Sayce, wrote that the ancient mountainous region 'Rowandiz seems also to have been regarded in Accadian mythology as the Olympos on which the gods dwelt.'[6] According to Sayce, mythical Rowandiz represented the spiritual mountain of the gods. Jefferson's reference to 'Rowanty', in preference to the better-known Mount Olympus of Greek myth, illustrates not only his learned eclecticism, but his direct identification of his mountain as classical and ancient.

At the same time, Jefferson extends his description of Monticello by giving it a Graeco-Roman character. In the detail of a 'spring, centrally situated', he highlights one of the defining features of the *locus amoenus* ('pleasant place') motif in ancient poetry.[7] The picture Jefferson paints of Monticello stems from one of his favourite Roman poets, Horace. In his *Commonplace Book*, which he began during his boyhood years in the 1750s, Jefferson inscribed a passage evoking the idealized image of a rural retreat from Horace's *Satires* 2.6.60-2: 'O rural home: when shall I behold you! When shall I be able, now with books of the ancients, now with sleep and idle hours, to quaff sweet forgetfulness of life's cares!' (*O rus quando ego te aspiciam? quando licebit / Nunc veterum libris, nunc somno et inertibus horis / Ducere sollicitae jucunda oblivia vitae?*)[8] Already as a schoolboy during the 1750s, Jefferson's typical eighteenth-century classical education primed him for a lifelong quest to seek and establish his own *locus amoenus* in Virginia. Jefferson's adult libraries contained four copies of Theocritus' *Idylls* in Latin and Greek; twelve copies of Virgil's complete works in various languages; eight editions of Horace's works; and many more modern writers who were inspired by these classical authors, such as Alexander Pope.[9] The *locus amoenus* motif features prominently in all of these authors. It was not commonplace in ancient Greek or Roman literature to locate *locus amoenus* scenes on mountains, but as both Douglas Whalin and Janice Hewlett Koelb show elsewhere in this volume, there are many examples from late antiquity and from the Renaissance, with Jefferson following in this tradition. The *locus amoenus* was also an important reference-point for gardeners and landscape designers during Jefferson's lifetime, particularly in England.[10] By grafting these traditions onto their own landscapes, these eighteenth-century authors and designers appropriated classical ways of thinking about space for their own purposes.[11] Jefferson in particular transformed Horace's *locus amoenus* from poetry to landscape.

As he constructed his home at the age of twenty-eight, Jefferson's mountain mindscape reflected a range of imaginative traditions. He was influenced by images of the spiritual mountains of antiquity in depicting it as a place close to the gods with a view of the world below. He was also influenced by the pastoral world-making of the classical poets. As Horace created his own *locus amoenus*, the Sabine Farm (more on that below), as both a real and an imagined place, Jefferson did the same at Monticello, infusing it with mythical and pastoral motifs. Jefferson's eighteenth-century manipulation of the mountain at Monticello illustrates his own distinctive ways of imagining the classical past, recast on the American landscape.

Jefferson romanticized his mountains especially when absent from them. While serving as the American Ambassador to France from 1784–9, Jefferson longed for the mountains of Virginia. Writing to his love interest, Maria Cosway, on 12 October 1786 (in an Epicurean letter called the 'Head and Heart Dialogue'), Jefferson tried to persuade the artist to accompany him to his beloved native landscape.[12] From 'The Falling spring, the Cascade of Niagara, the Passage of the Potowmac thro [sic] the Blue mountains, [and to] the Natural bridge', Jefferson painted for Cosway his picturesque native land, and attempted to encourage her to come to Virginia.[13] He continued:

> It is worth a voiage [sic] across the Atlantic to see these objects; much more to paint, and make them, and thereby ourselves, known to all ages. And our own dear Monticello, where has nature spread so rich a mantle under the eye? mountains, forests, rocks, rivers. With what majesty do we there ride above the storms! How sublime to look down into the workhouse of nature, to see her clouds, hail, snow, rain, thunder, all fabricated at our feet! And the glorious Sun, when rising as if out of a distant water, just gilding the tops of the mountains, and giving life to all nature![14]

Jefferson's perspective is like that of a god viewing nature from on high: 'we there ride *above* the storms'; he looked '*down* into the workhouse of nature'; and his view saw where nature had 'spread so rich a mantle *under* the eye'.[15] Jefferson's sublime view is depicted as the work of Nature herself – she produces this pleasant place for Jefferson to till and admire.

Jefferson did not reserve his sublime mountain visions solely to Virginia. A year later during 1787, Jefferson crossed the Alps from France into Italy. He imagined the possibility of following Hannibal's route through the mountains during 218 BCE, as described by

Livy, (*History of Rome* 21 30.7-8) and Polybius. Jefferson wrote from France to his mentor and fellow classicist, George Wythe, about his ancient quest:

> In the latter country my time allowed me to go no further than Turin, Milan, and Genoa; consequently I scarcely got into classical ground. I took with me some of the writings in which endeavors have been made to investigate the passage of Annibal [*sic*] over the Alps, and was just able to satisfy myself, from a view of the country, that the descriptions given of his march are not sufficiently particular to enable us at this day even to guess at his tract across the Alps.[16]

Partially frustrated in his search for 'classical ground',[17] Jefferson nevertheless succeeded in casting himself as an investigator and classicist during his journey, eager to retrace and reconstruct the experiences Livy described in his *History*.

A decade later in Virginia, Jefferson continued to try and persuade his European friends to visit his mountain region. During the spring of 1796, Jefferson wrote to the Comte de Volney on the 'groves of poplars, towering mountains, rocks and rivers, blue skies balsamic air yet pure and healthy' of his landscape.[18] Nearly exactly a year later, Jefferson further expressed his sentiments on the paradise of his mountains to Volney: 'Indeed my experience of the different parts of America convinces me that these mountains are the Eden of the US.'[19] In these attempts to convince his friends to visit Virginia, Jefferson continued to represent the landscape as his personal *locus amoenus*, albeit in this instance one expressed not through classical references but rather through the language of the Old Testament.

Years later during 1809, Margaret Bayard Smith – friend of the retired president and chronicler of early America – recollected her first impressions of Jefferson's Monticello. Her reflections illuminated Jefferson's lifelong plan of his personalized *agrotopia*. After calling the Rivanna river 'wild & romantic', Smith characterized Jefferson's land as an 'undisturbed dominion'.[20] Her first recorded impression upon reaching the summit of Monticello was of a 'sublime scenery'.[21] Beyond the wild forests, gardens, Mulberry Row and the villa itself, 'arose the blue mountains, in all their grandeur', which, from the height of Monticello, resembled endless blue waters. Smith's experience of Monticello as commanding 'one of the most extensive views [of] any spot of the globe' resembled Jefferson's own 1771 description of the panoramic views and of Monticello as 'Rowanty', which resembled 'the mountain of the world'.[22]

Seven years later during 1816, Richard Rush, the son of the renowned doctor Benjamin Rush, visited Jefferson's classical mountain: 'If it had not been called Monticello, I would call it Olympus, and Jove its occupant . . . Now, figure to yourself . . . that house, thus as it were in the sky, decked off with art and wealth, and you have Monticello'. Once again, Greek classicism was conflated with other traditions, as Rush concluded that 'his mountain is made a sort of Mecca'.[23] Inside, Jefferson furthered this syncretism, decorating his villa with marble busts of the American founders and paintings of his favourite philosophers and even included Native American artefacts and objects of his own invention in the foyer. Rush positioned Monticello up in Elysium, aligning Jefferson with

Jove, overseeing the world (and plantation) from its summit. Jefferson impressed Rush with his architectural wonder atop the mountain, and his nearly godlike ability to build it. These impressions from Jefferson's visitors later in his life tend to emphasize the kind of links between mountains and divine viewpoint which were prominent in classical literature, as well as elsewhere.[24]

Years earlier during the winter of 1783, Jefferson wrote to his friend, Eliza House Trist, about his mountain seat. From Annapolis, Maryland, Jefferson composed his letter: 'I have now in my eye a mountain where nothing but the eagle can visit you which I think would suit your present taste for retirement. It looks down on mine as a giant does on a dwarf'.[25] Importantly, Jefferson regarded his mountains as suitable places for retirement because of their panoramic, sublime views. There is a precedent for that view in the opening section of Lucretius, *De Rerum Natura* 2.7-10: 'nothing is more delightful than to possess lofty sanctuaries serene, well-fortified by the teachings of the wise, whence you may look down upon others and behold them all astray, wandering abroad and seeking the path of life'. In much the same way, the tranquillity of Jefferson's mountaintop provided an Epicurean freedom from public affairs (which he valued during his retirement and frequently wrote about in his letters), and the pleasure of private contemplation from on top and within his *locus amoenus*.

Jefferson believed that yeomanry, of the kind praised by Horace in the description of his Sabine Farm in *Satires* 2.6,[26] was the only suitable lifestyle for a virtuous American. He also connected his emulation of Epicurean lifestyle to the rugged landscape through his political philosophy: agrarian republicanism.[27] Jefferson regarded the American landscape in light of the Augustans' *novus ordo seclorum*, his new order of the ages.[28] Jefferson believed that cultivators of the earth 'are the most virtuous and independent citizens' because they do not compromise their values (autonomy, integrity) for economic profit.[29] For Jefferson, the precise type of rural landscape suitable for a virtuous American, whether that be a garden, farm or mountain, did not matter.[30] So long as his fellow citizens cultivated the soil, they cultivated their virtue. Jefferson's native Virginia mountains provided him the ideal landscape for cultivating virtue. Up on his mountains, Jefferson designed his natural world: plantation, gardens, farms and vineyard. Aligning the Virginia landscape with classical motifs gave him a sense of cultural and ancestral legitimacy for his identity as a learned, wealthy planter and a member of the Virginia gentry.

Jefferson's love for his native mountains fused with his sense of American identity. Writing from France during 1785, for example, Jefferson called himself a 'savage of the mountains of America' in a letter to Charles Bellini.[31] Jefferson frequently called himself a mountain-man throughout his lifetime as he leisured in his villas, Poplar Forest and Monticello, desiring to be free from travel and politics. However, these places of American identity were also profoundly marked by classicizing influences. Jefferson designed his Palladian (and thus Vitruvian) villas especially for tranquil retirement. In Bedford County, westward from his great plantation villa, Monticello, Jefferson constructed a quaint, octagonal villa close to the western mountains, intended as a retreat from the public sphere. Jefferson even designed Poplar Forest's bowling green in the Roman rectangular style, while the front lawn included Lancelot 'Capability' Brown's famous 'clumps' of trees. Jefferson seems to have envisaged a strong connection between the Classics and gardening, having gone on a garden tour during 1784, visiting classically-inspired gardens like Stowe and the Leasowes. Moreover, he kept Thomas Whately's *Observations on Modern Gardening* as his guidebook, which was itself full of classical quotations by Virgil and Horace.

The dining room of Poplar Forest resembled a classical temple. In the central room, he designed the white Doric entablature in the style of Diocletian's baths. Jefferson then used the temple of Fortuna Virilis as inspiration for his parlour.[32] While Jefferson designed the octagonal villa in the Palladian style reminiscent of the Lateran Baptistery in Rome, he used bricks made of Virginia red clay for the material for the house itself, rather than adhering to typical Palladian materials. Jefferson thus fused his Roman design motifs with natural materials found in his native Virginia. Importantly, Poplar Forest existed for Jefferson primarily as an idealized sanctuary for retirement and retreat, not function, which can be seen in his eclectic design of the villa.

During his retirement after 1809, Jefferson expressed classical (particularly pastoral and Epicurean) sentiments more frequently than at any other time in his life. He increasingly valued the private life of Epicureanism over the public life required for civic duty. In 1812, for example, Jefferson wrote: 'on the political events of the day I have nothing to communicate. I have retired from them, and given up newspapers for more classical reading'.[33] Such sentiments stemmed from the philhellenic Roman poets, and from ancient Epicurean thinking, which valued retiring from public life and the city, and living a life in the natural landscape amongst family and friends. An example of the kind of verse texts that influenced Jefferson can be found in Statius' description of the villa of Pollius Felix at Sorrento: 'free of cares as you are, mind composed in tranquil virtue, ever master of yourself? Why should I rehearse the thousand rooftops and the changing views? Every room has its own delight' (Statius, *Silvae* 2.2.71-3). Like Jefferson, Statius' villa patrons pursued *otium* ('leisure') in direct contrast to political life in Rome. As President in 1804, Jefferson felt the pull of *otium* very strongly:

> I sincerely regret that the unbounded calumnies of the Federal party have obliged me to throw myself on the verdict of my country for trial, my great desire having been to retire at the end of the present term to a life of tranquility [*sic*], and it was my decided purpose when I entered into office. they force my continuance. if we can keep the vessel of state as steady in her course for another 4. years, my earthly purposes will be accomplished, and I shall be free to enjoy … my family, my farm, & my books.[34]

In retirement he continued to write in similar terms. 'Tranquillity', wrote Jefferson, 'is the summum bonum of that age. I wish now for quiet, to withdraw from the broils of the world, to soothe enmities and to die in the peace and good will of all mankind'.[35] Jefferson received his retirement like an old friend. For the Epicurean, the pastoral villa life was an ideal setting in which to live without stress or discomfort.

It was also important to Jefferson that his retirement should be among the mountains. During 1814, Jefferson told Thomas Clark: 'I live among the mountains'.[36] In the summer of 1821, Jefferson wrote to President James Monroe: 'retired, as I am, among the mountains of our interior country, I see nobody but the farmers of my neighbourhood'.[37] He also wrote to the French revolutionary, the Marquis de Lafayette, in the autumn of 1822: 'on our affairs little can be expected from an Octogenary, retired within the recesses of the mountains, going nowhere, seeing nobody but in his own house, & reading a single newspaper only, & that chiefly for the sake of the advertisements'.[38] And again a month later to William Annesley, Jefferson wrote that he was 'born & bred among the mountains'.[39] As he aged, Jefferson expressed a greater connection to his mountainous landscape than he had ever done before.

In an 1809 letter to Jefferson, Philip Freneau, poet and friend of Jefferson, composed a lengthy poem on Jefferson and his retirement from the presidency. Besides beginning the poem with a line from Horace's *Epistles* 2.1.15 – *Præsenti tibi maturos largimur honores* ('Upon you, while still among us, we bestow premature honours') – Freneau envisioned Jefferson as he envisioned himself, as an Epicurean gardener. Freneau wrote:

All this you braved – and now, what task remains,
But silent walks on solitary plains:
To bid the vast luxuriant harvest grow,
The slave be happy and secured from woe
[...]
Whether, with NEWTON, you the heavens explore,
And trace through Nature the creating power.

Freneau envisioned Jefferson retiring to his landscapes, indulging in the *otium* of his pastoral villas and engaging in the natural sciences, which included both cosmological queries and gardening.[40] Moreover, Freneau's inclusion of Jefferson's favourite Roman poet, Horace, fits well with Jefferson's Epicurean vision of himself, most importantly because Horace also wrote about retirement in the country in order to avoid the public affairs of the city. A year into his retirement, Jefferson wrote to Charles Holt, expressing his connection between himself and Horace: 'but I wish at length to indulge myself in more favorite reading, in Tacitus & Horace, and the writers of that philosophy which is the old man's consolation & preparation for what is to come'.[41] As he attempted to remove himself from the public and immerse himself in classical reading atop his mountain, Jefferson sought the solitude of his villas' libraries. Jefferson longed for rest and welcomed death as he aged into the nineteenth century: 'and when that is done, you and I may retire to the tranquillity which our years begin to call for, and reprise with satisfaction the efforts of the age we happened to be born in, crowned with compleat [*sic*] success'.[42]

For the Roman writers who influenced Jefferson, the visual pleasures of the place of retirement were an important source of happiness. Jefferson's tendency to describe his native mountainous Virginia through visual language, which we have observed already, was in line with that tradition. In his 1787 *Notes on the State of Virginia*, he described the mountains of Virginia's Shenandoah Valley as a painting, calling the landscape a 'picture' upon which nature gave a 'distant finishing'.[43] He called the view 'placid and delightful', and 'wild and tremendous' after contrasting the background of the Shenandoah Valley with its 'foreground', using terms of modern art critique. 'For the mountain being cloven asunder', he continued, 'she presents to your eye, through the cleft, a small patch of smooth blue horizon … Here the eye ultimately composes itself … This scene is worth a voyage across the Atlantic'.[44] With the *Notes*, Jefferson as viewer and critic envisioned his mountainscape through the modern artistic lens, perceiving nature as designed through repeated use of words like 'picture', 'foreground', 'scene' and mentions of 'the eye'. He viewed nature, and indeed his own backyard, as an artist viewed a painting. Moreover, as Jefferson levelled his mountaintop and 'cut out the superabundant plants', he in effect cast himself as the artist and curator of the Virginia landscape.[45]

The Natural Bridge and Jefferson's mountain aesthetics

A consideration of the importance of the visual in Jefferson's representation of retirement raises questions about the aesthetic categories Jefferson used in his representations of mountain scenery. Reaching 65.5 metres high in solid grey limestone, the Natural Bridge in Rockbridge County, Virginia, which now belongs to the State of Virginia, once belonged to Jefferson himself. He began his inquiry into purchasing the Natural Bridge during 1773, and he received ownership of the rock bridge the next year. Jefferson wrote his observations and recollections of the Natural Bridge largely in the language of the sublime. In his only book, the *Notes on the State of Virginia* (1787), Jefferson wrote that the Natural Bridge is 'the most sublime of nature's works'.[46] Jefferson experienced a sublime moment atop the rocky structure: as he walked along the edge of its rocky cliff with the wind rushing past his face and pushing him off balance, Jefferson experienced vertigo from on-high, feeling the force of gravity. Such an experience was similar to what Alain Corbin called the 'emotions in the soul that create sublime moments'.[47] Corbin suggests that 'the sight of the incommensurable forces man to experience his finite nature; it arouses passions in his soul in which the aesthetics of the sublime take root'.[48] Jefferson himself recorded that kind of experience in the *Notes*:

> Though the sides of this bridge are provided in some parts with a parapet of fixed rocks, yet few men have resolution to walk to them, and look over into the abyss. You involuntarily fall on your hands and feet, and creep to the parapet, and peep over it. Looking down from this height about a minute, gave me a violent headache. If the view from the top be painful and intolerable, that from below is delightful in an equal extreme. It is impossible for the emotions arising from the sublime to be felt beyond what they are here; so beautiful and arch, so elevated, so light, and springing as it were up to heaven! The rapture of the spectator is really indescribable![49]

For Jefferson, the sublime was an emotional experience, something to be felt, not merely understood. Atop this vertiginous rocky arch, Jefferson's nature shock threw him into an experience both frightening and heavenly. The combination of the sublime with feelings of fear in that passage are characteristic of depictions of the natural sublime in other eighteenth-century writing too.

Jefferson's engagement with classical literature, however, complicates the 'modernness' of his engagement with landscape. His juxtaposition of classical references with aesthetic vocabulary that was newly in vogue during his lifetime is a good example of Jefferson's attempt to bridge between ancient and modern ways of experiencing mountains.[50] Jefferson's familiarity with the sublime extended both to England and the classical world. Jefferson's English source for the sublime is likely to have been Edmund Burke's *A Philosophical Enquiry into the Origin of Our Ideas of the Sublime and Beautiful* (1757), a copy of which Jefferson owned.[51] But he was also directly familiar with Longinus' *On the Sublime*, and was more-than-familiar with Lucretius' *On the Nature of Things*, an important text for him given his interest in Epicureanism.[52]

The importance of Lucretius as a forerunner is apparent in the way in which the view from Monticello over the Blue Ridge Mountains was compared by Jefferson with a view over water, and more specifically with a view over the sea by many visitors to the site. There are some striking classical parallels. The site of Tiberius' villa at Sperlonga included a natural grotto within the rough coastline: such a perilous place provided Epicurean tranquillity and contemplation paired with the sublime terror of the ever-changing sea. The apparent irony of a *locus amoenus* paired with the terror of the sublime is characteristically classical, especially Epicurean. In *De Rerum Natura* 2.1-19, for example, Lucretius described the pleasure to be gained from a terrifying sight: the wild tempest out at sea.[53] Such a sublime place leads to contemplation and recognition of *ataraxia* for the Epicurean.[54] Notwithstanding his political attitudes toward nature, i.e. his agrarian republicanism,[55] Jefferson believed, as a self-proclaimed Epicurean,[56] that true human happiness could be found most effectively in communion with the natural world, amongst one's native landscape, especially in contrast to industrialization and city-life.

Nor was it just the villa landscape of Monticello that was associated with contemplation and Epicurean retreat: those associations came to be applied even to the sublime terrain of the Natural Bridge. A year before the publication of the *Notes*, Jefferson wrote to William Carmichael: 'You will find in them that the Natural bridge had found an admirer in me also … I sometimes think of building a little hermitage at the Natural bridge'.[57] Jefferson's vision of building a place of contemplation on a mountaintop followed him during his European adventures. In his 'Hints to Americans Travelling in Europe' of 1788, Jefferson suggested that his fellow American travellers to France should explore mountain hermitages themselves: 'On the hill impending over this village is made the wine called Hermitage, so justly celebrated. Go up to the hermitage on the top of the hill, for the sake of the sublime prospect from thence'.[58] Earlier during his travels through the French countryside in 1786, Jefferson himself frequented a mountain hermitage. His daughter, Martha, later recalled that her father 'was in the habit of taking his papers and going to the hermitage, where he spent sometimes a week or more till he had finished his work'.[59]

Whether in the guise of a Catholic hermitage or a Roman villa, Jefferson often explored mountaintops as places of contemplation and learning.

Jefferson also saw the landscapes of Virginia as representative of distinctively American aesthetic characteristics. Back in the United States in 1791, for example, Jefferson wrote to the American artist John Trumbull on the picturesque characteristics of the Natural Bridge. Jefferson was particularly keen to have an American artist represent the sublime structure because he regarded the Natural Bridge as uniquely American – an American version of Europe's ancient monuments. Jefferson wrote:

> There I hope it will meet you in good health, and resolved to return by the way of the Natural bridge. Remember you will never be so near it again, and take to yourself and your country the honor of presenting to the world this singular landscape, which otherwise some bungling European will misrepresent.[60]

Jefferson treated the Natural Bridge as a national monument. Only an American, who was by nature hardy, rustic and who thrived in the wild New World, could depict it with any real likeness. Jefferson's vision of landscape and American identity was connected with his interest in promoting a new form of classically-inspired architecture. One hint of this can be seen in a letter that Jefferson composed in 1809 in which he similarly encouraged the British-born architect, Benjamin Henry Latrobe to sketch Monticello. Jefferson equated the achievements of nature at Monticello with the classical architecture of the Capitol:

> but what nature has done for us is sublime & beautiful and unique. you could not fail to take out your pencil & to add another specimen of it's [sic] excellence in landscape to your drawing of the Capitol & Capitol hill.[61]

Jefferson in fact spent decades attempting to generate a unique, classically-influenced style of American art and architecture, known as 'republican art'. He even encouraged the Virginia Legislature to design the new state capitol in Richmond after the Roman temple, the Maison Carrée. In 1785, Jefferson wrote a vehement plea from Paris to James Madison in an attempt to persuade the statesman to propose a classical design for the Virginia State Capitol:

> We took for our model what is called the Maison quarree [sic] of Nismes, one of the most beautiful, if not the most beautiful and precious morsel of architecture left us by antiquity ... It is very simple, but it is noble beyond expression, and would have done honor to our country, as presenting to travellers a specimen of taste in our infancy, promising much for our maturer age.[62]

Jefferson also wrote a nearly identical letter to Edmund Randolph on the same day. In the letter to Madison, Jefferson made no explicit mention of republicanism and the republican models of antiquity, but this does not mean that the letter was not inherently political. Instead, Jefferson highlighted the virtues of beauty as a stronghold for the United States' reputation on the world stage. Jefferson observed that the United States' lack of historical beauty within the greater context of the enlightened eighteenth century was almost laughable, as the United States began to compete for prominence alongside the greater powers like England and France. Despite their corrupt regimes, the European powers nonetheless possessed a political and cultural legitimacy that would ensure their longevity in a way that the United States could not. Jefferson wanted American architecture to emulate that of the Europeans because he saw the United States as the *novus ordo seclorum* for its political and cultural history. Jefferson tried to develop a style of American architecture in order to showcase America's greatness to the world by emulating the architecture of antiquity. For Jefferson, the federal and, worse, colonial architectural styles were poor imitations of the Italianate and Georgian styles. As he put it in his *Notes on the State of Virginia*, colonial architecture was 'rarely constructed of stone or brick; much the greatest proportion being of scantling and boards, plastered with lime. It is impossible to devise things more ugly, uncomfortable and happily more perishable'.[63] Americans lacked artistic and historic inspiration for their architecture, especially because of the materials used. Given the United States' infancy, Jefferson saw the period after the Revolution as an opportunity for the American landscape to emulate the grandeur of Europe's classical architecture, though without the corrupted governments. For Jefferson, America's natural monuments (mountains), coupled with its national monuments (classical architecture), provided the key to America's entrée on the world stage. With the beginning of the nineteenth century came a new opportunity for America to generate its own aesthetic reputation through its wild nature. Jefferson's interest in classical styles of architecture paralleled his interest in classical styles of engagement with landscape.

Garden design was an important focus for Jefferson as he sought to articulate that distinctive blend of classical heritage and American identity. In the garden, Jefferson saw Roman republicanism in an aesthetic environment – that is, an ideal reasoned and romantic landscape. The connection between Rome and the eighteenth century was more prevalent in the garden than perhaps anywhere else. 'Here and there indeed,' wrote historian of Roman art, Mortimer Wheeler:

> amongst the carved and painted landscapes of the end of the Republic and the earlier Empire, we have something strangely akin to the Romantic Movement of the eighteenth and early nineteenth centuries. There can of course be no complete identity between one age and another; but the conscious cult of Nature, seen somewhat as an elegant curiosity from the window of a comfortable and sophisticated room, is in harmony with the spirit of both 'Augustan' periods … Park scenery, often with elements of fantasy, had become a normal part of the genteel environment.[64]

As Wheeler observed, both the Romans of the Augustan Age and the Europeans of the eighteenth century (the 'New Augustans') sought to create garden spaces for polite, learned members of the elite. The idea was to design a space where discourse on politics, art and philosophy could happen while overlooking and walking through natural scenery. English gardens in particular had much in common with their bucolic classical equivalents.[65] It was the presence of the shepherd, the kitchen garden and the imagined wild mountains beyond that made English gardens so characteristic of the pastoral vision of Rome's gardens. It was this quality that attracted Jefferson to a tour of English gardens and the subsequent adoption of such motifs in his own garden in Virginia.[66] Jefferson delighted in the gardens of England's country estates, though he lamented their over-ornamentation. Jefferson believed that classicizing English garden design, when coupled with the sublime American background, could help foster a distinctively American nature aesthetic.

The beauty of the picturesque garden and the sublimity of the mountainside thus merged for Jefferson into a national aesthetic. Historian Charles Miller has made similar observations in analysing Jefferson's 1786 'Head and Heart Dialogue' (already discussed above) in Paris: 'in the dialogue, the Heart describes France, with its hills, rainbows, and the gardens at St. Germains, as beautiful. The sublime it reserves for America, particularly for the view of Monticello'.[67] Having American artists such as Trumbull and Latrobe paint the Natural Bridge and Monticello allowed Jefferson to construct a space for the American landscape in the emerging nineteenth-century Romantic artistic movement. Miller notes the way in which Jefferson moves beyond 'Reynolds's neoclassical idea that the keys to beauty and taste were the "immutable laws of nature"', favouring instead the notion of 'an art that was related to the other understanding of nature, wild, dynamic'.[68]

Monticello real and imagined

Jefferson's classicizing vision of Monticello was largely a product of his imagination. Despite the bountiful gardens, four farms and commanding views of his world, Jefferson's little mountain functioned as a working plantation. Down from his villa at the summit, Jefferson designed tiers along the sides of the mountain as sites for labour production. On top of the mountain in his own back yard rested the very visible Mulberry Row, a place where Jefferson's workers, enslaved and free, laboured in workshops and storehouses. It was the industrial centre of Jefferson's agricultural plantation. Outside Mulberry Row and elsewhere in his 5,000 acres of land, over 100 enslaved peoples tilled and cultivated Jefferson's landscape at any given time. Over the course of his lifetime, more than 200 enslaved persons worked for Jefferson and worked toward his classical vision for his mountain. His mountainscape not only included tulips, beans and poplar trees, but also enslaved African Americans who lived and worked on the mountain.

Those characteristics of Jefferson's mountain villa force us to reassess its significance. Jefferson regarded his land as a place of retirement and retreat. For over 200 people (including his own children), however, whom Jefferson owned over the course of his lifetime, this mountain was a site of enslaved labour, not the liberating, sweet leisurely labour that he often romanticized in his letters.[69] Although Jefferson's Virginia mountainscape may have resembled the sublime for him and his free white visitors, such visions bore vastly different meanings for different viewers. Where Jefferson stood on his mountaintop envisioning his plough as his paintbrush, enslaved African Americans were granted no such autonomy in relation to the mountain they laboured to transform.[70] The reality of eighteenth- and nineteenth-century Southern plantations starkly contrasted with their mythology. Jefferson's admirers may have regarded the 'sage of Monticello' as a Horace or a Jove, in line with his own self-image, but he nevertheless existed alongside his classical persona as a patriarch and planter, similar to many American landowners in the South. This double character of Thomas Jefferson as both planter and pastoralist speaks to the complexity of his mountain landscape as a place of both beauty and exploitation: Jefferson's romantic visions of Monticello would not have existed without enslaved labour.

Jefferson, in other words, was able to embark on his explorations of the ancient and of the sublime due to his special circumstance: his advantages of race, wealth and gender. Larson has observed that:

> a mansion library like Byrd and Jefferson's, had the effect, as a men-only space, of narrowing the lives of the women of the house, while, simultaneously, widening that of its male owner. Not only did such a library provide a space for the man of the house to entertain, in person, an extra-familial male social circle, but on a more metaphysical level, its books and writing-desk afforded access to, and means of communication with the minds of other men of his class, both past and present, in a transatlantic world of scholars.[71]

Jefferson's inheritance as the owner of a mountain was due to his wealthy station and the laws of Virginia. Jefferson's formal education in and exposure to the Classics while in school and university at the College of William and Mary was due to his position in Virginian society. Even though Jefferson remarked that 'those who labor in the earth are the chosen people of God',[72] the reality for his enslaved workers was not so privileged. Jefferson's classical education exposed his Enlightenment imagination to the poetry of Lucretius' sublime vistas, Virgil's Arcadia, Horace's Sabine Farm and Statius' villa visits. But his desire to translate this imagination into reality was predicated on the productions of enslaved people. From the moment of his birth until his last breath, Jefferson was surrounded by slavery.

Jefferson died on his mountaintop on 4 July 1826, exactly fifty years after the signing of the Declaration of Independence. Jefferson's sublime visions of Virginia lived on beyond his death and were replicated by artists, poets and writers for decades thereafter. Monticello, still stands today as an icon of Jefferson's genius and of America's exploitation of the classical heritage, but also of the underlying role of slavery in that process. Jefferson's adventures in the mountains, and his sending of explorers into the West, speak to his desire to define a nation by its wild, unknown landscapes. He developed classicizing versions of ideas about retirement, pastoralism and the sublime into an American identity for the public, but also an Epicurean identity for himself. Jefferson incorporated the ancient world of Greece and Rome within his uniquely American attitude towards nature and cultivated landscapes.

Notes

1. Temple 1908: 12.
2. See Smart 1938; Larson 2017; one of my goals here is to build on Larson's conclusions by bringing Jefferson's classical books off the shelves and understanding how they contributed to Jefferson's response to the world outside the library, in the rural mountains of Virginia.
3. For more on classical reception in the English picturesque: see O'Loughlin 1978; Stack 1985; Bowe 2013; Johnson 2015. Brown 1991 traces the influence of 'Augustan' (English) gardens as places of *otium* and retirement on the garden designs adopted by wealthy Virginians, with reference not just to Jefferson but also to others like William Byrd II. That article has influenced my approach here, but I differ from Byrd in looking beyond the formal gardens of Virginia at Jefferson's engagement with more rugged, natural sites.
4. Jefferson began construction on his mountain during 1768 at the age of twenty-five by levelling the mountaintop, but he did not finish constructing and renovating until 1808, the year before his retirement at the age of seventy-five. For literature on Jefferson's house and landscape, see McLaughlin 1988; Stein 1993; Hatch 2001. Jefferson also owned another mountain called Montalto, which rises 410 feet above Monticello, with panoramic views of Monticello and the Blue Ridge Mountains.
5. Jefferson (3 August 1771), Letter to Robert Skipwith, with a List of Books for a Private Library (Boyd et al. 1950–: I, 76–81).
6. Sayce 1892: 34.
7. For more on the *locus amoenus*, see Horace, *Ars Poetica* 1.14-18 and Spencer 2010: 22.
8. Jefferson 1989: 83.
9. For a comprehensive list of Jefferson's libraries, see the Sowerby Catalogue: http://tjlibraries.monticello.org/transcripts/sowerby/sowerby.html (accessed 28 September 2020).
10. See Røstvig 1958.
11. For British gardeners envisioning their own landscapes in this tradition, see Hunt 1988.
12. The letter is Epicurean in the sense that it is a dialogue between Jefferson's emotional heart and his rational mind, in which they discuss the benefits of love and pleasure to pure intellect. In the end, the Heart triumphs over the Head.
13. Jefferson (12 October 1786), Letter to Maria Cosway (Boyd et al. 1950–: X, 443–55).
14. Ibid.
15. Emphases my own.
16. Jefferson (16 September 1787), Letter to George Wythe, with Enclosure (Boyd et al. 1950–: XII, 127–30).
17. See Duffy 2013 on the importance of that concept for eighteenth-century understandings of the sublime as an experience that is sensitive to the cultural and historical resonances of landscape.
18. Jefferson (10 April 1796), Letter to Volney (Boyd et al. 1950–: XXIX, 61).
19. Jefferson (9 April 1797), Letter to Volney (Boyd et al. 1950–: XXIX, 352–3).
20. Smith, M., Account of a Visit to Monticello, 29 July–2 August 1809 (Looney et al. 2004–: I, 386–401).

21. Ibid.
22. Sayce 1892: 143.
23. Rush, R. (9 October 1816), Letter to Charles Jared Ingersoll (Looney et al. 2004–: X, 442–3).
24. See de Jong 2018.
25. Jefferson (11 December 1783?), Letter to Eliza House Trist (Boyd et al. 1950–: VI, 382–3) .
26. Horace, *Satires* 2.6, esp. lines 1-4: 'This is what I prayed for! – a piece of land not so very large, where there would be a garden, and near the house a spring of ever-flowing water, and up above these a bit of woodland'.
27. Other figures in early American history were similarly linked with the virtues of agriculture in the classical world. George Washington was dubbed 'Cincinnatus' due to his planter background and willingness to lead the Continental Army during the American Revolution, and subsequently the new nation, though he himself was not formally educated in the Classics.
28. The phrase, *novus ordo seclorum*, which rests on the U.S. dollar bill, stems from Virgil's *Eclogues* 4.5.
29. Jefferson [1787] 1964: 165. Other American founders believed likewise, including George Washington: 'I think with you that the life of a Husbandman of all others, is the most delectable', (Washington to Alexander Spotswood, February 13, 1788). Cf. Jefferson [1787] 1964: 157.
30. Jefferson wrote in 1787 that 'ours are the only farmers who can read Homer': Jefferson (15 January 1787), Letter to St. John de Crèvecoeur (Boyd et al. 1950–: XI, 43–5).
31. Jefferson (30 September 1785), Letter to Charles Bellini (Boyd et al. 1950–: VIII, 568–70).
32. See Kimball 1916.
33. Jefferson (2 February 1812), Letter to Benjamin Galloway (Looney et al. 2004–: IV, 470–1).
34. Jefferson (3 March 1804), Letter to Elbridge Gerry, (Boyd et al. 1950–: XLIII, 24–5).
35. Jefferson (24 December 1821), Letter to Archibald Theweatt. For more on Jefferson and tranquillity, see: Jefferson to John Randolph, 26 August 1775; to James Madison, 9 June 1793; to Pierre Samuel Du Pont de Nemours, 18 January 1802; to Edward Dowse, 19 April 1803; to Benjamin Rush, 21 April 1803; to William Duane, 12 August 1810; to William Short, 28 November 1814; to Spencer Roane, 6 September 1819; to Benjamin Waterhouse, 19 July 1822.
36. Jefferson (20 March 1814), Letter to Thomas Clark (Looney et al. 2004–: VII, 256–7).
37. Jefferson (13 August 1821), Letter to James Monroe.
38. Jefferson (28 October 1822), Letter to Marie-Joseph-Paul-Yves-Roch-Gilbert du Motier, Marquis de Lafayette.
39. Jefferson (20 November 1822), Letter to William Annesley.
40. During his retirement years, Jefferson exchanged dozens of letters with the Reverend Joseph Priestly on Epicureanism in religion and cosmology.
41. Jefferson (23 November 1810), Letter to Charles Holt (Looney et al. 2004–: III, 227).
42. Jefferson (31 December 1803), Letter to George Clinton (Boyd et al. 1950–: XCII, 214–15).
43. Jefferson [1787] 1964: 15.
44. Ibid.
45. Jefferson (19 June 1788), Hints to Americans Travelling in Europe (Boyd et al. 1950–: XIII, 264–76).
46. Jefferson [1787] 1964: 21.
47. Corbin 1994: 128.

48. Ibid. 127.
49. Jefferson [1787] 1964: 21.
50. Cf. König in this volume for a similar argument on Edward Dodwell.
51. Jefferson (3 August 1771), Letter to Robert Skipwith, with a List of Books for a Private Library (Boyd et al. 1950–: I, 76–81).
52. Jefferson owned two copies of Longinus in Latin and Greek, and seven copies of *De rerum natura*. On Lucretius as one of the ancient authors who anticipates modern conceptions of the sublime most extensively, see Porter 2016: esp. 445–54.
53. Relevant also is Thomas Cole's great painting *The Oxbow* (1836). Cole was associated with John Trumbull, Jefferson's friend and portraitist. *The Oxbow* depicts the aftermath of a devastating storm leading to tranquillity, viewed from Mount Holyoke, reminiscent of this passage from Lucretius.
54. One is reminded of an inscription from the opening line of Lucretius' *De rerum natura* Book 2 (*suave mari magno*) at the House of Fabius Rufus in Pompeii, which was built according to Vitruvian aesthetics, and looked out to the sea: see Beard 2008: 114–15. Jefferson's own 'sea view' stood in this tradition.
55. On Jefferson's agrarian republicanism, see Martinez 2005 and Sturges 2011.
56. Jefferson (31 October 1819), Letter to William Short: 'As you say of yourself, I too am an Epicurean. I consider the genuine (not the imputed) doctrines of Epicurus as containing every thing [sic] rational in moral philosophy which Greece & Rome have left us.'
57. Jefferson (26 December 1786), Letter to William Carmichael (Boyd et al. 1950–: X, 632–5).
58. Jefferson (19 June 1788), Hints to Americans Travelling in Europe (Boyd et al. 1950–: XIII, 264–76).
59. Jefferson (18 October 1787), Letter to Madame de Corny (Boyd et al. 1950–: XII, 246–7). See Randolph 1871.
60. Jefferson (20 February 1791), Letter to John Trumbull (Boyd et al. 1950–: XIX, 298–301).
61. Jefferson (10 October 1809), Letter to Benjamin Henry Latrobe (Looney et al. 2004–: I, 595–6).
62. Jefferson (20 September 1785), Letter to James Madison (Rutland and Rachal 1973: 366–9).
63. Jefferson [1787] 1964: 153.
64. Wheeler 1964: 185–6.
65. Ibid. 197.
66. Jefferson, Notes of a Tour of English Gardens [2–14 April] 1786 (Boyd et al. 1950–: IX, 369–75).
67. Miller 1988: 102.
68. Ibid.; cf. Corbin 1994: 126 for a similar account of the changes that lead towards Romanticism.
69. Jefferson fathered six children with an enslaved woman whom he owned, Sally Hemings, herself the child of a white planter and enslaved woman. For historiography on slavery at Monticello, see especially Miller 1977; Stanton 2000 and 2012; Gordon-Reed and Onuf 2016.
70. Jefferson (17 April 1813), Letter to Charles Willson Peale (Looney et al. 2004–: VI, 68–70).
71. Larson 2017: 246.
72. Jefferson 1964: 157.

CHAPTER 8
EDWARD DODWELL IN THE PELOPONNESE: MOUNTAINS AND THE CLASSICAL PAST IN NINETEENTH-CENTURY MEDITERRANEAN TRAVEL WRITING[1]

Jason König

Introduction

When the Irish traveller and painter Edward Dodwell finally reached the summit of Mount Ithome in southern Greece on 6 February 1806, having been delayed by a gun battle involving some bandits in a nearby village – an incident we will read more of below – he was impressed by what he saw. 'Few places in Greece, he tells us, combine a more beautiful, and at the same time a more classical view'.[2] That brief phrase sums up neatly one of the most typical features of Dodwell's treatment of landscape in his travel writing, in its combination of aesthetic and historical interests: his appreciation of the beauty of mountain scenery is repeatedly combined with an interest in mountains as places where the classical past is visible and present to an unusual degree. Far from being an exclusively new and modern phenomenon, his interest in mountain landscape is here represented as something that is rooted in and intertwined with the classical past.

My argument in this chapter, in response to this passage and many others like it in the work of Dodwell and his contemporaries, is that a full account of modern responses to mountains needs to give more attention to the influence of classical precedents and models;[3] and more specifically that eighteenth- and nineteenth-century travel writing from the Mediterranean, and especially from mainland Greece, offers fertile ground for seeing that influence in action. As we have seen in the introduction to this volume, there has been a tendency to tell a simplistic story about the disjunctions between modern and premodern engagement with mountains.[4] It is commonplace in modern writing on the subject to focus on descriptions of the Alps as a paradigm for experiences of mountains and mountaineering over the last two centuries or more, as a locus for encounters with the sublime and as a playground for the first modern mountaineers.[5] My hypothesis here is that looking beyond the Alps at Greece and the wider Mediterranean can help to complicate that picture. The writers I examine in this chapter, much more obviously so than their Alpine counterparts, were immersed in classical literature and keen to anchor their own responses in classical precedents, and to represent the mountains of Greece as places of special connection with the classical past.[6]

In examining those tensions this chapter also has the supplementary aim of offering some models for a reassessment of the large body of northern European travel writing from eighteenth- and nineteenth-century Greece. In particular I aim to shed new light on the work of Edward Dodwell, whose work has a fascination, for me, that is not reflected in any of the scholarly treatments I have come across. That body of work, both by Dodwell and by his contemporaries, has had some attention from scholars interested in the history of Ottoman Greece, or in the history of specific archaeological sites, but I am not aware of any sustained discussion of their importance for the history of landscape understanding in European culture. Nor have I seen many accounts that acknowledge the rewards of reading these texts from end to end as complex and sophisticated creations in their own right. As we shall see further below, many of these authors cover similar ground to each other, visiting similar sites, and displaying a shared interest in the way in which the classical past is both present and tantalizingly absent within the landscape of Greece. At the same time all of them have their own distinctive worldviews and thematic preoccupations:[7] hence my interest here in reading Dodwell's remarkable work in depth in order to show how his interest in landscape is threaded through his text in quite idiosyncratic ways.[8]

Mountains and the classical past in Ottoman Greece

Eighteenth- and nineteenth-century travellers' accounts from Greece can help us to recreate a more expansive and varied picture of the places and modes of expression that were available for mountain appreciation in Europe beyond the Alps. With the Napoleonic Wars, the conventional Grand Tour routes became inaccessible to British travellers, and the Alps were for a time much less visited.[9] During that time Greece and the mountains of Greece came to play an important role in the development and consolidation of new models of landscape appreciation. Those new models had much in common with the approaches that had already been developed in the Alps and elsewhere in Europe, but generally with a less exclusive emphasis on the awe-inspiring scale of mountain scenery as a source of the sublime, perhaps not surprisingly given the smaller size of the mountains of Greece, and a correspondingly greater emphasis on their historical associations.[10] Recent work by Cian Duffy has stressed the importance of what he calls 'classic ground' in eighteenth- and nineteenth-century experience of the sublime.[11] But for the most part, the landscape of Greece tended to be associated much more with the idea of the 'picturesque', which was generally envisaged as standing halfway between the 'beautiful' and the 'sublime' (although the concept tended to be used quite indiscriminately in practice, often in combination with either or both of those terms,[12] as we shall see later for Dodwell). That concept was even more closely suited to the landscapes of the Mediterranean, partly because of the increasing interest, in the second half of the eighteenth century, in associating the picturesque with places that carried a sense of decay and of the passing of time, especially through the presence of ruins. That association made Greece a particularly appropriate venue for picturesque tourism.[13] The ancient travel-writer Pausanias in particular was often taken as a forerunner of the picturesque, for example in the influential work of Uvedale Price, whose work *Essays on the Picturesque* was first published in 1794.[14] In some respects that association is remarkable, given that Pausanias was almost completely uninterested in describing scenery, but it clearly owed a great deal to his interest in the historical texture of the Greek landscape, and in its ruins, which for him expressed a sense of the continued but always precarious and elusive presence of the pre-Roman past.[15] It is not surprising that Pausanias' interest was shared by the northern European travellers who took him as their constant companion in their search for traces of the classical heritage.[16] The classical past was of course a key part of the attraction for travellers to Greece in other respects too, putting aside their engagement with landscape specifically.[17]

There has been very little work, however, that attempts to draw out the significance of that interest in the classical past specifically for the history of human engagement with mountains in European culture. The most important exception is Veronica della Dora's work on Mediterranean mountains as memory theatres which gave the opportunity for an embodied encounter with the past to northern European travellers who were distinguished both by their classical education and by their interest in mountaineering.[18] Two features of that phenomenon are of particular importance, both for the authors della Dora discusses and for many other travellers' accounts too, Edward Dodwell included. The first is the phenomenon whereby ascending to the top of a hill or a mountain seemed to make the past more clearly visible, as if the sordid details of life under Ottoman rule vanished from view with the elevated, distant view provided by the Mediterranean summit position. For example, della Dora discusses Edward Daniel Clarke's travel journals, and more specifically his account of climbing Mount Gargarus in Asia Minor: 'Clark's ascent activated a temporal descent from the present to the past … Finally, on the top of the mountain, Clarke gained a bird's-eye view of the lands and landmarks of the classical world'.[19] That way of viewing had ancient precedents. Viewing from above, and especially viewing from mountaintops, was enormously important for the ancient Greeks and Romans as it is for us. The 'summit position' has also been crucial to modern mountaineering culture, as Peter Hansen has shown.[20] Ancient Greeks and Romans were different in the sense that they did not give much weight to the idea of being first on a summit; often what ancient responses valued was precisely the experience of returning to the summits that others had stood on before over many centuries, for example in the rituals of mountaintop sacrifice that were repeated over many centuries or even millennia. The idea of retracing famous routes and ascents is not alien to modern mountaineering culture, of course, but it does often stand side by side with an interest in being first which is hard to parallel in ancient Mediterranean culture. Despite that difference, however, our fascination with the idea of looking down from above surely owes a great deal to its prevalence in ancient literature. It tended to be associated with various kinds of authority: divine authority, military authority, historiographical authority.[21] The pilgrimage writing of the early Christian writer Egeria is an obvious example. She travelled to the Sinai Peninsula and on to Palestine in the late fourth century CE, and has left detailed accounts among other things of looking down from the summits of Mount Sinai and Mount Nebo at places associated with the biblical past.[22] And so when the nineteenth-century travellers look down from the mountain summits of Greece they are communing with the classical past not only because their position makes it specially visible, but also because they are replicating classical ways of viewing.

There are examples spread very widely through the travel writing of the early nineteenth century in particular. Thomas Smart Hughes' *Travels in Sicily, Greece and Albania*, published in 1820, is an account of travels in 1813. Chapter 7 of that work opens with an account of the view from Larissa, the acropolis of Argos, at sunrise. Hughes' opening words seem to acknowledge in passing that his reader might expect a predominantly aesthetic response to the view: 'The view from hence was transcendantly beautiful; but even more interesting by its association than by its natural magnificence'.[23] The implication seems to be that his own intense experience of the historical resonances of this panorama goes beyond the aesthetic response that one would standardly expect. Hughes then lists, over the course of nearly four pages, some of the key sights (and sites) that are visible to him:

> Before me lay that plain where knowledge was first transplanted into Europe from the prolific regions of the east; a plain so identified with the earliest ages of Grecian story that every object upon which my eye rested might have formed a subject for the muse: the very cradle of demi-gods and heroes, the scene of the most impassioned writings of the Grecian poets.[24]

Then further below:

> Amidst the retreating folds of that fine semicircle of mountains which enclose the plain, my eye caught the majestic summits of Arcadian Cyllene, the parent of the Grecian lyre; from thence passing over two conical peaks which tower aloft behind imperial Mycenae ... it rested upon the heights of Arachnaeum, where that last light gleamed in the beacon-train which announced the fall of Troy. In the plain itself appeared the ruins of Mycenae and Tiryns ... .[25]

From where he stands Hughes sees some of the most famous and ancient places of Greek myth laid out before him. His reference to the famous chain of mountaintop beacons that carry news of the fall of Troy back to Agamemnon's wife Clytemnestra in Mycenae, in Aeschylus' *Agamemnon* 281–316,[26] offers us an image of the mountains of Greece as an interconnected network. It also allows Hughes to fantasize about the idea that his view of the summit of Mount Arachnaeum (Arachnaion), south of Corinth, replicates a view that others saw or at least imagined seeing thousands of years before.

For a rather later example one might look at the work of Henry Fanshawe Tozer.[27] His book *Researches in the Highlands of Turkey: Including Visits to Mounts Ida, Athos, Olympus, and Pelion, to the Mirdite Albanians, and Other Remote Tribes, with Notes on the Ballads, Tales, and Classical Superstitions of the Modern Greeks*, was published in 1869. It is a composite account of three journeys, from the 1850s and 1860s. The subtitle of Tozer's work tells its own story. Mountains are not incidental landmarks for him, to be examined en route to elsewhere: they structure his whole journey. Often on the plains

Tozer becomes preoccupied with details of the peoples he encounters and their way of life in their present-day landscapes. But as he climbs upwards his gaze is almost invariably directed more and more to the classical world. On the summit of Mount Olympus, for example, the mountain offers him a panorama of the Greek past:

> There followed other lofty summits close to us, beyond which, to the west, as far as the eye could reach, the numerous ranges of the Cambunian chain filled all the view; while at our feet was the entrance of the deep defile forming the pass of Petra, through which Xerxes entered Greece, with yawning chasms and impassable precipices descending towards it, the 'barrier crags of precipitous Olympus' of the Orphic poet of the *Argonautica* ... Athos rose majestic above all. A magnificent view indeed it was, together with the wide expanse of sea, which on this day was in colour a delicate soft blue ... The heights on which we were standing were no unworthy position for the seat of the gods.[28]

For Tozer, Mount Olympus is a place of special connection with the classical world: his gaze reaches out from there to the great landmarks of classical history – another good example of della Dora's identification of mountains as 'memory theatres'.

The second key phenomenon, not discussed by della Dora, is the tendency to see the classical and the aesthetic as inextricably combined with each other, in line with the classicizing conceptions of the picturesque already outlined above. That sometimes involved enlisting classical authors as ancestors not just for present-day antiquarian interests but also for contemporary aesthetic appreciation of mountain landscapes, in a way which implies a continuity between the past and the present. It is important to stress that this is not a uniform phenomenon. Some authors took a particularly austere approach to the task of antiquarianism: Leake's *Travels in Northern Greece* and *Travels in the Morea* are obvious examples, with their monumental and painstaking topographical knowledge-gathering, which is rarely interrupted by considerations of beauty or sublimity.[29] In other cases, however, historical reflection is regularly interspersed with aesthetic judgements about landscape and quotations from Romantic poetry. Robert Pashley, who travelled around Crete in 1833, and whose account, *Travels in Crete*, was published in 1837, is a typical example. The work opens with Pashley's sighting of the White Mountains of Crete, 'which well deserve the name bestowed on them by both ancients and moderns', and which his companions mistake for Mount Ida: in drawing attention to their error he presents himself there as someone with a careful knowledge of the island's summits and their ancient history.[30] That impression is reinforced by the final words of the book, as Pashley describes his sense of loss at leaving behind the scenery of the Samarian gorge:

> On leaving these most grand and most beautiful of Nature's works; it is not without a feeling of regret that I have only been allowed to gaze on them for a few hours ... I am indeed leaving
>
>> A land whose azure mountain-tops are seats
>> For gods in council, whose green vales, retreats

>   Fit for the shade of heroes, mingling there
>   To breathe Elysian peace in upper air.[31]

That final quotation, from William Wordsworth,[32] suggests the compatibility of a Romantic appreciation of mountains with a sensitivity to the classical heritage. It is one of many quotations from Wordsworth and other Romantic poets, most often in relation to mountain scenery, elsewhere in the work. Alternatively one might look at Aubrey de Vere's work *Picturesque Sketches of Greece and Turkey*, published in two volumes in 1850:

> The scenery of Delphi and its neighbourhood, I have no hesitation in saying, is the finest that I have ever seen; and I have visited all the most beautiful regions of Europe ... Nor do I believe that the Swiss mountains rise to a greater height from the level of any of the lakes which they adjoin, than Parnassus rises from the Gulf of Lepanto – that noblest of lakes, whose breadth, vast as is the expanse, is never too great for beauty; and whose shores are enriched successively with associations, Egyptian, heroic, classical, Roman, Crusading, Venetian, and Turkish.[33]

Once again antiquity and aesthetics are addressed side by side here. The mountains of Greece are not only represented as no less elevated than the Alps, at least in relation to the bodies of water that lie beneath them, but also as far richer in beauty and historical depth. De Vere's sweeping claim about the multi-cultural character of the Gulf of Lepanto is made casually and allusively, as if for a discriminating reader who is able to envisage that complex history without further explanation, in a way which suggests that the capacity to see beauty and history as mutually reinforcing components of mountain scenery is something not everyone shares.

To summarize: for many of these nineteenth-century travellers mountains were places for accessing history; they were also places where beauty and antiquity were inextricably combined with each other. Both of these phenomena helped to portray the mountains of Greece as places where the classical past was strongly present, and where nineteenth-century ways of viewing and experiencing mountains were deeply rooted in the classical past. In that sense these texts challenge long-standing assumptions about the dissonance between ancient and modern responses to mountain landscape.

Edward Dodwell: bandits in the Peloponnese

My main case study for those phenomena is Edward Dodwell.[34] Dodwell's journeys through Greece took place in the first decade of the nineteenth century, although he waited until 1819 to publish them, with the title *Classical and Topographical Tour through Greece during the years 1801, 1805, and 1806*, in two volumes. He is best known for his many watercolour paintings of Greece.[35] His text is regularly quoted in passing by scholars interested in the antiquarian travel culture of this period, but there seems to be relatively little interest in reflecting on the reading experience it offers when one reads it from beginning to end. Dodwell too, like so many of his classical predecessors[36] and like so many of his contemporaries, offers us (among other things) a powerful and intricate landscape narrative, a story of his developing engagement with the mountains of Greece. The mountains stand always in the background to his travels; they are threaded through the work in a way which invites us to read intratextually and to think about how Dodwell's different encounters with the high places of Greece relate to each other and what they add up to.

There is a clue to the importance of mountains at the very beginning of the work. The map that stands at the end of the preface (Fig. 8.1) gives striking prominence to the mountains even by the normal standards of nineteenth-century cartography: they seem almost to rise up from the page, dark ridges of rock standing out from the background of the Greek mainland as writing does from a blank page, or like a skeleton, as if they are the true structure underlying the flesh of Greece. And for Dodwell, as for the other

Figure 8.1 J. Walker, 'Map of Greece', from Edward Dodwell (1819), *Classical and Topographical Tour through Greece during the Years 1801, 1805, and 1806*, London: Rodwell and Martin: Volume I, facing p. x. Cambridge University Library.

authors we have looked at already, mountains seem to be special in part because of the way in which they symbolize the continuities between past and present. On just the second page of his preface we find the very Pausanian claim (probably the most frequently quoted passage from Dodwell's work) that: 'its mountains, its valleys, and its streams, are intimately associated with the animating presence of the authors by whom they have been immortalized. Almost every rock, every promontory, every river, is haunted by the shadows of the mighty dead'.[37] We see that connection over and over again for the mountains of Greece as we read on into the main text.[38]

Dodwell approaches Greece from the north. He travels by sea, from Venice. As he and his fellow travellers make their way down the Dalmatian coast, he offers us repeated accounts of the towns they pass and the people who inhabit them, very much in the manner of ancient geographical writing. Several times he confidently records the warlike quality of the inhabitants of the mountains that he sees from on board ship, in a way which implies that they have remained unchanged over many centuries. In those passages the mountains are represented as zones of continuity with the past, as though the assessment of classical authors like Polybius of these harsh lands on the edge of civilization still holds good.[39] Dodwell seems, in fact, to quote from ancient authors most often of all when he is talking about mountains. He quotes Livy on the location of Mount Scodrus.[40] He quotes from Horace, Cassius Dio, Pliny the Elder, Procopius and Strabo on the Acroceraunian mountains and their inhabitants,[41] and then a wide range of authors on the phenomenon of fire coming out of the ground in mountainous places: Strabo, Vitruvius, Pliny, Aelian, Plutarch, Cassius Dio, Pausanias.[42] That approach may be partly as a substitute for autopsy, because of the difficulty he has in exploring them himself, but it nevertheless leaves us with the impression that these are places specially intertwined with classical literature.

Dodwell travels on to Athens, from where he makes regular trips into the countryside of Attica. He then returns north into Thessaly, and then south into the Morea (the medieval name for the Peloponnese, which was still regularly in use in the early nineteenth century). In all of this he repeatedly seeks out the mountains and especially their summits. But over and over again as the narrative goes on we see the people who inhabit the mountains getting in the way of his ideals of continuity between past and present, rather than reinforcing them. The mountains may be places of special encounter with the past, but they are also full of dangerous people, ready to make the antiquarian's job difficult, or contemptible people who fall far short of their classical predecessors. Like many of his contemporaries Dodwell tends to contrast the poverty of present-day Greece with its glorious past,[43] and in that sense his appreciation of the mountains as places linked with classical history is an elitist assertion of his own northern European learning and good taste, as engagement with the mountains so often was in the early nineteenth century in other parts of Europe too.[44]

The Peloponnese in particular, as Dodwell represents it, is full of bandits. The mountain bandits of mainland Greece were often associated with resistance to the occupying Turks,[45] and Dodwell does acknowledge that in places.[46] For the most part, however, Dodwell plays down those associations with resistance, and emphasizes instead more predatory motives for their activity,[47] making it clear that they are resented by the local population and by the Turks alike.[48] Not only that, but bandits also repeatedly get in the way of Dodwell's attempts to visit classical sites. That had been the case even early on in his journey. Halfway along the Gulf of Corinth, for example, he spots the mountains Chalcis and Taphiassos: 'I wished to land, and examine the coast between the two mountains; but so strong is the dread of robbers, I could prevail on no-one to accompany me.'[49] He has to content himself with speculating about the possibility that there are many unexplored 'forts and cities of ancient times' between the two peaks.

That theme of bandits as a distraction reaches an extraordinary climax in Dodwell's account of visiting Mount Ithome. Finally here he loses patience with all the warnings and obstructions. The locals warn him not to go because 'the country that we wished to explore was at that time infested with banditti', but Dodwell is 'incredulous'[50] and sets out anyway. As they get closer to Ithome, they come within musket range of a fortress occupied by the remnants of the bandits – the rest are engaged in a battle in the village of Alitouri at the foot of the mountain, with 140 bandits facing a force of 100 Greek villagers and 60 Turks – and they hear gunfire. The next morning they ascend a nearby hill to get a view of the fighting, which Dodwell, temporarily viewing the bandits as worthy of interest (he describes the battle as 'this curious incident'),[51] sketches with the help of his camera obscura. But as we read on, the bandits once again come to be characterized as obstructions to the real object of Dodwell's interest. He is determined to continue with his plan, and finally on 6 February 1806, four days after setting out, he manages to make his way up to the summit of Mount Ithome. Here he launches into a detailed account of the classical history of Messene, as if his arrival at the top of the mountain is the thing that makes that narrative possible, even though he could just as well have told it at some other point: once again, the summit of a mountain is represented here as a place of special access to the classical past.[52] His focus is particularly on the Messenian wars against Sparta, which saw the Messenians besieged on the summit: he imagines them crowded together there, with their houses scattered all over the mountainside beyond the acropolis walls too. Should we see here a parallel between those ancient wars of resistance and the fighting Dodwell has sketched for us down below, as if the mountain is still alive with the vestiges of ancient heroism? Or does he want us to see instead the differences? His rather undignified description of the deserted monastery on the summit suggests the latter: he tells us that 'the monks of this monastery had also fled, on account of the thieves. The door was full of fresh bullet-holes, as the banditti had a short time before amused themselves with firing at it, for want of other recreation.'[53] Moreover, any interest Dodwell might have had in the bandits seems to have been replaced once again by irritation. He puts his umbrella up to keep the sun out of his eyes as he sketches. His companions tell him to take it down in case it attracts the attention of the thieves. But even then he carries on with his work stubbornly, focusing his mind on the past rather than the present: 'I had taken one view of the gate, and begun another, when we were alarmed by the cry of thieves! I was however determined to finish my view, which, by the aid of the camera-obscura, I accomplished in a hasty, but accurate manner.'[54]

But we should not dismiss too quickly the idea that the bandits do in some respects stand for the real classical past that Dodwell is seeking. For much of the work they distract from his antiquarian researches, but there are other moments where they seem almost to be relics of the ancient Greek past themselves. In that sense they contribute to Dodwell's understanding of the mountains as places of historical depth as well as aesthetic value. Certainly they share with that past one very striking characteristic, that is their elusiveness. Dodwell, like Pausanias and like many of his contemporaries, is fascinated by ruins. The ruins of the classical past are often hard to find. Dodwell glimpses them beneath the undergrowth and between the rocks; the local populations are aware of them, but do not always know exactly where to look for them. The bandits are similarly evasive. Over and over again Dodwell is warned about them. The narrative tantalizes us through these repeated references. Early on in the text, while Dodwell is still in Ithaca off the coast of north-west Greece, one of the local robber captains comes to meet the travellers, together with some of his band of Albanian bandits, to offer their services as an escort, which Dodwell and his companions decline.[55] But there is no further physical encounter with bandits before that incident on Mount Ithome, which comes in chapter 9 of the second volume (i.e. the 25th chapter of 28 overall). At times Dodwell seems almost to doubt their existence: 'we sometimes strongly suspected that these stories were invented by our attendants, who preferred travelling on the high road, and loitering in towns, to the climbing of rocks and mountains'.[56]

But when they do burst into Dodwell's narrative of the Morea they do it spectacularly. Almost immediately after the climb of Ithome, Dodwell has a second encounter with them. This one is completely different in character. Suddenly here Dodwell throws off his air of antiquarian detachment: now the bandits have his full attention. It is 10 February, four days later. They have travelled a little way to the north. They are setting out from the village where they have stayed overnight when they see the women and children rushing into their cottages, driving in their cows and shutting the doors, calling out that there are thieves. Dodwell is as usual undaunted. He and his companions arm themselves and set out, accompanied by about twenty of the villagers. They 'plung[e] into a thick forest of oaks' and soon come across a small band of thieves 'secreted in the wood'.[57] They catch one of them and tie him up; the rest run away; Dodwell and the others chase after them but fall into an ambush, 'in an inextricable labyrinth of bushes and morasses'.[58] There is an exchange of fire; two of Dodwell's men are badly wounded; and they are saved only by the sudden arrival of a band of Turkish soldiers, who initially take them for the robbers and begin to trample them with their horses, before realizing their mistake and going off in pursuit of the real bandits through the woods. We might see this incident again as a distraction from the search for the classical that Dodwell is preoccupied with. This is a confrontation with the mundane world of early nineteenth-century Greece: when they are finally captured, it turns out that the bandits are 'badly clothed, extremely dirty, and had very little ammunition'.[59] It is striking, however, that Dodwell goes out of his way to characterize this incident as an encounter with the physical landscape, in his repeated descriptions of the labyrinthine undergrowth. The bandits seem to have an organic connection with that terrain: 'they dispersed, and were indebted for their safety to the dense intricacies of the forests, and the precipitous ruggedness of the mountains'.[60] This is an irruption of the real into Dodwell's antiquarian researches – a confrontation with the real, physical landscape of Greece, its forests and rocks, which had always been there, and with the people who belong there – and for a short time at least he seems to be excited by it. Dodwell is not unusual in that: other travellers too were drawn to Greece by the thrilling realness of its landscape, as well as by their idealized visions of the classical past, and were fascinated by the tension between the two.[61]

The bandits fade from view again, as if they had never been there, and Dodwell carries on with his travels. But there is one final encounter in store for him which illustrates again the odd combination of elusiveness and realness that has characterized his interaction with the bandits throughout the work. On 22 February he approaches Mount Lykaion. Once again, he is in rough, remote terrain, which had been a stronghold of the bandits until just a few days before:

> In one of these passes we found a human head, which, from the state of preservation, appeared not to have been cut off more than two days, and from the tonsure of the hair, it was evidently an Albanian Christian, and it had the appearance of a beardless youth with a fine physiognomy. It had no wound, except some bruises, caused perhaps by its having been thrown down the rocks at some distance from the place where it was severed from the body.[62]

Dodwell explains that the bandits cut off the heads of their fallen comrades in order to prevent the Turks from carrying them off and using them to claim rewards. They bury the head beneath an oak tree and then struggle on to the summit; one of their horses falls over a precipice and has to be rescued with a rope; they finally reach the top to be greeted by 'a cold, bleak wind', snow, thunder and the sound of musket-fire from below in the valley. And then as always Dodwell launches into an account of the different places he can see from the summit, and of the classical ruins and Pausanias' account of them.[63]

The head is startlingly real and physical; at the same time it stands as an emblem of the elusive nature of Dodwell's encounter with the bandits. Dodwell sees traces of them, but a full understanding of them is always out of reach. In that sense the head is strikingly similar to some of the classical ruins Dodwell comes across elsewhere. Over and over again he finds old mutilated statues; also ancient coins, whose heads are described in great detail. In Athens he tells us that the heads of many of the figures on the frieze of the monument of Lysikrates are broken.[64] When he visits the Parthenon, we hear that 'the head of the male figure in the western tympanon, which is said to have been knocked off by a Turk, is in my possession'.[65] In Attica he finds 'a marble lion, admirably sculptured in the style of those at Mycenae: it is in a recumbent posture ; its length is four feet nine inches ; but its head is mutilated'.[66] In the cave of Pan at Rapsana, also in Attica, he finds a mutilated lion's head carved into the rock; also the headless statue of a woman.[67] Visiting Marathon, he tells the mythical story of the burial of the head of Eurystheus, after his death at the hands of the sons of Hercules.[68] The remnant of the 'beardless youth with a fine physiognomy' on Mount Lykaion is just one of this long series of severed heads which recur throughout the narrative. Dodwell's bandits, although they seem at times to distract from that encounter with the past, in other respects are a part of it, as relics of the rough mountain populations of antiquity, both thrillingly real and elusive at the same time.

Edward Dodwell: the picturesque and the classical

Mountains, then, are places where Dodwell experiences a complex sense of both the presentness and the absence of the classical past. In that sense he offers us a view of what mountains signify that is very different from the Alpine visions that tend to take centre stage in histories of eighteenth- and nineteenth-century mountain history. It is important to stress, however, that this historical vision of the mountains of Greece does not replace the aesthetic dimension that so often characterizes Romantic representations of the sublime and the picturesque in mountain landscapes; instead it supplements it and combines with it, so that the two become almost inextricable in Dodwell's prose.[69]

For a first illustration, let us stay with Dodwell on the summit of Mount Lykaion. It is not only the storm he sees there: 'no words can convey an adequate idea of the enchanting scene which burst upon us. The snow-crested summits of Taygeton [i.e. Taygetos] rose in rugged majesty, and towering pride, above the smooth and even surface of the Messenian gulf. Nothing can be more impressive and interesting than the varied outline of this renowned mountain'.[70] Then after a catalogue of all the places he can see, he tells us that 'the nearer view is gratified by the sight of abrupt precipices and wooded masses receding one behind another, varied with intervening glens and plains, and adorned with every variety of tint that nature ever combined in her most fantastic mood, and most smiling hour'.[71] As it happens, Pausanias had mentioned the view too.[72] Dodwell mentions that precedent as if Pausanias straightforwardly shares his own preoccupations: 'Great part of the Peloponnesos was, according to Pausanias, visible from this spot'.[73] But that passage from Pausanias is just a brief passing mention. It is also extremely rare – in fact it is the only example of Pausanias describing a summit view – and part of a notorious lack of interest on Pausanias' part in detailed description of the natural features of the countryside he travels through. For Dodwell, by contrast, this is just one of dozens of passages in the work which offer extensive aesthetic assessments of mountain views. Dodwell describes the landscape with the eye of a painter, and with a particular interest in the quality of variety, which was standardly viewed as one of the key features of the picturesque[74] ('every variety of tint that nature ever combined'). He tells us that 'we quitted Lycaeon, after we had remained upon its summit for several hours; during which I traced the panorama of the Peloponnesos with my camera obscura'.[75] Dodwell is in fact even more obsessed with aesthetic judgements than most other British and Irish travellers from the same period, no doubt in part simply because he was interested in landscape painting as one of the major goals of his trip. Similarly when he writes about his visit to the Vale of Tempe – 'We made several drawings, and certainly no part of Greece affords so much grandeur of line, or so many exquisite combinations of the sublime and the picturesque'[76] – his immersion in the idioms of contemporary landscape appreciation is impossible to miss.

Once again, however, these descriptions are not an alternative to classical ways of viewing but an integral part of them. As we have seen, Dodwell is interested in the way in which mountains give us access to an overarching vision of classical geography and the classical past but he extends that fascination by making it inextricable with physical beauty. Over and over again he suggests that the two go together. On a hill near Missolonghi in north-west Greece he says that 'we were deeply impressed by the view which it displayed. The features are truly beautiful; and the objects are rich in classical interest'.[77] At Thermopylae 'the beauty of the scenery was illuminated by many reflections from the lustre of the classic page'.[78] It is not surprising, then, that he expects the beauty of the landscape to become more and more pronounced as he approaches the heart of Greece. As they sail down the Dalmatian coast 'the outlines [i.e. of the coastline] increased in beauty the nearer we approached to Greece'.[79] Later: 'as we approached the pass of Thermopylae, the scenery assumed at once an aspect of more beauty and sublimity'.[80] Often his reactions seem almost to be predetermined by his classical reading, for example in his initial mention of Thessaly 'the pastoral beauties of which had been deeply impressed upon my imagination by the writers of antiquity'.[81]

His sense of thrill at the accessibility and the reality of this classical beauty is reflected in his paintings too. Further north in Thessaly he tells us that 'we stopped some time to make a drawing of Mt Olympos, the grandeur and beauty of which appeared to increase at every step we took from Larissa,'[82] a claim which is immediately and characteristically followed by citations from Plutarch and Homer. Fig. 8.2 is one of the images from his book *Views in Greece*, published two years after his *Classical and Topographical Tour*, in 1821. Whether it is a version of the image he refers to in this passage is not completely clear, but it shares the

Figure 8.2 'Mount Olympus as seen between Larissa and Baba', from Edward Dodwell (1821), *Views in Greece*, London: Rodwell and Martin. Humbox.

idea of a landscape that stands out from everything around it. The colours in the image become lighter as our gaze moves from the wooded foreground to the high peak in the distance, which stands apart in its whiteness, and the path winding forward towards the mountain picks up on the phrase 'at every step we took from Larissa'. The text which introduces the picture in the 1821 volume mentions a number of Homeric and Hesiodic epithets for the mountain, including the words 'snowy', 'with many ridges' and 'with many glens'. The painting seems to illustrate precisely those characteristics, for example in the folded texture of the mountain and its foothills, which are depicted with remarkable precision. Dodwell's illustration thus works in parallel with his text in emphasizing the continuing relevance of ancient descriptions of the mountain for its present-day appearance.

In one case especially, Dodwell makes a concerted effort to reinvent the classical authors he quotes in his own image, as if they share his own contemporary interest in landscape. Towards the end of Volume I, he sets out to climb Mount Hymettos just outside Athens, together with Pomardi, the professional artist who travelled with him, in the belief 'that its summit would present one of the most extensive views in Greece'.[83] They reach the monastery of Sirgiani, four and a half miles from the centre of Athens, in the evening, only to find it deserted with the doors shut. They climb the walls of the monastery 'with a great deal of difficulty and some danger'. Inside they find that

> a deep silence prevailed throughout the cells; the occupants of which seemed to have recently retired. The store-rooms were open, and well furnished with jars of Hymettian honey, ranged in neat order: next were large tubs of olives; and from the roof hung rows of grapes, pomegranates, and figs ... We took complete possession of the place, and feasted on the produce of the deserted mansion, which seemed to have been prepared for our reception.[84]

In the morning, they ride to the summit, 'over the bare and shining surface of the rocks'. The view surpasses even Dodwell's elevated expectations:

> I had already seen in Greece many surprising views of coasts and islands, and long chains of mountains rising one above another, and receding in uncertain lines, as far as the eye could reach: but no view can equal that from Hymettos, in rich magnificence, or in attractive charms. The spectator is sufficiently elevated to command the whole surrounding country, and at the same time not too much so for the full impression of picturesque variety; and I conceive, that few spots in the world combine so much interest of a classic kind, with so much harmony of outline.[85]

As so often, aesthetic, painterly judgement (the 'attractive charms', the 'picturesque variety', the 'harmony of outline') is combined with antiquarianism. Even by Dodwell's normal standards the catalogue of what can be seen from the summit is extraordinarily detailed, stretching for six whole pages. The pages preceding the arrival at the summit include extensive references to Ovid, Pliny the Elder, Pausanias and Plato. Up here they seem to be alone with the classical. The jars of Hymettian honey, which Hymettos had been famous for even in the ancient world, and which wait for them in such abundance in the monastery, seem to signal the fact that the mountain is welcoming them into a place where antiquity is still alive in the present. They pass several more days drawing on the summit, and sleeping in the monastery, and then they go back down to Athens.

The painterly quality of this account is hard to parallel in any description of a mountain anywhere in classical literature. And yet in the case of Ovid at least Dodwell is keen to suggest that his ancient sources share his own sensitivity to landscape. He quotes from Ovid's description of Mount Hymettos and its 'purple hills' (*purpureos colles*),[86] and then launches into a detailed justification of the accuracy of Ovid's description:

> Hymettos is remarkable for its purple tint, at a certain distance; particularly from Athens, about an hour before sun-set, when the purple is so strong, that an exact representation of it in a drawing, coloured from nature, has the appearance of exaggeration. The other Athenian mountains do not assume the same colour at any time of the day ... It seems clear, that in speaking of the *colles* of Hymettos, Ovid had in view the number of round insulated hills at the foot of the mountain; which are particularly remarkable and numerous near Sirgiani.[87]

That attention to colour and to shape ascribes to Ovid an artistic sensibility akin to Dodwell's own. And the phrase 'had in view' asks us to imagine Ovid standing there for himself, as Dodwell himself clearly has, gazing down at the vista beneath him.

For Dodwell, then, the mountains of Greece are places where his own distinctively modern aesthetic sensibility is combined with a sensitivity to the continuing presence of the classical past in the present-day landscape of Ottoman Greece. It is not just that those two perspectives can co-exist with each other side by side; rather they seem to be inextricably intertwined. Dodwell has his own idiosyncrasies: the fascination of his work comes in part from the alternation between dispassionate antiquarianism and very personal anecdote. However, his writing is also representative of motifs of landscape description that recur over and over again in the landscape description of his contemporaries too, who like him repeatedly appreciated mountains in ways which were rooted in engagement with the classical past.

Notes

1. I am grateful to Dawn Hollis and Alexia Petsalis-Diomidis for their comments on drafts of this chapter, and to the other contributors for their suggestions at the volume workshop in December 2018.
2. Dodwell 1819: II, 363.
3. For a later example of that phenomenon one might look at the influence of ancient Greek and Roman educational, philosophical and athletic ideas over nineteenth- and twentieth-century mountaineering culture. I am grateful to Jonathan Westaway for discussion of his not-yet-published work on that topic. For a brief account in relation to late nineteenth-century British and German mountaineering, see Westaway 2009: 591.

4. See especially 2–4, above, esp. on the continuing influence of Nicolson 1959.
5. Cf. Debarbieux and Rudaz 2015: 34–6 on 'the Alps' status as the prototype for the organization of knowledge about mountains' (35).
6. Even those who wrote about the Alps as a new frontier in human experience were in some cases more heavily influenced by classical literature than they initially appear. For example, John Addington Symonds represented a love of Classics as incompatible with a love of the Alps: 'the classic nations hated mountains. Greek and Roman poets talk of them with disgust and dread' (from the essay 'Love of the Alps' in Symonds 1874: 296, quoted in the anthology of Irving 1938: 29); elsewhere in his work, however, he is fascinated by the mountains of Greece and Italy as emblems of their classical heritage: e.g. Symonds 1874: 195–206 ('Etna') and 207–33, esp. 231–2 ('Athens').
7. Cf. Constantine 2011: 210.
8. None of the recent survey works on Mediterranean antiquarian travel-writing offers extensive analysis of individual authors, although both Stoneman 2010 and Constantine 2011 include many brief but perceptive comments; see also Eisner 1991: 103 for dismissive comments on Dodwell ('an amazing amount of dull, albeit learned, information'), which seem to me to be misguided.
9. See Stoneman 2010: 140–1.
10. See della Dora 2008a: 219: 'climbing Aegean peaks was a form of mountaineering intellectually more sophisticated than Alpinism, for it rested on humanistic as much as on scientific and muscular training'; also della Dora 2016a: 158: 'unlike the Western Alps, Hellas' peaks were not perceived as sublime or chaotic, but rather as inspiring poetic objects, as beautiful, well-defined landmarks for orientation . . . and as privileged nodes within a complex web of memory'.
11. See Duffy 2013, esp. 9–10: 'time and again in the texts which I consider here, this concept is invoked to characterize the encounter with the "natural sublime" as involving either a landscape or an environment which already exists as what might be called "classic ground" in the European cultural imagination, that is, which already possesses a range of culturally determined and topographically specific associations'.
12. See Buzard 2002: 47: 'the very imprecision of the term seems to have aided its dissemination'.
13. See Andrews 1987: 39–66 on ruins and the picturesque; cf. Stoneman 2010: 141–2, as part of a wider discussion of the association between Greece and the picturesque more broadly at 136–47.
14. See Elsner 2010 for Uvedale Price's ingenious association of the picturesque with Pausanias; also Stoneman 2010: 145–6; and a good example of the high aesthetic value he attaches to ruins at Price 1810: I, 51.
15. See Porter 2001.
16. See Pretzler 2007: 130–49 on the importance of Pausanias for Mediterranean travellers, but not with any detailed discussion of his portrayal of mountains.
17. E.g. see Dolan 2000: 113–51; also Cheeke 2003, e.g. 29–34 and 68 and Leask (2004), esp. 102–6 on Byron's ambivalence about the tendency to view modern Greece through an ancient lens.
18. della Dora 2008a and 2016a: 155–9.
19. della Dora 2016a: 156.
20. Hansen 2013.
21. See de Jong 2018.
22. E.g. see della Dora 2016a: 109–11.
23. Hughes 1820: I, 201.
24. Ibid. I, 201–2.
25. Ibid. I, 203–4

26. Discussed in detail below by Bray, 191–3.
27. Discussed by della Dora 2008a: 223, 225–6, but only in relation to his ascent of Mount Athos.
28. Tozer 1869: II, 20–1.
29. See Stoneman 2010: 155–62, contrasting Leake with some of his contemporaries.
30. Pashley 1837: I, 1–2.
31. Ibid. II, 272–3.
32. William Wordsworth, 'Humanity' (1829) lines 73–6.
33. de Vere 1850: II, 14–15.
34. Mentioned only in passing by della Dora 2008a: 222.
35. The best starting-point for Dodwell is the set of introductory essays in Camp 2013; see esp. Sloan 2013 on Dodwell's drawings, especially his use of the camera obscura. Dodwell is also mentioned in a number of survey works on travellers to Greece, but usually with only very brief passing analysis: e.g. see Stoneman 2010 147–8; and n. 8, above, on Eisner 1991.
36. For the concept of 'landscape narratives' and for the intratextual sophistication of a lot of ancient Greek and Roman representations of landscape, see König 2016, on mountains in Strabo.
37. Dodwell 1819: I, iv.
38. For a good example not discussed in the main text here, see Dodwell's first glimpse of Mount Taygetos at ibid. II, 352.
39. For good examples see ibid. I, 5 and I, 95.
40. Ibid. I, 18.
41. Ibid. I, 21–2 and I, 26.
42. Ibid. I, 24–5.
43. See McNeal 1993: 84–7 for a negative portrayal of Dodwell's condescension and indifference towards the present-day Greek population; and 1995 for similar discussion of disappointment with contemporary Greece as a motivation for Dodwell's idealized landscape painting; cf. Hionidis 2014 for similar assumptions in later writers from 1832–70.
44. Cf. Archer in this volume, 197; also Petsalis-Diomidis 2019: 45–7 on Dodwell's references to ancient vases in the possession of local populations, and on the way in which those populations are represented in denigratory terms.
45. On the Turkish campaign against the klephts in 1806, which Dodwell gets dragged into, see Alexander 1985: 89–101.
46. E.g. see Dodwell 1819: II, 373–4.
47. E.g. see ibid. II, 353 on the inhabitants of the village of Kleisoura, many of whom subsist by large-scale robbery: 'whole villages are plundered, flocks of sheep, and herds of cattle, are driven away from the rich pastures of Messenia'.
48. See Angelomatis-Tsougarakis 1990: 80–2 for the suggestion that Dodwell's reluctance to give much attention to their resistance to the Turks is entirely typical of British travellers in this period (by contrast with French travellers, who tend to be more sympathetic).
49. Dodwell 1819: I, 125.
50. Ibid. II, 351.
51. Ibid. II, 356.
52. For a good parallel from Dodwell, see his description of the view from Acrocorinth, at ibid. II, 190: 'the finest regions of classic interest, where the arts had most flourished, and poetic inspiration most prevailed, were expanded before my eyes'.

53. Ibid. II, 363.
54. Ibid. II, 366.
55. Ibid. I, 72–4.
56. Ibid. II, 92.
57. Ibid. II, 371.
58. Ibid. II, 372.
59. Ibid. II, 373.
60. Ibid.
61. Cf. Güthenke 2008 on German travellers and authors, emphasizing especially their fascination with the physical materiality of the Greek landscape as a key part of their idealization of it.
62. Ibid. II, 390.
63. Ibid. II, 392–3.
64. Ibid. I, 290.
65. Ibid. I, 325.
66. Ibid. I, 525.
67. Ibid. I, 551 and 553.
68. Ibid. II, 163.
69. Cf. McNeal 1995 for discussion of the way in which Dodwell's obsession with the remains of the classical past are central to the picturesque quality of his painting.
70. Dodwell 1819: II, 392.
71. Ibid.
72. Pausanias, *Periegesis* 8.38.7.
73. Dodwell 1819: II, 393.
74. E.g. see Price 1810: I, 21–3.
75. Dodwell 1819: II, 394.
76. Ibid. II, 118.
77. Ibid. I, 95.
78. Ibid. II, 72. Cf. MacGregor Morris 2000 on beauty and the sublime in Dodwell's account of Thermopylae, and its relationship with similar sentiments in the work of other travellers from the same period.
79. Dodwell 1819: I, 12.
80. Ibid. II, 67.
81. Ibid. II, 51.
82. Dodwell 1819: II,105. Larissa here is the city in Thessaly, different from the acropolis of Argos, also called Larissa, which is discussed above in relation to Thomas Smart Hughes.
83. Ibid. I, 483
84. Ibid. I, 485–6.
85. Ibid. I, 490.
86. Ovid, *Ars Amatoria* 687, quoted at I, 487.
87. Dodwell 1819: I, 487.

CHAPTER 9
THE TOP STORY: TRUTH AND SUBLIMITY IN PATRICK BRYDONE'S ACCOUNT OF HIS 1770 ASCENT OF MOUNT ETNA

Gareth D. Williams

The Etna encountered by most classicists as they range over the Graeco-Roman literary canon is rarely the bare and literal object of real-life experience and observation. Far more common is the *idea* of Etna, that stimulus to the imagination that licenses writers from Hesiod onwards to generate their own highly creative, often powerfully symbolic versions of the mountain.[1] My purpose in what follows is to contemplate Etna through this bifocal lens, but to approach this hybrid experience of the mountain – the different but sometimes combined strands of physical and literary visitation of the volcano – via one particular category of mountain experience: the feigned ascent, or what we might *suspect* to be the fabricated ascent, of a given peak.

If the Graeco-Roman tradition of fictive embellishment had long brought Etna to life as a storied volcano of vast symbolic possibility, the idea of the feigned ascent of that and other peaks opened up new pathways of literary experimentation in the voicing of mountain experience down to the Renaissance and beyond. A celebrated case in point is Petrarch's account of his climb of Mont Ventoux in 1336:[2] the spiritual connotations of his conversion-like experience at the summit after his trial-and-error progress to those heights provide a strong symbolic motivation for a version of events whose truth-value is in any case arguably suspect for other reasons, as we shall see. The suspicion that Petrarch fabricated part or whole of his account has important implications, I argue in section 1 below ('Two storied ascents'), for the Venetian humanist Pietro Bembo's version of climbing Etna in his *De Aetna* of 1495; but the classical accent of both Petrarch's and Bembo's accounts, and the ways in which each flirts with fictive elaboration in describing his climb, will set the stage for my focus on the fact-stretching credentials of my Exhibit A in this chapter: the account offered by Patrick Brydone (1736[3]–1818) of his ascent of Etna in his famous *A Tour Through Sicily and Malta in a Series of Letters to William Beckford, Esq. of Somerly in Suffolk*, first published in two volumes in 1773 and 'a milestone in the history of travel literature'.[4]

My focus on Brydone is dictated in part by his importance as an Anglophone pioneer of the eighteenth-century travelogue subgenre that introduced Sicily in particular to a northern European consciousness.[5] But it is also prompted by the bifurcated nature of Brydone's coverage of Etna, by which I mean the tension between his eye-witness reportage of the mountain's topography on the one hand and, on the other, his allusive eye for source text(s) as he embroiders and perhaps even invents certain aspects of his climb. Given the suggestion in section 1 below that Petrarch and Bembo at least partially feigned aspects of their experience on (respectively) Mont Ventoux and Etna, the possibility that Brydone might equally indulge a certain freedom of invention is neither startling nor revelatory in itself; what matters is the particular literary-aesthetic motive that caused him to take liberties with the truth in describing his ascent. Why, then, did he resort to what looks, as we shall see, like high fiction on so many fronts? Various answers suggest themselves, such as Brydone's cultivation of an engaging storyline, his perhaps partial or selective memory of the climb, or the penchant that he shows more broadly within his *Tour* for painting with vivid colours in the pictorial word; but most important for now is his enterprising approach to articulating sublime experience.

In an age when the sublime was undergoing fresh examination, definition and diagnosis through (most notably) Burkean and Kantian modes of analysis, Brydone's Etna narrative makes its own distinctive contribution to that larger aesthetic movement. His portrayal of the sublimity that he experienced at Etna's summit is no spontaneous revelation, I propose, but one mediated through a preconceived literary filter.[6] I argue that he captures the ambiguity of sublime experience – that visualization of a transcendent state of being that struggles for articulation in ordinary language – by creating an in-between state in his own narrative: the Etna on which he treads is in tension with the Etnean summit that seems beyond his literal reach but which he nevertheless attains through imaginative projection and allusive borrowing from the classical and post-classical literary tradition. If it is hard to know where the plausible facts of his climb end and projection begins, that indeterminacy is itself *precisely* meaningful; for what he ultimately captures in his in-between narrative, I contend, is that delicate transition point (as when two shades of a rainbow just begin to fade away from their merging with each other) between 'real' description high up the mountain and the giddy sublimity of a heightened inner condition. My claim is hardly that Brydone was the first to recognize or articulate the delicacy of this transition point, but rather that he captures it with unusual nuance in the haze he generates between fact and possible fiction in his Etna letters.

Central to the picture offered below of the texts on which Brydone relied for filling out his own Etna narrative are the volcanological writings of Sir William Hamilton.[7] Before we embark on our tour of Brydone's *Tour*, however, and before Hamilton is introduced into our proceedings, Petrarch and Pietro Bembo offer initial orientation on the literary phenomenon of the feigned ascent.

Two storied ascents

Brydone nowhere refers in his *Tour* to Bembo's ascent of Etna, let alone to Petrarch's climb of Mont Ventoux, and there is no evidence to prove his first-hand familiarity with either text. In briefly touching on both climbs, then, I hardly posit any direct influence on Brydone. Rather, my goal is to offer a snapshot of the ways in which seemingly embroidered, exaggerated or even invented claims of climbing achievement had long predated Brydone's experimentation in this same direction. Whether or not he consciously writes in and under the explicit influence of this tradition, my further aim is to offer a comparandum for his Etna narrative so as to differentiate and highlight certain striking features of his own exposition.

Brydone's *Tour* teems with allusions to the classical past and to Graeco-Roman authors and antiquities,[8] as if his visit to Sicily marks his movement through time as well as topography. This fusion of chronological and spatial reach was of course hardly a new literary development: already in his 1495 *De Aetna* Bembo deployed a similar technique of mnemonic topography (i.e. revisiting the past through experience of landscape) that was itself well established in classical precedents such as Virgil's *Aeneid* and Lucan's *Bellum civile*,[9] and Brydone too is implicated in this same evolving tradition almost 300 years later. But Bembo modifies the idea of mnemonic topography by introducing a contemporaneous figure – the Italian humanist and Franciscan friar Urbano Bolzanio (1442–1524)[10] – who was in a sense the very embodiment of antiquarian travel and recovery of the classical past through the collecting of manuscripts and epigraphic remains. Bembo tried, he claims, to emulate Urbano in reaching the higher of the two craters at Etna's summit, but he failed in the attempt because of the extreme force of the winds at such an elevation. As for Urbano, 'a few days before he'd carefully examined the summit during a period of the utmost calm' (*De Aetna* 28).[11] Bembo climbed Etna in late June or July 1493; in stating that Urbano made his ascent 'a few days before', he presumably means the climb that he attributes later in *De Aetna* 46 to 1 June of that year. In reality, however, it is far from certain that Urbano was or could have been in Sicily on or around that date: varied testimony places him in Venice in the early to mid-1490s, and the harsh practicalities of travel to Sicily tell against his making any brief journey to and from the island and Etna in May/June 1493; hence the implication that the ascent reported by Bembo may have been a literary construction. Even if (as other evidence indicates) Urbano did indeed climb the volcano at some point in his Mediterranean peregrinations over many years, Bembo's dating of that ascent to 1 June 1493 finds no corroborating evidence, and it comes under serious challenge from a different possibility: wanting to fill out his account of his own incomplete ascent of Etna, Bembo consulted Urbano only *after* he, Pietro, returned to Venice in 1494, and he modified that record of events in plotting his Etnean adventure in *De Aetna*.[12] In sum, Urbano's is a feigned ascent at least in the sense that it appears misdated and hence misreported in *De Aetna* 46.

But the plot thickens when *De Aetna* is viewed in relation to Petrarch's ascent of Mont Ventoux on 26 April 1336 as reported in a famous letter (*Epistolae familiares* 4.1) addressed to his close friend and erstwhile confessor, Dionigi da Borgo San Sepolcro (*c*. 1300–42). Petrarch was motivated to make his climb with his brother Gherardo, he claims, 'solely by the desire of seeing what so great a height had to offer' (1).[13] When he finally reached the summit, he was dazed at first by the panoramic view (17), but he then turned his gaze within, moving from the spatial plane to that of time and memory: 'Today it is ten years since you [sc. Petrarch in self-address] completed your youthful studies and left Bologna. Eternal God and immutable Wisdom, how many and how extensive are the changes that this intervening period has seen in your character!' (19). Petrarch had progressed, but it was not yet three years since he had renounced carnal passion (22), and he foresaw ten more years of struggle before him (23). Then, opening at random the text of the *Confessions* that he apparently always carried with him (26), a cherished gift from Dionigi, he fell upon a passage at the beginning of Augustine's discussion of the power of the mind discovered in memory (*Confessions* 10.8.15). Stunned, Petrarch closed the book, angry at himself for still admiring but earthly commodities when 'nothing is wonderful but the soul' (28); he had seen enough of the mountain, and instead turned his inward eye on himself (29) as he made the descent in silence.

But just how credible is Petrarch's account of his climb? Even if the climb cannot be dismissed as a complete fiction, an event that he demonstrably never undertook in 1336 or in any other year, his version of events surely arouses suspicion. He may conceivably have made it up and down the mountain in a single day, but it is harder to believe that he still had the energy to pen so artfully crafted a letter while the servants prepared supper that night (35). Then the symbolic contrast between Gherardo's fast and direct route up the mountain and Petrarch's detour-filled slowness towards the summit becomes far more pointed if the letter was composed only *after* Gherardo's 'lightning conversion'[14] and entry into the Carthusian monastery in Montrieux in 1343. Moreover, the rich texture of literary allusion that belies Petrarch's claim to hasty composition[15] includes references to works that had yet to come to his attention, prominent among them Cicero's letters, that formative model for his own *Epistolae familiares* that he discovered only in 1345 in Verona. Such factors make a compelling case for a date of composition after 1336, and even after Dionigi's death in 1342; hence Giuseppe Billanovich's influential dating of the work to 1353.[16] For present purposes, however, the suggestion of large-scale fictive embellishment in Petrarch's account has important implications for Bembo's response to that obvious guiding model in recounting his own ascent of Etna.

The path to conversion in Petrarch's letter[17] suggestively pre-conditions *De Aetna* as another story of conversion, albeit of a secular kind: the young Pietro undergoes a rite of passage on Etna, a test of courage that quickly grows the man. But if we concede that Bembo on Etna consciously vies with Petrarch on Mont Ventoux, could it be that Urbano Bolzanio takes on added significance as a Gherardo-like figure in *De Aetna*? To press the analogy, Gherardo, like the Franciscan Urbano, reaches the summit while Petrarch makes far slower progress to it and Bembo fails to reach the topmost crater on Etna. If the analogy is accepted, Bembo not only emulates (and even outdoes?) Petrarch's climb in the first place; through a convenient historical coincidence – or, just possibly, through his *own* distortion of historical fact (just as Petrarch may have distorted chronological fact) – Pietro also has his own Gherardo near at hand. To put the point more bluntly: does Bembo respond to the fictive properties of Petrarch's account by positing a fictional ascent by Urbano on 1 June 1493? If so, his depiction of Urbano is crucially conditioned by the dictates of his Petrarchan subtext, and the 'truth' of his account succumbs to the claims of literary *aemulatio*.

Petrarch and Bembo offer two powerful precedents, then, for the phenomenon of the feigned ascent that will now be explored in the case of Patrick Brydone's *Tour*. The view taken of Brydone's Etna narrative below hardly presupposes that he had any direct contact with or knowledge of those precedents; but the differences of literary agenda that are already evident in Petrarch's and Bembo's respective treatments of the phantom-climb theme nevertheless set the stage for our analysis of Brydone's own distinctive experimentation with this versatile phenomenon. So to Italy, and after Bembo's inventive reaction to Petrarch's letter, we now turn to Brydone's dialogical relation with an important source text supplied by Sir William Hamilton.

Brydone in the footsteps of Hamilton

On the evening of 18 January 1770 Brydone was in Naples, where he had arrived on 6 December in the previous year with the then seventeen-year-old William Fullarton in his charge.[18] While in Naples he came to know Sir William Hamilton (1730–1803), the British Ambassador to the Court of Naples from 1764 to 1800 who had already acquired considerable renown as an antiquarian collector and accomplished volcanologist.[19] On that same day, 18 January 1770, a letter of Hamilton's was read in London before the Royal Society, of which he had been elected a Fellow in 1766.[20] This letter, dated 17 October 1769, was included in a double dispatch sent to the secretary of the Royal Society, Matthew Maty (1718–76), one part of it intended as a cover letter for Maty's eyes alone, the other designed for dissemination within the society.[21] The theme of this second missive was Hamilton's account of the expedition to the summit of Etna on which he had embarked on 24 June 1769 in the company of Lord Fortrose[22] and one Canon Recupero, that 'ingenious priest of Catania, who is the only person there, that is acquainted with the mountain'.[23] Their ascent took two days, with the summit reached just before sunrise on the third day; hence the stunning view as 'the sun arose and displayed a scene that indeed passes all description'.[24] After being read to the Society in January 1770, this letter was included in the collection of *Observations on Mount Vesuvius, Mount Etna, and Other Volcanos, in a Series of Letters Addressed to the Royal Society* that was first published in London by Thomas Cadell in 1772.[25] This work was followed by the publication in Naples in 1776 of Hamilton's two-volume *Campi Phlegraei: Observations on the Volcanos of the Two Sicilies as They Have Been Communicated to the Royal Society of London*; a third, supplementary volume was added in 1779.[26]

Perhaps inspired at least in part by Hamilton's visit to Sicily in 1769, Brydone embarked at Naples on 14 May 1770 on the *Charming Molly* en route for Messina in the company of Fullarton and a certain [John?] Glover.[27] His Tour took in Taormina, Catania, his climb of Etna, Syracuse and then an excursion to Malta; returning to Sicily, he visited Agrigentum and subsequently enjoyed a prolonged stay in Palermo before finally embarking on 29 July for Naples, where he arrived on 1 August. Of the thirty-six missives that constitute the original 1773 edition of Brydone's *Tour of Sicily and Malta*, his ascent of Etna that began on 29 May 1770 is recounted in *Letters* VIII to XI; yet beyond these four letters, the mountain casts a long shadow (as we shall see below) over the rest of the collection, as if replicating in its immanent presence across the collection the volcano's unique status within Sicily as both topographical landmark and the island's epicentre of mythological projection. For present purposes, however, the feature of Brydone's ascent that warrants special scrutiny is the tension between the different modes of coverage that he offers: even as he observes the mountain for himself, the many points of contact with Hamilton's account of *his* climb indicate that Brydone is simultaneously engaged in two types of reading of Etna, one topographical, the other textual: as if with one eye on the volcano, the other on Hamilton's letter, his narrative yields striking overlaps with, departures from, and also targeted modifications (even corrections) of Hamilton that we shall first briefly sample before taking stock of Brydone's competitive relationship with his eminent predecessor on Etna. In turn, these contact-points affirm that, for all their obvious differences of genre (letter to the Royal Society vs popular travelogue), target audience, and degree of scientific rigour, Brydone's Etna narrative is, like, Hamilton's, 'a good example of the kind of intermediate discourse, between imaginative literature and natural history, that grows up around the [eighteenth-century] description of natural catastrophes'.[28]

The Advertisement to Brydone's *Tour* asserts that he wrote his letters not for wide distribution but 'for the amusement of his friends, and as an assistance to his memory'.[29] Such imperfections as they may contain are therefore to be excused on the grounds that publication was never originally intended; and, in a further formulaic gesture of modesty, 'one principal motive' for the eventual publication was not so much authorial self-assertion as 'the desire of giving to the world ... a monument of his friendship with the gentleman to whom [the letters] are addressed', William Beckford.[30] Yet for all Brydone's insistence on the unvarnished immediacy of his writing, and despite his pose of modesty as he takes his first diffident steps towards publication, the dissimulating literariness of his self-effacement in his Advertisement is exposed by what *is* known of his efforts at revision before his *Tour* entered the world. David Hume for one, in a letter to his publisher William Strahan of 3 June 1772, acted as an intermediary for Brydone, commending the latter's 'Travels thro Sicily and Malta' to Strahan.[31] Pursuing the matter, Strahan soon found Brydone a hard bargainer who was all too alive to the commercial possibilities of his undertaking.[32] In reply, Hume denies any involvement on the financial side,[33] but he stands by his positive judgement of the book, albeit urging certain revisions.[34] Beyond this revision process, the Advertisement already reveals his knowing fluency in the language of self-deprecation by which the eighteenth-century travel writer could 'set the stylistic tone of sincere plainness and honesty'.[35] But if Brydone's teasing exploitation here of one of the genre's staple tropes already makes the Advertisement more literary than literal in its claims, the understated artifice of his allegedly spontaneous effusions in real time in his *Tour* is still more apparent in his allusive engagement with Hamilton's account of his 1769 ascent.

While allowance naturally has to be made for the coincidental overlap between two narratives that cover the same ground on Etna and between two tours that apparently featured the same guide (Canon Recupero), the contact-points in this case are surely too numerous, too frequent, and too close in verbal detail and choice of emphasis to be systematically explained away as chance occurrences. Consider the following examples (of many that could be cited) of how Brydone echoes, augments or enhances Hamilton's account. In his letter of 17 October 1769 Hamilton describes his party's initial progress through Etna's lower region, called by locals La Regione Piemontese: 'It is well watered, *exceedingly fertile*', the volcanic lava eventually softening and gathering 'soil sufficient for vegetation, which I am convinced from many observations, unless assisted by art, *does not come to pass for many ages*, perhaps a thousand years or more'.[36] So Brydone on this same region: it 'forms *the most fertile country* in the world on all sides of it ... It is composed almost entirely of lava, which, *after a great number of ages*, is at last converted into the most fertile of all soils'.[37] Arriving after a gradual ascent of four or so hours at 'a little convent of Benedictine monks, called St. Nicolo dell'Arena, about thirteen miles from Catania', Hamilton describes the effects as witnessed from there of 'the last very great eruption in the year 1669' – an eruption emanating from 'within a mile' of the convent.[38] Brydone too reaches Nicolosi, named for the monastery of San Nicolo; but whereas Hamilton focuses solely on the effects of the 1669 occurrence, and on a mountain that was raised by that eruption and 'is not less than half a mile perpendicular in height',[39] Brydone focuses first on a mountain 'known by the name of Montpelieri' that was formed by an eruption before 1669 and 'does not rise in perpendicular height above 300 feet'.[40] As if first filling out a picture of the volcanic past that Hamilton has left half drawn, Brydone only then turns to the 1669 occurrence: after flowing around Montpelieri, the lava's two branches merge into a single stream which, 'laying waste the whole country betwixt that [sc. Montpelieri] and Catania, scaled the walls of that city, and poured its flaming torrent into the ocean'.[41] Brydone's account here condenses and (in the detail about the lava flow dividing around Montpelieri) adds nuance to Hamilton's extended description of the effects on Catania (the lava 'reached Catania, and destroyed part of its walls, ... and ran a considerable length into the sea, so as to have once formed a beautiful and safe harbour; but it was soon after filled up by a fresh torrent of the same inflamed matter').[42] Hamilton then visits the lava-source of the 1669 event: 'At the foot of the mountain raised by the eruption of the year 1669, there is a hole, through which, by means of a rope, we descended into several subterraneous caverns'.[43] Brydone appears to follow Hamilton step-by-step, at least as far as the hole's entrance: 'We went to examine the mouth from whence this dreadful torrent issued, and were surprised to find it only a small hole, of about three or four yards diameter'.[44]

In the mountain's second region, La Selvosa,[45] Hamilton reports on a majestic chestnut tree of legendary size, the famous Castagna di Cento Cavalli, adding in a footnote in the 1772 printing of his letter that he has 'heard since, from some of our countrymen who have measured this tree, ... that they could perceive some signs of *four stems having grown together*, and formed one tree'.[46] Given the detour he would have had to make, Hamilton did not himself visit this tree; but Brydone did so, and he appears to go out of his way to 'correct' Hamilton's insinuation that the tree was formed from the merging of multiple stems: although it 'does not seem to be one tree, but a bush of five large trees growing together', he writes, his guides 'unanimously assured us, that by the universal tradition and even testimony of the country, all these were once *united in one stem* ... We began to examine it with more attention, and found that there is an appearance that these five trees were really once *united in one*'.[47] Later, as Hamilton nears the summit with his party, he observes that in many places the snow is covered with a bed of ashes, thrown out of the crater, and the sun melting it in some parts makes this ground treacherous; but as we had with us, besides our guide, a peasant well accustomed to these valleys, we arrived safe at the foot of the little mountain of ashes that crowns Etna, about an hour before the rising of the sun.[48]

Brydone goes into greater detail on these perils underfoot, informed as he is by the expert guide known as 'the Cyclops' (does Brydone here have one eye on Hamilton's 'peasant', who appears disappointingly anonymous by comparison?):

> He told us, that it often happened, that the surface of the mountain being hot below, melted the snow in particular spots, and formed pools of water, where it was impossible to foresee our danger; that it likewise happened, that the surface of the water, as well as the snow, was often covered over with black ashes, that rendered it exceedingly treacherous; that however, if we thought proper, he should lead us on with as much caution as possible.[49]

The 'little mountain of ashes that crowns Etna', reports Hamilton, 'is situated in a gently inclining plain, of about nine miles in circumference; it is about a quarter of a mile perpendicular in height, very steep'.[50] Brydone's description is broadly similar ('its circumference cannot be less than ten miles ... We found this mountain excessively steep');[51] but even if the coincidence with Hamilton here is deemed more incidental than deliberate, the verbal echoes when Brydone describes the early morning view from near the summit are surely unmistakable.

Here comes the sun: 'Soon after we had seated ourselves on the highest point of Etna', writes Hamilton,

> the sun arose, and displayed *a scene that indeed passes all description.*[52] The horizon lighting up by degrees, we discovered the greatest part of Calabria, and the sea on the other side of it; the Phare of Messina, the Lipari Islands, Stromboli with its smoking top, though at above seventy miles distance, seemed to be *just under our feet*; we saw the whole island of Sicily, its rivers, towns, harbours, &c. *as if we had been looking on a map* ... The pyramidal shadow of the mountain *reached across the whole island* and *far into the sea* on the other side.[53]

Now Brydone:

> *But here description must ever fall short*; for no imagination has dared to form an idea of so glorious and so magnificent a scene ... The body of the sun is seen rising from the ocean, immense tracks both of sea and land intervening; the islands of Lipari, Panari, Alicudi, Strombolo, and Volcano, with their smoking summits, appear *under your feet*; and you look down on the whole of Sicily *as on a map* ... On the sun's first rising, the shadow of the mountain extends *across the whole island*, and makes a large track visible *even in the sea* and in the air.[54]

Fundamental to the illusion of spontaneous, 'authentic' narration in Brydone's *Tour* is his attempt directly to engage his reader in the real-time movement of his day-to-day narrative. For Charles Batten, in seeking 'to seize the reader's imagination and to carry it with him on his tour' Brydone injects 'more autobiographical and fictional material than had his predecessors';[55] and his colourful interludes on, say, going after swordfish, or hunting (and eating) porcupine, or vainly trying to land a turtle at sea, or the delicacy of the morene eel,[56] are all designed to capture the imagination of a readership unused to such Mediterranean exotica. But the effort to recruit the reader as a fellow-traveller is all-important. The aim is to seize the reader's imagination and, as Brydone puts it, to 'carry it along with us through every scene, and make it in a manner congenial with our own; every prospect opening upon him with the same light, and arising in the same colours, and at the same instant too, as upon us'.[57] His addressee, William Beckford, thus becomes an absent presence along the way, even 'one of the party',[58] so that when Brydone wishes his friend 'Adieu' at the journey's end and the book's conclusion, he hails him as 'our faithful companion during this tour'.[59] But Hamilton too is in a sense one of Brydone's party, as if carried in the latter's pocket: in persistently recalling Hamilton's account of Etna, our author can be seen to engage with the volcano not just empirically but also textually, and so to replicate *in his own case* the very effect that he seeks to have on his own reader; for his step-by-step engagement with Hamilton on the mountain models the very immediacy of impact – that sense of an imagination carried by a guiding text – that Brydone wills for his own narrative. My proposal, in effect, is that Hamilton's Etnean footprint in Brydone's *Tour* does more than merely acknowledge an influential precursor on the mountain, perhaps with a certain deference to one whose letters of introduction opened doors around Sicily;[60] Hamilton's sub-presence provides a dialogical yardstick against which to measure not just the plausibility of Brydone's account of his climb, but also the different, still more self-conscious literary ambition of Brydone's venture – perhaps most of all his greater ambition to 'paint like nature'[61] as he surveys the sunrise at Etna's peak, where his picturesque description (its sublime accent as much articulating an inner condition as an external view)[62] rapturously outshines even Hamilton's luminous description. But then a dark cloud: what if Brydone never in fact came close to reaching Etna's summit?

Brydone's detractors

A telling anecdote is recounted by the diarist Joseph Farington (1747–1821) of the elusive Mr Glover who accompanied Brydone on his Tour.[63] In his entry for 20 October 1805, Farington records an encounter with a certain Mr Tathem, erstwhile Consul General in Sicily, who 'spoke of Brydone's tour in Sicily and called it a *romance*'; for Tathem

> spoke to Mr. Glover who accompanied Brydone to the top of Mount Etna respecting the description given by Brydone of the vast extent of country, and of

Sea, and of Circumstances which He saw from the Summit of that mountain. Mr. Glover said that if Brydone saw such things He must have had better eyes than Mr. Glover possessed who saw nothing but *Clouds*.[64]

If for Glover the view from the top was impeded, other rumour had it that Brydone was prevented by injury from making any attempt on the summit in the first place. He does indeed mention an injury, but one incurred only on his descent from the upper reaches, and with symbolic implications that may themselves invite suspicion about the sincerity of his account. In a pleasing symmetry between mental elevation and his heightened station at Etna's summit, Brydone's serene view-from-above induces an inner serenity:

> Here, where you stand under a serene sky, and behold, with equal serenity, the tempest and storm forming below your feet . . . the mind considers the little storms and thunder of the human passions as equally below her notice.[65]

But then disaster: 'In the very midst of these meditations, my philosophy was at once overset' when, as he ran across the ice, 'my leg folded under me'.[66] The sprain is painfully exquisite in its timing in Brydone's telling, graphically reducing him to 'a poor miserable mortal'[67] as he comes down from the sublime heights; but the truth of the matter was rather different, at least by alternative report. So Thomas Watkins describes how in Catania he encountered an innkeeper who

> told us, that Mr. _____, who has published such a minute description of his journey to the crater of Aetna, was never there, but sick in Catania, when his party ascended, he having been their guide.[68]

By the early nineteenth century the sceptical view had seemingly hardened among Anglophone observers, at least to judge by the matter-of-fact dismissals of George Russell, say, in his 1819 *A Tour Through Sicily in the Year 1815* ('. . . the more we must admire [Brydone's] fancy, which enabled him to speak with such rapture of the prospect from the double summit of the highest crater, without having ever ascended it'),[69] or Richard Grenville, 1st Duke of Buckingham and Chandos (1776–1839), in his diary entry for 4 November 1827:

> The memory of Brydone is now laughed at. For a long while his stories did us honour. Their effect is now passed away. It is now acknowledged and known that Brydone never proceeded further up Etna himself than the Benedictine Convent [sc. at Nicolosi].[70]

While the seductive charms of Brydone's *Tour* won it many admirers, its success also provoked jealousy and harsh critique on the Continent,[71] notably in the Polish-born Michel-Jean de Borch's *Lettres sur la Sicile et sur l'île de Malthe* (Turin 1782), written in 1777 and ostensibly – or ostentatiously – designed as a supplement of sorts (even a rival) to Brydone's *Tour*.⁷² Brydone's slighting allusions to the French also drew the ire of his critics, foremost among them Jean-Benjamin de la Borde (1734–94), author of the first French translation (5 volumes, Paris, 1785–7) of Henry Swinburne's *Travels in the Two Sicilies in the Years 1774, 1778, 1779 and 1780* (London 1783–5).⁷³ In this vein Joseph-Antoine de Gourbillon (*c.* 1770–?), in his *Voyage critique à l'Etna en 1819* (2 volumes, Paris 1820), repeated the assertion that Brydone never made it to the top crater, injured as he was in Nicolosi and then transported to the Benedictine convent where he awaited the rest of his party after they had made it to the summit.⁷⁴ Gourbillon's informants, he goes on to relate,⁷⁵ had apparently heard as much from none other than Canon Recupero himself, who had his own axe to grind with Brydone: in the scientific component of his Etna narrative Brydone had seemingly drawn on Recupero's unpublished work on the topic. Gourbillon's Recupero thus set the record straight about Brydone's tall story of reaching the summit, but there was also another score to settle.⁷⁶ In his *Tour* Brydone reports that Recupero's researches on Etna's lava formations had led him to conclude that the eruption producing the earliest accretions 'must have flowed from the mountain at least 14,000 years ago'⁷⁷ – a view glaringly incompatible with the Mosaic Chronology that (after the influential biblical chronologies of Archbishop James Ussher of Ireland, 1581–1656) dated the creation to 4004 BCE. Embarrassed by his discoveries, the Canon chose the path of discretion, only for Brydone to betray that reticence. Recupero's response to that betrayal⁷⁸ was amplified, even sensationalized, by Brydone's critics, Borch chief among them,⁷⁹ but Samuel Johnson shows a lighter touch in scorching Brydone with wit: 'The information which we have from modern travellers is much more authentic than what we had from ancient travellers; ancient travellers guessed, modern travellers measure ... If Brydone were more attentive to his Bible, he would be a good traveller'.⁸⁰

If at this point the more extreme, agenda-driven charges of such hostile critics as Borde and Gourbillon are laid to one side, the fact remains that a certain licence was inveterate to the eighteenth-century travel genre; the creative writer in Brydone might be expected to massage the truth-quotient of his Etna narrative without compromising his scientific rigour as he investigates the volcanic landscape, measures barometric pressure, or tests the properties of electricity. Yet his *suspected* liberties may nonetheless still disconcert: his (feigned?) progress almost to the summit, his (fabricated?) account of the ineffable sunrise that he witnessed there, his claim to have sustained an injury only on his descent – and all this in addition to what we might, at least on one reading, perceive as his undisguised reliance on Hamilton's account of his prior ascent. Let us momentarily concede, then, Brydone's potential fabrications and mountain of debt to textual allusion, but without reverting to the dead-end of trying to define the limits of his fictional enhancements. What matters more for now is Brydone's conversion of his 'real' experience on the mountain into an aesthetic experience at the summit – as if his priority in recounting his climb has not been to detail the wonders of Etna *per se*, but to explore the psychological experience that the ascent facilitates. His exploration of external nature thus evolves into a more internally focused production; the nitty-gritty problem of his truth-telling recedes before the different challenge that the text now poses, of assessing Brydone's ability to find (not least through Hamilton's help) a rhetorical match for the natural sublime; and even if our doubt that he reached the summit wins out, his imaginative power in projecting the rapture of that pinnacle achievement suddenly takes centre stage in his Etna narrative.

Etna's shadow over Brydone's *Tour*

As we survey the larger landscape of Brydone's *Tour* from atop Etna in *Letter* X, the imaginative capacities that shape his ascent can now be seen to radiate down from the mountain and to infiltrate the general design of his work. If his conceptual map of Sicily is centred on Etna, the volcano is similarly central to Brydone's text. So, for example, when he observes of the impressive ancient theatre at Taormina that 'The seats exactly front mount Aetna, which makes a glorious appearance from this place; and no doubt has often diverted their attention from the scene',[81] his own writing, like the theatre audience, is diverted by that star attraction. In turning to Catania in *Letter* VIII, he is transported once more: 'But this amazing mountain perpetually carries me away from my subject; I was speaking of this city'.[82] On 31 May 1770 Brydone departs from Catania for Syracuse, but there is no escaping Etna in *Letter* XII: 'The view of mount Aetna, for the whole of this little voyage is wonderfully fine ... The view of the mountain from the sea is much more complete and satisfactory than any where on the island'.[83] Now in Malta in *Letter* XIV, he inevitably contemplated the volcano on the outward voyage there: 'We were now on the main ocean, and saw no land but mount Aetna; which is the perpetual polar star of these seas'.[84] In *Letter* XXX he writes from Palermo, recounting how from the top of the nearby Monte Pelegrino 'the prospect ... is very beautiful and extensive. Most of the Lipari islands are discovered in a very clear day, and likewise a large portion of mount Aetna, although at the distance of almost the whole length of Sicily'.[85] In his last letter actually penned on the island (*Letter* XXXV, Palermo, 29 July 1770; contrast *Letter* XXXVI, Naples, 1 August), his final remarks on Etna are retrospective in feel, as if summing up the volcano's centrality throughout his *Tour*:

> But it would be endless to give you an account of all the various commodities and curious productions of this island; Aetna alone affords a greater number than many of the most extensive kingdoms, and is no less an epitome of the whole earth in its soil and climate, than in the variety of its productions.[86]

Already before he reached Sicily, Brydone's eye for wonder had found much to admire in and around Naples, where

> the country ... abounds so much in every thing that is curious, both in art and nature, and affords so ample a field of speculation for the naturalist and antiquary, that a person of any curiosity may spend some months here very agreeably, and not without profit.[87]

If the appetite is thus whetted in Naples for the still greater wonders that await in Sicily, Brydone's passing commentary on the Lipari islands, Stromboli, etc., in his lead-up to the Etna sequence in *Letters* VIII to XI functions as a rehearsal of sorts for his treatment of 'that venerable and respectable father of mountains'.[88] His many evocations of classical antiquity (whether through literary or archaeological allusion) represent a comparative reach into the past that is dwarfed by his superlative leap into Etna's deep geological time;[89] and for all his scientific inquiries on Etna into barometric pressure and the 'fifth element' of electricity,[90] those efforts are belittled by the many aspects of the volcano's functioning that defy conventional explanation. Hence the 'absurdity', for example, of attributing to 'the power of suction' the emanation of boiling water from the volcanic crater,[91] and hence the reticence imposed on Canon Recupero when the evidence of the lava layers leads him to infer that the volcano must surely predate 4004 BCE.[92]

Many further illustrations could be given of how Brydone embeds Etna in the larger literary geology of his *Tour*, and of how that embedding process combines with other structural devices to create thematic balance across the letters. So, for example, the narrative highpoint of the Etna sequence in *Letters* VIII to XI is suggestively offset by Brydone's extended coverage of Palermo in *Letters* XX to XXXV: just as Etna is a marvel of paradoxical admixture in its snow-clad fieriness and heavenly hellishness,[93] so the elegance of Palermo's high society underscores the paradox of Sicily itself as both a crucible of volcanic rawness and a cradle of cultured civility; in this respect, the feast of St Rosalia as pictured in *Letter* XXVIII arguably balances the spectacle of Etna earlier in the *Tour*, the festive lights and fireworks[94] perhaps implicitly (even poignantly) contrasted with the volcano's natural pyrotechnics. The sirocco, that hot south-east wind, appears early in the *Tour*, infecting Naples with that 'degree of lassitude, both to the body and mind, that renders [the Neapolitans] absolutely incapable of performing their usual functions'.[95] Brydone achieves a breezy symmetry by returning to the sirocco in Palermo in *Letter* XXVII, albeit it is now differently felt ('Now, in Naples, and in many other places in Italy, where its violence is not to be compared to this, it is often attended with putrid disorders').[96]

Beyond the sirocco's recurrence, as if in ring-composition, early and late in the *Tour*, the sickliness associated with it is also relatable to the atmospherics of illness (figurative as well as literal) that Brydone imputes to Sicily more generally. So the mini-drama when his boat arrives in Messina: since one of the entourage's servants was accidently omitted from the ship's bill of health, he would have to undergo a long quarantine if discovered; and so he is hidden away, in a plot-line that persists into the next letter.[97] This minor episode is in keeping with the diaristic feel of the *Tour*; or could it yet be more contrived than ingenuous? After all, while the authorities work to prevent the importation of disease into Sicily, Brydone portrays the island as itself a symbolically infectious 'country of fable':

> You have, therefore, only to suppose that these regions are still *contagious*; and call to mind that mount Aetna has ever been the great mother of monsters and chimeras both in the antient [*sic*] and the modern world. However, I shall, if

possible, keep free of the *infection*, and entertain you only with such subjects as fall under my own observation.[98]

But while Brydone resists this figurative infection, his *Tour* shows infirmity in other ways. When his leg folds under him 'in the very midst of these [sublime] meditations' high up the mountain, his 'philosophy was at once overset, and in a moment I found myself relapsed into a poor miserable mortal':[99] whether or not his rude awakening here gently evokes the fate that befell Empedocles, that rather more famous philosopher made mortal on Etna,[100] Brydone certainly shows a keen sensitivity to the rhythm of coming to be and passing away, or of fortunes transformed over time, that is emblematized by Etna's volcanic changefulness. So Taormina, for example: 'This famous city is now reduced to an insignificant burgh; yet even these small remains give a very high idea of its former magnificence'.[101] The undulating fertility of 'the beautiful country near Hybla' that is famed for its honey is duly reflected in its change of name from Mel Passi to Mal Passi after one eruption of Aetna, and then to Bell Passia after it recovered – only for it to revert once more to Mal Passi after the eruption of 1669.[102] Then Syracuse: 'But, alas! how are the mighty fallen!', exclaims Brydone; 'This proud city, that vied with Rome itself, is now reduced to a heap of rubbish'.[103] Agrigentum (for but one further example) similarly attests to this nostalgia for a lost grandeur,[104] a conspicuous feature of the *Tour* that may be motivated in part by Brydone's Scottish Enlightenment credentials as a Liberal and Rationalist committed to technological innovation and economic entrepreneurship; hence, as his *Tour* progresses, he takes oblique aim at the absolutist Spanish regime that, he implies, has crushed the Sicilian spirit of enterprise through bureaucratic inertia, a culture of disincentive, and a lack of technological advancement.[105]

What, then, to make of these recurrent themes as we finally take stock of Brydone's *Tour* as a whole? That certain preoccupations should surface in different missives is no surprise, of course; yet the structural coherence that is aided by that recurrence does nothing to allay the suspicion that the day-to-day spontaneity that he claims for the letters is more illusory than real. The air of improvisation certainly draws attention to itself: so in *Letter* II, for example, his updates in moving from his first setting of pen to paper on 15 May to resuming on the next day and in increments thereafter ('17th in the morning'; '17th. Three o'clock'; then 'Eleven at night') nicely capture the clock ticks of epistolary time.[106] Interruptions as he writes,[107] his hasty additions in 'P.S.',[108] his fitful routine,[109] his occasionally sagging energies,[110] and his improvised positions as he sets pen to paper now (for example) 'on the end of a barrel' and now in bed:[111] such features may give his descriptions 'the appearance of being immediate and hence accurate',[112] but the 'truth' they project is itself hardly reinforced by the ubiquity of the immediacy trope in eighteenth-century travel writing. No: the imaginative elaborations that he builds into his Etna sequence in *Letters* VIII to XI are typical, we surely infer, of the inventiveness that extends from the volcanic slopes to so many other aspects of the *Tour*. Hence the subtlety of vision that Sir William Hamilton for one praises in Brydone, albeit perhaps with a coyness of tone that puts us on our guard. He hails Brydone as 'a very ingenious and accurate observer'[113] whose measurements of temperature and barometric pressure on Etna he then reports; but is it vain to hope that Hamilton, ever the diplomat, used that phrase with an ironic charge, knowing full well that Brydone was far more ingenious than truthful in so many aspects of his Etna narrative as ultimately published in 1773?

Conclusion

If, *in fine*, we infer that Brydone never truly witnessed the sunrise at Etna's summit, his projection to that effect amounts to a coalescence between factual assertion on the one hand and fictive elaboration on the other; and this merging of properties, I have argued, captures the amorphous transition point as 'real' experience gives way to a state of sublime transcendence – sight to insight, so to speak – high on the volcanic slopes. For all his particularized focus on Sicily and Etna, Brydone's exploration of the mountain thus expands into an exploration of mountain experience, and of sublime experience, more generally – a breadth of appeal that may in part explain why his *Tour* was so well received that multiple further editions followed soon after its first publication. As we follow Brydone up Etna, then, we become members of his party not just as vicarious visitors of that magic mountain, but also as his fellow travellers on a seminal path of eighteenth-century aesthetic experience: in touring Etna he explores the imaginative capacities involved in sensing and articulating the sublime. Along the way he exploits the phenomenon of the feigned ascent that we have also explored in the cases of Petrarch and Pietro Bembo. Even if Brydone is not directly indebted to them for his own elaboration of that phenomenon, he shares with Bembo in particular a highly creative approach to the literary stylization of Etna. Steeped as he was in the classical tradition, Brydone's articulation of the sublime in and through his progress up the mountain is arguably informed by what he knew to be the many ingenious symbolic meanings that had been attributed to the volcano from Hesiod onwards. Brydone is no captive to that tradition, however: in describing his (feigned?) path to the summit, he tells what looks suspiciously like a tall story, but a *novel* tall story nonetheless, crucially inflected as it is by his peak performance of the sublime.

Notes

1. On the Graeco-Roman Etna tradition, Buxton 2016 with Williams 2017: 23–71 and now Duffy in this volume.
2. *Epistolae familiares* 4.1; bibliography in Williams 2017: 95–101.
3. *Not* 1743, as sometimes claimed: see Portale 2004: 23 and 47, n. 1.
4. For orientation on Brydone's life, Portale 2004 with Evans 2014. On the *Tour* as a 'milestone', Smecca 2003: 52, with stress on its 'new elements' – the Sicilian setting, the myth of Etna, and 'the sublime note, which appears here for the first time in the work of a typical Enlightenment, rationalistic *voyageur-philosophe*'. For the successive editions and translations of the *Tour* that followed soon after its first publication, Evans 2014: 127–30. My own approach to Brydone in this essay is designed to complement Duffy's fine treatment elsewhere in this volume (see esp. 43–5), and also that of Hollis 2020.

5. Background: Ruta 2016 with Tuzet 1945, 1955 and 1988; Falzone 1963; di Carlo 1964; Smecca 2005. John Dryden, the poet's second son, had in fact already toured Sicily and Malta in 1700–1; for his account of that adventure (*A Voyage to Sicily and Malta, in the Years 1700 and 1701*), prompted into publication in 1776 by the appearance of Brydone's *Tour* three years before, see Duffy 37–43 in this volume.
6. Cf. the important formulation in Duffy and Howell 2011: 19: 'Brydone ... responds, here [sc. in his Etna narrative], as much to a cultural as to a natural phenomenon: his engagement with the volcanic sublime is in no sense a "disinterested" aesthetic judgement'.
7. For Hamilton see also Duffy 46 in this volume.
8. Cf. Duffy 43 in this volume on Brydone's 'indebtedness to classical writing about Etna'.
9. Further on mnemonic topography, Williams 2017: 74–9.
10. For whom Gualdo Rosa 1986 with Scapecchi 2001.
11. The full text of Bembo's *De Aetna* is translated in Williams 2017: 310–53.
12. Further on these points, Williams 2017: 88–9.
13. Translation of Petrarch my own; text and subsection numbers from Stoppelli 1997.
14. Billanovich 1966, 397; on the circumstances of Gherardo's sudden conversion 'from a wayward and unstable young man into a firm and constant one' (*Epistolae familiares* 16.9), Robbins 1991: 59–60.
15. For the wide net of biblical and classical allusions, Billanovich 1966: 394–5 with Courcelle 1963: 339–42, Martinelli 1973 and Durling 1977: 305.
16. Billanovich 1947: 193–8 with 1966: esp. 399.
17. For this Petrarchan conversion as itself a partial imitation and reaction against the Augustinian conversion experience see Falkeid 2009.
18. Chronology: Portale 2004: 26 with Evans 2014: 70–1. For Fullarton (1754–1808), Portale 2004: 81–2 with Evans 2014: 63–4.
19. On the antiquarian and geological aspects, Sleep 1969 with Jenkins and Sloan 1996 and Constantine 2001: esp. 32–44 ('Vases and the volcano').
20. Fothergill 1969: 84.
21. On this combination of letters, Wood 2006: 72–3.
22. I.e. Kenneth Mackenzie, 1st Earl of Seaforth (1744–81).
23. Hamilton 1770: 3 = 1772: 57; further on Giuseppe Recupero (1720–78), Candela 2016 with Tuzet 1955: 486–91. For the prevalence of volcanology in eighteenth-century Royal Society debate, Stokes 1971.
24. Hamilton 1770: 12 = 1772: 74.
25. For details on its three editions between 1772 and 1774, Sleep 1969: 319.
26. For orientation on this edition, Wood 2006 with Cheetham 1984.
27. For the details of his itinerary here and below, Portale 2004: 29. For the elusive Glover (the water-colorist John Glover, d. 1849?), Portale 2004: 82–3 with Greig 1924: 118–19.
28. Heringman 2003: 124.
29. Succinctly on this and other familiar tropes (e.g. the pose of modest stylistic accomplishment, the rapidity of composition, etc.) in the eighteenth-century travel letter, Batten 1978: 31–46 with Smith 1998.
30. Brydone 1773: I, 'Advertisement'. On this Beckford of Somerly (1744–99), *not* his cousin William T. Beckford (1759–1844) of *Vathek* fame, Portale 2004: 75–81.

31. Hill 1888: 249, *Letter* LXIII.
32. Ibid. 257, n. 3.
33. 30 January 1773 = Hill 1888: 255, *Letter* LXVI: 'I never, that I remember, mention'd to Cap^n Braidon [*sic*] any particular Sum which he might expect'.
34. 30 January 1773 = Hill 1888: 255, *Letter* LXVI.
35. Batten 1978: 45.
36. Hamilton 1770: 3 = 1772: 57–8; my emphasis.
37. Brydone 1773: I, 155.
38. Hamilton 1770: 4 = 1772: 59–60.
39. Hamilton 1770: 6 = 1772: 65.
40. Brydone 1773: I, 161.
41. Ibid. I, 163.
42. Hamilton 1770: 7 = 1772: 65.
43. Hamilton 1770: 7 = 1772: 66.
44. Brydone 1773: I, 164.
45. Hamilton 1770: 8 = 1772: 68.
46. Hamilton 1770: 9; footnote in 1772: 69 (my emphasis).
47. Brydone 1773: 1.109–10; my emphasis. Further on this episode, Watkins 2014: 91–3.
48. Hamilton 1770: 11 = 1772: 72.
49. Brydone 1773: I, 182.
50. Hamilton 1770: 11 = 1772: 72–3.
51. Brydone 1773: I, 186.
52. See Heringman 2003: 125 on the tension between this 'retreat from description' and 'the insistence on measurements' in Hamilton's *modus scribendi* – a tension hinting at 'a Burkean sublime of obscurity', and one that resurfaces in Brydone's own appeal to scientific measurement on Etna on the one hand, the ineffability of sublime natural description on the other.
53. Hamilton 1770: 12 = 1772: 74–5; my emphasis.
54. Brydone 1773: I, 187, 189, 194–5.
55. Batten 1978: 118.
56. Brydone 1773: I, 15 (porcupine), I, 66, II, 218–20 (swordfish, on the Sicilian techniques and perils of fishing for which see Gudger 1940), I, 263–5 (turtle), II, 4 (morene eel).
57. Ibid. I, 100.
58. Ibid.
59. Ibid. II, 286.
60. See, e.g. ibid. I, 350 and esp. II, 65 (Hamilton's 'recommendations we have ever found to be the best passport and introduction').
61. From James Thomson's *Spring* (1728, part of *The Seasons* sequence), cited by Batten 1978: 101.
62. Brydone 1773: I, 187–92.
63. For Glover, 169 and n. 27 above.
64. Greig 1924: 118–19.

65. Brydone 1773: I, 201–2.
66. Ibid. I, 202.
67. Ibid.
68. Watkins 1792: II, 21.
69. Russell 1819: 220.
70. Temple-Grenville 1862: I, 169.
71. See in general Portale 2004: 135–93 (on 'Ammiratori e detrattori').
72. For Borch (1751–1810), Portale 2004: 158–9 with Tuzet 1955: 53–9.
73. See Portale 2004: 140–2 and 163–4 with Tuzet 1955: 53–66.
74. Gourbillon 1820: I, 393–4, with 395–8 on the seeming impracticality of Brydone's claimed itinerary in Sicily; on Gourbillon, see Portale 2004: 164–8 with Tuzet 1955: 51–2.
75. Gourbillon 1820: I, 394 and n. 1 with Portale 2004: 165–6.
76. On the ensuing anecdote, now Duffy 2013: 78–80.
77. Brydone 1773: I, 132.
78. And perhaps also to Brydone's irreverent flippancy in stating (ibid.) that 'Moses hangs like a dead weight upon him [sc. Recupero], and blunts all his zeal for inquiry'.
79. See Tuzet 1955: 51 with Portale 2004: 160 and Duffy 2013: 79–80.
80. Croker 1876: 617; the quip dates to a 1778 meeting between Dr Johnson and William Fullarton.
81. Brydone 1773: I, 97–8.
82. Ibid. I, 140.
83. Ibid. I, 253, 256.
84. Ibid. I, 305.
85. Ibid. II, 200.
86. Ibid. II, 281.
87. Ibid. I, 12–13.
88. Ibid. I, 154.
89. Deep time: Duffy 2013: 69–72, and further discussion in this volume above, 9.
90. See esp. Brydone 1773: I, 207–28.
91. Ibid. I, 107.
92. Ibid. I, 131–2, on which 175 above.
93. Brydone makes much of such paradox (e.g. ibid. I, 173: 'It is indeed a curious consideration, that this mountain should reunite every beauty and every horrour; and, in short, *all the most opposite and dissimilar objects in nature*. Here you observe a gulph, that formerly threw out torrents of fire and smoke, now covered with the most luxuriant vegetation; and from an object of terrour, become one of delight' [my emphasis]); further, Giardina 1995: esp. 250–4.
94. Brydone 1773: II, 161, 171.
95. Ibid. I, 6.
96. Ibid. II, 144, part of an extended discourse on the sirocco's effects in Palermo (142–6).
97. Ibid. I, 47–8 (*Letter* II), 55–6 (*Letter* III).
98. Ibid. I, 90; my emphasis.

99. Ibid. I, 202.
100. Ibid. I, 199–200, on Etna throwing up Empedocles' shoe after he had leapt into the volcano, his vanishing act 'that he might be looked upon as a god' thereby exposed; for 'by his death, as well as life, he only wanted to impose upon mankind, and make them believe that he was greater than they'. Further on Empedocles, see Duffy, 44 and 46, this volume.
101. Ibid. I, 97.
102. Ibid. I, 160.
103. Ibid. I, 265; the lament recurs at 284–5.
104. Ibid. I, 351–9 (*Letter* XVIII).
105. On these points, Farrell 1992: 294–7 and 2014: 79–81.
106. Brydone 1773: I, 25–6.
107. E.g. *Letter* IV, ibid. I, 70 ('I have just been interrupted by an upper servant of the prince's'); XVIII at I, 359 ('But I am interrupted by visitors'); XIX at I, 360 ('The interruption in my last…').
108. E.g. *Letter* IV, ibid. I, 86; XXVIII at II, 137.
109. E.g. *Letter* XVIII, ibid. II, 1: 'When I have nothing else to do, I generally take up the pen'.
110. E.g. *Letter* XVIII, ibid. II, 22: 'These two fellows are still as sound as pigs. In a few minutes I shall be so too, for the pen is almost dropping out of my hand'.
111. *Letter* V, ibid. I, 101; IX at I, 179; X at I, 206.
112. Batten 1978: 71.
113. Hamilton 1772: 80n.

CHAPTER 10
MOUNTAINS OF MEMORY: A PHENOMENOLOGICAL APPROACH TO MOUNTAINS IN FIFTH-CENTURY BCE GREEK TRAGEDY

Chloe Bray

In the study of ancient literature, it is often difficult to comment on unspoken, culturally shared understandings of broad concepts such as space and landscape. As various chapters in this volume show, modern authors and explorers often record their sensory and imaginative responses to mountainous landscapes in detail; ancient authors, by comparison, rarely address such experiences. In scholarship on ancient Greek tragedy, this has led to the opinion that tragedians were generally disinterested in landscape.[1] Scholars who do acknowledge the significance of setting for tragedy have been primarily interested in structural contrasts between the city and the wilderness, or in identifying 'liminal' spaces which symbolize death.[2] These dialogues have created a general perception of the ancient Greek mountain as a space of violence, which is physically and conceptually distant from the civilized world. Whether directly or indirectly, such perceptions may have contributed to the wider belief in a premodern 'mountain gloom' which is set out in the introduction to this volume. Drawing on approaches from phenomenology, I aim to show another side of mountains in Greek tragedy. Though the marginality and violence of mythical mountain space which scholars such as Richard Buxton have discussed is clearly important in the reading of tragic texts,[3] phenomenology can help to illuminate an equally important perception of mountains as connective places of heightened sensory experience which facilitate acts of memory. In this way, I will demonstrate that aspects of the modern experience of mountains as places of spatial, temporal and imaginative connectivity can also be recognized in Greek tragedy, even in the briefest of descriptions.

Phenomenology is concerned with the human experience of landscape. Moving away from the traditional approach to viewing, where distance and disconnection is assumed between the viewer and the landscape, phenomenology seeks the meaning of landscape through the engaged relationship between viewer and landscape, in practices, emotions and sensations which transcend cognitive and visual terms.[4] In his *Phénoménologie de la Perception* (1945), Merleau-Ponty stresses that the world is not perceived as a series of distinct, external phenomena but as a whole, where any sight, sound or smell can only be understood in relation to those around it and to the body of the one engaged in perception.[5] This idea has been more recently developed by anthropologist Tim Ingold, who addresses the immersive experience of light, sound and feeling as the creation of an atmosphere, concluding that sensory experience sweeps the perceiver not into landscape as a fixed surface one stands upon but into atmosphere as an 'all-enveloping' awareness.[6] These ideas are part of the wider understanding of *embodiment*, a term used in landscape phenomenology to describe the immersive experience of the sensing, moving body in landscape, as opposed to the static view of landscape as an observed medium separate from the body.[7] In literature, references to movement are essential in recreating embodied experience; researchers in discourse analysis and cognitive psychology have acknowledged the difference between the disembodied, static representation of space as a map, and the dynamic, internal perspective of space in narrative, in which the reader is taken on a 'tour' from the perspective of a moving object.[8] The movement of characters within or through the represented space 'stimulates the embodied experience of a traveler'.[9] These ideas form a useful framework for looking at ancient descriptions of landscape, since theories of embodied experience are concerned with automatic human responses which are not culturally or temporally specific. This makes it possible to assess whether the highly sensory experience of mountains which is evidenced in the modern period can also be traced in ancient accounts of mountains.

While mountains in Greek tragedy are often discussed in terms of their separation from society and normal behaviours, phenomenology provides an insight into the connectivity of mountains, as locations of heightened sensory experience where memory is uniquely tied to landscape. Veronica della Dora characterizes mountains as performative landscapes, which allow an embodied and multi-sensorial spatial act of recollection.[10] Examining the appeal of mountaineering for philhellenic tourists of the nineteenth century, della Dora discusses the necessity of performance in landscape's potential to stimulate memory: it was in dynamic, embodied encounters that those hoping to experience the past were satisfied.[11] This can partly be explained by the views from mountains, which visually draw together distant places. From an elevated position, it is possible to gain a broader perspective on landscapes in the form which Ingold has called 'taskscapes',[12] or landscapes as the lasting accruement of past and present human lives and activity. Moreover, anyone who has stood on a mountain knows that light and shadow create dramatic contrasts on peaks, valleys, cliffs and rock formations. In terms of narratives which describe movement, it is relevant that travelling on mountain paths often necessarily increases the attention a traveller pays to their own position in the landscape. Lorimer describes the heightened awareness experienced by a long-distance runner climbing a slope, even where the terrain is familiar: sight and sensation are enclosed to immediate surroundings, and as a result 'ascension can be remembered most intensely'.[13] It is not unreasonable to suppose that a similar single-mindedness might be reached by a fifth-century BCE herdsman climbing a familiar mountain path, or by an urban Athenian travelling to a mountain sanctuary. This experience can also be transferred to a theatre audience or a reader. Behavioural and neuroimaging experiments have demonstrated that when sentences involving bodily movement are processed, areas of the brain are activated which correspond to those activated in the physical movement of the same body parts.[14] This process, known as 'motor resonance',[15] means that upon hearing or reading the description of movement, an audience is likely to experience the sensory traces which accompany that movement as part of its relational memory schema. A reader or audience member receiving descriptions of movement in landscape, such as climbing a mountain, will therefore undergo elements of the embodied experience of the terrain, enabling acts of memory in a reduced but similar way to real, physical encounters with landscape.[16] It is with this body of theory in mind that the following discussion proceeds.

Euripides' *Bacchae* and Mount Kithairon

Euripides' *Bacchae* ('Bacchic Women'), first performed in 405 BCE, dramatizes the myth of Dionysus' arrival in Greece. It is set at the palace of Thebes, but much of the action in the play takes place on the slopes of nearby Mount Kithairon, and is reported back to the characters in the city by messengers. When Pentheus, the king of Thebes, refuses to recognize Dionysus as a god, Dionysus afflicts the women of Thebes with madness; they abandon the city and their children for Mount Kithairon to live as wild women, dancing, singing and performing miracles for Dionysus. Failing to capture Dionysus or the Theban women, Pentheus eventually climbs the mountain himself, but when the women see him they tear him to pieces. Pentheus' mother triumphantly carries his head back to Thebes, where her madness lifts and the royal family is forced to see their error in rejecting Dionysus. Most discussions of Mount Kithairon in Euripides' *Bacchae* focus on the dangerous, uncivilized nature of the mountain and its separation from the city.[17] However, a phenomenological approach reveals that Mount Kithairon is also connective, as a vividly experienced location which draws together the audience's memories of myth and religious experience with narrative space.

The importance of mountains and movement is clear from the outset of the play. The chorus, a group of Lydian women who have accompanied Dionysus on his journey through Asia to Greece, repeatedly cry 'to the mountain, to the mountain' (εἰς ὄρος εἰς ὄρος) (Euripides, *Bacchae* 116, 162), emphasizing the role of not just Mount Kithairon, but the journey there. There are also numerous descriptions of Dionysus or his band of followers (*thiasoi*) dancing wildly in mountain settings (306-9, 723-7). The introduction (*parodos*) is particularly effective in building an immersive atmosphere, of the sort that Ingold describes as part of the embodied experience of space. Seaford identifies the *parodos* as dithyrambic: it includes elements which are emblematic of the dithyramb, a form of collective religious dance praising Dionysus.[18] These elements include elaborate compound epithets for Dionysus (100, 102, 108, 112, 117, 122, 123, 124), repetition (107, 116), the mythical narratives of Dionysus' birth, and an unrestrained metre.[19] The effect of the rhythmic changes in metre, beginning with the religious tone of ionics before turning to choriambs, glyconics and fast-paced dactyls, builds momentum and pace as the chorus sing of rushing to the mountains.[20] This feeling of motion was surely complemented by the instances of self-reflexivity.[21] This technique, where the chorus refers to their own performance as they dance, blurs the lines between narrative and reality, inviting the audience to become participants in the ritual action of the play. The chorus describe themselves crying in Bacchic frenzy (Βάκχιον εὐαζομένα) (67-8), and refer to established songs for Dionysus, introducing their odes as hymns (71-2). The chorus also sing of a worshipper in the mountains, who shakes the *thyrsos* (80), the ivy staff associated with the followers of Dionysus, as they dance. It is likely that the chorus would have shaken their own *thyrsoi* as they described the worshipper in the mountains, integrating the space of the theatre, the narrative space outside the palace of Thebes where they dance, and the imagined mountainside where the worshipper shakes his *thyrsos*.[22] It is also possible that as they described a bacchant as a foal who 'moves swift-footed in her leaps' (166), the chorus themselves may have leapt like foals in their own dance too.

This visual and descriptive recreation of dithyrambic movement is significant to the understanding of the relationship between movement, memory and landscape. Many members of the audience would have had first-hand experience of dithyrambic performance. In its classical form, danced competitively between the tribes of Attica by around a thousand citizens at the annual dramatic festival, the City Dionysia, the dithyramb has been identified by Kowalzig and Wilson as 'the most intense expression of civic cohesion through public ritual that we have of the radical Athenian democracy'.[23] The dithyrambic qualities of the *parodos* would therefore have involved the audience on a visceral level, allowing them through their memories of their own participation in collective dance to become part of the play's Dionysiac atmosphere. As Merleau-Ponty shows, space is perceived in relation to the body by the sensation of movement, and senses are not a series of distinct phenomena but part of a multi-sensory whole.[24] Thus, in triggering the memories of movement and the collective, multi-sensory atmosphere of dithyramb, the audience are brought more firmly into contact with narrative space.

However, the narrative space most vividly constructed is not the chorus's location before the palace of Thebes, but the Dionysiac mountain. The *parodos* makes no less than ten references to mountains ('sacred Mount Tmolos', 65; 'celebrating the rites of Dionysus in the mountains', 76; 'from the mountains of Phrygia', 86; 'to the mountain, to the mountain!', 116; 'welcome/pleasant in the mountains', 135; 'in the mountains of Phrygia, of Lydia', 140; 'joy of gold-flowing Mount Tmolos', 154; 'to the mountain, to the mountain!', 164). Alongside the evocation of dithyrambic movement, the audience is also drawn beyond the narrative space to the figurative mountain space by vivid appeals to the senses. The account of the invention of the *tympanon*, a drum associated with Dionysiac song, in a cave on the Cretan Mount Ida, and the accompaniment of the 'frenzied Bacchic dance' (βακχείᾳ) (126) and the 'sweet-sounding breath of Phrygian flutes' (ἀδυβόα Φρυγίων αὐλῶν πνεύματι) (127-8), presents a rich aural atmosphere of Dionysiac worship. These sounds are linked to the City Dionysia by the mention of satyrs, and to contemporary religious practice by reference to Dionysus' biennial festivals at which the *tympanon* is played. The scene painted in most detail is the Phrygian mountainside where the unnamed worshipper of Dionysus is described running from a band of the god's followers:

> He is welcome in the mountains, when from the running *thiasoi* he falls to the ground, wearing the sacred garment of fawnskin, hunting bloodshed of slaughtered

goats, delight in eating raw flesh, rushing to the mountains of Phrygia, of Lydia. The leader is Bromios. *Euoi*. The ground flows with milk, it flows with wine, it flows with the nectar of bees. Like the smoke of Syrian frankincense the Bacchic god holds aloft the bright-burning flame of the pine-torch, he darts with the fennel-stalk, with running and dances, arousing wanderers with cries and springing, throwing his delicate locks into the ether. Together with these Bacchic shouts, he roars: 'O onward bacchants, o onward bacchants, joy of gold-streaming Tmolos, celebrate Dionysus with song and dance with the loud-roaring drum, exalting the god of Bacchic cries with Bacchic cries among the Phrygian shouts and calls, when the melodious sacred flute rings its sacred playing, joining movement to the mountain, to the mountain'. And then joyfully, like a foal with her grazing mother, the bacchant moves swift-footed in her leaps.

135-66

The abundance of rich, sensory language and memory cues is immediately clear in this section, as is the recurrence of the mountain landscape. Bacchic worship is depicted in constant motion (running, falling, rushing, flowing, darting, dancing, springing, throwing). The joyful song and dance with Bromios as the leader (*exarchos*) merges the image of the tragic chorus with dithyrambic performance.[25] The soundscape of Bacchic shouts and Phrygian calls among the drums and pipe-playing constructs Kithairon as an Asiatic and Dionysiac mountainscape, complemented by the smell of Syrian frankincense. The pine-torch may have recalled the torchlit procession of Dionysus Eleuthereus at the beginning of the City Dionysia, leading in the god's image from the temple on the road to Eleutherai.[26] The image of the blazing torch and smoke creates a striking contrast, surely remembered by the audience from the nocturnal atmosphere of the procession.

Similarly, the flowing milk, wine and honey, as well as painting a striking visual picture, stimulate olfactory and gustatory senses. All three are associated with Dionysus, and are used in libations together in other tragedies such as Euripides' *Orestes* (115) and *Iphigenia in Tauris* (163-5).[27] Taste is also evoked in a manner which is all the more graphic for its less savoury nature in the eating of raw flesh; this element (alongside torchlight) is also present as part of Bacchic initiation in Euripides' satyr-play, the *Cretans* (*Tragicorum Graecorum Fragmenta* 5.1, fr. 472). Seaford suggests that this act may have had some reflection in ritual, even if real maenads did not literally engage in the bloody tearing and eating of raw flesh as their mythical counterparts do.[28] In this way, the dithyrambic *parodos* appeals not to events or objects so much as to a sensory experience, which sweeps the audience into an atmosphere which they perceive as participants.[29] As preparation for the events of the play, the audience are transported to the Dionysiac mountain as a dynamic medium, not 'embodied' in the sense of becoming more firmly rooted to their physical location but caught in the current of light, sound and feeling which creates place. Rather than isolated and oppositional, here the mountain is connective; through its vivid description, the experience of narrative space is stimulated by the evocation of the remembered experiences of the audience.

Sophocles' *Oedipus Tyrannos* and Mount Kithairon

Similar processes are evident in Sophocles' *Oedipus Tyrannos* ('Oedipus the King') (*OT*). This play, first performed in 429 BCE, concerns the Theban king Oedipus and his discovery that he has unknowingly committed patricide and incest. Raised as the son of the king of Corinth, Oedipus leaves his home to avoid fulfilling a prophecy that he will kill his father and marry his mother. At the crossroads on the road to Delphi he kills an unknown man after a dispute, and after defeating the Sphinx he arrives in Thebes and marries the queen, Jocasta. The play begins many years later, when an oracle demands that Oedipus learn the identity of the former king's murderer. He summons the blind prophet Teiresias, and learns that the man he killed at the crossroads was his father, and that Jocasta, with whom he has four children, is his mother. His parents abandoned him as an infant on Mount Kithairon, where he was saved by shepherds before being adopted by the king of Corinth. When Oedipus realizes what he has done, he blinds himself in horror.

As in the *Bacchae*, Mount Kithairon looms as a backdrop to the events of the play. The mountain is presented as somehow specifically suited to Oedipus, as his 'proper tomb' (κύριον τάφον) (*OT* 1453), where Oedipus wishes that he had died as his parents intended. Oedipus refers to the mountain as 'this Kithairon which is called mine' (ἔνθα κλήζεται / οὑμὸς Κιθαιρὼν οὗτος) (1451-2), reaching beyond the narrative to the future when his story has become myth, and his relationship with Mount Kithairon has become well known.[30] This suggestion creates a complicity between Oedipus and the audience of Sophocles' play, referring to shared knowledge of his story.[31] As well as being appropriate to Oedipus, the prominent scholar of tragedy Oliver Taplin suggests that Kithairon was famously resonant, particularly where violent acts are concerned; in Herodotus' *Histories*, the northern slopes of the mountain are the setting of the death of the Persian general Masistios, and the echoes of Persian lamentations are exaggerated by the environs to the extent that they are heard across Boeotia.[32] In the *Bacchae*, the 'crags of Kithairon' (λέπας Κιθαιρώνειον) (1045) resound with the screams of Pentheus and the ritual cries of the bacchants as they tear him apart. The references to Kithairon in *Oedipus Tyrannos* conjure the echoes of Kithairon's history, of which Oedipus is part. The significance of this is clear in Tiresias' enigmatic prophecy concerning Oedipus' future wandering, when he goes into exile at the end of the play. The literal translation is as follows: 'What kind of harbour will there not be for your cry; what kind of Kithairon will not soon call out in unison, when you find out the wedding-song, the one without anchorage in your house, that you sailed into, after winning a fair voyage?' (*OT* 420-3).[33] Taplin points out that the human sounds of the cry and the wedding-song are appropriate to the sounds of Kithairon, Oedipus' mountain, echoing his misery.[34] The evocation of sound in a landscape is used to connect elements of the audience's mythological knowledge, and the aural phenomenon of echoing is used to connect unhappy events through time, making Kithairon a spatial and temporal background of tragedy to the character of Oedipus.

The acknowledgement of senses, landscape and memory in the phenomenological framework allows us to take Taplin's observations a step further. There is a certain parallelism between the reactions of Pentheus' mother Agaue in the *Bacchae* and Oedipus in *Oedipus Tyrannos* to the tragic realization of their crimes. This parallelism suggests that the multi-sensory, performative experience of mountains is relevant to both plays. After she murders her son in a Bacchic frenzy, Agaue goes into exile, hoping that she will come to a place where 'neither blood-stained Kithairon may see me, nor my eyes see Kithairon' (μήτε Κιθαιρὼν ἔμ' ἴδοι μιαρὸς / μήτε Κιθαιρῶν' ὄσσοισιν ἐγώ) (1384-5). Not only does this draw attention to the role of sight in memory, but it addresses the idea that a mountain could serve as a visual trigger of remembered events. For Agaue, the mountain has become a symbol of what occurred there. Similarly, Kithairon becomes a symbol of Oedipus' crimes, hailed first as his nurse and mother (1094), then as the mountain which allowed him to live an unlucky life by sheltering him as an abandoned infant (1391-3), and finally as his proper tomb (1451-3). Kithairon's role in both plays finds agreement in the phenomenological identification of mountains as 'topographical memory places',[35] whose concrete visibility evokes a sense of temporal continuity and connection with the past. It is interesting in this light that as Agaue seeks to avoid memory by avoiding sight, Oedipus blinds himself, and claims that he would have deafened himself too if he knew how (1370-90).[36] While Oedipus does not specifically do so to avoid the sight of Kithairon, in both plays mountains and the act of seeing preserve knowledge, and characters flee the pain of that knowledge by avoiding a sight, whether of one place in Agaue's case or all things in Oedipus's. This suggests that the conceptual link between mountains, sight and memory, which is more commonly associated with later literature, was present enough in the imagination of fifth-century audiences that tragedians could manipulate the theme.

Aeschylus' *Agamemnon* and the mountains of the 'Beacon Scene'

These observations show the potential for mountains to form conceptual networks, where place, time and memory are linked by mountain landscapes. This is demonstrated in a particularly literal way by the beacon scene of Aeschylus' *Agamemnon*. In this scene, Clytemnestra, the unfaithful wife of the Greek war leader Agamemnon, tells the chorus of old Argive men that Troy has fallen. The news was delivered to her in a single night via mountaintop beacons, which she has ordered to be set in place so that she would have warning of Agamemnon's return. From lines 281 to 319, eight mountains are mentioned. The beacon is lit on Ida, and Clytemnestra names the flame Hephaestus, god of craft and blacksmith's fire, personifying the fire as a messenger (281). Next is the Hermaean crag of Lemnos, then the summit of Zeus on Athos. Two lines of text are missing, before the flame reaches Makistos and Messapion, both mountains of uncertain location.[37] Next is Kithairon near Thebes, then a mountain ambiguously named Aigiplanktos, or 'ranged over by goats', then Arachnaion, where it is finally visible to Clytemnestra's watchman in Argos.

Clytemnestra identifies the flame which the watchman saw as 'this very fire not undescended from the flame of Ida' (φάος τόδ' οὐκ ἄπαππον Ἰδαίου πυρός) (311); it is not simply a new fire lit on Arachnaion in response to the sight of a fire on Aigiplanktos, but the same flame that has travelled from mountaintop to mountaintop from Ida to Argos. Through the visual network of mountains, the vast distance between Troy and Argos has been bridged. The flame embodies both the enormity of the distance and the close connection between the distant events and people. Unlike the 'unfledged rumour' (ἄπτερος φάτις),[38] which the chorus assume has informed Clytemnestra's news (276), the flame represents the certain knowledge which gives Clytemnestra power and the ability to plan for Agamemnon's return. This is almost a literal version of the way that the mountains of Asia form a backdrop to the mountains of Greece in the *Bacchae*, or the temporal backdrop of Kithairon's past and future behind Oedipus' references to the mountain in the *Oedipus Tyrannos*. As myths travel in the imagination of the audience from mountain to mountain, past to future, here a message travels across them.

The role of memory becomes apparent in the conceptual links that are made by the mountains in the chain, as it is the audience's wider knowledge of the mountains that provides meaning as the flame makes its way to Argos. That Clytemnestra names Hephaestus, Hermes and Zeus in association with the first three mountains of the flame's journey may indicate that she imagines a journey begun with good omen and divine support.[39] As part of a triad alongside Hephaestus and Hermes, the count of Mount Athos as 'third' (τρίτος) alludes to 'Zeus the Third' (τρίτος Ζεύς). This ritual title refers to Zeus' role as the third and greatest deity to receive dedication in any ritual triad.[40] Resonance between these summits and their associated deities increases the sense of mountains as places which allow the far sight of gods, which is possibly reinforced by the use of the word φάτις, for the report the fire brings, which can translate to 'report' or 'rumour' but also 'voice from heaven' or 'oracle'.[41] Zeus also links Mount Athos and Mount Arachnaion, which were both considered seats of Zeus, and were weather indicators for sailors in the northern archipelago and for people in the area surrounding Argos respectively.[42] These famous landmarks were vital to both trade and war in the decades preceding the production of the *Oresteia*,[43] allowing audience members to follow Clytemnestra's narration through their own geographical knowledge, whether or not they had visited such places.

The effect of this 'spatial sweep', opening the world of the play to briefly encompass the breadth of the Greek world,[44] is to position the events of the *Oresteia* within the epic framework of Homer's *Iliad* and *Odyssey*. Tragedy often reimagines the various myths whose canonical version existed in Homer. The journey from mountaintop to mountaintop transports the audience into the space of myth and imagination, not to the Argos of their present day but Homer's Argos. The use of these mountains in reporting the fall of a great city also has darker undertones in recent history; it is likely that the Persian general Mardonios used a nearly identical system in the opposite direction to report the capture of Athens to Xerxes in Sardis during the Persian War, in the fourth century BCE.[45] The comparison aligns the Greeks at Troy with the Persians at Athens in the audience's recent history, burning shrines and wreaking destruction.[46] In this light, Clytemnestra's identification of the flame having travelled from Ida across the mountaintops links the beacon fires with the fires blazing in Troy, as though the distant city's destruction can be seen from Argos.[47] Whether communicating positive, divine associations, or more troubling memories of violence, mountains are presented as thoroughly integrated into organized human activity. As in the *Bacchae* and *Oedipus Tyrannos*, the mountains of the *Agamemnon*'s beacon scene link places, myth, characters, remembered history and personal experience.

Phenomenology, mountains, and tragedy

These analyses are made possible through a phenomenological approach. Classicists must constantly avoid the assumption that an ancient audience would have had similar responses to a modern reader when interpreting any text. Phenomenology, rooted as it is in automatic sensory responses, helps us to imagine the otherwise unknowable realm of unspoken associations and subconscious responses to landscape. Having acknowledged the importance of senses, movement and memory to the embodied experience of landscape, it is possible to see that the mountain scenes of the *Bacchae*, *Oedipus Tyrannos* and *Agamemnon* go far beyond vivid imagery. In the *Bacchae*, the chorus' recreation of a multi-sensory, Dionysiac mountainscape enacts Merleau-Ponty and Ingold's concepts of the perceiving subject embedded in the space that surrounds them. The audience's own memories of dance blend with the chorus' descriptions of rushing to the mountains; the intensity of remembered and imagined movement together, as evidenced by studies on motor resonance and the immersive experience of climbing a slope, draws the audience into the narrative space as participants. This is also made possible by the uniquely temporal nature of mountains, which has been acknowledged in modern travel accounts of Greek mountains by della Dora.[48]

This element is particularly clear in *Oedipus Tyrannos*. Oliver Taplin's suggestion of a resonance on Mount Kithairon, where both sound and memories of myth were carried across the landscape, already acknowledges the relationship between memory and senses on a mountain in the ancient imagination. The additional points made here on sight and memory establish the understanding of mountains as icons of memory; just to look at or hear of Kithairon is to remember the myths of Oedipus, or the crimes of Agaue in the *Bacchae*. Finally, in the *Agamemnon*, the views from mountaintops are used to link far distant places. The role of mountains and memory is apparent in the myths and religious associations of each peak as the flame travels from Troy to Argos. In a manner which is not unlike the experience of Victorian tourists travelling in Greece, feeling transported to antiquity by the view from a mountain,[49] the audience of the *Agamemnon* is transported to the heroic world of Homer by the description of the mountain chain which leads to Troy.

It is therefore clear that in the ancient world, mountains were performative locations, deeply rooted in the past. Tragedians of the fifth century BCE demonstrated a keen awareness of mountains as places where sensory experience is heightened, and described mountains accordingly in order to draw their audiences into narrative space. Phenomenology reveals the ancient understanding of mountains as icons of memory, linking times, places and characters together in a network of meaning. Not only does this allow insights into mountains in antiquity which go beyond their common identifications as liminal, isolated spaces; it also advocates the use of phenomenological theory in studies of the past. Studies which acknowledge such automatic cognitive responses to landscape offer a promising method of enquiry into perception, imagination and associations which are otherwise unspoken, and Classics can benefit greatly from its valuable outcomes. Furthermore, these conclusions demonstrate the value of viewing ancient representations of mountains within the context of a broader history of human responses to landscape. While the close readings I have provided here are firmly rooted within the cultural context of fifth-century BCE Athens, an awareness of the human experience of mountains throughout history has exposed these texts to new questions. A cross-disciplinary perspective, drawing particularly on phenomenological approaches, can provide new and valuable insights into the range of responses which mountains might have triggered in ancient audiences.

Notes

1. Whitehead 1986: 328–38 notes the momentary detail of a meadow in Sophocles' *Trachiniae* 180-99; Roy 1996: 100 considers the natural scenery of Euripides' *Hippolytus* (73-81, 121–30, 208–31) detailed but generic, and in Sophocles' *Oedipus Tyrannos* he observes a complete dismissal of descriptive detail when the infant Oedipus is discovered on Mount Kithairon, with the exception of the line ναπαίαις ἐν Κιθαιρῶνος πτυχαῖς, 'in the wooded vale of Kithairon' (1026); Krummen 1990: 212 allows that rural locations are used to root Sophocles' *Oedipus Coloneus*, Euripides' *Supplices*, and Euripides' *Iphigenia in Tauris* in a recognizable locality, but only to the extent that they appear basically believable and relatable to the audience.
2. See e.g. Segal 1978; Vidal-Naquet 1988; Serghidou 1991.
3. Buxton 2013 asserts that while myths reflect human experiences, they also *refract*, reducing a wide range of real activities and experiences to a small, extreme selection with 'symbolically productive characteristics' (18). The occasional presence of e.g. bandits on mountains might therefore have led to myths in which mountains were always dangerous.
4. Rose and Wylie 2011: 222.
5. Merleau-Ponty 1945: 4, 21, 22, 132, 136. This approach is part of existential phenomenology (see Rose and Wylie 2011: 221–34 for summary), which builds upon the philosophies of Husserl 1973, who proposed that the perceiving consciousness cannot be separated from the object it perceives, and Heidegger 1996, who proposed that the understanding of such a relationship must be preceded by the understanding of the structure of existence in which both the perceiving consciousness and the object of perception are situated.
6. Ingold 2011: 95–139, with this phrase at 134.
7. Rose and Wylie 2011.
8. Linde and Labov 1975: 929–31.
9. Ryan 2003: 218.
10. della Dora 2008a: 220. These ideas draw on Deleuze's (1988: 56–9) notion of the 'ontological past', where past and present are coexisting elements. della Dora notes that this is consistent with the visual nature of memory in Aristotle and Plato, where memory is an imprint on the

mind like the mark of a signet-ring on wax (Aristotle, *De memoria et reminiscentia* 450a 25; Plato, *Theaetetus* 191d-e). See also Carruthers 1990: 16–17, 21. Similarly, della Dora 2008b discusses Mount Athos as *Mons Sanctus* and *Locus Memoriae*, and its vivid representation as a mnemonic device on medieval maps.

11. della Dora 2008a: 229.
12. Ingold 2000: 189 discusses this in relation to the network of paths visible in the distance of Bruegel's 1565 painting *The Harvesters* (The Metropolitan Museum of Art, Rogers Fund, 1919, 19.164).
13. Lorimer 2012: 254–5.
14. Fischer and Zwaan 2008.
15. Kuzmičová 2012: 29.
16. Ibid. 24. This theory is well suited to spaces whose description has been considered sparse, since while simulation of movement has been identified as a powerful method of immersion in space, the degree of detail has little effect on the vividness of spatial imagery.
17. Segal 1997: 27–54; Buxton 2013: 26–7.
18. Kowalzig and Wilson 2013: 2–3. According to Aristotle, *Poetics* 1449a, tragedy originated from this performative genre, which seems to have developed from its seventh-century form as a range of local, Bacchic cult songs to a highly sophisticated spectacle by the classical period. See also Revermann 2006.
19. Seaford 1981: 270. The τύμπανον, a drum associated with the worship of Dionysus, is referenced indirectly. Such indirect references to ritual equipment are typical of dithyramb.
20. Dodds 1960: 72–4.
21. Henrichs 1994: 57–9.
22. Seaford 1996: 155. Similarly, they refer twice to the crowns of ivy which surely formed part of their own costumes (81, 106), and to their whole costume (107–14) in inviting all of Thebes to adorn themselves.
23. Kowalzig and Wilson 2013: 2–3.
24. Merleau-Ponty 1945: 139.
25. Seaford 1996: 165. An *exarchos* appears as the leader of lament (Homer, *Iliad* 24.721) and Dionysiac dithyramb (Aristotle, *Poetics* 4). This role may indicate one of the respects in which Dionysus was imagined to act in ritual.
26. This torchlit procession celebrated the arrival of Dionysus in Athens from Eleutherai, and as Seaford 1994: 250 notes, participants would have easily imagined Dionysus crossing from Thebes to Attica, staying in Eleutherai on the slopes of Kithairon before entering Athens. The processional origin of dithyramb, as evoked by Pindar (fr. 70b.1-5; *Ol.* 13.9, 18-9), seems to have been remembered as part of its traditional past to the extent that Aeschylus could figuratively associate it with the κῶμος, the informal procession through the city following the symposium (Aeschylus, *TrGF* iii, 355; see Hedreen 2013: 172). It is also possibly reflected in the use of the word κῶμος in the fragmentary *Fasti* inscription, detailing the Dionysia from 473–328 BCE (Csapo and Slater 1995: 40–1). Therefore, when the chorus, in a *parodos* which Seaford 1981: 270 has identified as evocative of public processional ritual, sing that they are 'leading Bromios down from the mountains of Phrygia to the broad streets of Greece' (Βρόμιον ... κατάγουσαι Φρυγίων ἐξ ὀρέων Ἑλλάδος εἰς εὐρυχόρους ἀγυιάς) (84-7), the audience would surely have in mind their own recent participation in leading Dionysus to Athens, accompanying the god on the last stage of his journey from the mountains of Phrygia but also from Eleutherai and the slopes of Kithairon.

27. Maenads are frequently imagined drawing honey and milk from the ground or rivers (e.g. Plato, *Ion* 534a); Dionysus conjures wine (Pausanias 6.26.2) and milk (Antonius Liberalis 10) and is credited with discovering honey (Ovid, *Fasti* 3.736-44).
28. Seaford 1981: 266 and 1996: 37.
29. Ingold 2011: 128–35 discusses vision as the experience of light; it is 'the experience of inhabiting the world of the visible' (128), where colour and brightness are variations and significance lies not in the confirmation of surfaces or objects but in the creation of an atmosphere. The same is true of sound and feeling.
30. Taplin 2010: 236.
31. Ibid.
32. Ibid. 237, with reference to Herodotus, *Histories* 9.22-4.
33. βοῆς δὲ τῆς σῆς ποῖος οὐκ ἔσται λιμήν, / ποῖος Κιθαιρὼν οὐχὶ σύμφωνος τάχα, / ὅταν καταίσθῃ τὸν ὑμέναιον, ὃν δόμοις / ἄνορμον εἰσέπλευσας, εὐπλοίας τυχών. Translation from ibid. 244.
34. Taplin ibid. 244–5 acknowledges that ποῖος Κιθαιρών is strange, and could accept πῶς σοι ('how will Kithairon not sound in unison ...'), or πᾶς σοι ('will the whole of Kithairon not sound in unison ...') instead.
35. Nora 1996: 15, 18.
36. For the link between sight and knowledge in *OT*, see Champlin 1969.
37. A mountain in Euboea: see Fraenkel 1950: 157.
38. Denniston and Page 1957: 94. The exact meaning of ἄπτερος in this context is unclear. In the *Odyssey* it is used four times (17.57, 19.29, 21.386, 22.398) to mean something one does not say, but here the most straightforward implication is that the rumour is premature. See also Goldhill 1984 for similar contrasts.
39. Fraenkel 1950: 154.
40. Also alluded to at *Agamemnon* 172, 246-7; *Choephoroi* 244-5, 578; *Eumenides* 759-60. See Fraenkel 1950: 154; Collard 2002: 124. See Burian 1986: 332–42 for Zeus the Third and triads in the *Oresteia*.
41. Liddell, Scott, Jones, *Greek-English Lexicon*, s.v. φάτις.
42. Wilamowitz 1931: 225.
43. Fraenkel 1950: 156.
44. Cook 1998: 561.
45. Rawlinson 1880: 373 n. 5; for more on the use of fire signals in antiquity see Polybius 10.43-7.
46. Tracy 1986: 258–60.
47. See Gantz 1977: 28–9 for the foreboding suggestions of the watchman waiting for the fire at 8-9 and 20-1, which further suggest that the beacon fires symbolized destruction rather than good news.
48. della Dora 2008a: 229.
49. della Dora 2008a, and further discussion by König in this volume.

CHAPTER 11
MOUNTAINS, IDENTITY AND THE LEGEND OF KING BRENNUS IN THE EARLY MODERN ENGLISH IMAGINARY[1]

Harriet Archer

In his *Illustrative Remarks upon the Scenery of the Alps*, William Wordsworth enjoined the Alpine traveller to 'surrender up his mind to the fury of the gigantic torrents, and take delight in the contemplation of their almost irresistible violence'.[2] Modern critical commentary has suggested that such ecstatic surrender would have been unthinkable prior to the Romantic apprehension of sublimity. However, Wordsworth's evocation of this 'irresistible' experiential force resonates powerfully with the sixteenth-century focus of this chapter, John Higgins' legend of the ancient British King Brennus, included in Higgins' collection of admonitory verse complaints, *The Mirror for Magistrates* (1587). One of the first-person narrators of this series of non-dramatic, tragic poems, Brennus observes during his own Alpine crossing 'waters wilde which from the mountaynes faling flow', and 'rockes . . . whence riuers rore of melting snow',[3] as part of a vivid, second-person description of Alpine travel. Delight, terror and opportunism mingle in Higgins' account, confounding the dominant narrative of mountains' reception in early modernity.

As suggested in Peter Hansen's *Summits of Modern Man*, there is a narrative affinity between modernity proper and the ways in which mountains have been understood.[4] The elite status of the 'summit position' indicates social, cultural, military or even moral supcriority, tied to the perceived modern vanquishing of pre-Enlightenment thought. The 'conquest' of the mountain figures a defeat, and externalization, of superstition, uncertainty and the nonhuman. In addition, though, 'the mountaintop measures a distance from humanity, and . . . a rising *above* humanity'.[5] It is a commonplace that, as a symbol of cultivated taste, the studied appreciation of mountains has been bound up with various kinds of privilege since Wordsworth complained that the mountains of England's Lake District were wasted on working-class day-trippers.[6] Yet, as for Ruskin who observes 'gloom' in the villages of the French Alps while enjoying the 'glory' of his own aesthetic competence, it is often mountain-dwelling peasants themselves, in contrast to sophisticated lowlanders, who bear the brunt of modern orophilic prejudice.[7] The mountain ascent as a heroic, solitary and multiply worldly feat eclipses the mundanity of local alpine aptitude, regularly dismissed as a more or less grubby ethnonational characteristic.[8]

The texts discussed below suggest that this dynamic plays out similarly in early modern mountain experience. This chapter explores a selection of sixteenth- and seventeenth-century English examples which trouble the clear-cut distinctions between elite and rustic mountain travel and inhabitation, as mountain identity is seen to be bound up with the simultaneous nobility and subordination of ancient British (or, as understood in Tudor England, Welsh) culture. Through their debt to the Latin texts with and against whose models Renaissance English humanists defined their emerging sense of national identity, literary mountains function as both vectors and barriers to figure the vexed interchange between early modern England, the classical world, and Renaissance Europe's competing cultures of Catholic and Protestant Christianity. While Debarbieux and Rudaz suggest that the 'image of the mountaineer' has functioned 'sometimes as a foil, sometimes as a model for the idea of the [emerging] nation' since the eighteenth century,[9] both functions coalesce in the early modern texts which explicitly resituate episodes from England's ancient British origin myths in mountainous terrain.

More 'a dynamic web than a site or location', place is 'the geographical expression of the interaction between individual action and abstract historical process', according to geographer Timothy Oakes.[10] It encapsulates what Oakes calls the 'paradox of modernity', in its simultaneous evocation of progress and loss, and of the global and local. Here, I explore how mountains work to articulate this paradox in early modern writing, through their relationships to identity and agency. In particular, I focus on the figure of King Brennus, an ancient British warrior adapted from a patchwork of Latin and vernacular sources, and the role mountain ascents play in Renaissance English iterations of his legend. While Brennus is regularly invoked across Tudor and Stuart exemplary literature as a stock warning against ambition, blasphemy and avarice, his dealings with mountains are startlingly depicted in two specific texts: John Higgins' compilation of verse histories, *The Mirror for Magistrates* (1587), and Jasper Fisher's Romano-British history play, *Fuimus Troes: The True Trojans* (1633). This chapter aims to set these texts' surprising emphasis on Brennus's alpinism within contemporary impressions of mountains' cultural significance.

But the chapter is as much concerned with the language of landscape as it is with mountains as a geographical feature, including the interplay between rhetoric, etymology and the idea of place. Early modern imaginative historiography is in many ways a topographic, or chorographic, medium. From the *topoi* of the humanist commonplacing tradition, compiled as part of the sixteenth-century grammar school's rhetorical education into curated collections of axiomatic examples, to the spatial morality of the tragic fall from 'high' status to 'low', British history operates for Renaissance poets and dramatists as the location – whether a storehouse, muniments room or dreamscape – out of which ethical *exempla* might be extracted. In the case of Brennus's story, his literal ascents and descents map onto his rise and fall on Fortune's wheel. More broadly, his mountain crossings chime with the metaphorical evocation of translation, adaptation and transformation around the 'Matter of Britain', the body of legendary narrative which dealt with the mythic foundation of Elizabeth I's dynasty by Aeneas's grandson, Brutus. A story fraught with shifts of ethnic identity effected by migrations (the Trojans 'become' Britons, who later 'become' Welsh), this series of myths was most familiar to later sixteenth-century readers through translations which foregrounded the time and space across which they were transmitted. Their retellings in early modern imaginative historiography's dominant fictive modes, like ethopoeia (the rhetorical impersonation of a subject) and drama, found readers and performers themselves momentarily embodying new identities. Meanwhile, the allegorical commentary on contemporary events afforded by exemplars drawn from British history encouraged readers to engage with its characters at the level of metaphor, understood in sixteenth-century poetics as 'an inuersion of sence by transport'.[11] Pertinent, too, is the spatial analogy Benedict Anderson uses in *Imagined Communities* to explain the difference between dynastic and modern models of sovereignty. Dynastic '[k]ingship organizes everything around a high centre', Anderson suggests, while 'in the modern conception, state sovereignty is fully, flatly, and evenly operative over each square centimetre of a legally demarcated territory ... In the older imagining, where states were defined centres, borders were porous and indistinct'.[12] The Tudor and Stuart texts discussed here could be thought of as negotiating between the workings of these two models, such that their ancient mountains function at once as the centres and the porous boundaries of cultural and territorial nationhoods.[13]

Mountains and national identity in Tudor and Stuart literature

While studies of early modern English literature and landscape continue to proliferate, Renaissance treatments of mountains – including ascents, crossings and daily mountain life – do not loom large in the field, perhaps because the traditionally canonical authors have relatively little to say about them. Two decades of criticism have been steeped in Spenser and Shakespeare's engagement with the materialities of national identity, but coastlines and rivers, for example, have received more attention than mountains as epistemological tropes. Studies by Wyman Herendeen and Lisa Hopkins have demonstrated the ways in which early modern accounts of river origins and courses engage the construction and dissemination of knowledge and identity.[14] Herendeen makes an etymological point about the 'place' of rivers, too: he suggests that 'the river in a unique way traverses the realm of geography, or our reaction to landscape, and language, the metaphoric constructs by which we expand our domain into the realm of the unknown. Living on the banks of one river or another, people have developed various riparian *topoi*, or rhetorical "topics" originating from their relation to the local landscape'.[15] The river encapsulates the 'humanistic response to the physical world', as a *topos* for the search for origins.[16]

While sharing this property in some respects, mountains also confound such a humanistic programme of interpretation, through their unexpected flux and occasional illegibility. It is the phenomenological encounter with mountain terrain, not its symbolic significance, which is most lexically and syntactically striking in early modern accounts. It is in the evocation of such sensory experience where these narratives begin to trouble the denial of a premodern sublime.

Edmund Spenser's admittedly infrequent engagements with mountain landscapes gesture towards the traditional alignment of high places with transcendence. This is hinted at in Patrick Cheney's recent work on *English Authorship and the Early Modern*

Sublime. The Redcrosse Knight's encounter with the hermit on the Mount of Contemplation in Book I of the *Faerie Queene* (1590), for example, leads to a 'transcendent vision' of 'surpassing brilliance', while 'nowhere is an aesthetic of sublime transport simultaneously more dumbfounding and ordained' than in Book I's closing, in the aftermath of Redcrosse's defeat of the dragon.[17] Spenser seems for the most part to adhere to Nicolson's stereotype of alternating indifference to and abhorrence of mountains, to the extent that they most frequently crop up in his writing as similes for waves; that is, mountains are at once a figure for the grotesque wildness of the nonhuman world, and practically absent from his imagined landscapes. In *Colin Clouts Come Home Againe* (1595),

> to the sea we came; the sea? that is
> A world of waters heaped vpon hie,
> Rolling like mountaines in wide wildernesse,
>   Horrible, hideous, roaring with hoarse crie.[18]

The image does effect a vertiginous disorientation comparable to the dramatic swell of a stormy seascape; it also poses an epistemological conundrum, by eliding the apparently static with the perilously moveable. This chimes with Porter's definition of the sublime as 'impossible Thing': 'Simultaneously fascinating and fearful, such an object resists integration into one's symbolic frameworks of understanding'.[19]

In common with this simile's evocation of mountains in proximity to the 'horrible' and 'hideous' in nature, as well as their uncanny property of 'rolling' turbulence, Spenser's depiction of Redcrosse's dragon mobilizes a cluster of mountain similes to convey his organic strangeness, and perhaps to set up the conditions for the sublime revelation which follows his defeat. The 'dreadfull Beast',

>   with his largenesse measured much land,
> And made wide shadow under his huge waste,
> As mountaine doth the valley overcast.
> Approching nigh, he reared high afore
> His body monstrous, horrible, and vaste.[20]
>
>   *The Faerie Queene* 1.11.8

His fiery breath is likened to a volcano, which in turn generates more rocky terrain:

> As burning Aetna from his boyling stew
> Doth belch out flames, and rockes in peeces broke,
> And ragged ribs of mountains molten new.
>
>   1.11.44

Finally, having been conquered by Redcrosse, 'So downe [the dragon] fell, and like an heaped mountaine lay' (1.11.54). Here, mountains are clearly in use as a symbol of awful size, as well as a container for danger, lumpen passivity, and, crucially, epistemological alienation. Beyond these evocative passages, though, Spenser's wandering knights might journey 'through mountains & through playns', but the haptic experience of mountain travel is never specifically broached.

Mountains are multiple, composite places, comprising peaks and passes; solids, liquids and vapours of differing kinds; animal, vegetable and mineral constituents; and a variety of climates, faces, aspects and atmospheres. They conjured a spectrum of possible moods in early modern English writing, from the holy and rarefied, through the rugged and uncouth, to the downright barbarous – coming full circle, perhaps, in the regularly invoked wellspring of pagan high culture, Mount Parnassus. But in Tudor historiography, these flavours coalesced in a collective inscription of ancient British, or Welsh, identity, and its fraught centrality to the nation's origin myth. The Welsh, as sixteenth-century historiographers' interlaced accounts had it, represented the remnants of the ancient British race which had been 'remooued ... out of the most part of the Ile into od corners and mountaines' by the Saxons, such that the supposedly impenetrable Welsh mountain ranges in particular became, in contemporary thought, geological repositories for the last vestiges of British alterity.[21]

Mountains served as evocations of Welsh identity in early modern literature in a number of different ways. In some examples, we see them bound up with disparaging national stereotypes: in Shakespeare's *Henry IV Part 2*, Falstaff is 'gross as a mountain' (2.4.219), and Owen Glendower's boast that 'at my birth / The front of heaven was full of fiery shapes' is qualified by the bathetic elaboration that 'The goats ran from the mountains' (3.1.36–8).[22] The capacity to navigate the mountain terrain also served to distinguish between the British of the first century CE and the Romans. Tudor authors highlighted classical texts which depicted the invading forces as poor alpinists. Holinshed notes, for example, that Agricola's 'Romans were sore troubled with the rough mountains and craggie rocks, by the which they were constreined to passe', while the Britons rely on 'the secret hauens and creekes of their countries', which 'were not easie to be woone, by reason of the thicke woods inuironed with deepe mareshes and waters, and full of high craggie rocks and mountains'.[23] Shakespeare, too, accesses this specific cultural landscape as the setting for the martial and ideological clashes between Britons and Romans dramatized in *Cymbeline* (c. 1609).[24] The Wales of Shakespeare's *Cymbeline* is, according to Huw Griffiths, 'truly primitive'; and he argues that 'The harshness of the Welsh terrain ... echoes a particularly English experience of Wales' impenetrability'.[25] In addition to this challenge, though, the play's depiction of mountain life offers an earthy, spiritually rich counterpoint to the Machiavellian tenor of its other plot-lines.[26] The sons of the British king, Cymbeline, are raised among the Welsh mountains by the falsely-disgraced general Belarius, who keeps them in ignorance of their identities and praises the values of a simple life. Belarius contrasts the health and prosperity of their 'mountain sport' (III.iii.10) with

> the art o' the court
> As hard to leave as keep; whose top to climb

> Is certain falling, or so slippery that
> The fear's as bad as falling.
>
> III.iii.46-9

Shakespeare's Belarius takes up medieval tragedy's spatial metaphor of fall from high to low, and inverts its force. Instead, the 'sweet content' of simple mountain life has a reputedly barren environment yield both material and spiritual sustenance. Tudor versifier Thomas Churchyard likewise contends that it is the valleys which 'nourish mischief' while 'A Mountain is a noble stately thing', which he compares 'vnto a King, / Who sits full fast on top of Fortunes wheele'.[27] Shakespeare's ghastly princeling Cloten identifies the disguised princes, Guiderius and Arviragus, as 'rustic' (IV.ii.100) and 'villain mountaineers' (IV.ii.71), a crude foil for his attempt at sophisticated Jacobean artifice. But Belarius integrates their nobility with the paradoxical gentility and rudeness of the Welsh landscape, an 'uncanny' wilderness-utopia haunted by fairies and outlaws, to bridge Welsh barbarity and British patriotism.[28] The boys are both 'as gentle / As zephyrs blowing below the violet', 'yet as rough / Their royal blood enchafed, as the rudest wind, / That by the top doth take the mountain pine, / And make him stoop to the vale' (IV.ii.171-6). Like the play's presentation of classical Romans and Italian characters redolent of contemporary revenge tragedy side by side, 'the double-edgedness and ambiguity of Welshness ... offers an English audience a dual position of simultaneous similarity and estrangement'.[29] As such, *Cymbeline* usefully articulates mountains' semiotic range in the ancient British context to which Brennus also belongs.

The composite identity of King Brennus

The Brennus with whom we are concerned here was the synthetic protagonist in one of the tragic complaints newly included in Higgins' *Mirror for Magistrates*, who went on to make a cameo appearance in Jasper Fisher's play, *The True Trojans*. The *Mirror* was originally conceived of in the 1550s as a sequel to John Lydgate's late fifteenth-century *Fall of Princes*, itself a translation and enlargement of Boccaccio's fourteenth-century moral compendium, *De casibus virorum illustrium*. These collections of tragic falls, written in the voices of deceased ancient and medieval rulers and rebels, began as a warning of fortune's fickleness, and evolved to address contemporary politics through topical allegory. Under the supervision of the printer and poet William Baldwin between 1554 and 1563, the *Mirror* focused on the cycle of English history between the reigns of Richard II and Richard III; in 1574, John Higgins extended Baldwin's coverage with *The First Part of the Mirror for Magistrates*, a prequel which detailed the tragic lives and deaths of legendary figures from the ancient British past. Higgins went on to produce an augmented compilation of his and Baldwin's tragedies in 1587. In the early seventeenth century, Brennus's ghost reappears in *The True Trojans* as part of the play's prologue, and subsequently to exhort the British soldier Nennius before battle with the invading Romans; the ghost of the Roman Marcus Camillus performs the same service for Julius Caesar in the play.

In the 1587 *Mirror*, Higgins's Brennus undertakes two mountain journeys, which evoke two distinct models for how late Elizabethan and Stuart ideas about identity – both national and personal – seem to work as properties of topography. As Brennus's itinerary unfolds he has cause, firstly, to cross the Alps – the high point, as far as the poem is concerned, of his achievements – and secondly to climb Mount Parnassus in a fatal attempt to rob the Temple of Apollo, where literal and metaphorical falls coincide in the gods' elemental retribution. Brennus as a *topos* in himself comes to contain tensions between ideas about rooted localism, and a new, mobile and acquisitive opportunism, as he pursues his transcontinental expedition.

In mid-sixteenth-century England, the relatively blank historical slate presented by ancient Britain offered post-Reformation historiography the chance to colonize its murky terrain in the service of a proto-Protestant narrative. Ancient Rome was regularly put to use as a proxy for continental Catholicism by revisionary Tudor accounts, which pitted the British descendants of the Trojan Brutus against the 'other' branch of Aeneas's patrimony.[30] Yet narratives of British resistance to Roman aggression necessarily sought legitimacy in Roman (and some Greek) textual sources, following attacks on the veracity of Geoffrey of Monmouth's *Historia Regum Britanniae*, such that the ur-text of British legend had to be supplanted by works produced within the very culture the *Historia*'s heroes strove to defeat. The printed paratext of Fisher's *True Trojans* draws attention to these difficulties in grand style, by grouping its *dramatis personae* into characters found in Livy, Julius Caesar and Geoffrey of Monmouth, followed by a collection of Fisher's own additions, listed under 'names fained'.

The intellectual landscape of early modern English writing was also deeply invested in the concept of *translatio imperii*, by which cultural and geopolitical authority was seen to have migrated towards the west, from the ancient empires of Greece and Rome to early modern London (and perhaps onwards to the New World). The history of ancient British resistance to Roman conquest therefore occupied a difficult space in this prevailing metanarrative, as the ancient British kings and tribal chiefs such as Cymbeline (Cunobelinus), Cassibelane (Cassivellaunus) and Arthur represented an oppositional pulse against the *translatio*'s current. As noted above, this did useful work in the contemporary opposition to Catholicism and the threat of invasion from the Holy Roman Empire, but also set Britain and ancient Rome at odds in ways which did not best serve the Tudor humanists' revivalist agenda.

The story of King Brennus becomes a flashpoint for these tensions. It threw into sharper relief the difficulty of establishing a reliable national history based solely on native sources. Still more troubling was the doubt cast on easy associations between territory and identity, associations which provided one basis for the politics and aesthetics of nationhood and empire. The Elizabethan and Stuart Brennus is a hodgepodge of legendary and historical namesakes, reported by Justin, Livy, Pausanias, Plutarch, Strabo and others, and identified variously as a Gaul, a Dane, a Briton, an Englishman, and 'kyng of Albany' – hinting at a Scottish link – in John Hardyng's *Chronicle*.[31] Around 390 BCE, the first of these Brennuses, a warrior from Gaul, is said to have led the Gallic Senones tribe over the Alps to sack Clusium and then Rome, after the Battle of Allia, whence they were routed by Marcus Camillus.³² The second Brennus is supposed to have led an army from Pannonia against Delphi in 279 BCE, where he suffered a cataclysmic defeat, and died at his own hand – either by stabbing himself, according to Justin, or, in Pausanias's version, drinking undiluted wine.³³ A third analogous figure receives brief mention in Livy's account of Hannibal's Alpine crossing of 218 BCE: Livy states that marching up the Rhone towards the Alps, Hannibal encountered 'Two brothers [who] were disputing the sovereignty [of their tribe]. The elder, Braneus by name, who had held sway before, was being driven out by a faction of juniors headed by the younger brother, whose right was less but his might greater' (Livy, *History of Rome* 21.31.6).

Geoffrey of Monmouth's Brennius combines the fourth-century Gallic Brennus and Livy's Braneus with the legendary Welsh figures Bran and Beli.³⁴ In the *Historia*, Brennius is the son of Mulmutius Dunwallo, who had succeeded in reuniting ancient Britain after the civil war which followed King Gorboduc's division of the kingdom between his sons, Ferrex and Porrex. Threatening to retrace Ferrex and Porrex's steps, Brennius and, here, his elder brother Belinus clash over the allocation of the south to the elder, and the north to the younger.³⁵ Brennius forms an alliance with the King of Norway and marches against Belinus, who has seized the northern territory in his absence. After an unsuccessful invasion attempt, Brennius is driven back to France, where he gains the Gauls' support to launch a second attack. Just as the brothers' armies are about to join battle, however, their mother delivers an impassioned speech dissuading them from further conflict. Instead, they combine their forces and lay siege to Gallic, Frankish and German territory on their way to Rome.

The medieval monk John Lydgate went on to adapt Boccaccio's story of the second 'Duke Brennyus' in his *Fall of Princes*.³⁶ Lydgate's Brennyus is a Dane, but he otherwise plays out the third-century Brennus's Greek tragedy. He tells how his desire for treasure, irreverence towards the 'Grekysshe goddys', and misreading of 'thynnocent simplenes' of his enemies, led to his destruction at Delphi. As in Pausanias, Brennyus and his troops drink immoderately before their mountain ascent, before the appearance of the gods drives them mad with panic; indeed, in Pausanias most explicitly, the army falls into disarray 'neither understanding their mother tongue nor recognizing one another's forms' (Pausanias, *Periegesis* 10.23.8). An earthquake and a hail of rocks seal their fate, and Brennyus commits suicide.

Brennus and his army are also classically associated with lasting ethnic confusion, which takes the Gauls' descendants back up to their wonted mountain haunts: Florus's *Epitome* notes that

> The race of the Gallo-Greeks, as their very name implies, was of mixed and confused origin; they were the remnants of those Gauls who had laid Greece waste under the leadership of Brennus, and then, taking an easterly direction, settled in the middle of Asia. And so, just as seeds of cereals degenerate in a different soil, so their natural ferocity was softened by the mild climate of Asia. They were, therefore, routed and put to flight in two engagements, although, at the approach of the enemy, they had left their homes and retired to the highest mountains.
>
> Florus, *Epitome of Roman History* 1.17

Such environmental determinism pursues Brennus through the history books.

Higgins' tragedy of Brennus, likely following the lead of Ranulph Higden's brief composite narrative in the *Polychronicon*, absorbed the accounts by both Geoffrey and Lydgate, to combine the three ancient warriors with the legendary British ruler.[37] Higgins' story, then, begins with the division of the British territory, and follows Brennus through his conflict with Belinus, their mother's intervention, the sacking of Clusium and Rome, and finally to Delphi where he brings about his fall and ignominious death. Brennus's identity is, thus, by the sixteenth century, complicated to say the least. Fisher's later play has Caesar and Camillus attempt to clear up the confusion, without great success. Caesar asks,

> Is this that Northerne route, the Scourge of kingdomes?
> Whose names till now vnknowne, We iudged Gaules;
> Their Tongue and Manners not vnlike?

To which Camillus replies that 'Gaules were indeed the Bulke, but *Brennus* led / Then Brother to the Britaine King'.[38]

In addition to incorporating multiple figures of history and legend, the character of Brennus also encompasses additional, allegorical identities dependent on the text and era in which he appears. Helaine Newstead suggested some time ago that Geoffrey seems to have 'embellished' his narrative of Brennius and Belinus with 'details recalling the stormy relations between Henry I and his brother Robert of Normandy', a contemporary twelfth-century conflict.[39] Higgins' Brennus and Belinus also carry topical potential. In the context of Higgins' 1587 *Mirror*, the tragedy of Brennus follows hot on the heels of those of Ferrex (or Forrex, as Higgins has it) and Porrex, a pair of complaints which seems to allude, in its narrative of north/south division and inter-familial rivalry and murder, to the sentencing of Mary Stuart to death for treason, just weeks before Higgins' work was completed.[40] Brennus's story also begins with a conflict brought about by the division of Britain between its monarch's sons, but as it unfolds, Brennus's and Belinus's exploits replay the tragic dealings of Ferrex and Porrex – or Elizabeth and Mary – in a major key. Like a counterfactual Tudor fantasy of British reunion, Brennus's and Belinus put aside their differences, as Belinus allows Brennus to come home from France and rule the northern portion of the island, and they unite to assail the Roman Republic and its territories. Their father Mulmutius Dunwallo's status as a ruler by martial victory rather than British descent, following the curtailment of Brutus's lineage with the deaths of Ferrex and Porrex and ensuing civil war, is sometimes presented as a serious flaw in the Galfridian legend's service of the Elizabethan dynastic myth, but only strengthens, in this case, the parallels with the Welsh Henry Tudor and his unification of the country after the Wars of the Roses.

What, though, is the relationship between mountains and identity in this legend, and in comparable English texts? In the ancient sources, Brennus's ethnic identity is of central importance in this regard. Plutarch's *Life of Camillus*, for example, presents Brennus's Gallic origin as crucial to the success of his alpinism, as part of his military tactics, and sack of Rome itself: mountaineering is a skill particular to the barbarians – as in ancient Wales and Scotland – and not mastered by their Roman opponents. Fisher's Cassibelane (Cassivellaunus) laments, by way of a reference to the brothers Brennus and Belinus, that if his own brother were alive,

> wee'de clime the Alpes;
> Like braue Mulmutius [Dunwallo's] sonnes; make Romulus' woolfe
> Howle horrour in their streets, and Rome looke pale.[41]

Cassibelane hopes to defeat Rome by appropriating Brennus's alpine skill, and Fisher's Brennus reinforces the association between the Britons and rocky terrain when he 'wonder[s] that such impudent Owles [as the Romans] should gaze / Against the splendour of our Britaine clifts',[42] like *Cymbeline*'s 'Neptune's park, ribb'd and pal'd in / With rocks unscaleable' (III.i.20-1). However, mountain travel itself also effects a destabilization of identities in these texts. *Cymbeline* is in many ways a play about the persistence of Welsh identity alongside the British integration with *Romanitas*, and Wales' mountains, building on contemporary historiographical understanding, have a part to play in this elision of authenticity and acculturation. The action thematizes the transformative effect of mountain journeys on identity, through the British princess Innogen's disguise as the (apparently somehow Gallic) youth Fidele, who in turn seems to Belarius, and her estranged brothers Guiderius and Arviragus, like 'a fairy' or 'angel' (III.vii.14-15), even while the truth of their own royal status is concealed. It is not only Fidele but also those who 'heare him speake' who are 'in Paradise the while', such that the agency of mountain places seems to act transformatively on both subject and observer.

Brennus's national identity is also contested in the historical record at large.[43] The 1546 *Abridgement of the Notable Woorke of Polidore*, for example, tells, apropos of a lexical quibble, how 'the Frenchemen' successfully sacked Rome 'by the valiauntnes of their captaine (Brennius that was an Englishe-man)', reassigning Brennus's country of origin, perhaps on the basis of the author Polydore Vergil's notorious scepticism towards Geoffrey of Monmouth's British pseudo-history.[44] Other historians hedge their bets. The 1637 edition of William Camden's contemporary chorographical edifice, *Britannia*, demonstrates Camden (in Philemon Holland's translation) puzzling over Brennus's etymological significance, when he wonders whether the ruined Welsh castle Dinas Bran is named after 'Brennius the Generall of the Galles', or whether its name means 'The Castle of the Kings Palace'. 'For,' Camden/Holland notes, 'Bren in British signifieth a King ... But others againe draw this name from the high situation upon an hill, which the Britans [also] tearme Bren.'[45] On a practical level, Camden's research makes plain the common interrelation of place and individual identity through naming, in this period and beyond. The semantic proximity of 'king', 'highness', and 'hill', though, also generates a suggestive cluster of meaning around Brennus which, while unfortunately linguistically dubious, shores up the mutual dependency of space, place and identity in the Elizabethan reception of the Brennus story.

While Brennus is noted briefly in numerous classical texts for his Alpine crossing, Higgins interpolates a detailed and visceral account, which describes the experience of a mountain journey – a fitting addition to this anomalous adventure narrative, but one which, unexpectedly, steals the show from Brennus's other triumphs. In particular, the passage speaks to an embodied engagement with the physical properties of the terrain, unique in the *Mirror for Magistrates*, which transcends the usual evocations of mountains in the service of more baldly symbolic aims. 'Renowned' throughout Europe, Brennus and Belinus are not content to excel only in battle.

> As *Hercules* to scale the *Alpes* did first contend:
> So wee agayne (a worke of toyle) the cloudy *Alpes* ascend.
>
> Great mountaynes, craggy, high, that touch the skies,
> Full steepe to climbe vnto, and penshot all,
> The Seas allow[d] doe rore, and foggy vapours rise,
> And from the hills great streames of waters fall.
> The pathes so strickte to passe the speede is small.
> The ise, snowe, cold, clouds, rombling stormes, and sights aboue,
> Are able constant harts with doubtfull feare to moue.
>
> For as you goe, sometimes y'ar fayne to reatch
> And hang by handes, to wend aloft the way:
> And then on buttockes downe an other breatch,
> With elbowes and with heeles your selfe to stay.
> Downe vnder well behold the streames you may,
> And waters wilde which from the mountaynes faling flow:
> Ore head the rockes hang down whence riuers rore of melting snow.[46]

Where might Higgins have found inspiration for this startling and evocative passage? Higgins himself is an unlikely candidate for early alpinism: a parish vicar in Somerset for most of his life, he probably would have noted, as part of his occasional autobiographical digressions in the *Mirror* and elsewhere, had his travels taken him to more adventurous mountain terrain than the Mendip Hills. Neither, though, is he reproducing these details from Geoffrey of Monmouth's narrative, who does not mention an Alpine crossing. And William Warner's historical poem *Albion's England*, almost exactly contemporary with Higgins' own and covering much of the same ground, notes that Brennus 'this side and beyond the *Alpes* subdewed all by fight', almost willfully omitting Brennus's journey through the mountains, as it locates his martial feats categorically on either side.[47]

Terms like 'craggy' and 'foggy' leap directly out of the vernacular historiography, but no comparable journey is portrayed in this way. However, Higgins might be drawing on Silius Italicus's description of Hannibal's Alpine crossing in his Flavian epic of the Second Punic War, which describes the Alps as,

> Covered with rime and hail that never thaws, and imprisons the ice of ages; the steep face of the lofty mountains rises stiffly up ... unsightly winter alone inhabits the gruesome heights and dwells for ever there ... All winds and storms, moreover, have set up their furious dominion in the Alps. The gaze turns giddy on the high cliffs, and the mountains are lost to the clouds ... Hercules was the first to set foot on these virgin fortresses; he was a sight for the gods as he cleft the clouds, mastered the steep ascent, and with main force tamed the rocks that no foot had ever trodden.
>
> <div align="right">Silius Italicus, <i>Punica</i> 3.485-99</div>

The unusual detail about Hercules is particularly suggestive in relation to Higgins' account. Otherwise, this closely reproduces in verse Livy's prose narration of the same event in *The History of Rome*, although both Silius and Higgins reject Hannibal's dismissive exhortation to his soldiers, which asks 'What else did they think that the Alps were but high mountains? ... Surely no lands touched the skies or were impassable to man' (Livy, *History of Rome* 21.30.7).[48] In (arguably) turning to classical accounts of Hannibal for details with which to embellish Brennus's story, Higgins once more generates a provocative interaction between Roman texts and ancient British history, while playing on Brennus's frequent alignment with Hannibal as parallel conquerors of Rome in other contemporary writing. Yet Higgins' Brennus does not share the *Punica*'s Hannibal's disdain for mountain travel. Despite his structural similarities with Hannibal's trajectory, Brennus's Galfridian heritage equates him rather more with the 'nimble mountaineers', 'whose speech and customs did not differ greatly from those of' the Gauls, according to Livy, who appear out of the rocks during the Carthaginians' laboured journey.

Turning to more recent potential sources, the sense of implicit thrill alongside the awe and fear inspired by the landscape may derive from the Swiss humanist Josias Simler's late-sixteenth-century accounts of his own Alpine ascents. Simler also cites Silius, and details 'the narrowness of the footpaths, or the precipices, or the ice, or the snow, or in the end the cold, wind, and suffering'. Higgins' focus on the flow of water down the mountain valley might echo, as well, Simler's evocation of the 'dizzying terror' inspired by 'the sight of the vallies extending below the feet of the travelers'.[49] Simler notes how Alpine travellers sometimes 'cut tree branches (generally pines), sit down and slide down as if they were on a horse',[50] which perhaps anticipates Higgins' evocation of a slippery descent. Also a contender is Livy's account of the Romans' crossing through the difficult terrain between Dion and Mount Olympus during the Second Macedonian War in Book 44, when some of Quintus Martius's elephants (in Philemon Holland's 1600 English translation) 'glid and kept themselves standing upright on their feet, others rested upon their buttockes', while his troops themselves sometimes went 'upright on their feet, but were faine most-what to tumble and roll over and over with their armour and fardels about them'.[51] However, this delineates another hapless and troubled mountain crossing, which Higgins' British Brennus transcends through his narrative style, and by displacing this echo of the Roman army's inelegant progress onto the experience of his audience.

What is unprecedented in all these possible sources, then, is Higgins' use of the second person to absorb the reader bodily into his narrative. Higgins' 1574 *Mirror* had modelled a similar mechanism. Following the tragedy of the Briton Nennius, the inscribed narrator becomes so caught up in Nennius's account of a battle that he starts casting about for a weapon to see off imagined Roman adversaries.[52] In Brennus's complaint, the narrative sleight of hand constructs an immersive sensory experience which seems to demand that we read ourselves into his story – in doing so we follow Brennus following Hercules, but also the textual Brennus following Silius's Hannibal, across a boundary between barbarian and Roman territory and text. Personal identity itself is presented as porous at this moment of geopolitical translation and transport, as the associated affect shifts from speaker to listener.

Brennus's second mountain ascent in Higgins' poem operates differently, as Brennus approaches his assault on Apollo's temple not with awe or empathetic transference, but with sarcasm. The 'riche and welthy gods', Brennus jokes, have no need of the offerings left to them, so they are free for his army to claim instead.[53] Stripped of his earlier apprehension of the mountain's sublimity, Brennus's troops are unequal to the ascent of Parnassus; they become aligned, in *Cymbeline*'s terms, with the valley-dwellers who 'worship dirty gods' (III.vii.28). Indeed, in an Augustan elegy, Propertius cites Brennus's attempted ransacking of the oracle as an example of the conflict between 'Noble Savagery and Corrupt Civilization' (Propertius, *Elegies* 3.13.51-4): 'Charred portals testify to the sacrilege of Brennus, when he attacked the Pythian realm of the unshorn god: and soon Parnassus shook its laurelled peak and scattered terrible snows upon the Gallic arms'. After drinking too heavily in the lowland villages Brennus and his army 'Forgate their feats of warre and playd the swine', before attempting the assault, 'brainesicke' and 'heedelesse'.[54] This drunken stupor, and the frightening weirdness of the priests of Apollo, sets the scene for the army's ultimate defeat amid something akin to a mountain panic. Brennus's attack on the mountain in Higgins' version is thwarted through the strategic use of the landscape by the temple's priests, who 'had fenste the easiest wayes, / So that against the rockes our force wee bend' while 'With stones the scaleing *Britaynes* downe they hend'.[55] 'Dazled', 'foule amazde' and 'orecome' (279), in this second ascent, Brennus is again confronted by a destabilization of identity. This time, though, the reader of Higgins' *Mirror* does not participate; rather, we are encouraged to 'Learne valiauntly',[56] and shun Brennus's negative example.

Having crossed the Alps, Higgins' Brennus seems to have been transformed. His assault on the 'insensate' mountain-dwelling priests and their 'deluding sprits'[57] comes to evoke not the aptitude of the indigenous mountaineer, or the thrilling, heroic conquest of alien terrain, but a prosaic counterpoint to the pagan divinity of high places, as he breaks down Delphi's monetization of the 'feare and wonder' inspired in other men by Parnassus's 'maiesty'.[58] The elision of Brennus's multiple histories forces these diverse facets of alpinism together, such that the Renaissance mountain's compound significance – summit and pass, refuge and conduit – is brought into focus, and something approaching tourism is mooted. Even though Brennus's raid fails, his changed attitude sketches out a new relationship to the landscape, grounded in international commerce.

As early modern examples of imaginatively reworked ancient history attest, the relationship between territorial demarcation and identity was a live issue in the British Isles during the long sixteenth century. Mountains presented a clear visual boundary: Silius, for example, describes the Pyrenees as dividing 'Spain from Gaul, making an eternal barrier between the two great countries' (Silius, *Punica* 3.418-19). His use of the mountain range motif has been framed in narratological terms, as 'a topological frontier', which 'polarizes the space of the plot between two antithetic spheres', divided by 'a mythological ethnocentric perspective of space', the violation of which has 'tragic consequences for the epic characters'.[59] Shorthand for otherness in the classical tradition, '*ultra montem*' translated to vernacular Tudor English usage, too, where 'beyond the mountains' in general, or 'beyond the Alps' in particular, had become a familiar means of identifying local difference.

Higgins' anomalous emphasis on Brennus's Alpine crossing certainly draws attention to the terrain's role as a 'topological frontier'.[60] As well as a practical impediment, though, mountains here and in the writing of his contemporaries serve as conspicuous conduits, both dividing and connecting territories, ethnic groups, cultures and chronological eras. When Fisher's ghost of Brennus appears in *The True Trojans*, he focuses on trans-European movement, and straightaway invokes his Alpine exploits to assert both British superiority and expansiveness. He begins,

> From the vnbounded Ocean, and cold climes,
> ...
> I first led out great swarmes of shaggy Gaules,
> And big-bon'd Britaines. The white-pated Alpes,
> Where snow and winter dwell, did bow their neckes
> To our victorious feete.[61]

Meanwhile, his appearance onstage as ghost plays on the particular capacity of mountain landscapes to elide disparate periods in history[62] – Raymond Williams' unfinished mid-twentieth-century series of novels, *People of the Black Mountains*, about the Roman invasion and colonization of not just Welsh territory but also recorded history, explores just this piling up of generations which are both 'distinct and all suddenly present'.[63] But the presentness of history engendered by early modern mountains is not just to do with embodied memory or psychogeography. The tongue-in-cheek greeting of Iachimo by Postumus on the 'speediness' (II.iv.31) of Iachimo's return to Rome from ancient Britain in *Cymbeline* jokes metatheatrically about Shakespeare's transgression of the unities of time and place, but also speaks to the counterintuitive mundanity of contemporary trans-European travel, particularly as regards the transalpine cultural exchange between Rome/Italy and early modern England.

The late sixteenth century was gripped with a new wave of anxiety about – stemming from evident enthusiasm for – Italian cultural borrowing, and the Alps play an increasingly prominent metonymic role in allusions to this process. In Churchyard's 1579 poem, 'The Troubles of Scotland', they designate the nefarious continental origins of a moral sickness that has taken hold north of the border. 'Bloodie brauls' are 'A tricke newe learnde, beyonde the Alps . . . A toye brought home, by those that trauell farre'.[64] Arthur Brooke, the author of verse narrative and Shakespearean source *Romeus and Juliet* (1562) also lays his scene 'beyonde the Alps, / [In] a towne of aunciente fame'.[65] The topographical situation of Verona is woven into broader conceptions of its civic virtue and value, while its location 'beyond the Alps' serves as a marker of distance, defamiliarization and invasive continental fashions. Crucially though, these poets employ the Alps as a boundary which may be crossed, symbolizing a foreignness which might be imported, as in William Byrd's seminal volume, *Musica Transalpina*, a collection of Italianate madrigals printed in 1588. Also imported, of course, were Petrarch's semi-allegorical progress up Mount Ventoux, recent, neo-Latin works such as Pietro Bembo's late fifteenth-century *De Aetna*, and descriptions of contemporary Alpine adventures by the likes of the sixteenth-century Swiss scholars Conrad Gessner, and Simler, only recently recognized as being not 'idiosyncratic forerunners of later developments, but . . . prominent exponents of an early modern trend among cultural elites'.[66] Another of *Cymbeline*'s metatextual jokes, whereby the lost British prince Guiderius is named 'Polydore' after Geoffrey of Monmouth's most vocal sixteenth-century critic, Polydore Vergil, (as well, perhaps, as Priam's errant son), sums up the irony of Italian humanism's new investment in mountain experience, by using a signifier of cosmopolitan intellectual exchange as an indigenous, rustic disguise.

As we have seen, narratives from the British Isles are also beginning to combine rugged authenticity with the modern 'pleasure' and 'delight' which continental European mountains inspire for Gessner.[67] In 1604, the Scottish Franciscan Simion Grahame detailed his own experience of mountain travel in his verse collection, *The Passionate Sparke of a Relenting Minde*. Grahame approaches his account of Alpine ascent through the framing of a pilgrim's exile from 'Scotland his Soyle'. The wandering Grahame is a 'vagabond astray', 'With trobled spri't transported here and there, / None like my selfe but this my selfe alone'. Walking through 'forreigne fieldes forlorne', the narrative voice is distraught, yet in a passage which bears striking similarity to Brennus and his analogues' Alpine crossings, Grahame presents the reader with a beset but exhilarated perspective:

You stately Alpes surmounting in the skyes
The force of floods that from your heights down falles
There mighty Clamors with my carefull Cries,
The Ecchoes voice from hollow Caues recalles.
The snow froz'n-clowds down fro[m] your tops do thu[n]der
Their voyce with mine doth teare the ayre a sunder

And Neptune thou when thy proude swelling wrath
Fro[m] gulphes to mountaines mou'd with Winters blast
. . .
Oft in thy rage, thy raging stormes I past
And my salt teares increast thy saltnes more,
My sighes with windes made all thy bowells rore.[68]

The assimilation of Grahame's voice, tears and sighs into the mountain land- and soundscape recuperates his exilic isolation, and once again articulates the capacity of alpinism to remake identity, and generate sensations of affinity as well as estrangement.

Conclusions

We might see in early modern literary mountains the notion of identity as a topographical property which facilitates two ways of meaning: indigenous identity rooted in the 'deep antiquity' of a specific landscape, on the one hand, and the crossing of geological/geographical boundaries, by people, stories or behaviours, as a means of recasting this identity, on the other. This is not at all to conclude, however, that the first is associated with stasis and the second with flux – in fact, I would frame the first as characterized by change, the second by exchange. Brennus's two mountains help to delineate such a contrast: the dynamic fluidity of the first, with its rising mists and snow melt, set against the chunky solidity of the second, whose weapons are rocks and hailstones. Broadly, it is possible to see the trope of the mountain working to figure authentic yet assimilative indigenous identities, as well as the fungibility of national characteristics in the early modern marketplace, embedded in an involved stratigraphy of source texts with their own associative freight. Higgins' brief but thrilling interpolation, and Brennus's successive mountain crossings in, and into, early modern imaginative literature, demonstrate some of these underlying trends in action.

Notes

1. I would like to thank the volume's editors and other contributors for their helpful revisions and suggestions, Alasdair MacDonald for the Simion Grahame reference, the St Andrews Medieval and Renaissance Research Group, and Paulina Kewes, Lorna Hutson, and the University of Oxford English and History Graduate Seminar for their comments on an earlier draft.
2. Wordsworth 1822: 111.
3. Higgins 1946: 271.
4. Hansen 2013.
5. Toliver 2011: 12.
6. Cf. Hollis 2019: 1040–2.
7. Ruskin 1856: 317–85.
8. Cf. König in this volume for related discussion of Ottoman Greece.
9. Debarbieux and Rudaz 2015: 74–5.
10. Oakes 1997: 510.
11. Puttenham 1589: 128, see also 148–9.
12. Anderson 2006: 19.

13. Cf. Debarbieux and Rudaz 2015: 283.
14. Herendeen 1981; Hopkins 2005: 4–7.
15. Herendeen 1981: 108–9.
16. Ibid. 127.
17. Cheney 2018: 95.
18. Spenser 1595: B2r.
19. Porter 2016: 5.
20. Spenser 1590.
21. Holinshed 1586: Preface.
22. Shakespeare 2002.
23. Holinshed 1587: 49; 98.
24. Shakespeare 2014. All references will be to this edition.
25. Griffiths 2003: 347. See also Hopkins 2005: 21.
26. Cf. Debarbieux and Rudaz 2015: 31 on the 'antimodernity' of this stance.
27. Churchyard 1587: M2v.
28. Hopkins 2005: 20. See also Cull 2016.
29. Hopkins 2005: 14.
30. Curran 2002: 124–5.
31. Hardyng 1543: 73v.
32. See, for example, Livy, *Ab Urbe Condita* 5.34-49; Diodorus Siculus, *Library* 14.113-17; Plutarch, Camillus 17-30; Polybius, *Histories* 2.18.
33. See Pausanias, *Description of Greece*, 10.23.13; cf. Strabo, *Geography*, 4.1.13; Justinus, *Epitome of Pompeius Trogus' Histories*, 24.4-8; Polybius, *Histories* 4.46.
34. See Newstead 1939; Koch 1990.
35. Geoffrey of Monmouth 1966: 90.
36. Lydgate 1494: Q4r-Q4v.
37. Higden 1482: 133v-4v; Curran 2002: 127.
38. Fisher 1633: D3r.
39. Newstead 1951: 58–9; see also Newstead 1939: 164–7.
40. See Kewes 2016 on fratricide as a topical theme in the *Mirror*; Archer 2017.
41. Fisher 1633: G4v.
42. Ibid. D2v.
43. See Curran 2002: 127–8.
44. Vergil 1546: 113v.
45. Camden 1637: 677.
46. Higgins 1946: 270–1.
47. Warner 1586: 66.
48. Cf. Polybius, *Histories* 3.47-8 on the illogic of historiographical presentations of Hannibal's Alpine expeditions.
49. Simler 2003: 22; 23.

50. Ibid. 23.
51. Holland 1600: 1173.
52. Higgins 1946: 203.
53. Ibid. 275.
54. Ibid. 279.
55. Ibid.
56. Ibid.
57. Ibid. 277.
58. Ibid. 276
59. Šubrt 1991: 226.
60. See Appian, *Roman History* 4.3.1-4 on ethnic distinctions between the Gauls and Romans.
61. Fisher 1633: A3r.
62. Cf. further discussion in the introduction to this volume, pp. 8–10.
63. Williams 1989: 3.
64. Churchyard 1579: D4r.
65. Brooke 1562: A1r.
66. Korenjak 2017: 182–3; see also Hooley and Ireton in this volume.
67. Korenjak 2017: 190.
68. Grahame 1604: E1r-E1v.

CHAPTER 12
UPLAND ON MONT VENTOUX
Peter H. Hansen[1]

'At the summit of the mountain, among pebbles, the terra-cotta trumpets of the men of the ancient white frosts chirped like little eagles'.[2] So wrote René Char in the poem 'Les dentelles de Montmirail' in 1960 after learning that archaeologists had unearthed terracotta trumpets atop Mont Ventoux. Since the nineteenth century, excavations to build meteorological observatories on the summit had uncovered many objects of piety from the last 500 years and fragments of terracotta trumpets that appeared to be from a much earlier date. The semi-circular pattern of trumpet fragments heralded the ruins of an ancient temple. In 1960, archaeologists thought the trumpets dated from antiquity, though more recent estimates place them in the twelfth or thirteenth centuries.[3] Twentieth-century potters still made terra-cotta trumpets for ecclesiastical clients in the region. Like summit chapels rebuilt on the mountain, the trumpets remained part of a living tradition.

Yet archaeological or poetic accounts barely influenced the prevailing interpretation that Petrarch's ascent of Mont Ventoux marked the arrival of the first modern man. A century earlier, in 1860, Jacob Burckhardt identified Petrarch's account of an ascent of Mont Ventoux, in a letter dated 26 April 1336, as the epochal moment when individual modern man broke the darkness that followed classical antiquity. Burckhardt took literally Petrarch's rhetorical claim that he had wanted to climb the mountain solely to enjoy the view. Since the 1960s, the remainder of Petrarch's letter has been read more often as an allegory for his own spiritual development. Petrarch ignored warnings to turn back from an aged shepherd and slowly mounted winding switchbacks while his brother climbed more directly to the top. After surveying the horizon from the summit of Ventoux, Petrarch reportedly opened Augustine's *Confessions* and read at random that men admire high mountains but pass themselves by. Chastened by precedents from scripture as well as late antiquity, Petrarch then descended the mountain in silence. Petrarch's ascent has prompted much commentary, but Burckhardt's view of the event as marking the arrival of the Renaissance and Western Civilization has remained surprisingly persistent.[4]

Burckhardtian images of Petrarch as the first modern man on Mont Ventoux are consistent with a cultural preference for epochal breaks between the past and present. Marjorie Hope Nicolson's *Mountain Gloom and Mountain Glory* (1959) echoed earlier dichotomous interpretations, especially John Ruskin's, with brevity, elegance, and alliterative rhythm in her title. Dawn Hollis[5] and other contributors to this volume have effectively questioned the wisdom of such a stark contrast across early modern and modern periods. Petrarch and those that followed in his footsteps on postclassical mountains have been in dialogue not only with classical or biblical precedents but also with local and provincial successors who view Petrarch and other predecessors as their contemporaries.

Archaeologists are not the only observers to identify multiple strata at the summit of Mont Ventoux. The palimpsestic layers at the highest point in Provence, the original Roman *Provincia*, also may provincialize the universalizing histories that so often accompany the summit position. The intersecting narratives of pagan practices, classical precedents, religious traditions and philosophical critiques on Mont Ventoux do not lead inexorably to the advent of modern man. In this respect, Mont Ventoux also provides a standpoint to reassess some contemporary representations of the Anthropocene with rhetorical echoes of Burckhardt that view our own time as the first to recognize human dominance of the earth. Scholars have noted that religious traditions, natural histories, nuclear war or the space age have offered earlier responses and examples of awareness of a changing climate.[6] René Char and his contemporaries were among many people reinterpreting postclassical mountains, and their local and provincial histories may help to locate our present predicaments in this longer continuum.

Modern Provençal pilgrimages

On 14 September 1851, a large group of 'modern pilgrims', including the printer François-Joseph Seguin and the poet Joseph Roumanille, ventured to the top of Mont Ventoux to celebrate a Provençal amalgam of local, religious and regional identities. As the pilgrims ascended, they paused 'at the stations of this new Calvary until reaching the summit with the first light of dawn'. According to Seguin, the chapel near the summit was too small for the 2,000 pilgrims so 'an altar was improvised on the highest point'. Re-occupying the place that had been used to make trigonometrical observations for maps of France, the pilgrims added stones to the base of an iron cross and replied to the sermon on this mount with cries of 'Vive la Croix/Vivo la Crous!' Seguin and Roumanille located their pilgrimage in a longer tradition by publishing an account of their ascent in French and Provençal along with contemporary translations of Petrarch's Ventoux letter and other documents as guides for excursionists.[7]

The summit of Mont Ventoux had been a pilgrimage site long before a cross or chapel was built in the eighth or ninth century, and continued to be so throughout the proceeding centuries.[8] In the fifteenth century, a bishop consecrated a summit chapel reputedly with a fragment of the 'real cross' guarded by a hermit. Annual summit pilgrimages were active in 1598 when the Swiss humanist Thomas Platter Jr made an ascent in search of medicinal plants, and in 1711 when the Jesuit priest Antoine de Laval measured Ventoux's longitude, latitude and height.[9] The surrounding region, known as the *Comtat Venaissin*, remained subject to papal control into the eighteenth century. Summit chapels were periodically repaired, and one was substantially rebuilt in 1818 before the dedication of the new iron cross in 1851.

Roumanille's 1852 anthology of poetry in Provençal, or Occitan, one of the *langues d'oc*, declared that he and his contemporaries were inheritors of the medieval troubadours of Provence.[10] In 1854, they founded the Félibrige, an association devoted to Provençal language, landscape and sociability that sponsored a literary almanac and cultural festivals. In his memoirs, Roumanille's pupil Frédéric Mistral described himself as the son of yeoman farmers 'who make a link between peasant and bourgeois', and the Félibrige self-consciously adopted this translational role. Mistral reported that they followed the advice of Romanian poets: 'when they wanted to revive their national language, which the bourgeois class had lost or corrupted, they sought it in the country and in the mountains among the least civilized peasants'. At the founding of the Félibrige, Mistral declared himself 'all ready to hurl the rallying cry to the mistral, to "hallo" (as the shepherds of the mountains say), and to plant the banner on Mont Ventoux'.[11]

During his ascent of Mont Ventoux in 1857, Mistral did not, in fact, plant a banner or occupy the positions attributed by contemporaries to Petrarch or to Catholic pilgrims. At the summit, Mistral's attention was drawn to 'the wide shadow of Ventoux extending its great triangular point down over the whole width of the Comtat Venaissin'. Under this benevolent shadow, Mistral celebrated the sociability of Provence in contrast to the officiousness of the French state. Mistral had felt humiliation when forced to speak French in school and vowed to 'raise and revive in Provence the traditional spirit that was being destroyed by all the schools and their false and unnatural education'.[12] Mistral was not at that time a religious pilgrim, though he converted to Catholicism decades later. On the descent, Mistral and his companions were arrested by a French policeman in one village and accosted by the mayor of another who both refused to believe they were artists on a walking tour of Ventoux. They were released after a prosperous farmer spoke up on their behalf because they spoke Provençal well and could confirm that 'it's true as they say that the sun hops three times when it rises on the summit of Mont Ventoux'. Shortly afterward, on learning they had come from Ventoux, a sunburned old man told them: 'Wise is he who does not go back, and mad is he who does'.[13]

Ventoux was climbed frequently by the Félibres and the many ascents by the entomologist and early member, Jean-Henri Fabre, illustrate his shifting positions on the summit. In 1842, Fabre climbed the peak at age eighteen with a former schoolmate. They received advice from a grey-haired herder who pointed out a winding path, but like others before them, they took a steeper and more direct route.[14] The summit cross, pilgrims' candles, and monuments of nature all prompted prayers before they admired the view and watched swallows flying above the peak.[15] Fabre then taught at a local lycée and became an entomologist. During a sunrise at the summit in 1865, the highlight was a 'glimpse of the sweet joys which await the naturalist on the summit of Mont Ventoux' – birds, wasps, ladybugs and butterflies fluttering among flowers.[16] In a later lecture, Fabre juxtaposed the swallows with summit observatories: 'Man has not the bird's strong wing, but he has something better – the strong will that laughs at obstacles'. During the second half of the nineteenth century, Fabre's object of awe had shifted from God in nature to the indomitable will of man. Man had built airships, planted observatories on mountaintops, and scaled the highest peaks: 'With what indomitable courage, with what ardent love of learning must he not be animated to brave the dangers that confront one on those awe-inspiring heights!'[17]

Ventoux/Ventour appeared frequently in verse, and Mistral's epic poems remained ambivalent about this expression of masculine will. The mountains provide the background for a love story in *Mirèio*,[18] which represents Ventour as a benevolent old shepherd watching over its flock. Ventoux takes a more decisive role in *Calendau*,[19] the story of a fisherman who wins a beautiful Provençal princess who had been married against her will to a brigand. She escapes to a mountain cave where the fisherman, Calendau/Calendal, sees a vision that persuades him to win her hand through deeds of valour. After a series of adventures, he makes the ascent of Mont Ventoux and realizes that 'on this mountain God only came at night.'[20] Calendau resolves to cut down the forest that covers Ventoux and for nine days trees fall and groan in a 'somber death rattle'. When he boasts of his conquest, the princess Estrello reprimands him for his machismo: 'You have dishonored the face of the Ventour! … The mountains, the elevated and imposing peaks, belong to God!'[21] In penitence, he makes a pilgrimage to the grotto of Mary Magdalene and wins her favour by reconciling factions of quarrelling Provençal journeymen. After the brigand perishes in a fire, the pair weds and love triumphs.

Ernest Renan, a decade after his influential lecture asking '*Qu'est-ce qu'une nation?*', told the Parisian Félibres in 1891 that he had first seen mountains in Provence and been enchanted by them. Provence, along with his native Brittany, still preserved the 'kingdom of enchantment, the only good that exists on earth'. He toasted these regions and 'our beloved French homeland, mother of these diversities, each amiable and excellent in its own way'.[22] Aspirations of a 'nation' did not require the erasure of particular identities, and their modernity was reaffirmed by the award to Mistral of the Nobel Prize for literature in 1904, which he shared with a Spanish playwright and used to establish a museum devoted to Provençal culture. *The Nation* thought the Nobel Prize for Mistral and others from 'minor nationalities' demonstrated that 'the spirit of modern imperialism is far from carrying everything before it'.[23] An appreciation of Mistral noted his emphasis on the landscape and legends of Provence: 'A particular discrepancy, in the midst of very human affairs, is the introduction of the supernatural. The fantastic side of Mistral's genius is evinced here, as well as his folkloristic desire to dwell on his compatriots' superstition'.[24] Mont Ventoux continued to cast shadows of discrepancy and provinciality that resisted incorporation into universalizing narratives of the metropoles. As the poet Roy Campbell observed in the 1950s: 'Calendal, as a character, exists to this day, wherever on the coast of Southern France it is uncomfortable for rich tourists to go'.[25]

Return to origins

Rebirth or a return to origins were understood very differently by historians, mountaineers or artists. Mistral's *Lou Tresor dóu Félibrige*,[26] a Provençal encyclopaedia, recorded that Ventoux owed its name to Ventour, a deity for the wind. Camille Jullian, historian of Gaul, confirmed 'Saint-Victoire and Mont Ventoux, the two most popular mountains in Provence, have their point of origin in the same Celtic or Ligurian name appropriate to the two summits which are partly covered in snow and wind'. The translation of names had led to variations: on Sainte-Victoire the deity took a Roman then Christian name, while on Ventoux it 'conserved its virile allure, secular and indigenous'.[27] An archaeologist likewise wrote that Ventoux was Ventour, 'undoubtedly derived from the divinity Venturius', the divinity of mountains in the region. Pilgrims on Mont Sainte-Victoire, near Aix-en-Provence, re-enacted pagan traditions that did not date from Christianity or the victory of Marius at the battle of Aix in 102 BCE. Rather, he argued that they owed their origins to the festival of the sun at the summer solstice, 'which was celebrated from time immemorial by Indo-European-speaking populations and of which traces remain in many of our villages'. The intervening years had blurred 'the eternal god of the sun, the Ligurian and pagan saint Venture, and the Christian Sainte-Victoire... Three conceptions absolutely distinct and irreducible one to another'.[28]

For Ernest Cézanne, founding President of the *Club Alpin Français* (CAF), mountains retained traces of 'ancient races' but were more important as national resources for engineering the future. As an engineer, this Cézanne built railways in France, Austria, Russia and the Ottoman Empire before returning to Paris during the Franco-Prussian war in 1870. After French defeat, Cézanne proposed brigades of alpine mountain troops to the National Assembly in 1873 and created the CAF with similar aims the next year. The club would foster national rebirth and 'snatch young people from the enervating idleness of cities' by exercising their minds and bodies on the mountains.[29] Following the example of alpine clubs in Britain, Switzerland, Germany and Italy, mountaineering for Ernest Cézanne was shaped by 'thinking like a state':[30] 'In our age of compulsory service, a prudent mother wants to familiarize her son with the trials of the mountain. France is certainly not disposed to provoke anyone; but, if attacked, it is in the Vosges, Jura and the Alps that it will repel the assault'.[31] In this pursuit of national regeneration, the CAF organized hundreds of school trips and thousands of club outings to the mountains over the following decades. The CAF graphically represented its patriotic ideals in its *Annuaire* (1903) with a shield depicting snow cliffs and an edelweiss flower below the motto 'Pour la patrie, par la montagne'.[32] The CAF celebrated the autonomy of its provincial sections which organized their own activities. A road was built to the top of Ventoux for a scientific observatory and the peak soon became the scene for automotive and bicycle races. Sainte-Victoire also became a popular destination for members of the Provence section of the CAF.

The artist Paul Cézanne refused the summit position of the alpinists and engineers. Among Parisian painters, Cézanne was a proud and recalcitrant provincial and he became an opponent of metropolitan, bourgeois manners and practitioner of a self-conscious, vernacular *provençalisme*.[33] He returned to Provence and painted Mont Sainte-Victoire from perspectives that aligned him with his friends among the Félibrige. An early Saint-Victoire painting from 1882–5, now at the Metropolitan Museum (Fig. 12.1), portrays this artistic cohabitation of mountain and modernity. A horizontal railway viaduct would cut the painting in half but for the dominant verticality of the mountain which, doubly framed by pine trees, anchors the composition, softens the railway line and waters the farms of the region. Nature abhorred straight lines, according to Cézanne, and mountains cannot be subdued by railway builders: 'To hell with the

Figure 12.1 Paul Cézanne (1839–1906). *Mont Sainte-Victoire and the Viaduct of the Arc River Valley*, 1882–1885. Oil on canvas. 25¾ x 32⅛ in. The Metropolitan Museum of Art, New York.

engineers!', he told a friend, 'we're not road surveyors.' Instead, for this Cézanne 'everything is connected', a sensibility that provided him a 'vague cosmic religious feeling'.[34]

Cézanne's series of Sainte-Victoire paintings searched for the remotest origins. He studied the mountain's structure and Neolithic sites and took crash courses on geology and philosophy.[35] Cézanne painted the mountain from quarries to plant its roots in the soil. He told his friend Joachim Gasquet, an active member of the Félibrige, that he hoped to discover geological foundations dating from the primordial collision of atoms and reaction of chemicals: 'I see rising these great rainbows, these cosmic prisms, this dawn of ourselves above the void. I saturate myself in them by reading Lucretius'.[36] Cézanne was proficient in Latin and admired and translated Virgil's *Ecologues* at an early age. Like Gasquet and other Félibres, Cézanne sought to re-envision Provence as a modern and French Arcadia based on Roman antecedents.[37]

The view from Les Lauves, on a hill above Cézanne's atelier, provided the point of view for his artistic ascents. Thick brush strokes of tawny yellows and burnt ochre, dabs of green, convex shadows and iridescent hues of blue that evaporate into grey. This palette provides a continuum from base to summit in which the mountain is poised in upward thrust, in a momentary equilibrium between earth and sky. Cézanne told Gasquet that everything was 'a bit of solar heat that has been stored up and organized, a reminder of the sun'. Cézanne wanted to extract its essence: 'Perhaps the earth's diffused morality represents the effort it's making to return to its solar origin. Therein lies the idea of God, its feeling, its dream of God'. He looked beyond arcadian models and wanted to free lines and colours and capture the spiritual quality of the light. 'Look at Sainte-Victoire there. How it soars, how imperiously it thirsts for the sun! How melancholy it is in the evening when all its weight sinks back ... Those blocks were made of fire and there's still fire in them.'[38]

Base and summit

For René Char, the Nazi and Vichy regimes in the 1940s had discredited a naïve search for origins in the mountains or elsewhere. A native of Provence whose poetry was inspired by the mountains, springs and rivers of the region, Char also identified the war with a broader threshold of religious doubt: 'the abandonment of the divine'.[39] Char had been part of the Surrealist movement in the early 1930s and a leader in the Resistance during the Second World War. Attempts by Surrealists, psychoanalysts and others in the 1930s to reconstruct the humanist individual had led, paradoxically, to theories of its dissolution and to Char's poetics of fragments, 'the taking apart of the self'.[40] Char was also deeply influenced by Heraclitus, whose 'poetry runs immediately to the summits, because Heraclitus possesses this sovereign ascensional power'.[41] Char's wartime journal, *Feuillets d'Hypnos*, recorded aphorisms of mountains, friendship and beauty. The mountains recur as a complex motif during the war, with men smelling of glaciers, resistance as hope, and poetry itself in a combative stance of 'furious ascension'.[42]

After the war, the cave drawings at Lascaux, discovered in the 1940s and then considered the earliest examples of human art, illustrated the suspicion Char shared with the philosophers Georges Bataille and Maurice Blanchot of the very notion of origin. To some, Lascaux represented the first 'modern art' if not the first 'modern man', and Bataille located the origins of art and of transgression at Lascaux.[43] In contrast, Char wrote that the only human figure painted on the walls of Lascaux was not the 'first' human representation but rather an 'abyss dancer, spirit, yet to be born'.[44] Blanchot compared Char to Heraclitus and Xenophanes and celebrated in Char's poetry the absence of origin and the presence of nature, not of earthly things – sun, water, wisdom or the infinity of the cosmos – but 'that which is already there before "all" ... Nature is the test of first things, a test in which poetry is exposed to the impact of a measureless freedom, a total absence of time, and from which its consciousness dawns, becoming the word of commencement'.[45] Reinterpreting earlier traditions, beginnings for Char and Blanchot were moments of open possibility that could not provide the panoramic perspective of the summit.

Mountains appear frequently in Char's works, but the only summit ever reached was Mount Everest in *L'Abominable homme des neiges* (1953), an argument in the form of a ballet. After Dr Hermez, the expedition leader, unties his rope to the Sherpas, an avalanche carries him over a precipice. A half-man, half-animal creature covered in fur emerges from the debris with a smaller figure and they both remove their disguise to reveal Venus with a young satellite star. Venus covers Hermez with her fur and falls in love with him. The climbers and Sherpas return Hermez to camp before making their final bid for the summit. The jealous satellite star dons Venus's disguise and fools Hermez into falling into an abyss where the climber dies.

> In the distance, one hears the voice of the explorers: 'Victory! The Mountain is conquered! Everest is climbed!' Thus succeeds what was only a limited material objective, while the hero succumbs, overcome by the imbrications of his sovereignty and his destiny ... Everest trampled, Venus will no longer return to earth. Impossible is now to be found in human affairs. What have we conquered, won?[46]

The summit was an illusion and conquest was annihilation. In this period Char compared the poet to the 'mountain climber constantly slipping backwards who is set on his feet again by the repeated assault of summits ... On the rasp of ridges and dizzying needles, exulting, he makes a smile. Meanwhile he dies'.[47]

The summit was an unattainable limit-point rather than the seemingly stable position occupied by mountaineers on Everest or Petrarch on Ventoux. In *Recherche de la base et du sommet* (1955), Char wrote 'Base and summit, provided that men bestir themselves and diverge, crumble rapidly. But there is the tension of this search'.[48] Conventionally, the summit had been associated with good and 'base' with evil, but these terms were reversed by Georges Bataille, who linked the 'moral summit' with decline. Bataille posited the summit as a point where life was pushed to an impossible limit.[49] In 1966, Char opened *Retour Amont*,[50] a collection of poetry, with this quotation from Bataille: 'This flight headed towards the summit (which is the constitution of knowledge – dominating the realms themselves) is only one of the paths of the *labyrinth*. But we can now in no way avoid this path which we must follow from attraction to attraction in search of "being"'.[51] Tensions between solitude and society and the competition for knowledge and power broke Ariadne's thread through the labyrinth, and the summit of these postclassical mountains became poetically unattainable and philosophically inaccessible.

Returning upland toward summits could not lead to a renaissance or rebirth. For Char, '*Returning Upland* does not mean a returning to the source. Far from it. Rather a sally, a returning to nourishment that has not been deferred from the source, and to its eye, upstream, that is, to the most forlorn place possible'.[52] The return upland resists reduction to nostalgia or philosophical categories of the 'summit' or 'eternal recurrence'. Scholars rightly emphasize Char's debt to pre-Socratic philosophers and Nietzsche,[53] though Char told Blanchot: 'I am a poet, not a philosopher in verse'.[54] In an interview in *Le Monde*, Char said that 'the return to the sources is one of the great illusions of man in regret. On the contrary, it is necessary to go "above" the sources to that which permits the sources to exist; there, where the nature of being is most inhospitable and where one finds the first fruits'.[55]

Uplands were threatened in June 1965 when the French government announced that it would install intermediate-range ballistic missiles in silos in the Plateau d'Albion, next to Mont Ventoux. Char organized 'Partisans de la Paix' to rally against the nuclear missile installation. During the war, Char and other members of the Resistance *maquis Ventoux* had taken refuge in the area chosen for the missile silos.⁵⁶ Char published a scathing pamphlet, *La Provence point oméga* (1965), which ridiculed the mayor of the village of Apt for trading hundreds of jobs for thousands of lives and poisoning the wells of the region. The *New York Times* compared displaced villagers to 'the inhabitants of various South Sea islands – primitives whose approval of the intrusion is clearly demonstrated by the absence – or weakness – of protest'.⁵⁷ Pablo Picasso joined Char's protest and issued a poster with a sketch of an eagle, sun and a satyr face sometimes considered Zeus hovering above the serrated summit ridge of the mountain. In 'Ruine d'Albion', Char identified this as the battle for the earthly crust: 'In our eyes this *site* is worth more than our bread, for it cannot be replaced'.⁵⁸

Nuclear missiles elicited a more radical critique than that articulated during earlier protests against pollution of streams in Provence. After the launch of the Sputnik satellite, Char wrote in 1959 in 'Aux riverains de la Sorgue' that 'Space man, whose day of birth it is, will be a thousand times less luminous and reveal a thousand fewer hidden things than the stone man' of Lascaux.⁵⁹ As *point omega*, the missiles on Mont Ventoux presented a deeper philosophical challenge. According to Blanchot, 'man has in a sense already rejoined the point omega. This means that there is no longer any Other other than man, and that there is no longer any Outside outside him'.⁶⁰ Man had included and comprehended everything within a closed circle of knowledge. Stone man and space man were succeeded by 'scorched earth man' in a Char poem of 1968.⁶¹

For Char, returning upland could lead, if not to the summit, then towards one Other other than man – wolves. Wolves were eliminated from Mont Ventoux after the summit observatory opened in the 1880s, but they left their trace on the mountain and in Char's poetry. In a 1980 interview, Char recalled that when wolves ate a sheep his grandfather was tending on Mont Ventoux in the 1830s, the boy hid in a grotto, where wolves prowled outside until he was able to flee during the next day. Char represented wolves as ennobled by their disappearance and waiting with the poet for an 'upland amplitude'.⁶²

This upland amplitude was a response to environmental awareness during the post-war years. 'Carelessly, we exalt and oppose nature and men', wrote Char in one of the Lascaux poems, and in other works he resembles a deist or refers to phenomena that appear supernatural.⁶³ Char's wolves on upland slopes embodied 'thinking like a mountain', Aldo Leopold's coinage from the 1940s in response to the disappearance of wolves in another provincial domain, the North American backcountry.⁶⁴ While Char's wolves in the 1940s echoed the *maquis Ventoux* of the Resistance, the wolves of *Retour Amont* in the 1960s evoked the search for being: 'We shall remain, to live and to die, with the wolves, filially, upon this teeming earth'.⁶⁵

Biospheres

A recent history of Mont Ventoux inevitably begins with Petrarch before describing in more detail the mountain's geology, geomorphology and hydrology, its climate, flora and fauna, and its human use through forestry, hunting, agriculture, industry and tourism. The archaeologist Guy Barruol then locates the mountain in a comparative context. Ventoux's social role and prominent conical silhouette compare favourably to Olympus in Greece, Ararat in Turkey, Canigou in Catalonia, Viso in the Alps, Kilimanjaro in Africa, or Fujiyama in Japan.[66] Mont Ventoux had long been a sacred site and compared to other mountains, but associations with Fujiyama and other 'global' sacred peaks were more recent developments. Tourist guidebooks disseminate references to Ventoux 'with its white cap and the allure of Fujiyama' and such global comparisons now circulate widely.[67]

In 1990, UNESCO and the French government declared Ventoux a 'biosphere reserve' which more formally recognized its place in a global network that combines conservation and sustainable development. These biosphere reserves are the most tangible achievement of UNESCO's 'Man in the Biosphere' initiative launched in 1970 at the same time as intermediate-range ballistic missiles were planted in the Plateau d'Albion. Twenty years later, at the end of the Cold War, the creation of the biosphere reserve and decommissioning of the nuclear missiles recast the image of Mont Ventoux once again. Or, to put the matter differently, events since the 1990s have provincialized the Burckhardtian representations of 'modern man' central to narratives of Western civilization that were once embodied in images of Petrarch astride Mont Ventoux.

The temptation remains to follow Petrarch's footsteps. Reporters from the *New York Times* periodically repeat the ascent, with one driving most of the way to the final switchbacks, while another felt a sense of anti-climax on the summit, 'hoping for an epiphany that never quite came'.[68] Would you believe that I ascended Mont Ventoux on April 26, a few years ago, following one of the routes that Petrarch could have taken from Malaucène? Naturally, there is no consensus on the route of a possibly fictional ascent, but the 600th anniversary of Petrarch's letter prompted speculation.[69] During my ascent, after leaving the source of the Groseau, paths diverged and most of the way was little used and largely overgrown. False summits appeared on the long, exposed ridge with snow nestled in shadows and small clusters of ladybugs basking in the sun. The chapel below the summit was still filled with snow and bypassed by nearly all the people who drove cars or rode bicycles to the top. The massive television tower dominated the fenced-off summit. The gift-shop bustled, cyclists posed for pictures and celebrated convivially, a gentle wind touched everyone; it was a glorious day for a first ascent of Mont Ventoux.

Char's wolves illustrate the tensions of any search for a stable position in the biosphere or Anthropocene. René Char was not the first to say that 'everything is a new beginning, always: to attain the summit is an illusion. But it is "necessary" to try'.[70] It remains to be seen whether embedding 'man' in the biosphere or in the Anthropocene will clear a space for Others other than man. Thinking like a mountain provincializes the code of homogenous, secular time by entangling past, present and future.[71] In these histories, wolves are not only in the past, even on a mountain such as Mont Ventoux on which they are extinct.

My ascent of Mont Ventoux took one of many possible routes through the histories that intersect on its slopes and at its summit. Like other postclassical mountains, Mont

Ventoux's histories are plural, and the moments of its past are not as distinct as geological strata or archaeological layers. They often blur or overlap rather than demarcate boundaries between epochs. Each moment in Ventoux's history remains available as a resource for the present, without claiming to be universal, or awaiting a rebirth, return or renaissance. Searching 'above' the sources does not mean searching for a higher summit position. On the contrary, perhaps returning upland on Mont Ventoux may summon the humility to locate ourselves on a continuum of time that extends into the future. We all stand on postclassical mountains now. 'Our earthly figure', as Char wrote in 'Lenteur de l'avenir', 'is only the second third of a continuous pursuit, a point, upland'.[72]

Notes

1. The author warmly thanks the editors and contributors in this volume for the stimulating discussion at St Andrews, and the Durham University Institute of Advanced Study for hospitality during revisions on this article.
2. Char 1995: 413.
3. Jully 1961; Barroul, Dautier and Mondon 2007: 193.
4. See Hansen 2013, esp. 12–22.
5. Hollis 2019.
6. Chakrabarty 2009; Chakrabarty 2012 and 2020.
7. Seguin 1852: 7, 12–13; Julian 1937; Brun 1977; Mondon 2003.
8. Seguin 1852: 118; Barroul, Dautier and Mondon 2007: 198–9, 231–2.
9. Clap 1976 ; LeRoy Ladurie 1977; Mondon 2003.
10. Roumanille 1852; Martel 1986; Roza 2003.
11. Mistral 1985: 3, 81, 152.
12. Ibid. 131.
13. Ibid. 226–31.
14. For the symbolic significance of the earlier winding path taken by Petrarch, see Williams, 167–8, this volume.
15. Mondon 2003: 39–45; Julian 1937: 171–82.
16. Fabre 1879: 181–93.
17. Fabre 1923: 190.
18. Mistral 1859.
19. Mistral 1867.
20. Ibid.: 298–9; Weiss 2005: 34–6.
21. Mistral 1867: 299, 301.
22. Renan 1904: 310–14.
23. Lesser 1914: 354.
24. Dargan 1914.
25. Campbell 1951: 281.

26. Mistral 1879: II, 1100.
27. Jullian 1899: 56–7; Jullian 1920: VI, 57, 329.
28. Clerc 1904: 278–82; Clerc 1906: 272, 274; Julian 1937: 337–9; d'Arnaud 1959.
29. Cézanne 1874.
30. Scott 1998.
31. Tissandier 1874; see Hoibian 2000; Drouet 2005.
32. Escudié 1903: 574.
33. Athanassoglou-Kallmyer 2003: 11.
34. Gasquet 1991: 165–6.
35. Athanassoglou-Kallmyer 2003: 176.
36. Gasquet 1921: 135–6; Tuma 2002: 56.
37. Athanassoglou-Kallmyer 2003: 187–92; Conisbee and Coutagne 2006.
38. Gasquet 1991: 152–4. The vision of mountains as coming from fire and thus still retaining some of the characteristics of fire can also be found in the writings of Conrad Gessner, discussed herein by Hooley, 25–6.
39. Char 1995: 255.
40. Caws 1977: 23; Dean 1994.
41. Char 1995: 720–1.
42. Ibid. 189.
43. Smith 2004.
44. Char 1995: 351.
45. Blanchot 1956: 37.
46. Char 1995: 1135.
47. Char 1956: 225; Char 1995: 1297.
48. Ibid. 631; Caws 1977: 32.
49. Bataille 1992: 33–40; Surya 2012: 429.
50. Char 1995: 656, 1377.
51. Bataille 1988: 86; Hollier 1990: 57–73.
52. Char 1995: 656; Caws and Griffin 1976: 199.
53. Née 2007.
54. Veyne 1990: 310.
55. Mora 1966.
56. Greilsamer 2004: 361–5; Coron 2007: 173–7; Leclair and Née 2015.
57. Schneider 1966.
58. Char 1995: 456. Picasso's 'La Provence – Point Oméga' is reproduced in Czwiklitzer 1968: 238.
59. Char 1995: 412.
60. Blanchot 1993: 207.
61. Char 1995: 466.
62. Ibid. 433, 1385; Leclair and Née 2015: 350–1.
63. Char 1995: 353.

64. Leopold 1949; Flader 1994.
65. Char 1995: 656; Caws and Griffin 1976: 199.
66. Barroul, Dautier and Mondon 2007: 8.
67. Ibid. 169.
68. Kimmelman 1999; Woodward 2006.
69. Champeville 1937.
70. Mora 1966.
71. Chakrabarty 2000; Hansen 2013.
72. Char 1995: 435.

BIBLIOGRAPHY

Addison, J. (1699), 'Ad Insignissimum Virum D. Tho. Burnettum, Sacræ Theoriæ Telluris Autorem' ['To the most distinguished man Dr Thomas Burnet, author of the Sacred Theory of the Earth'], in *Musarum Anglicanarum Analecta*, Vol. II, 284–6, Oxford: E. Theatro Sheldoniano, Impensis Tim. Child, ad insigne Albi Cervi in Coemeterio D. Pauli.

Addison, J. (1701), *A Letter from Italy*, London: H. Hills.

Alexander, J. C. (1985), *Brigandage and Public Order in the Morea, 1685–1806*, Athens: [s.n].

Allen, P. (1987), 'Some Aspects of Hellenism in the Early Greek Church Historians', *Traditio*, 43: 368–81.

Altick, R. (1978), *The Shows of London*, Cambridge, MA: Harvard University Press.

Anderson, Benedict (2006), *Imagined Communities: Reflections on the Origin and Spread of Nationalism*, revised edition, first published in 1983, London: Verso.

Anderson, Ben (2020), *Cities, Mountains and Being Modern in fin-de-siècle England and Germany*, London: Palgrave Macmillan.

Andrews, M. (1987), *The Search for the Picturesque: Landscape Aesthetics and Tourism in Britain, 1760–1800*, Aldershot: Scolar.

Andrews, M. (1999), *Landscape and Western Art*, Oxford: Oxford University Press.

Angelomatis-Tsougarakis, H. (1990), *The Eve of Greek Revival: British Travellers of Early Nineteenth-Century Greece*, London: Routledge.

Archer, H. (2017), *Unperfect Histories: The Mirror for Magistrates, 1559–1610*, Oxford: Oxford University Press.

Armbruster, K. and K. R. Wallace, eds (2001), *Beyond Nature Writing: Expanding the Boundaries of Ecocriticism*, Charlottesville: University Press of Virginia.

Ascoli, A. R. (1991), 'Petrarch's Middle Age: Memory, Imagination, History, and the "Ascent of Mount Ventoux"', *Stanford Italian Review*, 10: 5–43.

Ashburn Miller, M. (2009), 'The Image of the Volcano in the Rhetoric of the French Revolution', *French Historical Studies*, 32: 555–85.

Assmann, J. (1998), *Moses the Egyptian: The Memory of Egypt in Western Monotheism*, Cambridge, MA: Harvard University Press.

Assmann, J. (2013), 'Communicative and Cultural Memory', in A. Erll and A. Nünning (eds), *A Companion to Cultural Memory Studies*, 109–18, Berlin: De Gruyter.

Athanassoglou-Kallmyer, N. M. (2003), *Cézanne and Provence: The Painter in His Culture*, Chicago: University of Chicago Press.

Athanassopoulos, E. F. (2010), 'Landscape Archaeology and the Medieval Countryside: Settlement and Abandonment in the Nemea Region', *International Journal of Historical Archaeology*, 14: 255–70.

Auzépy, M.-F. (1997), *La vie d'Étienne le Jeune par Étienne le Diacre*, Aldershot: Ashgate.

Bainbridge, Simon (2020), *Mountaineering and British Romanticism: The Literary Cultures of Climbing, 1770–1836*, Oxford: Oxford University Press.

Bainbridge, William (2020), *Topographic Memory and Victorian Travellers in the Dolomite Mountains: Peaks of Venice*, Amsterdam: Amsterdam University Press.

Barnard, T. (2015), 'The Lure of the Volcano in the Female Literary Imagination', in T. Barnard (ed.), *British Women and the Intellectual World in the Long Eighteenth Century*, 33–51, London: Routledge.

Bibliography

Barroul, G., N. Dautier and B. Mondon (2007), *Le mont-Ventoux: encyclopédie d'une montagne provençale*, Forcalquiere: Alpes de Lumière.
Barton, W. (2017), *Mountain Aesthetics in Early Modern Latin Literature*, Abingdon: Routledge.
Bataille, G. (1988), *Inner Experience*, Albany: State University of New York Press.
Bataille, G. (1992), *On Nietzsche*, New York: Paragon House.
Bates, R. H. (2000), *Mystery, Beauty and Danger: The Literature of the Mountains and Mountain Climbing Published before 1946*, Portsmouth, NH: Peter E. Randall.
Bätschmann, O. (2008), *Giovanni Bellini*, London: Reaktion Books.
Batten, C. (1978), *Pleasurable Instruction: Form and Convention in Eighteenth-Century Travel Literature*, Berkeley: University of California Press.
Bayburtluoğlu, C. (2005), *Arykanda: The Place Near the High Rocks*, Istanbul: Homer Kitabevi.
Beard, M. (2008), *Pompeii: The Life of a Roman Town*, London: Profile.
Beaumont, J. (1693), *Considerations on a Book, entituled the Theory of the Earth. Publisht some Years since by the Learned Dr. Burnet*, London: Printed for the Author.
Beekes, R. S. P. (2010), *Etymological Dictionary of Greek*, Leiden: Brill.
Bentley, R. (1693), *A Confutation of Atheism From the Origin and Frame of the World. The Third and Last Part. A Sermon preached at St Mary-le-Bow, December the 5th 1692. Being the Eighth of the Lecture Founded by the Honourable Robert Boyle, Esquire*, London: Printed for H. Mortlock.
Bernard, A. (2018), 'Greek Mathematics and Astronomy in Late Antiquity', in Keyser, P. T., J. Scarborough and A. Bernard (eds) *Oxford Handbook of Science and Medicine in the Classical World*, 869–94, Oxford: Oxford University Press.
Bernbaum, E. (1997), *Sacred Mountains of the World*, Berkeley: University of California Press.
Billanovich, G. (1947), *Petrarca letterato, 1. Lo scrittoio del Petrarca*, Rome: Edizioni di storia e letteratura.
Billanovich, G. (1966), 'Petrarca e il Ventoso', *Italia medioevale e umanistica*, 9: 389–401.
Black, J. (1992), *The British Abroad*, London: St. Martin's.
Black, J. (2003), *Italy and the Grand Tour*, New Haven: Yale University Press.
Blanchot, M. (1956), 'The Beast of Lascaux', tr. D. Paul, in *René Char's Poetry: Studies by Maurice Blanchot, Gabriel Bounoure, Albert Camus, Georges Mounin, Gaëtan Picon, René Ménard, James Wright*, 27–40, Rome: Editions de Luca.
Blanchot, M. (1993), *The Infinite Conversation*, Minneapolis: University of Minnesota Press.
Borch, M.-J. Comte de (1782), *Lettres sur la Sicile et sur l'île de Malthe de monsieur le comte de Borch de plusieurs académies à M. le C. de N. écrites en 1777. Pour servir de supplément au Voyage en Sicile et à Malthe de monsieur Brydonne. Ornées de la carte de l'Etna, de celle de la Sicile ancienne et moderne avec 27. estampes de ce qu'il y a de plus remarquable en Sicile,* 2 volumes, Turin: Reycends.
Bowe, P. (2013), 'The Garden Grotto: Its Origin in the Ancient Greek Perception of the Natural Cave', *Studies in the History of Gardens & Designed Landscapes*, 33: 128–38.
Bowersock, G. W., P. Brown and O. Grabar, eds (1999), *Late Antiquity: A Guide to the Postclassical World*, Cambridge, MA: Harvard University Press.
Boyd, J. et al., eds (1950–), *The Papers of Thomas Jefferson*, 44 volumes, publication ongoing, Princeton: Princeton University Press.
Bradley, R. (2000), *An Archaeology of Natural Places*, London: Routledge.
Brady, E. (2012), 'The Environmental Sublime', in T. Costelloe (ed.), *The Sublime: From Antiquity to the Present*, 171–82, Cambridge: Cambridge University Press.
Brock, S. P. (ed.) (1990), *St Ephrem the Syrian: Hymns on Paradise*, Crestwood, NY: St. Vladimir's Seminary Press.
Brock, S. P. (2006), *An Introduction to Syriac studies*, revised edition, first published in 1980, Piscataway, NJ: Gorgias Press.
Brooke, A. (1562), *The Tragicall Historye of Romeus and Juliet*, London: Richard Tottell.
Brown, A. C. (1991), 'Eighteenth-Century Virginia Plantation Gardens: Translating an Ancient Idyll', *Regional Garden Design in the United States*, 15: 125–62.

Brown, P. (1989), *The World of Late Antiquity: AD 150-750*, New York: Norton.
Brown, G. T. (1934), 'Early Mountaineering', in S. Spencer (ed.) *Mountaineering*, 17-39, London: Lonsdale Library of Sports, Games and Pastimes.
Brun, G. (1977), *Le Mont Ventoux*, Carpentras: Le Nombre d'or.
Brush, S. B. (1984), 'The Anthropology of Highland Peoples', in P. D. Beaver and B. L. Purrington (eds) *Cultural Adaptation to Mountain Environments*, 159-67, Athens, GA: University of Georgia Press.
Brydone, P. (1773), *A Tour Through Sicily and Malta in a Series of Letters to William Beckford Esq. of Somerly in Suffolk from P. Brydone, F.R.S*, 2 volumes, London: W. Strahan and T. Cadell.
Buell, L. (2005), *The Future of Environmental Criticism*, Malden, MA: Blackwell.
Burian, P. (1986), 'Zeus ΣΩΤΗΡ ΤΡΙΤΟΣ and Some Triads in Aeschylus' *Oresteia*', *American Journal of Philology*, 107: 332-42.
Burnet, T. (1684-91), *The Theory of the Earth: Containing an Account of the Original of the Earth, and of all the General Changes Which it hath Already Undergone, or is to Undergo, Till the Consummation of all Things*, 2 volumes, London: Printed by R. Norton for W. Kettilby.
Burnet, T. (1690), *An Answer to the Late Exceptions Made by Mr Erasmus Warren*, London: Printed by R. Norton for W. Kettilby.
Burnet, T. (1691), *A Short Consideration of Mr Erasmus Warren's Defence of His Exceptions*, London: Printed by R. Norton for W. Kettilby.
Busine, A. (2015), *Religious Practices and Christianization of the Late Antique City (4th-7th Century)*, Leiden: Brill.
Buxton, R. (1992), 'Imaginary Greek Mountains', *Journal of Hellenic Studies*, 112: 1-15.
Buxton, R. (1994), *Imaginary Greece: The Contexts of Mythology*, Cambridge: Cambridge University Press.
Buxton, R. (2013), 'Imaginary Greek Mountains', in R. Buxton, *Myths and Tragedies in Their Ancient Greek Contexts*, 9-32, Oxford: Oxford University Press, revised version of Buxton 1992 and Buxton 1994: 81-96.
Buxton, R. (2016), 'Mount Etna in the Graeco-Roman *imaginaire*: Culture and Liquid Fire', in J. McInerney and I. Sluiter (eds), *Valuing Landscape in Classical Antiquity: Natural Environment and Cultural Imagination*, 25-45, Leiden: Brill.
Buzard, J. (1993), *The Beaten Track*, Oxford: Oxford University Press.
Buzard, J. (2002), 'The Grand Tour and After (1660-1840)', in P. Hulme and T. Youngs (eds) *The Cambridge Companion to Travel Writing*, 37-52, Cambridge: Cambridge University Press.
Byron, G. G., Lord (1982), *Byron's Letters and Journals*, ed. L. Marchand, 12 volumes, Harvard: Harvard University Press.
Cajori, F. (1929), 'History of Determinations of the Heights of Mountains', *Isis* 12: 482-514.
Camden, W. (1637), *Britain, or A Chorographicall Description of the most Flourishing Kingdomes, England, Scotland, and Ireland, and the Ilands Adjoining*, tr. P. Holland, London: F. Kyngston, R. Young, and J. Leggatt for G. Latham.
Cameron, Alan (2011), *The Last Pagans of Rome*, New York: Oxford University Press.
Cameron, Averil (1999), 'Remaking the Past' in Bowersock, G. W., P. Brown and O. Grabar, eds (1999), *Late Antiquity: A Guide to the Postclassical World*, 1-20, Cambridge, MA: Harvard University Press.
Cameron, Averil (1998), 'Education and Literary Culture', in Averil Cameron and P. Garnsey (eds) *The Cambridge Ancient History. Vol. 13. The Late Empire, A.D. 337-425*, 665-707, Cambridge: Cambridge University Press.
Camp, J. M. II, ed. (2013), *In Search of Greece: Catalogue of an Exhibit of Drawings at the British Museum by Edward Dodwell and Simone Pomardi*, Los Altos, CA: Packard Humanities Institute.
Campbell, R. (1951), *Light on a Dark Horse*, London: Hollis and Carter.
Candela, A. (2016), 'Recupero, Giuseppe', *Dizionario biografico degli italiani* 86: 695-8.
Carrier, N. and F. Mouthon (2011), *Les communautés montagnardes au Moyen Age*, Rennes: Presses Universitaires de Rennes.

Bibliography

Carruthers, M. (1990), *The Book of Memory*, Cambridge: Cambridge University Press.
Caws, M. A. (1977), *René Char*, Boston: Twayne.
Caws, M. A. and J. Griffin (1976), *Poems of René Char*, Princeton: Princeton University Press.
C. E. F. (1905), 'Review of *Josias Simler et les Origines de l'Alpinisme jusqu'en 1600* by W. A. B. Coolidge', *Bulletin of the American Geographical Society*, 37: 568–70.
Cézanne, E. (1874), *Club Alpin Français*, Paris: Chamerot.
Chakrabarty, D. (2000), *Provincializing Europe: Postcolonial Thought and Historical Difference*, Princeton: Princeton University Press.
Chakrabarty, D. (2009), 'The Climate of History: Four Theses', *Critical Inquiry*, 35: 197–222.
Chakrabarty, D. (2012), 'Postcolonial Studies and the Challenge of Climate Change', *New Literary History*, 43: 1–18.
Chakrabarty, D. (2020), 'The Human Sciences and Climate Change: A Crisis of Anthropocentrism', in *Climate Crisis in India: Issues and Concerns, Science and Culture* Special Issue, January–February 2020: 46–8.
Champeville, P. de (1937), 'Sur le chemin de Pétrarque au Mont Ventoux', *La Montagne: revue mensuelle du Club alpin français*, 285: 261–7.
Champlin, M. W. (1969), '"Oedipus Tyrannus" and the Problem of Knowledge', *Classical Journal*, 64: 337–45.
Char, R. (1956), *Hypnos Waking*, New York: Random House.
Char, R. (1965), *La Provence point oméga*, [s.l.]: [s.n.].
Char, R. (1966), *Retour amont*, Paris: Gallimard.
Char, R. (1995), *Oeuvres complètes*, Paris: Gallimard.
Chard, C. (1999), *Pleasure and Guilt on the Grand Tour*, Manchester: Manchester University Press.
Cheeke, S. (2003), *Byron and Place: History, Translation, Nostalgia*, New York: Palgrave Macmillan.
Cheetham, M. A. (1984), 'The Taste For Phenomena: Mount Vesuvius and Transformations in Late 18th-Century European Landscape Depiction', *Wallraf-Richartz-Jahrbuch*, 45: 131–44.
Cheney, P. (2018), *English Authorship and the Early Modern Sublime: Spenser, Marlowe, Shakespeare, Jonson*, Cambridge: Cambridge University Press.
Churchyard, T. (1579), *The Miserie of Flaunders, Calamitie of Fraunce, Misfortune of Portugall, Unquietnes of Ireland, Troubles of Scotlande: And the Blessed State of Englande*, London: Andrew Maunsell.
Churchyard, T. (1587), *The Worthines of Wales: Wherein are More then Severall Thousand Things Rehearsed*, London: G. Robinson for Thomas Cadman.
Clark, G. (2011), *Late Antiquity: A Very Short Introduction*, Oxford: Oxford University Press.
Clark, K. (1979), *Landscape into Art*, revised edition, first published in 1949, New York: Harper and Row.
Clark, R.W. (1953), *The Victorian Mountaineers*, London: B. T. Batsford.
Clark, R.W. (1959), *An Eccentric in the Alps: The Story of W. A. B. Coolidge, the Great Victorian Mountaineer*, London: Museum Press.
Clark, T. (2019), *The Value of Ecocriticism*, Cambridge: Cambridge University Press.
Clarke, M. ed. (2010), *The Concise Dictionary of Art Terms*, 2nd edition, first published in 2001, Oxford: Oxford University Press.
Clap, V. (1976), *Le Mont-Ventoux au XVIIIme siècle*, Montpellier: Dehan.
Clerc, M. (1904), 'Sainte-Victoire et Sainte-Venture', *Annales de la Société d'Études Provençales*, 1: 278–82.
Clerc, M. (1906), *Bataille d'Aix*, Paris: Fontemoing.
Clugnet, L. (ed.) (1903), 'Vie de saint Auxence. Texte grec', *Revue de l'Orient Chrétien*, 8: 1–14.
Coates, P. (1998), *Nature: Western Attitudes since Western Times*, Cambridge: Polity Press.
Coffey, D. (2002), 'Protecting the Botanic Garden: Seward, Darwin, and Coalbrookdale', *Women's Studies*, 32: 141–64.
Coghen, M. (2015), 'The Poet as Volcano: The Case of Byron', *Studia Litteraria Universitatis Iagellonicae Cracoviensis*, 10: 79–91.

Bibliography

Collard, C., ed. (2002), *Aeschylus, Oresteia*, Oxford: Oxford University Press.
Colley, A. C. (2010), *Victorians in the Mountains: Sinking the Sublime*, Farnham: Ashgate.
Conisbee, P. and D. Coutagne (2006), *Cézanne in Provence*, New Haven: Yale University Press.
Constantine, D. (2001), *Fields of Fire: A Life of Sir William Hamilton*, London: Weidenfeld and Nicolson.
Constantine, D. (2011), *In the Footsteps of the Gods: Travellers to Greece and the Quest for the Hellenic Ideal*, revised edition, first published in 1984, London: Tauris Parke paperbacks.
Conte, G. B. (1994), *Genres and Readers: Lucretius, Love Elegy, Pliny's Encyclopedia*, Baltimore: Johns Hopkins University Press.
Cook, A. (1998), 'Space and Culture', *New Literary History*, 29: 551–72.
Coolidge, W. A. B. (1904), *Josias Simler et les origines de l'alpinisme jusqu'en 1600*, Grenoble: Allier Frères.
Coolidge, W. A. B. (1908), *The Alps in Nature and History*, New York: E. P. Dutton and Co.
Cooper, J. E. and M. J. Decker (2012), *Life and Society in Byzantine Cappadocia*, Basingstoke: Palgrave Macmillan.
Corbin, A. (1994), *The Lure of the Sea: The Discovery of the Seaside 1750–1840*, Berkeley: University of California Press.
Coron, A. (2007), *René Char*, Paris: Gallimard.
Cosgrove, D. (1984), *Social Formation and Symbolic Landscape*, London: Croom Helm.
Courcelle, P. (1963), *Les Confessions de Saint Augustin dans la tradition littéraire. Antécédents et postérité*, Paris: Études Augustiniennes.
Croft, H. (1685), *Some Animadversions upon a Book Intituled the Theory of the Earth*, London: Printed for C. Harper.
Croker, J. W., ed. (1876), *Boswell's Life of Johnson, including their Tour to the Hebrides*, London: John Murray.
Csapo, E. and W. Slater (1995), *The Context of Ancient Drama*, Ann Arbor: Michigan University Press.
Cull, M. R. (2016), 'Contextualizing 1610: *Cymbeline*, *The Valiant Welshman*, and *The Princes of Wales*', in W. Maley and P. Schwyzer (eds), *Shakespeare and Wales: From the Marches to the Assembly*, 127–42, London: Routledge.
Curran, J. E. (2002), *Roman Invasions: The British History, Protestant Anti-Romanism, and the Historical Imagination in England, 1530–1660*, Newark: University of Delaware Press.
Curtius, E. R. (1983), *European Literature and the Latin Middle Ages*, tr. W. R. Trask, Princeton: Princeton University Press.
Czwiklitzer, C. (1968), *290 Affiches de Pablo Picasso*, Paris : L'Auteur Art-C.C.
Dargan, E. P. (1914), 'Frédéric Mistral', *The Nation*, 98: 360.
d'Arnaud, A. B. (1959), 'Toponymie et histoire de la Montagne Sainte-Victoire', *Bulletin philologique et historique (jusqu'à 1715) du Comité des travaux historiques et scientifiques*, 1958: 34–42.
Darwin, E. (1791), *The Botanic Garden*, London: J. Johnson.
Davis, W. (2011), *Into the Silence: The Great War, Mallory and the Conquest of Everest*, London: Bodley Head.
Dean, C. J. (1994), *The Self and Its Pleasures: Bataille, Lacan and the History of the Decentered Subject*, Ithaca, NY: Cornell University Press.
Debarbieux, B. and G. Rudaz (2011), '"Mountain Women": Silent Contributors to the Global Agenda for Sustainable Mountain Development', in *Gender, Place and Culture: A Journal of Feminist Geography*, 19: 1–20.
Debarbieux, B. and G. Rudaz (2015), *The Mountain: A Political History from the Enlightenment to the Present*, tr. J. M. Todd, first published in French in 2010, Chicago: Chicago University Press.
de Gourbillon, J.-A. (1820), Voyage critique à l'Etna en 1819, 2 volumes, Paris: P. Mongie l'aîné.
de Jong, I. (2018), 'The View from the Mountain (*oroskopia*) in Greek and Latin Literature', *Cambridge Classical Journal*, 64: 23–48.
de Vere, A. (1850), *Picturesque Sketches of Greece and Turkey*, 2 volumes, London: R. Bentley.

Bibliography

de Voragine, J. (2012), *The Golden Legend: Readings on the Saints*, tr. William Granger Ryan, Princeton: Princeton University Press.
Delehaye, Hippolyte (1962), *Les Saints stylites*, Subsidia hagiographica 14, Brussels: Société des Bollandistes.
della Dora, V. (2008a), 'Mountains and Memory: Embodied Visions of Ancient Peaks in the Nineteenth-Century Aegean', *Transactions of the Institute of British Geographers*, 33: 217–32.
della Dora, V. (2008b), 'Mapping a Holy Quasi-Island: Mount Athos in Early Renaissance *Isolarii*', *Imago Mundi*, 60: 139–65.
della Dora, V. (2011), *Imagining Mount Athos: Visions of a Holy Place from Homer to World War II*, Charlottesville: University of Virginia Press.
della Dora, V. (2012), 'Setting and Blurring Boundaries: Pilgrims, Tourists, and Landscape in Mount Athos and Meteora', *Annals of Tourism Research*, 39: 951–74.
della Dora, V. (2016a), *Mountain: Nature and Culture*, London: Reaktion Books.
della Dora, V. (2016b), *Landscape, Nature, and the Sacred in Byzantium*, Cambridge: Cambridge University Press.
Deleuze, G. (1988), *Bergsonism*, tr. H. Tomlinson and B. Habberjam, first published in French in 1966, New York: Zone Books.
Denniston, J. and D. Page, eds (1957), *Aeschylus:* Agamemnon, Oxford: Clarendon Press.
d'Este, I. (2018), 'Correspondence with Giovanni Bellini', in D. Gasparotto (ed.) *Lives of Giovanni Bellini*, tr. Frank Dabell, 115–57, Los Angeles: J. Paul Getty Museum.
Dhar, A. (2019), 'Travel and mountains', in N. Das and T. Young (eds), *The Cambridge History of Travel Writing*, 345–60, Cambridge: Cambridge University Press.
di Carlo, E. (1964), *Viaggiatori stranieri in Sicilia nei secoli XVIII e XIX*, Palermo: Tipografia Montaina.
di Palma, V. (2014), *Wasteland: A History*, New Haven: Yale University Press.
Dodds, E. R. (1960), *Euripides: Bacchae*, Oxford: Oxford University Press.
Dodwell, E. (1819), *Classical and Topographical Tour through Greece during the Years 1801, 1805, and 1806*, 2 volumes, London: Rodwell and Martin.
Dolan, B. (2000), *Exploring European Frontiers: British Travellers in the Age of Enlightenment*, Basingstoke: St Martin's Press.
Drake, H. A. and A. R. Brown, eds (2006), 'Hellenic Heritage and Christian Challenge: Conflict over Panhellenic Sanctuaries in Late Antiquity', in H. A. Drake (ed.) *Violence in Late Antiquity: Perceptions and Practices*, 309–20, Aldershot: Ashgate.
Drouet, Y. (2005), 'The "CAF" at the Borders: Geopolitical and Military Stakes in the Creation of the French Alpine Club', *The International Journal of the History of Sport*, 22: 59–69.
Dryden, J. (1697), *The Works of Virgil: Containing His Pastorals, Georgics, and Æneis*, London: Printed for J. Tonson.
Dryden, J. (1776), *A Voyage to Sicily and Malta . . . in the Years 1700 and 1701*, London: J. Bew.
Duffy, C. (2013), *The Landscapes of the Sublime 1700–1830: Classic Ground*, Basingstoke: Palgrave Macmillan.
Duffy, C. and P. Howell, eds (2011), *Cultures of the Sublime: Selected Readings, 1750–1830*, Basingstoke: Palgrave Macmillan.
Dunn, M. (2000), *The Emergence of Monasticism: from the Desert Fathers to the Early Middle Ages*, Oxford: Blackwell.
Durling, R. J. (1965), 'Conrad Gesner's *Liber Amicorum*: 1555–65', *Gesnerus*, 22: 134–59.
Durling, R. M. (1977), 'Il Petrarca, il Ventoso e la possibilità dell'allegoria', *Revue des Études Augustiniennes*, 23: 304–23.
Eisner, R. (1991), *Travellers to an Antique Land: The History and Literature of Travel to Greece*, Ann Arbor: University of Michigan Press.
Elsner, J. (2010), 'Picturesque and Sublime: Impacts of Pausanias in Late-Eighteenth- and Early-Nineteenth-Century Britain', *Classical Receptions Journal*, 2: 219–53.

Elsner, J. (2013), 'Paideia: Ancient Concept and Modern Reception', *International Journal of the Classical Tradition*, 20: 136–52.
Escudié, A. (1903), 'Chronique du club alpin Français: rapport annuel', *Annuaire du Club Alpin Français*, 30: 555–75.
Evans, H. C. (2004), *Saint Catherine's Monastery, Sinai, Egypt: A Photographic Essay*, New Haven: Yale University Press.
Evans, J. (2014), *A Quite Remarkable Man: The Life of Patrick Brydone and His Family (1736–1818)*, Stroud: Amberley Publishing.
Fabre, J.-H. (1879), *Souvenirs Entomologiques*, Paris: Delagrave.
Fabre, J.-H. (1923), *This Earth of Ours*, London: Albert & Charles Boni.
Falkeid, U. (2009), 'Petrarch, Mont Ventoux, and the Modern Self', *Forum Italicum*, 43: 5–28
Falzone, G. (1963), *Viaggiatori stranieri in Sicilia tra il '700 e l'800*, Palermo: G. Denaro.
Farrell, J. (1992), 'Patrick Brydone, Enlightenment Traveller', in E. Kanceff and R. Rampone (eds) *Viaggio nel Sud, I. Viaggiatori stranieri in Sicilia*, Biblioteca del viaggio in Italia 36, 291–305, Geneva: Slatkine.
Farrell, J. (2014), '"A Reverend Pilgrim": Patrick Brydone in Sicily', in G. Tulloch, K. Agutter and L. D'Arcangeli (eds) *Sicily and Scotland: Where Extremes Meet*, 72–83, Kibworth Beauchamp: Troubador Publishing.
Felton, D. (ed.) (2018), *Landscapes of Dread in Classical Antiquity: Negative Emotions in Natural and Constructed Spaces*, London: Routledge.
Fischer, H. (1966), *Conrad Gessner (26. Marz 1516 – 13. Dezember 1565): Leben und Werk*, Zurich: Naturforschende Gesellschaft.
Fischer, M. H. and R. A. Zwaan (2008), 'Embodied Language: A Review of the Role of the Motor System in Language Comprehension', *Quarterly Journal of Experimental Psychology*, 61: 825–50.
Fisher, J. (1633), *Fuimus Troes: The True Trojans*, London: John Legatt for Robert Allot.
Fitter, C. (1995), *Poetry, Space, Landscape: Toward a New Theory*, Cambridge: Cambridge University Press.
Flader, S. L. (1994), *Thinking Like a Mountain: Aldo Leopold and the Evolution of an Ecological Attitude Toward Deer, Wolves, and Forests*, Madison, WI: University of Wisconsin Press.
Fleming, F. (2000), *Killing Dragons: The Conquest of the Alps*, London: Granta Books.
Fothergill, B. (1969), *Sir William Hamilton: Envoy Extraordinary*, New York: Faber & Faber.
Fraenkel, E. (1950), *Aeschylus' Agamemnon: Volume II, Commentary on 1–1055*, Oxford: Clarendon Press.
Frankfurter, D. (1990), 'Stylites and Phallobates: Pillar Religions in Late Antique Syria', *Vigiliae Christianae*, 44: 168–98.
Frankfurter, D. (2018), *Christianizing Egypt: Syncretism and Local Worlds in Late Antiquity*, Princeton: Princeton University Press.
Fremantle, H. ed. (1980), *The Principal Works of St. Jerome*, reprint edition, first published in 1954, Grand Rapids, MI: Wm. B. Eerdmans.
Freshfield, D. W. (1904), 'On Mountains and Mankind', *The Geographical Journal*, 24: 443–60.
Freshfield, D. W. (1906), 'Review of *Josias Simler et les Origines de l'Alpinisme jusqu'en 1600* by W. A. B. Coolidge', *The Alpine Journal*, 171: 76–80.
Gabra, G. and T. Vivian (2002), *Coptic Monasteries: Egypt's Monastic Art and Architecture*, Cairo: American University in Cairo Press.
Gantz, T. N. (1977), 'The Fires of the *Oresteia*', *Journal of Hellenic Studies*, 97: 28–38.
Garnsey, P. (1988), 'Mountain Economies in Southern Europe: Thoughts on the Early History, Continuity and Individuality of Mediterranean Upland Pastoralism', in C. R. Whittaker (ed.), *Pastoral Economies in Classical Antiquity*, 75–86, Cambridge: *Proceedings of the Cambridge Philological Society*, Supplementary volume 14, reprinted with a brief addendum in P. Garnsey (1998), *Cities, Peasants and Food in Classical Antiquity: Essays in Social and Economic History*, 166–80, Cambridge: Cambridge University Press.

Bibliography

Gasquet, J. (1921), *Cézanne*, Paris: Bernheim-Jeune.
Gasquet, J. (1991), *Joachim Gasquet's Cézanne*, New York: Thames and Hudson.
Gemeinhardt, P. (2012), 'In Search of Christian Paideia: Education and Conversion in Early Christian Biography', *Zeitschrift für Antikes Christentum / Journal of Ancient Christianity*, 16: 88–98.
Gentili, A. (2004), 'Bellini and Landscape', in P. Humfrey (ed.) *The Cambridge Companion to Giovanni Bellini*, 167–181, Cambridge: Cambridge University Press.
Geoffrey of Monmouth (1966), *The History of the Kings of Britain*, tr. L. Thorpe, London: Penguin.
Gessner, C. (1937), 'A Letter to Jacob Avienus: On the Admiration of Mountains from the Hand of Conrad Gesner, Physician,' tr. H. B. D. Soulé, in *Conrad Gesner*, 5–15, San Francisco: Grabhorn.
Gessner, C. (2003), 'On the Admiration of Mountains', tr. A. S. Weber, in A. S. Weber (ed.), *Because It's There: A Celebration of Mountaineering from 200 B.C. to Today*, 16–21, Lanham: Taylor Trade Publishing.
Gessner, C. (2020), 'Letter to Jakob Vogel on the Admiration of Mountains' and 'Description of Mount Fractus, Commonly Called Mount Pilate,' tr. D. Hooley, in S. Ireton and C. Schaumann (eds), *Mountains and the German Mind: Translations from Gessner to Messner, 1541–2009*, 23–46, Rochester, NY: Camden House.
Giardina, L. (1995), 'Topos e scrittura: l'Etna di Brydone', in E. Kanceff and R. Rampone (eds) *Viaggio nel Sud, III. Il profondo Sud: Calabria e dintorni*, Biblioteca del viaggio in Italia 42, 249–60, Geneva: Slatkine.
Goffen, R. (1989), *Giovanni Bellini*, New Haven: Yale University Press.
Goldhill, S. (1984), *Language, Sexuality, Narrative: the Oresteia*, Cambridge: Cambridge University Press.
Gordon-Reed, A. and P. Onuf (2016), *"Most Blessed of the Patriarchs": Thomas Jefferson and the Empire of Imagination*, New York: W. W. Norton and Company.
Grahame, S. (1604), *The Passionate Sparke of a Relenting Minde*, London: Humfrey Lownes for Christopher Pursett.
Grand-Carteret, J. (1903–4), *La Montagne à travers les âges. Rôle joué par elle, Façon dont elle a été vue*, 2 volumes, Grenoble/Moutiers: Dumas/Ducloz.
Greig, J., ed. (1924), *The Farington Diary by Joseph Farington, R. A: Volume III (September 14, 1804, to September 19, 1806)*, London: Hutchinson.
Greilsamer, L. (2004), *L'éclaire au front: La vie de René Char*, Paris: Fayard.
Griffiths, H. (2003), 'The Geographies of Shakespeare's *Cymbeline*', *English Literary Renaissance*, 34: 339–58.
Grosart, A. B. (ed.) (1876), *The Prose Works of William Wordsworth*, Volume 2, *Aesthetical and Literary*, London: Edward Moxon, Son, and Co.
Gualdo Rosa, L. (1986), 'Dalle Fosse (Bolzanio), Urbano,' *Dizionario biografico degli italiani*, 32: 88–92.
Gudger, E. W. (1940), 'The Perils and Romance of Swordfishing', *Scientific Monthly*, 51: 36–48.
Güthenke, C. (2008), *Placing Modern Greece: The Dynamics of Romantic Hellenism, 1770–1840*, Oxford: Oxford University Press.
Hahn, J. (2008), *From Temple to Church: Destruction and Renewal of Local Cultic Topography in Late Antiquity*, Leiden: Brill.
Hall, J. (1974), *Dictionary of Subjects and Symbols in Art*, New York: Harper & Row.
Hamilton, W. (1770), 'An account of a journey to Mount Etna, in a letter from the Honourable William Hamilton, His Majesty's Envoy Extraordinary at Naples, to Mathew Maty, M. D. Sec. R. S.', *Philosophical Transactions*, 60: 1–19.
Hamilton, W. (1772), *Observations on Mount Vesuvius, Mount Etna, and Other Volcanos, in a Series of Letters Addressed to the Royal Society from the Honourable Sir W. Hamilton*, London: T. Cadell.

Bibliography

Hamilton, W. (1774), *Observations on Mount Vesuvius, Mount Etna, and Other Volcanos: A New Edition*, London: T. Cadell.
Hansen, P. (2013), *The Summits of Modern Man: Mountaineering after the Enlightenment*, Cambridge, MA: Harvard University Press.
Hardie, P. (1986), *Virgil's Aeneid: Cosmos and Imperium*, Oxford: Oxford University Press.
Hardison, O. B. and E. H. Behler (1993), 'Topos', in A. Preminger et al. (eds) *The New Princeton Encyclopedia of Poetry and Poetics*, Princeton: Princeton University Press.
Hardyng, J. (1543), *The Chronicle of Ihon Hardyng*, London: Richard Grafton.
Harrison, M. (2001), *Mountain and Plain: From the Lycian Coast to the Phrygian Plateau in the Late Roman and Early Byzantine Period*, Ann Arbor: University of Michigan Press.
Hatch, P. (2012), *"A Rich Spot of Earth": Thomas Jefferson's Revolutionary Garden*, New Haven: Yale University Press.
Hedreen, G. (2013), 'The Semantics of Processional Dithyramb', in B. Kowalzig and P. Wilson (eds) *Dithyramb in Context*, 171–97, Oxford: Oxford University Press.
Heidegger, M. (1996), *Being and Time: a translation of Sein und Zeit*, SUNY series in contemporary continental philosophy, tr. J. Stambaugh, first published in German in 1927, Albany: State University of New York Press.
Henrichs, A. (1994), '"Why Should I Dance?": Choral Self-Reflexivity in Greek Tragedy', *Arion*, 3: 56–111.
Herendeen, W. (1981), 'The Rhetoric of Rivers: The River and the Pursuit of Knowledge', *Studies in Philology*, 78: 107–27.
Heringman, N. (2003), 'The Style of Natural Catastrophes', *Huntington Library Quarterly*, 66: 97–133.
Heringman, N. (2004), *Romantic Rocks, Aesthetic Geology*, Ithaca: Cornell University Press.
Higden, R. (1482), *Polychronicon*, London: William Caxton.
Higgins, J. ([1587] 1946), 'King Brennus', in L. B. Campbell (ed.), *Parts Added to the Mirror for Magistrates*, Cambridge: Cambridge University Press.
Highet, G. (1985), *The Classical Tradition: Greek and Roman Influences on Western Literature*, Oxford: Oxford University Press.
Hill, G. B. (ed.) (1888), *Letters of David Hume to William Strahan*, Oxford: Clarendon Press.
Hiltner, K. (2015), 'General introduction', in K. Hiltner (ed.) *Ecocriticism: The Essential Reader*, xii–xvi, Abingdon: Routledge.
Hionidis, P. (2014), 'Travelling and the Shaping of Images: Victorian Travellers on Nineteenth-Century Greece', *International Journal of Cultural and Digital Tourism*, 1: 30–40.
Hoibian, O. (2000), *Les alpinistes en France 1870–1950 : une histoire culturelle*, Paris: Harmattan.
Holinshed, R. (1586), *The Third volume of Chronicles, beginning at duke William the Norman, commonlie called the Conqueror*, London: Henry Denham.
Holinshed, R. (1587), *The first and second volumes of Chronicles, comprising 1 The description and historie of England, 2 The description and historie of Ireland, 3 The description and historie of Scotland*, London: Henry Denham.
Holland, P., tr. (1600), *Livy, The Roman History*, London: Adam Islip.
Hollier, D. (1990), *Against Architecture: the Writings of Georges Bataille*, Cambridge, MA: MIT Press.
Hollis, D. (2017a), 'Re-thinking Mountains: Ascents, Aesthetics, and Environment in Early Modern Europe', PhD thesis, University of St Andrews.
Hollis, D. (2017b), 'Rethinking Mountain Gloom', *Alpinist*, 57: 105–8.
Hollis, D. (2019), 'Mountain Gloom and Mountain Glory: The Genealogy of an Idea', *Interdisciplinary Studies in Literature and the Environment*, 26: 1038–61.
Hollis, D. (2020), 'Aesthetic Experience, Investigation and Classic Ground: Responses to Etna from the First Century AD to 1773', *Journal of the Warburg and Courtauld Institutes*, 83.
Hooley, D. (2012), 'Prelude: Classical Mountain Landscapes and the Language of Ascent', in S. Ireton and C. Schaumann (eds), *Heights of Reflection: Mountains in the German Imagination from the Middle Ages to the Twenty-first Century*, 20–32, Rochester, NY: Camden House.

Bibliography

Hopkins, L. (2005), *Shakespeare on the Edge: Border-crossings in the Tragedies and the Henriad*, Aldershot: Ashgate.
Horden, P. and N. Purcell (2000), *The Corrupting Sea: A Study of Mediterranean History*, Oxford: Blackwell.
Hughes, J. D. (1996), *Pan's Travails: Environmental Problems of the Ancient Greeks and Romans*, Baltimore: Johns Hopkins University Press.
Hughes, T. S. (1820), *Travels in Sicily, Greece and Albania*, 2 volumes, London: J. Mawman.
Hunt, A. and H. Marlow, eds (2019), *Ecology and Theology in the Ancient World: Cross-Disciplinary Perspectives*, London: Bloomsbury.
Hunt, J. D. (1988), *The Genius of the Place: The English Landscape Garden, 1620–1820*, Cambridge: MIT Press.
Husserl, E. (1973), *Cartesian Meditations: An Introduction to Phenomenology*, The Hague: Nijhoff.
Hyde, W. (1916), 'The Volcanic History of Etna', *Geographical Review*, 1: 401–18.
Ingold, T. (2000), *The Perception of the Environment: Essays on Livelihood, Dwelling and Skill*, London: Taylor and Francis.
Ingold, T. (2011), *Being Alive: Essays on Movement, Knowledge and Description*, London: Routledge.
Iozzo, M., F. Borghesi and A. Magnelli (2001), *Art and History of Greece and Mount Athos*, tr. P. Boomsliter, Florence: Bonechi.
Ireton, S. and C. Schaumann, eds (2012), *Heights of Reflection: Mountains in the German Imagination from the Middle Ages to the Twenty-First Century*, Rochester, NY: Camden House.
Ireton, S. and C. Schaumann, eds (2020), *Mountains and the German Mind: Translations from Gessner to Messner, 1541–2009*, Rochester, NY: Camden House.
Irving, R. L. (1938), *The Mountain Way: An Anthology in Prose and Verse*, London: J. M. Dent and Sons.
Isserman, M. and S. Weaver (2008), *Fallen Giants: A History of Himalayan Mountaineering from the Age of Empire to the Age of Extremes*, New Haven: Yale University Press.
Jacobs, I. (2012), 'The Creation of the Late Antique City: Constantinople and Asia Minor during the "Theodosian Renaissance"', *Byzantion*, 82: 113–64.
Jameson, M. H. (1989), 'Mountains and the Greek City States', in J.-F. Bergier (ed.), *Montagnes, fleuves, forêts dans l'histoire: barrières ou lignes de convergence?*, 7–17, St Katharinen: Scripta Mercaturae Verlag.
Janin, R. (1975), *Les églises et les monastères des grands centres byzantins: Bithynie, Hellespont, Latros, Galèsios, Trébizonde, Athènes, Thessalonique*, Paris: Institut français d'études byzantines.
Jefferson, T. (1964), *Notes on the State of Virginia*, first published in 1787, New York: Harper Touchbook.
Jefferson, T. (1989), *Jefferson's Literary Commonplace Book*, ed. D. Wilson, Princeton: Princeton University Press.
Jenkins I. and K. Sloan, eds (1996), *Vases and Volcanoes: Sir William Hamilton and his Collection*, London: British Museum Press.
Johnson, J. W. (2015), *The Formation of English Neo-Classical Thought*, reprint edition, first published in 1967, Princeton: Princeton University Press.
Johnson, M., and C. Wilson (2007), 'Lucretius and the History of Science', in S. Gillespie and P. Hardie (eds), *The Cambridge Companion to Lucretius*, 131–48, Cambridge: Cambridge University Press.
Johnson, S. F. (2006), *Greek Literature in Late Antiquity: Dynamism, Didacticism, Classicism*, Aldershot: Ashgate.
Johnson, W. R. (2015), *Lucretius and the Modern World*, London: Bloomsbury.
Johnston, P. (1996), 'Under the Volcano: Volcanic Myth and Metaphor in Vergil's *Aeneid*', *Vergilius*, 42: 55–65.

Bibliography

Jost, M. (2007), 'Pausanias in Arkadia: An Example of Cultural Tourism', in C. Adams and J. Roy (eds), *Travel, Geography and Culture in Ancient Greece, Egypt and the Near East*, 104–22, Oxford: Oxbow Books.
Julian, P. (1937), *Le Pèlerinage littéraire du Mont Ventoux*, Carpentras: Editions du 'Mt Ventoux'.
Jullian, C. (1899), 'Notes gallo-romaines: Saint Victoire', *Revue des études anciennes*, 1: 56–7.
Jullian, C. (1920), *Histoire de la Gaule*, Paris: Librairie Hachette.
Jully, J. J. (1961), 'Deux trompettes en terre cuite du Mont Ventoux', *Ogam*, 13: 427–30.
Kahlos, M. (2012), 'Pagan-Christian Debates over the Interpretation of Texts in Late Antiquity', *Classical World*, 105: 525–45.
Kakalis, C. and Goetsch, E., eds (2018), *Mountains, Mobilities and Movement*, London: Palgrave Macmillan.
Kakavoulis, A. K. (1986), *An Introduction to Byzantine Education: Early Patristic Educational Thought*, Athens: [s.n.].
Kaldellis, A. (2015), *The Byzantine Republic: People and Power in New Rome*, Cambridge, MA: Harvard University Press.
Kazhdan, A., and A.-M Talbot (1998), 'Dumbarton Oaks Hagiography Database', Available online: https://www.doaks.org/research/byzantine/resources/hagiography/hagiointro.pdf (accessed 22 September 2020).
Keill, J. (1698), *An Examination of Dr. Burnet's Theory of the Earth*, Oxford: Printed at the Theater.
Keill, J. (1699), *An Examination of the Reflections on the Theory of the Earth*, Oxford: Printed at the Theater.
Kelly, J. N. D. (1975), *Jerome: His Life, Writings, and Controversies*, London: Duckworth.
Kewes, P. (2016), 'Romans in the Mirror', in H. Archer and A. Hadfield (eds), *A Mirror for Magistrates in Context: Literature, History, and Politics in Early Modern England*, 126–46, Cambridge: Cambridge University Press.
Kimball, F. (1916), *Thomas Jefferson, Architect*, Cambridge: Riverside Press.
Kimmelman, M. (1999), 'NOT Because It's There', *New York Times*, June 6.
Koch, J. T (1990), 'Brân, Brennos: An Instance of Early Gallo-Brittonic History and Mythology', *Cambrian Medieval Celtic Studies*, 20: 1–20
Koelb, J. H. (2009), '"This Most Beautiful and Adorn'd World": Nicolson's *Mountain Gloom and Mountain Glory* Reconsidered', *Interdisciplinary Studies in Literature and the Environment*, 16: 443–68.
Kofler, W., M. Korenjak and F. Schaffenrath, eds (2010), *Gipfel der Zeit: Berge in Texten aus fünf Jahrtausenden*, Freiburg: Rombach Verlag.
König, J. (2013), 'Landscape and Reality in Apuleius' *Metamorphoses*', in M. Paschalis and S. Panayotakis (eds), *The Construction of the Real and the Ideal in the Ancient Novel and Beyond*, 219–42, Leiden: Brill.
König, J. (2016), 'Strabo's Mountains', in J. McInerney and I. Sluiter (eds), *Landscapes of Value: Natural Environment and Cultural Imagination in Classical Antiquity*, 46–69, Leiden: Brill.
König, J. (2019), 'Mountain and City in Dio Chrysostom's *Euboicus*', in M. Taufer (ed.), *La montagna nell'antichità – Berge in der Antike – Mountains in Antiquity*, 327–45, Freiburg: Rombach Verlag.
Korenjak, M. (2017), 'Why Mountains Matter: Early Modern Roots of a Modern Notion', *Renaissance Quarterly*, 70: 179–219.
Kowalzig, B. and P. Wilson, eds (2013), *Dithyramb in Context*, Oxford: Oxford University Press.
Krummen, E. (1990), 'Athens and Attica: Polis and Countryside in Greek Tragedy', in A. H. Sommerstein, S. Halliwell, J. Henderson and B. Zimmerman (eds), *Tragedy, Comedy and the Polis: Papers from the Greek Drama Conference, Nottingham*, 191–217, Bari: Levante Editori.
Kruschwitz, P. (2015), 'Getting on Top of Things: Form and Meaning in the Pseudo-Vergilian *Aetna*', *Habis*, 46: 75–97.

Bibliography

Kuzmičová, A. (2012), 'Presence in the Reading of Literary Narrative: A Case for Motor Enactment', *Semiotica*, 189: 23–48.
Langdon, M. K. (1976), *A Sanctuary of Zeus on Mount Hymettos*, Princeton, NJ: *Hesperia* Supplement XVI.
Langdon, M. K. (2000), 'Mountains in Greek Religion', *Classical World*, 93: 461–70.
Larson, V. T. (2017), 'Byrd and Jefferson's Libraries: Roman otium "att the end of the world"', *Pacific Coast Philology*, 52: 238–54.
Lavan, L. and W. Bowden (2001), *Recent Research in Late-Antique Urbanism*, Portsmouth, RI: *Journal of Roman Archaeology* Supplementary Series 42.
Leask, N. (2004), 'Byron and the Eastern Mediterranean', in D. Bone (ed.) *The Cambridge Companion to Byron*, 99–117, Cambridge: Cambridge University Press.
Leclair, D. and P. Née (2015), *Dictionnaire René Char*, Paris: Classiques Garnier.
Leopold, A. (1949), *A Sand County Almanac*, Oxford: Oxford University Press.
Lemprière, J. (1788), *A Classical Dictionary*, Reading: T. Cadell.
Lent, F. (1915), 'The Life of St. Simeon Stylites: A Translation of the Syriac Text in Bedjan's Acta Martyrum et Sanctorum, Vol. IV', *Journal of the American Oriental Society*, 35: 103–98.
LeRoy Ladurie, E. (1977), *The Beggar and the Professor: A Sixteenth-century Family Saga*, Chicago: University of Chicago Press.
Lesser (1914), 'The Lesser Literatures', *The Nation*, 98, April 2: 354–5.
Levine, J. M. (1999), *Between the Ancients and the Moderns: Baroque Culture in Restoration England*, New Haven: Yale University Press.
Lillie, A. (2007), 'Fiesole: *locus amoenus* or Penitential Landscape?', *I Tatti Studies in the Italian Renaissance*, 11: 11–55.
Linde, C. and W. Labov. (1975), 'Spatial Networks as a Site for the Study of Language and Thought', *Language*, 51: 924–39.
Linxweiler, E. and M. Maude, eds (2017), *Mountaineering: The Freedom of the Hills*, 9th edition, Seattle: The Mountaineers.
Looney, J. J. et al., eds (2004–), *The Papers of Thomas Jefferson: Retirement Series*, 16 volumes, publication ongoing, Princeton: Princeton University Press.
Lorimer, H. (2012), 'Surfaces and Slopes: Remembering the World-Under-Foot', in O. Jones and J. Garde-Hansen (eds), *Geography and Memory: Explorations in Identity, Place and Becoming*, 253–7, Hampshire: Palgrave Macmillan.
Louargant, S., ed. (2013), 'Lever le voile: les montagnes au masculin-féminin', *Revue de géographie alpine*, 101–1. Available online: https://journals.openedition.org/rga/1973 (accessed 22 September 2020).
Lovell, A. (1696), *A Summary of Material Heads which may be Enlarged and Improved into a Compleat Answer to Dr. Burnet's Theory of the Earth*, London: Printed by T. B[raddyll].
Louth, A. (1988), 'St. Athanasius and the Greek "Life of Antony"', *Journal of Theological Studies*, 39: 504–9.
Lydgate, J. (1494), *Here Begynnethe the Boke Calledde Iohn Bochas Descriuinge the Falle of Princis Princessis [and] Other Nobles*, London: Richard Pynson.
Macfarlane, R. (2003), *Mountains of the Mind: A History of a Fascination*, London: Granta.
MacGregor Morris, I. (2000), '"To Make a New Thermopylae": Hellenism, Greek Liberation, and the Battle of Thermopylae', *Greece and Rome*, 47: 211–30.
McInerney, J. (1999), *The Folds of Parnassos: Land and Ethnicity in Ancient Phokis*, Austin, TX: University of Texas Press.
McLaughlin, J. (1988), *Jefferson and Monticello: The Biographer of a Builder,* New York: Holt.
McNeal, R. A. (1993), 'Nicholas Biddle and the Literature of Greek Travel', *Classical Antiquity*, 12: 65–88.
McNeal, R. A. (1995), 'Athens and Nineteenth-Century Panoramic Art', *International Journal of the Classical Tradition*, 1: 80–97.

McNee, A. (2016), *The New Mountaineer in Late Victorian Britain: Materiality, Modernity, and the Haptic Sublime*, Basingstoke: Palgrave Macmillan.
McNeil, J. R. (1992), *The Mountains of the Mediterranean World: An Environmental History*, Cambridge: Cambridge University Press.
Mango, C. A., ed. (1990), *Saint Nicephorus, Short History*, Washington, DC: Dumbarton Oaks, Research Library and Collection.
Martel, P. (1986), 'Le Félibrige', in P. Nora, *Les Lieux de Memoire, III: Les France, 2: Traditions*, 567–611 ,Paris: Gallimard.
Martinelli, B. (1973), 'Del Petrarca e il Ventoso,' in *Studi in onore di Alberto Chiari*, II, 767–834, Brescia: Paideia.
Martinez, M. J. (2005), 'Jeffersonian and Hamiltonian Views of Nature in the Early American Republic', *Politics & Policy*, 33: 522–52.
Mathieu, J. and Boscani Leoni, S., eds (2005), *Die Alpen! Zur europäischen Wahrnehmungsgeschichte seit der Renaissance / Les Alpes! Pour une histoire de la perception européenne depuis la Renaissance*, Berne: Peter Lang.
Mathieu, J. (2005), 'Alpenwahrnehmung: Probleme der historischen Periodisierung', in J. Mathieu and S. Boscani Leoni (eds), *Die Alpen! Zur europäischen Wahrnehmungsgeschichte seit der Renaissance / Les Alpes! Pour une histoire de la perception européenne depuis la Renaissance*, 53–72, Bern: Peter Lang.
Matthews, G. (1957), 'A Volcano's Voice in Shelley', *English Literary History*, 23: 191–228.
Meckien, R. (2013), 'Cultural Memory: The Link between Past, Present, and Future'. Available online: http://www.iea.usp.br/en/news/Cultural-Memory-The-Link-between-Past-Present-and-Future (accessed 22 September 2020).
Meiss, M. (1964), *Giovanni Bellini's Saint Francis in the Frick Collection*, New York: Princeton University Press.
Meiss, M. (1974), 'Scholarship and Penitence in the Early Renaissance: The Image of St. Jerome', *Pantheon*, 32: 132–40.
Merleau-Ponty, M. (1945), *Phénoménologie de la Perception*, Paris: Éditions Gallimard.
Miller, C. A. (1988), *Jefferson and Nature: An Interpretation*, Baltimore: Johns Hopkins University Press.
Miller, J. C. (1977), *The Wolf by the Ears: Thomas Jefferson and Slavery*, New York: The Free Press.
Mistral, F. (1859), *Mirèio: pouèmo prouvençau*, Avignon: J. Roumanille.
Mistral, F. (1867), *Calendau*, Avignon: Roumanille.
Mistral, F. (1879), *Lou Tresor dóu Felibrige, ou, dictionnaire provençal-français, embrassant les divers dialectes de la langue d'oc moderne*, Aix-en-Provence: Veuve Remondet-Aubin.
Mistral, F. (1985), *The Memoirs of Frédéric Mistral*, New York: New Directions.
Moloney, B. (2013), *Francis of Assisi and his "Canticle of Brother Sun" Reassessed*, New York: Palgrave Macmillan.
Mondon, B. (2003), *Voyages au Mont Ventoux: petit florilège littéraire*, Avignon: A. Barthélemy.
Mora, E. (1966), 'Dernière étape d'un voyage. René Char commente son retour amont', *Le Monde*, May 28.
Morley, H. (1871), 'Conrad Gesner', in *Clement Marot and other Studies*, 97–131, London: Chapman and Hall.
Née, P. (2007), *René Char: Une poetique du Retour*, Paris: Hermann.
Newstead, H. H. (1939), *Bran the Blessed in Arthurian Romance*, New York: Columbia University Press.
Newstead, H. H. (1951), 'About Geoffrey of Monmouth', *Latomus*, 10: 53–9.
Nicolson, M. H. (1959), *Mountain Gloom and Mountain Glory: The Development of the Aesthetics of the Infinite*, Ithaca: Cornell University Press.
Nora, P. (1996), *Realms of Memory: Rethinking the French Past*, Volume 1: *Conflicts and Divisions*, tr. A. Goldhammer, first published in French in 1992, New York: University of Columbia Press.

Bibliography

Oakes, T. (1997), 'Place and the Paradox of Modernity', *Annals of the Association of American Geographers*, 87: 509–31.
Ogilvie, B. W. (2006), *The Science of Describing: Natural History in Renaissance Europe*, Chicago: University of Chicago Press.
O'Loughlin, M. (1978), *The Garlands of Repose: The Literary Celebration of Civic and Retired Leisure*, Chicago: University of Chicago Press.
Osgood, C. G., ed. (1930), *Boccaccio on Poetry*, Princeton: Princeton University Press.
Parker, S. (1700), *Six Philosophical Essays Upon Several Subjects,* London: Printed by J.H.
Pashley, R. (1837), *Travels in Crete*, 2 volumes, London: John Murray.
Petsalis-Diomidis, A. (2019), 'Local Engagements with Ancient Greek Vases in Ottoman and Revolutionary Greece, c. 1800–1833', in E. Richardson (ed.) *Classics in Extremis: The Edges of Classical Reception*, 35–58, London: Bloomsbury.
Pitches, J. (2020), *Performing Mountains*, London: Palgrave Macmillan.
Pope, A. (1711), *An Essay on Criticism*, London: Printed for W. Lewis in Russel-Street, Covent-Garden.
Portale, R. (2004), *La meteora Brydone*, Viaggi e viaggiatori in Sicilia 9, Sarzana: Agora.
Porter, J. I. (2001), 'Ideals and Ruins: Pausanias, Longinus, and the Second Sophistic', in S. E. Alcock, J. Cherry and J. Elsner (eds) *Pausanias: Travel and Memory in Roman Greece*, New York: Oxford University Press: 63–92.
Porter, J. I. (2016), *The Sublime in Antiquity*, Cambridge: Cambridge University Press.
Porter, R. (2000), '"In England's Green and Pleasant Land": The English Enlightenment and the Environment', in K. Flint and H. Morphy (eds), *Culture, Landscape, and the Environment*, 15–43, Oxford: Oxford University Press.
Poulios, I. (2014), *The Past in the Present: A Living Heritage Approach – Meteora, Greece*, London: Ubiquity Press.
Pretzler, M. (2007), *Pausanias: Travel Writing in Ancient Greece*, London: Duckworth.
Price, M. (2015), *Mountains: A Very Short Introduction*, Oxford: Oxford University Press.
Price, U. (1810), *Essays on the Picturesque, As Compared with the Sublime and the Beautiful; and on the Use of Studying Pictures, for the Purpose of Improving Real Landscape*, 3 volumes, revised edition; first published in 1794, London: J. Mawman.
Puttenham, G. (1589), *The Arte of English Poesie Contriued into Three Bookes: the First of Poets and Poesie, the Second of Proportion, the Third of Ornament*, London: Richard Field.
Randolph, S. N. (1871), *The Domestic Life of Thomas Jefferson Compiled From Family Letters and Reminiscences*, New York: Harper.
Rawlinson, G. (1880), *History of Herodotos*, Volume 4, London: John Murray.
Ray, J. (1692), *Miscellaneous Discourses Concerning the Dissolution and Changes of the World. Wherein the Primitive Chaos and Creation, the General Deluge, Fountains, Formed Stones, Sea-Shells found in the Earth, Subterraneous Trees, Mountains, Earthquakes, Vulcanoes, the Universal Conflagration and Future State, are largely Discussed and Examined,* London: Printed for S. Smith.
Renan, E. (1904), 'Discours d'Ernest Renan', in Les Félibres de Paris, *Li Soluleiado: poésies et documents littéraires, 1879–1903*, 310–14, Paris: L. Duc.
Revermann, M. (2006), 'The Competence of Theatre Audiences in Fifth- and Fourth-Century Athens', *Journal of Hellenic Studies*, 126: 99–124.
Reynolds, L. D. and N. G. Wilson (1991), *Scribes and Scholars: A Guide to the Transmission of Greek and Latin Literature*, 3rd edition, first published in 1968, Oxford: Clarendon Press.
Rigby, K. (2004), *Topographies of the Sacred: The Poetics of Place in European Romanticism*, Charlottesville: University of Virginia Press.
Ring, J. (2000), *How the English Made the Alps*, London: Murray.
Rizos, E., ed., (2017), *New Cities in Late Antiquity: Documents and Archaeology*, Turnhout: Brepols.
Robbins, J. (1991), *Prodigal Son/Elder Brother: Interpretation and Alterity in Augustine, Petrarch, Kafka, and Levinas*, Chicago: University of Chicago Press.

Robinson, D. and A. Wilson, eds (2011), *Maritime Archaeology and Ancient Trade in the Mediterranean*, Oxford: Oxford Centre for Maritime Archaeology.
Romano, D. G. and M. E. Voyatzis (2010), 'Excavating at the Birthplace of Zeus: The Mount Lykaion Excavation and Survey Project', *Expedition*, 52: 9–21.
Rosand, D. (1988), 'Giorgione, Venice, and the Pastoral Vision', in R. Caffritz, L. Gowing and D. Rosand (eds) *Places of Delight: The Pastoral Landscape*, 20–81, New York: Crown Publishers.
Rosand, D. (1992), 'Pastoral Topoi: On the Construction of Meaning in Landscape', *Studies in the History of Art*, 36: 161–77.
Rose, M. and J. W. Wylie. (2011), 'Landscape: Part Two', in J. Agnew and J. S. Duncan (eds), *The Wiley-Blackwell Companion to Human Geography*, 221–34, Oxford: Wiley-Blackwell.
Rossi, P. (1984), *The Dark Abyss of Time: The History of the Earth and the History of Nations from Hooke to Vico*, tr. L. G. Cochrane, first published in Italian in 1979, Chicago: University of Chicago Press.
Røstvig, M.-S. (1958), *The Happy Man: Studies in the Metamorphoses of a Classical Ideal, Vol. II: 1700-1760*, Oslo Studies in English 7, Oslo: Oslo University Press.
Roumanille, J. (1852), *Li Prouvençalo: poésies diverses*, Avignon: Seguin aîné.
Roy, J. (1996), 'The Countryside in Classical Greek Drama, and Isolated Farms in Dramatic Landscapes', in G. Shipley and J. Salmon (eds), *Human Landscapes in Classical Antiquity: Environment and Culture*, 98–118, London: Routledge.
Roy, J. (2009), 'Living in the Mountains: Arkadian Identity in the Classical Period', in C. Gallou and M. Georgiadis (eds), *The Past in the Past: The Significance of Memory and Tradition in the Transmission of Culture*, 57–65, Oxford: BAR Publishing.
Roza, J. P. (2003), 'French Language and French Nationalism: The Félibrige, Occitan, and the French Identity of Southern France, 1854–1914', PhD diss., University of Washington.
Rudwick, M. (2005), *Bursting the Limits of Time*, Chicago: University of Chicago Press.
Ruskin, J. (1856), *Modern Painters*, Volume 4, London: Smith, Elder and Co.
Russell, G. (1819), *A Tour Through Sicily in the Year 1815,* London: Sherwood, Neely and Jones.
Russell, J. B. (1997), *A History of Heaven: The Singing Silence*, Princeton: Princeton University Press.
Ruta, C. (2016), *Storia del viaggio in Sicilia dalla tarda antichità all'età moderna*. Ragusa: Edizioni di storia e studi sociali.
Rutherglen, S. and C. Hale, eds (2015), *In a New Light: Giovanni Bellini's St. Francis in the Desert*, New York: The Frick Collection.
Rutland, R. A. and W. M. E. Rachal, eds (1973), *The Papers of James Madison, Volume VIII, 10 March 1784-28 March 1786*, Chicago: University of Chicago Press.
Ryan, M.-L. (2003), 'Cognitive Maps and the Construction of Narrative Space', in D. Herman, (ed.) *Narrative Theory and the Cognitive Sciences*, 214–42, Stanford, CA: Publications of the Center for the Study of Language and Information.
Salzman, M. R., M. Sághy and R. Lizzi Testa, eds (2016), *Pagans and Christians in Late Antique Rome: Conflict, Competition, and Coexistence in the Fourth Century*, Cambridge: Cambridge University Press.
Sanders, G. D. R. (2004), 'Problems in Interpreting Rural and Urban Settlement in Southern Greece, AD 365–700', in N. Christie (ed.) *Landscapes of Change: Rural Evolutions in Late Antiquity and the Early Middle Ages*, 163–93, Aldershot: Ashgate.
Sandys, G. (1632), *Ovid's Metamorphosis. Englished, Mythologiz'd, and Represented in Figures*, Oxford: Printed by J. Lichfield.
Sanzaro, F. (2018), 'Keep Our Mountains Free. And Dangerous', *New York Times*, 13 January. Available online: https://www.nytimes.com/2018/01/13/opinion/sunday/keep-our-mountains-free-and-dangerous.html (accessed 22 September 2020).
Sarris, P., M. Dal Santo and P. Booth, eds (2011), *An Age of Saints? Power, Conflict, and Dissent in Early Medieval Christianity*, Leiden: Brill.

Bibliography

Sayce, A. (1892), *Fresh Light from the Ancient Monuments*, 7th edition, first published in 1865, London: The Religious Tract Society.
Sayre, H. M. (2009), *Writing About Art*, 6th edition, first published in 1989, Upper Saddle River, NJ: Prentice Hall.
Scapecchi, P. (2001), 'Vecchi e nuovi appunti su frate Urbano', in Pellegrini, P. (ed.) *Umanisti bellunesi fra quattro e cinquecento: Atti del Convegno di Belluno, 5 novembre 1999*, 107–18, Florence: Olschki.
Schama, S. (1995), *Landscape and Memory*, London: Harper Collins.
Schaumann, C. (2020), *Peak Pursuits: The Emergence of Mountaineering in the Nineteenth Century*, New Haven: Yale University Press.
Schliephake, C. (2017), *Ecocriticism, Ecology, and the Cultures of Antiquity*, Lanham, MD: Lexington Books.
Schneider, P. E. (1966), 'What We Can't Cover with Plants, We'll Paint', *New York Times Magazine*, 14 August.
Scott, J. C. (1998), *Seeing like a State: How Certain Schemes to Improve the Human Condition have Failed*, New Haven: Yale University Press.
Seaford, R. (1981), 'Dionysiac Drama and the Dionysiac Mysteries', *Classical Quarterly*, 31: 252–75.
Seaford, R. (1994), *Reciprocity and Ritual: Homer and Tragedy in the Developing City-State*, Oxford: Clarendon Press.
Seaford, R. (1996), *Euripides: Bacchae*, Warminster: Aris and Phillips.
Segal, C. (1978), 'Pentheus and Hippolytus on the Couch and on the Grid: Psychoanalytic and Structuralist Readings of Greek Tragedy', *The Classical World*, 72: 129–48.
Segal, C. (1997), *Dionysiac Poetics and Euripides' Bacchae*, revised edition, first published in 1982, Princeton: Princeton University Press.
Seguin, F. (1852), *Pèlerinage au Mont-Ventoux; suivi de "Santo-Croux, douas lettro a ma bravo sore Touneto", par J. Roumanille. Avec un appendice relatif au Mont-Ventoux, comprenant la lettre de Pétrarque, une notice sur M. Requien, et autres documents divers*, Avignon: F. Seguin aîné.
Serghidou, A. (1991), 'La mer et les femmes dans l'imaginaire tragique', *Metis: Anthropologie des mondes grecs anciens*, 6: 63–88.
Serrai, A. (1990), *Conrad Gesner*, ed. M. Cochetti, with a bibliography of Gesner's works by M. Menato, Rome: Bulzoni editore.
Setzer, S. (2007), '"Pond'rous Engines" in "Outraged Groves": the Environmental Argument of Anna Seward's "Colebrook Dale"', *European Romantic Review*, 18: 69–82.
Seward, A. (1811), *Letters of Anna Seward*, ed. A. Constable, 6 volumes, London: Longman.
Seward, A. (2016), *The Collected Poems of Anna Seward*, ed. L. Moore, 2 volumes, London: Routledge.
Shakespeare, W. (2002), *Henry IV Part 1*, London: Bloomsbury.
Shakespeare, W. (2014), *Cymbeline*, London: Bloomsbury.
Shams, A. (2011), 'The Treasures of the Holy Monastery of Saint Catherine at Mount Sinai: From the Treasury of 6th Century CE to the Museum of 21st Century CE', *Predella Journal of Visual Arts*, 29. Available online: http://www.predella.it/archivio/index9632.html?option=com_content&view=article&id=165&catid=74&Itemid=100 (accessed 22 September 2020).
Sher, R. (2006), *The Enlightenment and the Book*, Chicago: University of Chicago Press.
Sim(m)ler, J. (1566), *Vita clarissimi philosophi et medici excellentissimi Conradi Gesneri Tigurini*, Zurich: C. Froschoverum.
Sim(m)ler, J. (1574), *Vallesiae descriptio, libri duo: De alpibus commentarius*, Zurich: Christoph Froschauer.
Sim(m)ler, J. (2003), *Vallesiae et alpinum descriptio* (excerpt), tr. A. S. Weber, in A. S. Weber (ed.) (2003) *Because It's There: A Celebration of Mountaineering from 200 B.C. to Today*, 22–8, Lanham: Taylor Trade Publishing.
Sleep, M. C. W. (1969), 'Sir William Hamilton (1730–1803): His Work and Influence in Geology', *Annals of Science*, 25: 319–38.

Sloan, K. (2013), 'Seen Through a Glass Darkly: Dodwell and Pomardi's drawings and Watercolors of Greece', in J. M. Camp II (ed.) (2013), *In Search of Greece: Catalogue of an Exhibit of Drawings at the British Museum by Edward Dodwell and Simone Pomardi*, 31–45, Los Altos, CA: Packard Humanities Institute.
Smart, G. K. (1938), 'Private Libraries in Colonial Virginia', *American Literature*, 10: 24–32.
Smecca, P. D. (2003), 'Cultural Migrations in France and Italy: Travel Literature from Translation to Genre', *Traduction et (im)migration*, 16: 45–72.
Smecca, P. D. (2005), *Representational Tactics in Travel Writing and Translation: A Focus on Sicily*, Rome: Carocci.
Smethurst, P. (2012), *Travel Writing and the Natural World, 1768–1840*, Basingstoke: Palgrave Macmillan.
Smith, A. E. (1998), 'Travel Narratives and the Familiar Letter Form in the Mid-Eighteenth Century', *Studies in Philology*, 95: 77–96.
Smith, D. (2004), 'Beyond the Cave: Lascaux and the Prehistoric in Post-War French Culture', *French Studies*, 58: 219–32.
Smolenaars, J. (2005), 'Earthquakes and Volcanic Eruptions in Latin Literature: Reflections and Emotional Responses', in M. Balmuth, D. Chester and P. Johnston (eds), *Cultural Responses to the Volcanic Landscape*, 311–30, Boston: Archaeological Institute of America.
Snow, C. P. (1959), *The Two Cultures and the Scientific Revolution*, Cambridge: Cambridge University Press.
Société des historiens médiévistes de l'Enseignement supérieur public, ed. (2004), *Montagnes médiévales: XXIV Congrès de la SHMES (Chambért, 23–25 mai 2003)*, Paris: Éditions de la Sorbonne. Available online: https://books.openedition.org/psorbonne/23225 (accessed 22 September 2020).
Speake, G. (2002), *Mount Athos: Renewal in Paradise*, New Haven: Yale University Press.
Speake, G. (2018), *A History of the Athonite Commonwealth: The Spiritual and Cultural Diaspora of Mount Athos*, Cambridge: Cambridge University Press.
Spencer, D. (2010), *Roman Landscape: Culture and Identity*, Cambridge: Cambridge University Press.
Spenser, E. (1590), *The Faerie Queene*, London: printed for William Ponsonby.
Spenser, E. (1595), *Colin Clouts Come Home Againe*, London: printed for William Ponsonby.
Stack, F. (1985), *Pope and Horace: Studies in Imitation*, Cambridge: Cambridge University Press.
Staedtke, J. (1965), 'Conrad Gesner als Theologe', *Gesnerus*, 22: 238–46.
Stanton, L. (2000), *Free Some Day: The African American Families of Monticello*, Charlottesville: University of North Carolina Press.
Stanton, L. (2012), *Those Who Labor for My Happiness: Slavery at Thomas Jefferson's Monticello*, Charlottesville: University of Virginia Press.
Stein, S. R. (1993), *Worlds of Thomas Jefferson at Monticello*, New York: Harry N. Abrams.
Stenger, J. R. (2016), 'Where to Find Christian Philosophy? Spatiality in John Chrysostom's Counter to Greek *paideia*', *Journal of Early Christian Studies*, 24: 173–98.
Stephens, W. P. (1986), *The Theology of Huldrych Zwingli*, Oxford: Clarendon Press.
Steppich, C. J. (2006), 'Inspiration through *imitatio/mimesis* in *On the Sublime* of Longinus and in Joachim Vadian's *De poetica et carminis ratione* (Vienna, 1518)', *Humanistica Lovaniensia*, 55: 37–69.
Stokes, E. (1971), 'Volcanic Studies by Members of the Royal Society of London 1665–1780', *Earth Science Journal*, 5: 46–70.
Stoneman, R. (2010), *Land of Lost Gods: The Search for Classical Greece*, revised edition; first published in 1987, London: Tauris Parke paperbacks.
Stoppelli, P. (1997), *Francesco Petrarca, Opera omnia*, CD ROM, Rome: Lexis Progetti Editoriali.
Sturges, M. (2011), 'Enclosing the Commons: Thomas Jefferson, Agrarian Independence, and Early American Land Policy, 1774–1789', *The Virginia Magazine of History and Biography*, 119: 42–74.

Bibliography

Šubrt, J. (1991), 'The Motif of the Alps in the Work of Silius Italicus', *Folia Philologica*, 114: 224–31.
Surya, M. (2012), *Georges Bataille*, Paris: Gallimard.
Sweetman, R. (2015), 'The Christianisation of the Peloponnese: The Case for Strategic Change', *Annual of the British School at Athens*, 110: 285–319.
Symonds, J. A. (1874), *Sketches in Italy and Greece*, London: Smith, Elder, and Co.
Talbot, A.-M. (1996), 'Life of St. Anthousa of Mantineon', in A.-M. Talbot (ed.) *Holy Women of Byzantium: Ten Saints' Lives in English Translation*, 13–19, Washington, D.C.: Dumbarton Oaks Research Library and Collection.
Talbot, A.-M. and S. F. Johnson, eds (2012), *Miracle Tales from Byzantium*, Dumbarton Oaks Medieval Library 12, Cambridge, MA: Harvard University Press.
Taplin, O. (2010), 'Echoes from Mount Cithaeron', in P. Mitsis and C. Tsagalis (eds) *Allusion, Authority, and Truth: Critical Perspectives on Greek Poetic and Rhetorical Praxis*, 235–48, Berlin: De Gruyter.
Temple, W. (1908), *Upon the Gardens of Epicurus, with other XVIIth Century Garden Essays*, London: Chatto and Windus.
Temple-Grenville, R., ed. (1862), *The Private Diary of Richard, Duke of Buckingham and Chandos, K.G.*, 3 volumes, London: Hurst and Blackett.
Thacker, C. (1983), *The Wildness Pleases: The Origins of Romanticism*, London: Croom Helm.
Thomas, K. (1983), *Man and the Natural World: Changing Attitudes in England, 1500–1800*, London: Allen Lane.
Thomasset, C. and D. James-Raoul, eds (2000), *La montagne dans le texte medieval: entre mythe et réalité*, Paris: Presses de l'Université de Paris-Sorbonne.
Thonemann, P. (2011), *The Maeander Valley: A Historical Geography from Antiquity to Byzantium*, Cambridge: Cambridge University Press.
Tissandier, G. (1874), 'Club Alpin Français', *La nature*, 2: 395.
Toliver, B. (2011), 'The Alps and the *Alpine Symphony*, and Environmentalism: Searching for Connections', *Green Letters*, 15: 8–21.
Tozer, H. F. (1869), *Researches in the Highlands of Turkey: Including Visits to Mounts Ida, Athos, Olympus, and Pelion, to the Mirdite Albanians, and Other Remote Tribes, with Notes on the Ballads, Tales, and Classical Superstitions of the Modern Greeks*, London: John Murray.
Tracy, S. V. (1986), 'Darkness from Light: The Beacon Fire in the *Agamemnon*', *Classical Quarterly*, 36: 257–60.
Tuan, Y.-F. (1971), *Topophilia: A Study of Environmental Perception, Attitudes, and Values*, New York: Columbia University Press.
Tuma, K. A. (2002), 'Cézanne and Lucretius at the Red Rock', *Representations* 78: 56–85.
Tuzet, H. (1945), *Voyageurs français en Sicile au temps du romantisme (1802–1848)*, Paris: Boivin.
Tuzet, H. (1955), *La Sicile au XVIIIe siècle vue par les voyageurs étrangers*. Strasbourg: P.-H. Heitz.
Tuzet, H. (1988), *Viaggiatori stranieri in Sicilia nel XVIII secolo*, Palermo: Sellerio Editore.
Vergil, P. (1546), *An Abridgement of the Notable Woorke of Polidore Vergile*, ed. T. Langley, London: Richard Grafton.
Veyne, P. (1990), *René Char en ses poèmes*, Paris: Gallimard.
Vidal-Naquet, P. (1988), 'Sophocles' *Philoktetes* and the Ephebeia', in J.-P. Vernant and P. Vidal-Naquet (eds) *Myth and Tragedy in Ancient Greece*, tr. J. Lloyd, first published in French in 1972, New York: Zone Books.
Waelkens, M. (1993), 'Sagalassos: History and Archaeology', in M. Waelkens (ed.) *Sagalassos I*, 37–82, Leuven: Leuven University Press.
Warner, W. (1586), *Albions England*, London: George Robinson for Thomas Cadman.
Warren, E. (1690), *Geologia: Or, a Discourse Concerning the Earth before the Deluge*, London: Printed for R. Chiswell.
Warren, E. (1691), *A Defence of the Discourse*, London: Printed by J. Southby.

Bibliography

Warren, E. (1692), *Some Reflections Upon the Short Considerations*, London: Printed by R. Roberts.

Wathelet, P. (1988), *Dictionnaire des Troyens de l'Iliade*, Liège: Université de Liège.

Watkins, C. (2014), *Trees, Woods and Forests: A Social and Cultural History*, London: Reaktion Books.

Watkins, T. (1792), *Travels Through Swisserland, Italy, Sicily, the Greek Islands, to Constantinople, Through Part Of Greece, Ragusa and The Dalmatian Isles: In a Series Of Letters To Pennoyre Watkins, Esq. From Thomas Watkins, A. M. in the Years 1787, 1788, 1789*, 2 volumes, London: T. Cadell.

Weber, A. S., ed. (2003), *Because It's There: A Celebration of Mountaineering from 200 B.C. to Today*, Lanham: Taylor Trade Publishing.

Weiss, A. S. (2005), *The Wind and the Source: In the Shadow of Mont Ventoux*, Albany: State University of New York Press.

Wellisch, H. (1975), 'Conrad Gessner: a Bio-bibliography', *Journal of the Society for Bibliography and Natural History*, 7: 151–247.

Welsh, J. (2014), 'How to Read a Volcano', *Transactions of the American Philological Association*, 144: 97–132.

Westaway, J. (2009), 'The German Community in Manchester, Middle-Class Culture and the Development of Mountaineering in Britain, c. 1850-1914', *English Historical Review*, 124: 571–604.

Wheeler, M. (1964), *Roman Art and Architecture*, London: Thames and Hudson.

White, L., Jr (1967), 'The Historical Roots of our Ecologic Crisis', *Science*, 155: 1203–7.

Whitehead, D. (1986), *The Demes of Attica 508/7– ca. 250 BC: A Political and Social Study*, Princeton: Princeton University Press.

Wilamowitz, U. (1931), *Der Glaube der Hellenen*, Volume 1, Berlin: Weidmann.

Williams, C. (1973), *Women on the Rope: The Feminine Share in Mountain Adventure*, London: George Allen & Unwin.

Williams, G. (2017), *Pietro Bembo on Aetna: The Ascent of a Venetian Humanist*, New York: Oxford University Press.

Williams, R. (1989), *People of the Black Mountains Volume I, The Beginning...*, London: Chatto and Windus.

Wilson, C. (2009), 'Epicureanism in Early Modern Philosophy', in J. Warren (ed.) *The Cambridge Companion to Epicureanism*, 266–86, Cambridge: Cambridge University Press.

Wood, K. (2006), 'Making and Circulating Knowledge through Sir William Hamilton's *Campi Phlegraei*', *British Journal for the History of Science*, 39: 67–96.

Woodward, R. B. (2006), 'In Provence, Honoring a Poet at 6,263 Feet', *New York Times*, 30 July.

Wordsworth, W. (1822), *A Description of the Scenery of the Lakes in the North of England; with Additions, and Illustrative Remarks upon the Scenery of the Alps*, 3rd edition, London: Longman, Hurst, Rees, Orme, and Brown.

Worman, N. (2015), *Landscape and the Spaces of Metaphor in Ancient Literary Theory and Criticism*, Cambridge: Cambridge University Press.

Wragge-Morley, A. (2009), 'A Strange and Surprising Debate: Mountains, Original Sin and "Science" in Seventeenth-Century England', *Endeavour*, 33: 76–80.

Wright, F. A., ed. (1933), *Select Letters of St. Jerome*, London: Heinemann.

INDEX

Acroceraunian mountains 154
Addison, Joseph 3, 38, 56
Aelian (*Varia Historia*) 62, 67, 154
Aeolian Islands *see* Lipari Islands
Aeschylus 40, 90, 150, 191–3
Agrigentum 44, 169, 178
Alpinism 73–88
   definitions of 77, 84
   premodern 23, 77, 79, 80 (*see also under* Brennus)
   see also mountaineering
Alps, the 7, 11, 32, 37, 58, 73–88, 133–4, 147–8, 152, 197, 203–11, 219, 224
   see also Dauphiné Alps
Amaseia 91
Anatolia 91, 93, 94
Anderson, Benedict 199
animals 22, 27, 31, 65–6, 82, 94, 118–22, 123, 189, 191, 217, 223
Anselm, Saint 110–11, 115
Anthony the Great, Saint 98, 101
Antioch 96, 113, 114
Apollo 89, 104, 203, 209
archaeology 4, 90–3, 98, 101, 148, 177, 215–16, 225
Aristophanes 61
Aristotle 22, 28, 30, 32, 60, 194 n.10, 195 n.18
Argos 150, 191–3
Armenia 95
Arykanda 91–2, 93
ascetic/asceticism 97, 100, 101–3, 106 n.34, 111, 112, 116, 118
Athena 104
Athens 154, 157, 161, 192, 194, 195 n.26
Attica 154, 157, 188, 195 n.26
Auxentios, Saint 101–3
   see also Mount Auxentios

Balmat, Jacques 23
Barton, William 3, 17 n.13, 34 n.15 and n.20, 71 n.75
Basil of Caesarea 93–5, 96, 97
Bataille, Georges 221, 222
Batten, Charles 173
Beaumont, John 59, 60, 62–3, 66
Bellini, Giovanni 109–29
   see also under Francis, Saint; Jerome, Saint; *locus amoenus*

Bembo, Pietro 23, 51–2 n.11, 125, 211
   potentially fabricated ascent of Etna 8, 13, 165, 166, 167–9, 179
Bentley, Richard 59, 66–7
Bethlehem 115, 119, 122
Bible/Biblical 9, 11, 57, 64, 67–8, 97–8, 102–4, 113, 116, 117, 125–7, 149, 175, 215
Blanchot, Maurice 221, 222, 223
Blue Ridge Mountains 139, 144 n.4
Boccaccio, Giovanni 126, 202, 204
Bolzanio, Urbano 167, 168
Bosporus 101, 103
botany 22, 32, 41, 73, 77
Breevort, Meta 75
Brennus, legendary king 197–214
   alpinism of 197, 198, 205–6, 207, 208, 209
   composite figure, as a 198, 202–5
   Hannibal, parallels with 204, 207–8, 209
   national identity of 204–6, 210
   see also Fisher, Jasper; Higgins, John
Brooke, Arthur 211
Brown, Lancelot 'Capability' 136
Brydone, Patrick 166–83
   and the classical past 42, 44, 45, 48, 49, 51 n.7, 167
   Etna, significance in his *Tour* 176–7
   fabricated ascent 13, 166, 173–6, 179, 182 n.74
   and Hamilton, William 169–73, 175, 178–9
   Seward, Anna, used by 46–7, 54 n.62
   and the sublime 44, 45, 166, 179
   see also deep time; myth
bucolic 27, 28, 32, 47, 49
   see also pastoral
Burckhardt, Jacob 80, 215–16, 224
Burke, Edmund 21, 28, 139, 166, 181 n.52
Burnet, Thomas 55–71
   ancient knowledge, use of 7, 55, 56, 59–60, 61–2, 63–6
   appreciation/denigration of mountains by 56, 57–8, 59
   origins of the world and of mountains, on 33 n.1, 55, 57, 61–2
   Scripture, use of 55, 57, 59, 62
Buxton, Richard 4, 9, 10, 41–2, 109–10, 117, 127, 185, 194 n.3
Byrd, William 211
Byron, George Gordon, Lord 37, 51 n.4, 162 n.17

Index

Camden, William 206
camera obscura 155, 158, 163 n.35
Canigou (mountain) 79
Cappadocia 91, 93
Cassius Dio 154
Catania 41, 45, 53 n.38, 169, 171, 174, 176
cave 32, 97, 99, 107 n.42, 125–6, 157, 188, 218, 221
  see also grotto
Cézanne, Ernest 219
Cézanne, Paul 219–21
Chalcedon 101
Chalcis/Chalkis (modern-day Varasova, mountain) 155
Chalkidean massif/Chalkis ad Bellum (city in Roman Syria) 113, 118, 123, 127
Chaos, the 9, 55, 61–3
Char, René 215, 221–3, 225
Christ 97–8, 100, 104, 112, 117, 122, 124
Christian/Christianity 15, 89–90, 94, 96–7, 98, 103, 115
  attitudes to nature 3, 110–12
  Catholic 47, 140, 198, 203, 217
  iconography 121
  and the pagan 47, 89, 91, 93–5, 104–5, 113, 118, 126, 127, 216, 219
  Protestant 47, 78, 198, 203
  see also Bible/Biblical; Christianization; monasteries; monastic; paradise; pilgrimage (*under* mountains)
Christianization 89, 90, 91, 94, 97, 103–4, 127
Churchyard, Thomas 202, 210
Cicero 3, 112, 168
Cilicia 89, 98, 104
Clark, Kenneth 110–11
Clarke, Edward Daniel 149
classic ground 3, 38, 51 n.9, 134, 148, 162 n.11
Claudian 83
climate 1, 93, 113, 176, 201, 204, 216, 223
Constantinople 90, 101, 103
Coolidge, W. A. B. 7, 21, 73–88
  grudge against Edward Whymper 75, 85 n.10
  reaction to Whymper party accident 87 n.45
  see also under Simler, Josias
Corbin, Alain 138
Corinth 150, 190
  Acrocorinth 163 n.52
  Gulf of 155
Cosgrove, Denis 14
Cosway, Maria 133
Croft, Herbert 58, 60, 62, 70 n.43
Crusades, the 97, 98, 104
cultural memory 18 n.26, 109–10, 113, 117, 123, 126–7
Cyclops 39, 48, 49, 50, 52 n.15, 172

da Borgo San Sepolcro, Dionigi 167–8
Dalmatian coast 154, 159

Dante 3, 117
Darwin, Erasmus 38, 47–51
Dauphiné Alps 78, 79–80, 83
de Borch, Michel-Jean 174–5
de Gourbillon, Antoine 175
de la Borde, Jean-Benjamin 175
de Vere, Aubrey *see under* picturesque, the
de Ville, Antoine *see* Mont Aiguille
Debarbieux, Bernard, and Gilles Rudaz 3, 12, 19 n.40, 162 n.5, 198
deep time 9, 43, 45, 53 n.39, 57, 68
della Dora, Veronica 9, 18 n.22, 162 n.10, 193
  mountains as memory theatres 10, 149, 151, 186
Delphi 152, 190, 204, 209
desert 93, 98, 103, 106 n.24, 109, 110, 111, 112, 113, 118, 119–20, 123
  see also wilderness
Dionysia (festival) 188, 189
Dionysus/Dionysiac 15, 187–9, 193, 195 n.26
dithyramb 187–9
Dodwell, Edward 7, 12, 14, 147–64
  as an artist 147, 152, 158–61
  attitudes to inhabitants of Ottoman Greece 149, 154
  encounters with bandits 154–7
  historic associations of Greek landscape 10, 153, 154, 156, 157, 159, 160–1
  and the picturesque 158, 160–1
Dryden, John, the younger 37, 38–9, 42–4
Duffy, Cian *see* classic ground

early modern 2, 4, 5, 9, 11, 21–36, 41, 55–72, 197–214
  bridging the ancient and the modern 73, 74
  challenging periodization 80, 81
  perceived break with modernity 16, 77
  see also modern; premodern
Eden/Edenic 21, 94, 96–7, 103, 111, 117, 127, 134
  see also paradise
Egeria 14, 149
Egypt 97, 98, 103, 109, 112
Egyptians, the 60, 61, 66
Elysian Fields, the/Elysium 63–4, 67, 134
Empedocles 44, 46, 178, 183 n.100
Enceladus 40, 43
  see also Typhon
environment/environmental humanities 5, 6, 8, 15, 47, 49, 80, 223–5
environmental determinism 12, 205
Ephraem of Syria, Saint 111, 115
Epicurus/Epicureanism 27, 36 n.48, 60, 62, 66
  Jefferson, Thomas, as an Epicurean 131, 133, 135–7, 139, 143
  see also under locus amoenus

250

Index

Etna *see* Mount Etna
Euripides 90
   Bacchae 20, 187–9, 193
   Cretans, the 189
   Hippolytus 194 n.1
   Iphigenia in Tauris 189, 194 n.1
   Orestes 189
   Supplices 194 n.1
Eustochium, Saint 112, 114, 115
Evagrius Ponticus 112, 113, 114, 115

Fabre, Jean-Henri 217
Farington, Joseph 173–4
Félibrige, the 217, 219, 220
Fisher, Jasper 198, 202, 203, 205, 206, 210
Florus, Julius 204
Francis, Saint, of Assisi 7, 109
   Bellini, Giovanni, depicted by 123–6
   see also under Jerome, Saint
Freneau, Philip 137

gardens
   classical ideas of 118, 136, 141
   Jefferson's 133, 135, 137, 142
   locus amoenus, as 117, 124
   moral status of 110–11
   see also Temple, William; Whately, Thomas; *see also under* paradise
Gardens of the Hesperides 64
gender 14–15, 46, 47, 49, 100, 104, 143, 218
Geoffrey of Monmouth 204, 205, 206, 207, 211
Gessner, Conrad 21–36, 77–9
   as both ancient and modern 4–5, 10, 23, 79, 84, 211
   classical authors, use of 25–8, 29–32, 35 n.29 and n.40, 36 n.48
   Descriptio Montis Fractis 23–4, 26–7, 31, 32
   de Montium Admiratione 22–3, 24, 25–6, 27, 29–30, 77, 78, 79
   mountain 'sublime' of 7, 28–33
   Mount Pilatus, ascent of 24, 32, 77
   and natural science 22, 33 n.8
   and volcanoes 25–6, 27, 34 n.27, 226 n.38
   as a Zwinglian 22, 34 n.11, 36 n.47
   see also under Romanticism
Grahame, Simion 211–12
Grand Tour 38, 148
Greek tragedy 8, 185–96
   see also Aeschylus; Euripides; Sophocles
Gregory of Nazianzus 94–5
Gregory of Nyssa 94, 95
Grenville, Richard 174
grotto 96, 101, 103, 139, 218, 223
   see also cave
Grynaeus, Simon 22, 30

hagiography 95–6, 97–103, 105, 119, 124
Hamilton, William 46, 48, 51
   see also under Brydone, Patrick
Hannibal 82, 133
   see also under Brennus; Livy
Hansen, Peter 2–3, 80, 84, 149, 197
   see also summit position
Hephaestus, 39–40, 50, 191, 192
   see also Vulcan; Cyclops
Heraclitus 27, 60, 221
Hercules 157, 207–8, 209
Hermes 192
hermit/hermitage 97, 98, 100, 102, 114, 118, 126, 200, 216
   see also Antony the Great, Saint; Stephen the Younger, Saint; *see also under* Natural Bridge (Virginia)
Herodotus 107 n.52, 190
Hesiod 39, 61, 160, 165
Higgins, John 8, 197, 198, 202–3, 205, 207–10
Homer 26–7, 28–9, 39, 94, 159–60, 192–3
   see also under locus amoenus
Horace 131, 132–3, 135, 136, 137, 143, 154
   see also Sabine Farm
Huber, Johannes Chrysostomus 22
Hughes, Thomas Smart 150
Hume, David 170

Iliad, the *see* Homer
Ingold, Tim 185, 186, 187, 193
Iris, river 95

Jefferson, Thomas 7, 10, 11, 12, 14, 15, 95, 131–46
   American landscape aesthetic 131, 133, 135, 140–2
   classical education of 131, 132–3
   Longinus, familiarity with 139, 146 n.52
   and the picturesque 132, 133, 140, 142, 144 n.3
   and the sublime 133–5, 138–9, 140, 142, 143
   see also Monticello; Natural Bridge; Poplar Forest; *see also under* Epicurus/Epicureanism; Lucretius; Romanticism
Jerome, Saint 7, 11, 95, 109–10, 111–23, 126–7
   biography of 112–17
   comparison with Francis, Saint 123–6
   depicted by Bellini, Giovanni 110, 118–23
   depicted in the mountains 111, 119, 121, 123
   see also under locus amoenus
Jerusalem 102
Jesus *see* Christ
John Chrysostom 96
Johnson, Samuel 175
Jullian, Camille 218

251

Index

Kant 21, 28
Keill, John 60–1, 63
Klovoka (mountain) see Taphiassos
Koelb, Janice Hewlett 3, 71 n.75, 85 n.4
Korenjak, Martin 3, 17 n.13, 21, 33 n.3, 85 n.5, 88 n.60

Lake District 37, 197
Lake Galilee 98
Larissa (city in Thessaly) 159–60
late antiquity 6, 11, 14, 89–107, 133, 215
Latrobe, Benjamin Henry 140, 142
Leake, William Martin 151
Lemprière, John see under Mount Etna
Letoon 91
Levant, the 97, 104
Libanius 117
Lipari Islands 172, 176–7
Livy 78, 154, 203
    Hannibal's Alpine crossing 133–4, 204, 208
    Philip's ascent of Mount Haemus 23
locus amoenus 14
    Bellini, Giovanni, presentation of 124, 126, 127
    Boccaccio, and 126
    Calypso's island in Homer 117
    Curtius, E. R., on 117
    in Epicurus 31
    Jefferson's Monticello as 132–3, 134, 135, 139
    and Jerome, Saint 110, 115, 117, 121, 122
    and Lucretius 32
Longinus 28, 29–30, 139
    see also under Jefferson, Thomas
longue dureé ix, 1–2, 21
Lovell, Archibald 63
Lucan 167
Lucretius 32, 220
    on Etna 40–1, 43, 44
    influence upon Jefferson, Thomas 131, 135, 139, 143, 146 n.52
    sublime, and the 28, 30–1, 48 n.36, 143, 146 n.52
Lycia 91–2
Lydia, mountains of 188, 189
Lydgate, John, 204 205

Macfarlane, Robert 2, 17 n.9, 69 n.9
Macrina, Saint 95–6
Madison, James 140
Malta 38, 169, 176
maps/mapping 7, 37, 82, 153
Marcella, Saint 115–16, 126
Marmara, Sea of 103
Marti, Benedict 22, 34 n.22
Maty, Matthew 169

medieval/middle ages 4, 18 n.19, 32 n.86, 78, 80, 91, 98, 104, 204, 216
    artistic and literary devices 117, 122, 194–5 n.10, 202
    attitudes to landscape 110–11
    Christianization of mountains 92 fig. 5.1, 103
Merleau-Ponty, Maurice 185, 188, 193
Messene 155
    Messenian Gulf 158
Messina 169, 172, 177
Meteora 101, 103
Miller, Charles 142
Milton, John 67, 117
Mistral, Frédéric 217, 218
modern/modernity 2, 6, 8, 16, 73, 74, 79, 80, 83, 84, 197, 198, 218, 219
    see also early modern; mountain gloom/mountain glory; premodern
monasteries 90, 97–9, 101–3, 119, 122, 124, 126, 155, 160–1, 171
monasticism 110, 112, 116, 118
Monroe, James (President) 137
Mont Aiguille 78–80, 86 n.28
Mont Blanc 23, 85 n.8, 86 n.28
Mont Sainte Victoire 8, 10, 218–21
Mont Ventoux 4, 8, 10, 11, 13, 15, 79, 166, 167–8, 211, 215–27
    see also Petrarch
Monticello 14–15, 95, 131, 132–8
    compared to Mount Olympus, 132, 134
    laudatory description of 132, 133, 140
    'new Rowanty', as 132, 134
    place of retirement and retreat, as 135, 139
    slavery at 142–3
    see also Poplar Forest; Sabine Farm; see also under locus amoenus
Morea, the 154, 156
    see also Peloponnese, the
Moses 60, 65, 98, 124
Mount Arachnaion/Arachnaeum 150, 191–2
Mount Athos 103, 107 n.52, 150, 151, 191, 192
Mount Auxentios 102–3
    see also Auxentios, Saint
Mount Calvary 97
Mount Carmel 97, 102
Mount Cyllene 150
Mount Etna 37–54, 165–83
    classical perspectives on 9, 11, 38, 39–46, 47, 48, 49
    and deep time 43, 45, 177
    Lemprière, John on 39
    and natural history 25, 175, 177
    famous/worthy of admiration 29, 37, 43–4, 45, 165–6, 177, 179
    Spenser, Edmund on 200

252

Index

see also Cyclops; Darwin, Erasmus; Dryden, John; Empedocles; Hamilton, William; Seward, Anna; Typhon; *see also under* Bembo, Pietro; Brydone, Patrick; Lucretius
Mount Gargarus 149
Mount Haemus 23, 76
Mount Horeb 97, 102
Mount Hymettos 160–1
Mount Ida 188, 191–2, 150, 151
Mount Ithome 147, 155–6
Mount Kadmos 18 n.24
Mount Kithairon 186, 190–1, 192, 193
Mount Lykaion 157, 158
Mount Nebo 149
Mount Olympus 132, 134, 150, 151, 159, 208
Mount Parnassos 15, 152, 201, 203, 209
Mount Scodrus 154
Mount Sinai 14, 97, 102, 149
Mount Tabor 97, 98–9, 102
Mount Taygetos 158, 163 n.38
Mount Tmolos 188, 189
Mount Vesuvius 30, 37, 38, 46
mountain gloom/mountain glory 2–4, 16, 17 n.6 and n.7, 68, 74, 80, 104, 185, 200, 215
mountain studies 1–2, 4–6, 12
mountaineer
    ambiguous definition 12
    as in climber 14, 23, 33 n.4, 74–5, 80, 222
    as in dweller 19, n.40, 198, 209
mountaineering 1, 2, 8, 9, 14, 21, 74, 75, 77, 79, 80, 81, 82–4, 109, 147, 149, 186, 206, 219
    see also Alpinism
mountains
    as spaces of connection 6, 21, 90–3, 150, 191–3
    and identity 4, 11–12, 131–46, 197–214, 215–27
    knowledge of 10–11, 22, 37–54, 55–71, 73–88, 151, 175, 192 (*see also* natural philosophy; science)
    as marginal 1, 10, 15, 18 n.17, 90–3, 109, 110, 117, 127, 185, 194, 197
    origins of 11, 16 n.4, 55–71, 220–1
    and temporality 8–10, 21, 25–6, 44–5, 55–71, 110, 127, 149–51, 155, 160–1, 175, 215–27 (*see also* deep time)
    as places of pilgrimage 18 n.19, 21, 97–8, 99, 101, 106 n.34, 149, 211, 216–18
    as places of retreat 7, 10, 14, 93–105, 109–29, 131–8, 139, 142
    as places of sacrifice 4, 9, 149
    as useful 13, 58–9, 94
Mummery, Albert 23
myth 8, 14–15, 24, 27–8, 29, 37–54, 113, 117, 118, 132, 150, 157, 169, 185–96, 198, 201, 205, 210
    and science 9–10, 41–2, 61

Naples 38, 169, 176–7
Natural Bridge (Virginia) 133, 138, 139–40, 142
natural philosophy 2, 38, 39, 41–2, 43, 45, 46, 49, 51, 55–71
    see also science
Naukratios, brother of St Macrina 95
Nicolosi (convent on Mount Etna) 171, 174, 175
Nicomedia, Gulf of 102
Nikephoros I, patriarch 101
Nicolson, Marjorie Hope *see* mountain gloom/mountain glory

Oakes, Timothy 198
Odyssey, the, *see* Homer
Oedipus 190–2, 193
oros 109–10, 111, 112–14, 118, 122, 127
otium 136, 137
Ovid 26, 63, 64–5, 67–8, 160–1, 144 n.3

Paccard, Michel-Gabriel 23
pagan *see under* Christian/Christianity
paideia 94
Palermo 169, 176, 177
Palestine 97, 98, 149
Palladius of Apsuna, hagiographer 96
Pamphylia 93
Pan 27–8, 157
Panarea (island) 172
Pashley, Robert 151
pastoral 117, 123, 125–6, 132–3, 136–7, 142–3, 159
    see also bucolic
paradise 56, 63–7, 103, 111, 116, 117–18, 119, 123, 127, 134
    see also Eden; Elysian Fields; Gardens of the Hesperides
Paul, Saint *see* Thekla, Saint
Pausanias 9, 19 n.43, 154
    on Brennus, on 203, 204
    and the picturesque 148–9, 158, 160
    and ruins 156, 157
Peloponnese, the 154, 158
Perge 91
Petrarca, Francesco ('Petrarch') 166–9
    a canonical figure 79
    fabricated ascent 8, 13, 166, 168, 179, 211
    father of humanism 122
    guide for modern excursions, as a 216, 224
    history of Mont Ventoux, start of 223
    identified as 'modern' 4–5, 80, 84, 129 n.46, 215–16 (*see also* Burckhardt, Jacob)
    love of mountains 80
    spiritual summit view 33 n.2, 165, 167, 180 n.17
    at the summit position 217, 222
Petrarca, Gherardo 167–8
phenomonology 8, 13, 185–96
    see also sensory experience of mountains

Index

Philo of Alexandria 26–7, 29, 34 n.27
Phrygia 91, 188–9, 195 n.26
Picasso, Pablo 223
picturesque, the
    America as 133
    Brydone, Patrick, and 173
    the classical and 7, 14, 132, 144 n.3, 151
    de Vere, Aubrey on 152
    Dodwell, Edward, and 158, 160
    Greece and 148, 158
    Pausanias as forerunner of 148–9, 162 n.14
    see also under Jefferson, Thomas
Pindar 39, 40, 42–3, 44, 45, 53 n.37
Pisidia 91, 92
Polybius 78, 134, 154
Pontus 91, 95
Pope, Alexander 1, 15–16, 47, 132
Poplar Forest 135–6
Porter, James 28, 30, 33 n.3
Pliny the Elder 19 n.29, 22, 52 n.17, 78, 129 n.43, 154, 160
Pliny the Younger 37
Plutarch 154, 159, 203, 205
premodern/premodernity 14, 80, 81
    continuity from antiquity, 28, 29 n.19, 74, 79, 83
    oversimplification of mountain attitudes, 2, 3–4, 6, 16, 147, 185 (*see also* mountain gloom/mountain glory)
    see also early modern, *see also* modern
Price, Uvedale 148–9
Procopius 154
Propertius 18 n.25, 209
Provence 216–23
Ptolemy 78

Quarrel of the Ancients and Moderns 56
Quintilian 3

Randolph, Edmund 140
Randolph, Martha Jefferson 140
Rapsana 157
Recupero, Giuseppe 169, 170, 175, 177, 182 n.78
Red Sea Mountains 98
Renaissance, the 1, 10, 12, 14, 22, 38, 104, 109, 110, 117, 126, 133, 165, 198, 199–202, 215
    see also modern
Renan, Ernest 80, 218
Rhellicanus, Johannes 22
Rivanna, river 134
rivers 172, 199
    of lava 29, 40
    noted alongside mountains 35 n.43, 133, 134, 154
    pleasing aspect of landscape 31–2, 67, 94, 117, 118
    produced by mountains 59

see also Arycandus, river; Iris, river; Rivanna, river; Strymon, river
Rocciamelone 79
Romantic *see* Romanticism
Romanticism
    and classicism 3, 46, 51 n.9, 141, 151–2, 158
    and Gessner, Conrad 23, 25
    and Jefferson, Thomas 141–2
    and landscape description 4
    and volcanoes 37–8, 45–51
    as a watershed in attitudes to nature 21, 68, 197
Rome 104, 112–15, 121, 136, 178, 203, 204, 205–6
Rotario, Bonifacio 80
Roumanille, Joseph 216–17
Royal Society, the 169, 170, 180 n.23
Rush, Richard 134–5
Ruskin, John 17 n.6, 197
Russell, George 174

Sabine Farm, 133, 135, 143
    see also Horace; Monticello
Sagalassos 91, 92
satyrs 27, 188
Sayce, Archibald Henry 132
Schama, Simon 9, 17 n.5, 19 n.29
science 1, 5, 11, 22, 23, 25, 26, 31, 37, 38, 45–6, 47, 51, 77, 79, 81, 137, 170, 175, 177, 178
    see also natural philosophy; *see also under* myth
Seguin, François-Joseph 216
sensory experience of mountains
    aural 31, 190
    embodied 32, 185–7, 189, 193
    olfactory 189
    visual 31–2, 189, 191
Seward, Anna 7, 9, 38, 46–51
Shaftesbury 21
Shakespeare, William 199, 201–2, 210
Silius Italicus 78, 83, 207–8, 209, 210
Simeon Stylites the Elder, Saint 98–101
Simler, Josias 7, 22, 73–88, 211
    awe and fear, evoking 208
    biography of 76–7
    classical sources 78, 83
    W. A. B. Coolidge, translated and transformed by 73, 75–6, 78, 81–2, 84
    De Alpibus Commentarius 73
    as the 'first Alpinist' 77
    Gessner, Conrad, friend to 22, 23, 33 n.7, 77
    technical mountain knowledge of 83–4, 87 n.55 and n.56
    see also under Strabo
Smith, Margaret Bayard 134
solitude 31, 95–6, 112, 114–16, 123, 126, 137, 222
Sophocles 90, 190–1
Spenser, Edmund 199–201
    see also under Mount Etna

Sperlonga 139
Statius 131, 136, 143
Stephen, Leslie 23, 80
Strabo 91, 154, 203
    as a source for Simler 78, 83
    on volcanoes 42, 43, 44
Strahan, William 170
Stromboli 172, 177
Strymon, river 94, 106 n.23
Stumpf, Johann 78
sublime, the 40–1, 45, 46–7 166, 173, 176, 179
    evoked by historical associations 3, 148, 158
        (*see also* classic ground)
    as a modern aesthetic 4, 7, 12, 14, 33 n.3, 147
    as a premodern aesthetic 7, 10, 24–33, 43, 199–200
    see also Burke; Kant; Longinus; Shaftesbury; *see also under* Jefferson, Thomas; Lucretius
summit position vii, 2–3, 8, 149–51, 197, 216, 219, 225
    viewing from the 133–8, 155, 158, 160–1, 167–8, 172, 173–4
Swinburne, Henry 175
Syracuse 169, 176, 178
Syria 97, 98–9, 100, 101, 103, 111, 113, 118

Tacitus 37, 78, 137
Taormina 169, 176, 178
Taphiassos (modern-day Klokova, mountain) 155
Tempe, Vale of 158
Temple, William 131
Thebes 187, 188, 190, 191
Thekla, Saint 89, 100, 104–5
Theophrastus 22, 25
Thermopylae 159, 164 n.78
Thessaloniki 103, 154, 159
Thessaly 67, 103, 154, 159
thinking like a mountain 80, 223, 224
Tozer, Henry Fanshawe 150–2
transfiguration, the 97–8
travel writing 3, 7–8, 9, 10, 37, 38, 43–5, 46, 147–64, 165–83
    see also Brydone, Patrick

Trist, Eliza House 135
Trumbull, John 140, 142
Tschudi, Aegidius 77, 78
Turks 102, 154–5, 157, 163 n.48
Typhon, 39, 40, 43
    see also Enceladus

Vadianus, Joachim 22
Venice 110, 122, 154, 167
Vesuvius *see* Mount Vesuvius
Villa of Tiberius *see* Sperlonga
Virgil 26, 167, 220
    Jefferson, Thomas, reception of by 131–2, 136
    Jerome, Saint, reception of by 112–13, 116
    paradise, ideas of 63–4, 67
    on, volcanoes 39, 40, 41, 43, 44, 45
Virginia, landscape of *see* Monticello; Natural Bridge
Vitruvius 135, 146 n.54, 154
Vogel, Jakob 22, 24
Vulcan 39, 48, 52 n.17
    see also Hephaestus
Vulcano (island) 172

Warren, Erasmus 58–9, 60, 62, 66
Weber, Alan 83
Whately, Thomas 136
Wheeler, Mortimer 141–2
Whymper, Edward 23, 85 n.2
    see also under Coolidge, W. A. B.
wilderness 101, 122, 126, 200, 202
    contrasted with the city 93, 96, 185
    mountains depicted as 6, 9, 14, 15, 94, 95
    as spiritual retreat 96, 99, 107 n.42, 109–10, 111, 113–14, 116, 118, 127
Williams, Gareth 23, 34 n. 22, 51 n. 11
Wordsworth, William 17 n. 7, 152, 197
Wythe, George 134

Xanthos 91
Xenophanes 60, 221
Xenophon 83

Zeus 39–40, 192, 223

www.ingramcontent.com/pod-product-compliance
Lightning Source LLC
Chambersburg PA
CBHW072136290426
44111CB00012B/1887